THE WESTIES

Inside New York's Irish Mob

T. J. English

BANTAM BOOKS
LONDON · TORONTO · SYDNEY · AUCKLAND · JOHANNESBURG

TRANSWORLD PUBLISHERS
61–63 Uxbridge Road, London W5 5SA
A Random House Group Company
www.randomhouse.co.uk

THE WESTIES
A BANTAM BOOK: 9780553819564

First published in the United States by G.P. Putnam's Sons
St Martin's Press edition published 2006

First publication in Great Britain
Bantam edition published 2008

15

Grateful acknowledgement is made to the following for permission
to use copyrighted material:
United Artists Television, Inc.: Dialogue from *Angels with Dirty Faces.* © 1938 by
Warner Bros. Pictures, Inc. Renewed 1966 by United Artists Television, Inc.
Music Music Music Inc.: Lyrics from 'The Ballad of the Green Berets,'
words and music by Barry Sandler and Robin Moore. © 1963, 1964 and 1966
by Music Music Music Inc.

Addresses for Random House Group Ltd companies outside the UK
can be found at: www.randomhouse.co.uk
The Random House Group Ltd Reg. No. 954009

Penguin Random House is committed to a sustainable future for
our business, our readers and our planet. This book is made from
Forest Stewardship Council® certified paper.

MIX
Paper from
responsible sources
FSC® C018179

Printed and bound in Great Britain by Clays Ltd, St Ives plc

For John Patrick English.
Wherever he might be.

ACKNOWLEDGMENTS

Contrary to popular opinion, no book – especially a first book by a novice author – is compiled in isolation. For their assistance I would like to thank my friend and colleague Bob Callahan, who got the project rolling in the first place, and my agent, Barbara Lowenstein. Gale Dick provided invaluable help with the historical research, and my brother, Terry English, formerly a Green Beret captain in Vietnam, showed me how to read often cryptic military records. I'd also like to thank my longtime friend and fellow journalist Frank 'the Crusher' Kuznik, who provided the encouragement and criticism any writer needs to slog his or her way through the muck; and Lisa Wager, my editor, who wasn't afraid to take the manuscript into a back room and slap it around a bit. I'm also indebted to William Urshal, Tom Dunne, and Michael Daly for their contributions.

There are hundreds of lawyers, cops, gangsters, and neighborhood people from the West Side of Manhattan whom I could thank. At the risk of leaving someone out (or, given the subject matter of the book, naming someone who would rather remain anonymous), I'll offer a blanket 'thank you' to all – you know who you are. I would be remiss, however, if I didn't offer special thanks to Lawrence Schoenbach, Esq., Richie Egan, and everyone at the law firm of Hochheiser and Aronson.

Finally, I'd like to thank Francis and Marcelle Featherstone for staying in touch as long as they could.

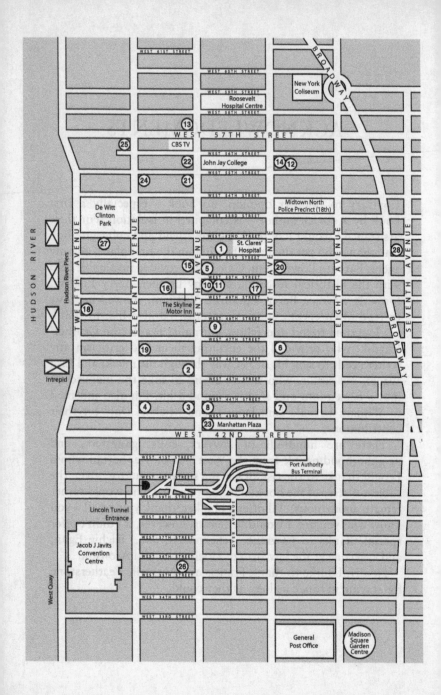

1 – Church of the Sacred Heart, 457 West 51st Street (between 9th and 10th Avenue): Michael 'Mickey' Spillane marries Maureen McManus, August 27, 1960; Billy Bokun marries Carol Collins, Flo and Tommy's daughter, May 26, 1985.

2 – The White House Bar, 637 10th Avenue (at 45th Street), extinct, now the site of the Tenth Avenue Jukebox Cafe: Mickey Spillane's place.

3 – 501½ West 43rd Street (between 10th and 11th Avenue): Mickey Featherstone's childhood home.

4 – The Market Diner, 572 11th Avenue (at 43rd Street).

5 – The Sunbrite, 736 10th Avenue (between 50th and 51st Street), extinct, now the site of Robert's Restaurant.

6 – Sonny's Cafe, 678 9th Avenue (between 46th and 47th Street), extinct, now the site of Midtown Bicycles: Mickey Featherstone gets a handgun from Jimmy Coonan to use at the Leprechaun Bar, September 30, 1970.

7 – The Leprechaun Bar, 608 9th Avenue (between 43rd and 44th Street), extinct, now the site of the Sea Palace.

8 – The 596 Club, 596 10th Avenue (at 43rd Street), extinct, now the site of J. T. Hudson's Restaurant: Jimmy Coonan's bar from 1972–79.

9 – 444 West 48th Street (between 9th and 10th Avenue): Home of Denis Curley.

10 – 452 West 50th Street (between 9th and 10th Avenue): Flophouse apartment shared by Billy Beattie and Paddy Dugan, among others.

11 – 442 West 50th Street (between 9th and 10th Avenue): 1975 home of Alberta Sachs, Jimmy Coonan's thirteen-year-old niece.

12 – Amy's Pub, 856 9th Avenue (between 55th and 56th Street): Mickey Featherstone meets Sissy, December 1975.

13 – The Stoplight, 875 10th Avenue (at 57th Street), extinct, now the site of Armstrong's Saloon: Michael Holly's bar.

14 – Tom's Pub, 854 9th Avenue (between 55th and 56th Street): Coonan and Featherstone pick up Rickey Tassiello, January 18, 1978.

15 – 747 10th Avenue (at 51st Street): Tony Lucich's apartment.

16 – New York Central Railroad tracks, 49th Street between 10th and 11th Avenue: Site of police diggings, October 1978.

17 – 434 West 49th Street (between 9th and 10th Avenue): Jimmy Coonan's childhood home.

18 – International Longshoremen's Association Headquarters, 12th Avenue at 48th Street; Vincent Leone's office.

19 – The Landmark Tavern, 11th Avenue at 46th Street: Coonan and Featherstone shake down ILA official John Potter, November 1978.

20 – Fran's Card Shop, 746 9th Avenue (between 50th and 51st Street), extinct, now the site of Carewell Pharmacy: Card shop was run by Fran, Tony Lucich's wife; drop site for some of Coonan's loanshark payments.

21 – Westway Candy Store, 827 10th Avenue (between 54th and 55th Street), extinct, now the site of Oscar's Deli and Grocery.

22 – 520 West 56th Street (between 10th and 11th Avenue), Apartment 15B: Mickey and Sissy's home in Hell's Kitchen.

23 – Manhattan Plaza, 400 West 43rd Street (at 10th Avenue): Henry Diaz's corpse thrown from a window, January 1981.

24 – Clinton Towers, 790 11th Avenue (between 54th and 55th Street): Jimmy McElroy and Tommy and Flo Collins's apartment building.

25 – The Madison Diner, 600 West 57th Street (at 11th Avenue): ILA officials John Potter and Tommy Ryan meet with Featherstone, McElroy, and Kevin Kelly, March 1984.

26 – 35th Street, between 10th and 11th Avenue: Michael Holly killed, April 25, 1985.

27 – Erie Transfer Co., 624 West 52nd Street (between 11th and 12th Avenue): Featherstone's place of employment 1984–85.

28 – Carpenters Local 608, 1650 Broadway (entrance on 51st Street): John O'Connor shot as he enters an elevator, May 7, 1986.

CONTENTS

Part Three

AUTHOR'S NOTE

What follows is a work of non-fiction. The events described are true and the characters are real.

While much of the dialogue in the book is taken directly from court transcripts, legal wiretaps, and electronic eavesdropping devices, in many cases it was based on interviews with the actual participants. It should be recognized that trial testimony and interviews sometimes produce conflicting versions of events. Where such conflict exists in testimony or recollection, the author has sought to provide a version of the facts which is in his opinion the most plausible. In addition, certain scenes have been dramatically re-created and in some cases a series of meetings or events condensed to provide narrative clarity.

'Good morning, gentlemen . . . Nice day for a murder.'

– Jimmy Cagney as Rocky Sullivan
in *Angels with Dirty Faces*

PROLOGUE

At approximately 6:30 A.M. on the morning of November 4, 1987, Francis Thomas 'Mickey' Featherstone awoke in a cold sweat. He tossed and turned in his bed, then sat upright. For a moment, he didn't know where he was. His heart was pounding and his eyes stinging as he peered into the surrounding darkness. Slowly, he was able to make out the familiar stone walls, the grungy toilet, the overhead bunkbed, and the forbidding metal door of his cell. Featherstone let out a sigh of relief and wiped the sweat from his brow with an already soaked bedsheet. Thank God, he said to himself, it's only prison.

Featherstone's night had been filled with bad dreams. He remembered seeing hundreds of human hands, pale and disembodied, reaching through the bars of a dingy prison cell. Then he saw himself on the floor of what looked like a hotel room, his wrists and ankles bound together with wire. He was surrounded by four or five conservatively dressed people – professional people. One of them, a man, put a gun to Featherstone's head and pulled the trigger. He felt the pain, saw the blood spurt past his eyes. Then he woke up.

Over the course of his often troubled thirty-nine years, Featherstone had grown accustomed to nightmares like this. But it had been a while since he'd seen the images so clearly. Not since the early 1970s anyway, when, after returning from a stint in Vietnam, his near sleepless nights were frequently filled with severed body parts, glistening blood, and the sounds of incoming fire. Over the years he'd talked to many psychiatrists about these dreams and they all told him the same thing. 'Post-traumatic stress syndrome,' they called it, using the popular post-Vietnam euphemism for battle fatigue.

As the years wore on and Featherstone gained distance from his war memories, the bad dreams subsided. More recent psychiatric evaluations gave him a clean bill of health. The nightmares would recur only if he were to engage in an 'anxiety-inducing undertaking,' according to a psychiatrist he'd seen just weeks earlier.

An anxiety-inducing undertaking. Featherstone had to laugh when he heard it put that way. With his eleventh-grade education, it was a phrase he'd never have used himself, though he had to admit in its own cold and clinical way it was a perfect description of what he was about to embark on.

Featherstone got up from his mattress and made his way to a porcelain sink near the toilet. He let the water run until it was good and cold, then cupped his hands under the faucet and splashed his face. He looked at his reflection in the mirror and saw the familiar crescent scar on his neck, the disheveled sandy-blond hair, the droopy mustache and hazel, forlorn eyes of a hardened convict.

The cool water ran down his chest and back, sending

a ripple of pleasure through his taut five-foot-nine-inch frame. The images of violence and terror from his dreams had already begun to recede.

Mickey Featherstone was ready to face the day.

Hours later, two United States marshals met Featherstone at his cell. Now dressed in a conservative light-brown suit, his hair newly trimmed and groomed, he submitted to a brief security check. Then the marshals led him down a long corridor which served as a passageway from New York City's Metropolitan Correctional Center (MCC), where he was incarcerated, to an adjacent building – the federal courthouse at Foley Square in lower Manhattan. Inside the courthouse, they took him to a sparsely furnished room with a large mahogany conference table, where he sat quietly until a breakfast of eggs, toast and coffee arrived. Featherstone tried to eat, but even this bland combination of tastes was too unsettling to his stomach. He pushed the food aside.

As a soldier stationed along the Mekong Delta during the war, then as a gangster and convicted killer back home in New York City, and finally as an inmate at Attica State Prison, Sing Sing, Rikers Island, and a half-dozen other federal and state penitentiaries, Featherstone had tried to eliminate fear from his emotional makeup. Too many times in his life he'd seen otherwise competent people paralyzed by fear at the moment of decision, usually resulting in the person's getting beaten, busted or something much worse. He'd learned over the years to submerge his own fears. The only place they had free rein was in his dreams.

19

But now, in this room on this morning in November of 1987, Featherstone's hand shook as he tried to drink his coffee. He was scared, no doubt about it. For in just a few short minutes he would be taken to Room 506 of U.S. District Court. There he would do something he'd always promised himself would never happen – he'd willingly take the stand to testify against his own people. To the court, the press, and the city-at-large, these people were known as the Westies, a gang of racketeers who had risen from the streets of Manhattan to the highest levels of organized crime. To Featherstone, they were the people he knew best, many of them close friends since childhood.

Mary Lee Warren, an assistant U.S. attorney for the Southern District of New York, entered the room to begin preparing Featherstone for the day's testimony. He heard her voice and the familiar litany of crimes they'd be covering, but the words had no impact. So many hours, days and months had been spent relating the details of his past to cops, lawyers and representatives of the federal government that they no longer felt like his memories. At times, it seemed to Featherstone like his entire past was now the property of the U.S. Attorney's office.

After Warren left the room, the two federal marshals led Featherstone down the hallway and onto a dingy freight elevator with metal caging. As the elevator descended, the fear Featherstone had been feeling that morning slowly gave way to a more familiar emotion: anger. He felt anger at those who'd forced him into this position; anger at those who'd made it impossible for him to look at himself in the mirror without feeling disgust; anger at everyone everywhere who'd ever done him wrong.

20

By the time the freight elevator clanged open and Featherstone entered the courtroom, he felt better. For the first time in many months, he could remember clearly why he was here. He could remember his motivation.

Revenge.

'Mr Featherstone,' asked Warren, standing in front of the jury box, 'have you ever heard the term "Westies"?'

'Yes.'

'Is that a term that you use?'

'No.'

'Is it a term you heard used?'

'Yes, ma'am.'

'Where have you heard it used?'

'The newspapers and the police.'

'And what do you understand the term "Westies" to apply to?'

'Me. People here. Different neighborhood people.'

'And during what period of time did this group operate?'

'Well, there's always been a group in my neighborhood, since I could remember, committing crimes.'

Featherstone was not being coy. The Westies had always been a nebulous group, and until he took his place on the witness stand, not even he had known exactly who the defendants would be. Nor did he know the specific charges. He had a vague idea, of course, since the bulk of the government's case was based on information he'd been giving them for the past eighteen months. But because he didn't know exactly how they would corroborate his claims, and since they were legally prohibited from discussing the case with him in any detail, he couldn't be sure who'd been indicted.

At first, he could hardly even tell where the defense area was. Room 506, known as 'the showroom' to the local press corps who regularly cover the courts, was a majestic, high-ceilinged affair presently overflowing with nearly 200 spectators, a dozen lawyers, twelve jurors, six alternate jurors, and a half-dozen federal marshals lining the walls. Even if Featherstone hadn't spent the last three years of his life cooped up in a tiny prison cell, it would have been an unnerving sight.

Eventually, after adjusting to the grandeur of the place, his eyes focused on the defendants and their attorneys, seated less than twenty feet away. Although dressed uncharacteristically in 'respectable' courtroom attire – suits, ties and plain-colored dresses – these were, for the most part, the people he'd expected to see, the people he'd run with in the tough Manhattan west side neighborhood known as Hell's Kitchen.

At the far left Featherstone saw the familiar faces of Tommy Collins and his wife Flo – both white-haired and in their fifties – looking like everybody's favorite Irish aunt and uncle. To their left was Richard 'Mugsy' Ritter, with thinning hair and a jet-black mustache, looking dapper in a brand-new pin-striped suit. Further down the table, seated with his attorney, was Billy Bokun, whose most notable feature was a large reddish birthmark that covered one whole side of his face. At thirty-one, Bokun was the youngest of the defendants.

At a ninety-degree angle, completing the expansive L-shaped seating arrangement, was another equally crowded table. First in line, as Featherstone looked from left to right, was lean, mean Johnny Halo, almost unrecognizable in wire-rimmed glasses and closely cropped black hair. Down the table from Johnny was James McElroy, known to Featherstone and just about everyone else on the West Side as Jimmy Mac. The tallest of the group at six-foot-one, McElroy had broad shoulders, dark hair, and the hardened good looks of a former boxer, which he was. And next to McElroy, seated with her attorney, was stout, formidable Edna Coonan, wife of James 'Jimmy' Coonan, the man the government had already identified as the leader of the Westies.

Finally, Featherstone came to the eighth and final defendant, who sat closest to him. More than any other, this was the man he'd been waiting to see; the man whose actions, he felt, were the main reason this group of West Siders now found themselves in this strange environment, where highly educated people wore fine new clothes and spoke with impeccable grammar.

At five-feet-nine-inches tall, with blond hair, blue eyes, and a broad, cherubic face, forty-year-old Jimmy Coonan didn't look like a cold-blooded killer. He looked more like a cop, perhaps, or an aging altar boy. But Featherstone knew this was only a facade. He'd stood by this man and at times actively participated with him in unspeakable acts of violence. Partly, he'd done so for business reasons. But also he'd done so out of allegiance, out of love.

In the old days, these violent acts had seemed almost acceptable to Featherstone. In Hell's Kitchen – the neighborhood where he and Jimmy had grown up together – you chose between good and evil at a young age. If you

23

chose evil, then violence became an important means of communication; a way of showing a friend just how far you were willing to go to prove your friendship. Featherstone had always believed that's what he and Jimmy were doing – sealing their friendship. Sealing it in blood.

But those days were long gone now, lost in a haze of angry, bitter memories.

According to the prosecution, Coonan was guilty of extortion, mail fraud, illegal gambling, drug dealing, loan-sharking, kidnapping, multiple murders, and attempted murders, all as leader of the Westies. To Featherstone, this was only half the story. Greed, treachery, betrayal – in traditional organized crime circles these were far greater crimes. And in Featherstone's mind, Coonan had already been charged with these crimes, tried and found guilty.

The sentence? Death. The executors of this sentence? Some of the very people Coonan now found himself seated next to, who, along with Featherstone, had been plotting his murder right up until their arrests for this trial.

As the witness looked out at the eight defendants seated in a large phalanx before the cold, imposing glare of U.S. District Court, his emotions shifted once again. Despite the enmity he had for many of these people and the justification he felt he had for testifying against them, he couldn't get used to the idea of being on the stand. Every time he thought about what he was doing he began to sweat. But as his testimony proceeded under the calm, probing tutelage of the assistant U.S. attorney, something came to him, something that seemed so obvious he couldn't believe it hadn't crossed his mind before.

24

For the first time since he'd begun his long life of crime, he, Mickey Featherstone, was in a position to tell the truth.

There was some satisfaction in that.

'Mr Featherstone,' said Warren, 'let me direct your attention to a night on or around January 18, 1978. Did you have an occasion to know personally a Rickey Tassiello?'

'Yes.'

'How did you know him?'

'I knew him all his life, since we grew up in the neighborhood. I got arrested with him once.'

'Do you know what Rickey Tassiello did for a living?'

'He pulled armed robberies and he gambled.'

'Do you know how he supported his gambling?'

'With money from armed robberies and money from shylocks.'

In the early hours of the afternoon, Warren had begun to lead Featherstone through some of the more gruesome charges in the indictment. Tall and frail, with hopelessly frazzled light-brown hair and a pale complexion, Warren was dressed in a white, frilly blouse and plaid skirt. She didn't look like the sort of person who would be comfortable talking about murder and dismemberment. She looked more like a grade school teacher, or a librarian. Yet, as she'd pointed out in her opening statement to the jury, throughout the trial she would be enumerating many horrible acts of violence. One of the worst, she cautioned, would be Act of Racketeering Number Nine: the Murder of Richard 'Rickey' Tassiello.

Before Featherstone took the stand, the court had heard

testimony on the Tassiello murder from Arthur Tassiello, a brother of the deceased, and from Anton 'Tony' Lucich, another Westie who, along with Featherstone, had become a government witness. Arthur Tassiello, a bartender on the West Side of Manhattan in 1977, told of meetings he had with Jimmy Coonan about his brother. According to Tassiello, Coonan told him that Rickey was behind on his illicit 'shylock' loans to the tune of $7,000, and he wanted the Tassiello family to either get Rickey to pay up or settle his debt for him.

It was Arthur who finally came up with the money. When he did, he pleaded with Coonan to stop making loans to his little brother because, as everyone in the neighborhood knew, Rickey was a 'sick gambler.'

A few months later, Coonan showed up at Arthur's place of business again. This time Rickey owed him $6,000. They worked out a payment schedule where Arthur would try to get his brother to pay $100 a week.

Months passed. Coonan showed up again. Rickey Tassiello had stopped making his payments. Exasperated, Arthur said there was nothing more he could do.

After Arthur Tassiello left the stand, Tony Lucich testified about the events following Rickey's murder, which took place in his Hell's Kitchen apartment at 747 10th Avenue. According to Lucich, he'd entered the apartment after the deed was done and helped cut up the body.

So the jury already knew there had been a murder, and they knew it was bloody. But neither Arthur Tassiello nor Lucich had witnessed the act itself.

Enter Mickey Featherstone.

The Market Diner, 11th Avenue and 43rd Street. Late afternoon, January 18, 1978. Featherstone and Coonan were sitting at the counter when Coonan got a phone call. He took the call and came back, telling Featherstone they had business to take care of at Tom's Pub, just a few blocks away. In the car on the way over, Coonan told Featherstone they were going to pick up Rickey Tassiello and take him to Tony Lucich's apartment.

Featherstone knew all about Rickey's outstanding shylock loans. He also knew that when Jimmy Coonan had a problem with one of his loanshark customers, he usually dealt with it swiftly and brutally. He knew this because he'd been there many times and helped administer the punishment.

But this time he didn't want to be a part of it. He'd known Rickey Tassiello all his life and couldn't see why the kid had to be killed, and he told Coonan this. 'While we were in the car,' said Featherstone quietly from the witness stand, 'Jimmy was telling me he's not gonna do nothin' to Rickey. He just wanted to warn him. And he and Tony were gonna offer him a job so he could pay his loan.'

They arrived at Tom's Pub on 55th Street and 9th Avenue. Jimmy went over to Rickey, who was seated with a group of friends, and said, 'Listen, everything is alright. We just want you to go up and apologize to Tony.' Tassiello had pulled a gun on Lucich and his wife the night before.

'Yeah,' said Rickey. 'Okay, I'll go up and see Tony.'

Ten minutes later the three of them arrived at Tony Lucich's 10th Avenue apartment. Mickey and Rickey sat down on the living room couch and Jimmy headed for a back room. 'I'll be right back,' said Jimmy. 'I'm going to get Tony. He's in bed, sick.' After Jimmy had left, Mickey got up and headed into the kitchenette area. 'You want anything?' he asked Rickey. 'I'm gonna get some Perrier water.' Rickey said no.

As Mickey was opening the refrigerator, he glanced through a doorway that opened onto the hall and saw Jimmy heading back towards the living room by himself. Then he heard the familiar sound of a round being loaded into the chamber of a gun. 'What the fuck's going on?' he heard Rickey shout from the other room. 'What are you doing!?'

The next thing he knew Rickey was running into the kitchenette area. Mickey heard the silencer go off and saw a shot hit the wall. Rickey started to reach for some knives in a rack on the kitchen wall. 'No!' shouted Mickey, as he grabbed Rickey to keep him from getting at the knives.

Just then, Jimmy stepped up behind Rickey and shot him in the back of the head. Rickey slumped down against the wall and the refrigerator, and Jimmy shot him twice more as he lay on the floor.

On the witness stand, Featherstone hardly moved, and his voice kept getting lower and lower. Four times the judge and prosecutor had to ask him to speak up, to enunciate more clearly. He told the jury that during the shooting he'd been hit in the head with something metallic, which later proved to be the casing from one of the bullets. But he didn't know that at the time. He thought maybe he'd been shot, so he panicked and ran for the door. At that moment, Tony Lucich walked in.

Both Lucich and Coonan told Featherstone to calm down. Together they dragged the body into the bathroom and dumped it face up in the tub. Then, said Featherstone, Coonan told him to stick a knife in Tassiello's heart, just to make sure.

'And what did you do?' asked prosecutor Warren.

'I stuck a knife in his chest.'

They went to the Market Diner after that. Jimmy and Tony sat in the dining area and ate a hearty meal, laughing and joking with the other patrons they knew. In the bar area, Mickey watched from a distance, drinking whiskey after whiskey until everything that was happening got blurry and quiet.

Around two o'clock in the morning, they went back to the apartment. Jimmy got some big kitchen knives with serrated edges, went into the bathroom and began hacking apart Rickey Tassiello's body. There was blood everywhere – the floors, the walls, the tub.

'About this time,' said Featherstone, 'Tony broke out some black plastic bags, and I started throwing up. I put a handkerchief over my mouth. Jimmy was joking about me not being able to take it . . .

'I vomited in the bathroom, in the toilet bowl. When he was goofing on me, I left the bathroom and went to the kitchen sink and finished vomiting in there. I sat on the couch in the living room and they called me in . . .

'I went in, and Jimmy was cutting his head off.'

'What was done with the body parts as they were removed?' asked the prosecutor.

'They were put in the black plastic garbage bags.'

'Who put them in the plastic bags?'

'Me and Tony.'

The plastic bags were then loaded into a number of cardboard boxes about three feet high and two feet wide. While they were doing that, Jimmy said to Lucich, 'Hey, you got any sandwich bags – you know, Baggies?'

'Yeah,' said Lucich.

'Go get some. I want you to put Rickey's hands in the Baggies and stick 'em in the freezer.'

'What!?'

'You heard me, I wanna stick the kid's hands in the freezer.'

Coonan explained that he had an upcoming murder in mind, and he wanted to plant Rickey's fingerprints on the gun. Lucich got the bags.

'Mr Featherstone,' asked prosecutor Warren, her voice steady and reassuring, 'do you have any idea how much money Rickey Tassiello owed James Coonan at the time of his death?'

The answer was $1,250.

A gasp came from some members of the jury. Featherstone wasn't surprised. He knew the viciousness of the killing would seem entirely out of proportion to the debt. He knew this, and he had to agree. Of all the beatings, stabbings, murders, and dismemberments, this was the one that bothered him the most.

That evening, in the Witness Protection Unit of the MCC, Featherstone stood under a steaming hot shower pondering his day on the witness stand. The Tassiello murder was something he'd never talked about to anyone until he began cooperating with the government. To relive it now in public was gut-wrenching. And yet, he knew what had to be done – for his own survival. Over the days that followed there would be more horrendous acts to describe, acts he often found hard to admit even to himself. If he hoped to get through it all, he knew he'd have to be willing to look out over that courtroom and say the words: 'Yes, I was a scumbag. I was a vicious killer.'

What really bothered him, though, were the reactions of those he knew in the gallery, many of them friends and relatives of the defendants. He'd seen them snicker and shake their heads in disbelief as he told his tales. It reminded him of the time, many months ago, when he had appeared publicly for the first time since it became known he'd flipped. It was at a pre-trial hearing and many of these same spectators were there. They'd snickered then, too, and made derisive comments. As he was led from the courtroom that day, his sister, *his own sister*, had shouted out, 'He should slit his fuckin' wrists!'

But these people – the neighborhood onlookers and some members of his own family – they didn't know the full story, he was certain of that. They didn't know of the deceit and betrayal that had led them all to this moment.

Well, before he was done, if he accomplished anything, the record would be set straight.

Then we'd see who was calling who a traitor.

That night Featherstone lay in his cell and stared at the wall. The events of his life played in his head like some weird, disjointed movie with all the reels shown out of sequence. He knew that in less than twelve hours the trial would resume, and once again he'd be asked to reveal his most shameful memories before a packed courtroom.

After that, the eight defense attorneys would all have their shot. No doubt they would dwell gleefully on the seamiest aspects of his undeniably seamy life – the troubled psychiatric history, drug addictions, sexual 'perversions,' and hopeless, sadistic propensity for violence.

He told himself the same thing he always did when he was having doubts. That this was not the end. This was the beginning . . . a new beginning.

He repeated it over and over like a mantra, then laid his head on the pillow, closed his eyes, and tried to dream he was somewhere far, far away from New York City.

PART ONE

PART ONE

1

THE GHOSTS OF
HELL'S KITCHEN

The victim never really had a chance. It was a moonless night and the sound of gunfire came so fast he could hardly believe what he was hearing.

The guy next to him got it first. Three quick shots and down he went. There was a strange sound coming from the guy's mouth as he struggled to say something.

Fuck this, thought the victim, time to split. He tried to run but only got a few steps before he heard another shot. The bullet hit him somewhere in the body – he knew that because he could feel the impact. But he couldn't tell where. So he just kept running. Then there was another shot. He knew *exactly* where that one hit him – in the left shoulder. The pain was immediate. Then a third shot. He wasn't sure where this one hit him, but he could feel his legs begin to give out. He fell on his back with a thud and for a minute he thought his arm had been blown clean off.

He heard the person who fired the shots walking across the gravel. He tried to focus, to raise himself up to see what was happening, but he had no strength at all. There was blood, lots of blood, coming from his upper body, and he felt the pain in his arm reverberate through his torso until he was sure his head was going to explode. The last thing he saw, through squinted eyes, was the gunman passing in front of the car's headlights. Then he heard laughter from the four people inside the car; laughter unlike anything he'd ever heard before. It was more like a cackle, really, and it was so loud it seemed to echo right inside his ears.

That was it. Darkness came next. For what seemed like an eternity there was complete silence. He thought he was dead. Then he heard someone talking. He thought maybe the gunmen had come back, but there were lights flashing now. An ambulance. Police cars.

'Hey,' he heard a voice ask. 'Can you hear me?'

He tried to move his lips.

'Listen,' the voice said. 'I'm a police officer. Your friend here is dead and you look pretty bad. You better tell us all you know.'

'Where's my left arm?' he asked in a whisper.

'Your arm's still there. Can you tell us what happened?'

Surprisingly, he was able to remember a lot. As he spoke, Patrolman Edward Gordon of the 108th Precinct in Queens jotted down what he could in a notepad and then followed the ambulance to the hospital. Once there, as the victim lay on a gurney in the emergency room, Gordon got the rest of the story . . .

Eight hours earlier, on the evening of April 3, 1966, twenty-six-year-old Charles Canelstein met a guy named Jerry Morales at the Luxor Baths, a steam room on East

46th Street in Manhattan. Canelstein and Morales had never met before, but they seemed to hit it off. After a while, Morales suggested they go for a bite to eat, then see if they couldn't pick up some women at the Pussycat Lounge. That sounded like a good idea to Canelstein. So they had dinner together at an East Side restaurant, a quick drink at a bar called the Living Room, and arrived at the Pussycat Lounge on 49th Street between 1st and 2nd avenues around 8:30 P.M.

Right away Canelstein started schmoozing with a girl named Karen who was sitting at the bar. He lost track of Morales, but that didn't really bother him. Since dinner, he'd begun to realize he didn't like the guy anyway – he was too loud and obnoxious. But Karen he liked. She was single, Jewish, and just in town from Los Angeles. What more could a guy ask for?

Things were going great with Karen until a brawny, brown-haired guy, later identified as thirty-six-year-old Eddie Sullivan, approached. 'See that stool you're sitting on?' Sullivan said to Canelstein. 'That's my stool. See that girl you're talking to? That's my girl.'

Canelstein didn't know what to make of all this, so he asked Karen if she knew the guy. When she shrugged and shook her head, Canelstein told Sullivan he must be mistaken. Sullivan had a few nasty words to say and Canelstein responded in kind. Then Sullivan left.

About twenty minutes later Sullivan returned with a police badge and a gun. Canelstein didn't know much about guns, but he could see this was a big one, with a barrel that looked to be about six inches long. It was pointed directly at his head.

'Alright,' said Sullivan, 'police business. You're comin' with me.'

'What's the charge?' asked Canelstein.

Sullivan grabbed him by the arm and started moving towards the door. 'Just get your ass outside.'

As soon as they stepped outside, Canelstein saw that another person already had Morales up against the wall. This guy was much younger than Sullivan. In fact, Canelstein was struck by how young the kid looked. He was short and stocky, with blond hair, and he looked to Canelstein to be about nineteen years old. Later, the kid would be identified as James Coonan.

Canelstein and Morales were hustled to a small compact car and forced into the backseat. Things were moving fast now, like a dream, hazy and fragmented. Canelstein could see there were two more guys in the car. The driver was young, but not as young as Coonan. And the kid in the back, he was young too, with blond hair just like Coonan's. Canelstein and Morales were wedged in the backseat, with Coonan on the right side and the other blond-haired kid on the left.

Sullivan sat in the front seat and kept his weapon pointed at them at all times. As the car headed north on 3rd Avenue, he smiled. 'You know, if you guys had $2,000 on you we could settle this thing right now.'

Canelstein let the words sink in slowly. At least now he knew what was up; it was a scam, a shakedown. Maybe he and Morales could scrape together enough to satisfy these guys. He told Sullivan they didn't have anywhere near $2,000, but if they were willing to drive by the

38

Luxor Baths he might be able to get $40 or $50 out of his locker.

That didn't seem to cut any ice with Sullivan.

There was a long period of silence as Canelstein and his kidnappers drove across the 59th Street bridge to Queens. The driver maneuvered his way through traffic along Queens Boulevard, past the Sunnyside railyard, past Long Island City, past Hunters Point Avenue. From the backseat, Canelstein could see the familiar sight of Calvary Cemetery, with its rolling hills of tombstones. That was the last thing he recognized.

'Are you sure you don't have any money?' It was the driver, speaking for the first time. He turned completely around to ask his question, taking his eyes off the road.

Canelstein just shook his head. He couldn't think of anything more to say.

A few minutes later the car pulled into a dark lot across the street from the Calvary Cemetery. It was after midnight now, and as Canelstein and Morales were taken from the car, the only illumination was from the headlights aimed at a brick warehouse wall. They were led across the debris-littered lot, stood up against the wall and searched one last time.

Suddenly, Morales turned around, pointed at his chest and started to shout, 'Go ahead, motherfuckers. Right here! Shoot me right here!'

That's when three gunshots rang out, with two of the bullets striking Morales in the face.

Canelstein started to run. There were three more gunshots, two of the bullets passing right through his abdomen and the third lodging in some bone marrow near his left armpit.

By the time the cops got to Canelstein they were lucky to get anything out of him. Not only had he been shot three times, but he was nearly in a state of shock. All he'd wanted was a drink and a night out, he told the cops. He didn't cheat anybody or do anything bad. A pickup, that's all he wanted, a nice single girl to bring home for the night.

What Canelstein did not know – what he could not have known – was that he had walked right into the middle of an old-fashioned gang war with roots on the West Side of Manhattan, in a neighborhood known as Hell's Kitchen.

From the descriptions Canelstein gave them, the cops were able to ID Coonan and Sullivan. Just twelve days earlier, in March, there had been another killing in the same precinct, no more than a few minutes drive from where the Canelstein/Morales shooting had taken place. The victim's name was Bobby Lagville – and Coonan and Sullivan were the prime suspects in that one too.

On the morning of April 5, 1966, the day after the Canelstein/Morales shooting, four detectives from the 108th Precinct in Queens were dispatched to the home of William 'Billy' Murtha, a suspected crime partner of Coonan's who lived at 412 East 50th Street in Manhattan. What the cops didn't know was that Murtha had been the driver on the night Canelstein and Morales were shot. When they arrived at Murtha's small studio apartment, he was still in his underwear. They told him to wake up and get dressed. They wanted to talk to him about a shooting.

As Murtha began to put on his clothes, Detective Martin Logan noticed there was a shoe on the floor that was about four sizes bigger than the ones Murtha was wearing. He looked around the apartment and heard a dog barking on the other side of a closed bathroom door. He took his gun out and told Murtha to open the door.

When Logan peeked inside he saw the silhouette of a man standing behind the shower curtain.

'Come out of there with your hands away from your body,' he commanded.

The curtain was pulled part way back and six-foot-two-inch Eddie Sullivan stepped out. Like Murtha, he was dressed only in his underwear.

Logan's partner slapped a set of handcuffs on Sullivan and led him out of the bathroom. Logan stepped towards the shower, his gun still poised, and pulled the shower curtain all the way back. In the shower, hunched all the way down and also in his underwear, was nineteen-year-old Jimmy Coonan.

At the 108th Precinct young Coonan was polite but firm. He swore he knew nothing about the Canelstein/ Morales shooting. Even when the cops informed him that Charles Canelstein had lived and would probably be able to identify his assailants, Coonan didn't budge – not yet, anyway.

To the cops in Queens it was no big deal. As far as they knew, Jimmy Coonan was just a petty crook from Manhattan, and they wouldn't have been surprised if his victim was too. There had been over 150 homicides in

Queens already that year. To them, this was just one more – and a seemingly insignificant one at that.

As of yet, they had no idea that the Canelstein/Morales shooting was the latest salvo in the Hell's Kitchen gang wars, a long tradition that, over some sixty-five years, had done more for the undertaking business in Manhattan than any criminal event in twentieth-century history.

Although most of the gangster element on the West Side knew young Jimmy Coonan was having a war with Michael 'Mickey' Spillane, leader of the Hell's Kitchen rackets in 1966, not many had known just how serious it was until the Canelstein/Morales incident. While Coonan, Sullivan, Murtha, and the man identified as the fourth person in the car, Jimmy Gallagher, were being held in custody, a story spread through the neighborhood. It went something like this: Spillane had called in two hit men from Texas to eliminate Coonan and his sidekick, Sullivan. The boys had found out about it, hunted the hit men down, and taken them out to Queens, where they were given a gangland-style farewell.

Never mind that Jerry Morales, a small-time burglar who'd once done a long stretch in San Quentin Prison, was from Los Angeles, not Texas. Whatever Morales had said to Eddie Sullivan at the Pussycat Lounge was enough to make Sullivan *think* he and Canelstein were hit men from Texas.

Since Spillane and Coonan had gone public with their feud, there had been lots of threats and accusations. One rumor was that Spillane had called hit men in from Boston. Another had him cutting a deal with Little Bobby

Lagville, a neighborhood kid, to kill just Eddie Sullivan. That rumor was taken seriously enough that Bobby Lagville disappeared from the neighborhood one evening. Later he was found dead out in Queens with six bullet holes in his body.

Coonan knew Spillane had boxed himself into a corner as far as violence was concerned. Dark and drop-dead handsome, with a courtly manner, Spillane was an old-time gentleman gangster with a much admired sense of loyalty to the neighborhood. He could not be seen to be condoning violence against a person from Hell's Kitchen or it would make him look bad in the eyes of his 'legitimate' friends. That's why Spillane had taken a contract out on Eddie Sullivan instead of Jimmy Coonan. Sullivan was from the East Side. He was fair game.

Little Bobby Lagville had been asked to do the killing because he was a close friend of Coonan's. 'Get rid of Sullivan,' Spillane supposedly told Lagville, 'then we can call a truce. Otherwise, your friend Coonan's gonna be history real soon.' When Jimmy Coonan and his buddies heard about this, they thought it meant Lagville was on Spillane's side. So they gave him a ride to 5th Street between 47th and 48th avenues, just across the East River in Long Island City. That's exactly where the police found the body, lying in a river of blood in the middle of the street at 4:30 A.M. on March 23, 1966.

Usually, that's how the Coonan/Spillane Wars were waged – in the quiet of the night on some dark street or in some back alley where there were few witnesses.

Sometimes, however, emotions boiled over. One popular story in the saloons and gambling dens of Hell's Kitchen had it that one afternoon Spillane and Coonan were seen exchanging words right on 10th Avenue. They both pulled guns and traded fire, just like an old-fashioned Western shoot-out.

Another time, it was reported, Spillane was headed to a late-night crap game on 46th Street between 11th and 12th avenues. He was with a group of seven or eight neighborhood buddies, including a young Tommy Collins and Julius 'Dutch' Grote. Suddenly somebody opened fire from the roof up above. They all ducked for cover as bullets sprayed down like rain.

'Holy shit!' somebody shouted. 'Who the fuck is that?'

They squeezed into the entryway of a tenement, pinned against the glass doors as the bullets hit the street and ricocheted off a nearby warehouse wall.

Spillane leaned forward, peering up towards the roof. 'It's that bug Coonan. He's got a machine gun!'

They had to stay like that for a while until Coonan disappeared. Then they scampered off to their dice game.

Most folks in Hell's Kitchen figured it was all about business. Spillane not only controlled the neighborhood policy games, but he was the area's primary bookmaker. Any neighborhood bets on sporting events or anything else of interest went through him. He also had influence with the unions, where various kickback rackets flourished, and all the neighborhood dice and card games. Plus, there was loansharking and his thriving robbery and hijacking operations. All in all, he was a well-rounded guy.

In the old days, the neighborhood rackets sprang out of one centralized scam like the illicit liquor trade or the waterfront. Now it was more of a hustle, and anyone who hoped to maintain control over a sprawling empire of gambling, loansharking and more would either have to do it through intimidation or, like Spillane, by establishing an impressive power base through legitimate as well as criminal connections.

But Mickey Spillane hadn't acquired his reputation overnight. As with earlier neighborhood gangsters, he'd had to build it slowly through assorted extortions. With Spillane, the extortion of choice had always been kidnapping. His modus operandi was simple enough. A well-connected neighborhood merchant might be shoved into the backseat of a car as he left his place of business at the end of the day. From there, he would be taken to an apartment or maybe to the rear of Spillane's own White House Bar at 45th Street and 10th Avenue. Phone calls would be made to the person's business partner or some other associate demanding ransom. Sometimes there might even be violence involved.

To an outside observer, this might have seemed like a high-risk proposition, given that most of the victims were people who knew Spillane. In some cases, they might even have lived down the block or around the corner from Spillane's own West 50th Street apartment. These people could easily have ratted to the police.

But Spillane knew that was unlikely. He was relying on something called the West Side Code, a tradition so sacred that even noncriminal types saw that it was adhered to. Simply stated, it went something like this: Under no circumstances does anyone talk to the cops. To do so would mean certain castigation within the community. It might also mean something very bad could happen to a member of your family.

The West Side Code wasn't based on any criminal impulse, per se. It was more a sign of solidarity against outside forces; a way to show loyalty and 'build character.' But over the years the gangsters were able to make the Code their own, and people like Mickey Spillane always knew they could bank on it.

Spillane never really liked the kidnap-for-ransom racket, unless it involved other mobsters. That was good business. But to kidnap somebody's uncle or cousin and hold him at gunpoint was uncivilized. As soon as he was in a position to give it up, he did so, and put out the word to all his underlings that kidnapping neighborhood people was now forbidden.

But Mickey Spillane could not rewrite his past. Like all the prominent Hell's Kitchen gangsters who had preceded him, he'd had to do some pretty nasty things to get where he was. And some people just weren't going to let him forget about it . . .

It had been a kidnapping not unlike all the others. Years before the Canelstein/Morales shooting, John Coonan, a neighborhood accountant who ran a tax office on West 50th Street, was snatched late one night and taken to the White House Bar. He was held there and pistol-whipped by Spillane and a few others. After a couple hours, a payment was made and he was let go.

After the kidnapping, Coonan was willing to let things slide. But his son Jimmy was not. For years, Jimmy would remember the humiliation his father had suffered at the hands of Mickey Spillane. It would fester inside like an illness, and he would swear time and time again that he would never be a victim like his father was. Never.

Given Coonan's strong feelings on the matter, it was a testament to his patience that he was, for the most part, willing to lie in wait. Oh, there were daily harassments, like machine gun fire from rooftops and occasional shoot-outs in the street. But that was just to prove he couldn't be pushed around. Coonan knew Spillane could not be removed overnight. He was too popular, too well-connected. If he removed Spillane now, no one would see him as the natural successor. He was much too young. What he had to do was make a name for himself first; muscle in on as much of Spillane's territory as he could; establish important alliances of his own, possibly with the Italians.

Coonan knew this would take time. But he was willing to build slowly to achieve his larger ambitions.

In the meantime, the plan was to fuck with Mike Spillane as much as possible.

Bounded on the south by 34th Street, on the north by 59th, and stretching from 8th Avenue west to the Hudson River, few neighborhoods have contributed more to the saga of New York City street life than Hell's Kitchen. Along the neighborhood's eastern flank stands Times Square, the city's world-renowned theater district, with its staggering array of Broadway and Off-Broadway theaters, restaurants, and movie palaces – not to mention a thriving drug, pornography, and prostitution trade. To the west, the Hudson River and the waterfront, once the most lucrative cargo and passenger port in the United States and an unending source of income for racketeers.

A number of popular legends concerning the origin of the name 'Hell's Kitchen' have now become part of the city's permanent record. Some say it came from a German couple named Heil who owned a diner popular with local dockworkers in the post-Civil War years. Somehow Heil's name was mispronounced as Hell, with Heil's Kitchen thus becoming Hell's Kitchen.

Another has it that two Irish cops, one a veteran and the other a rookie, stood watching a small riot on West 39th Street. 'This place is hell itself,' the rookie is supposed to have said.

'Hell's a mild climate,' responded the veteran. 'This is Hell's Kitchen, no less.'

Whatever the origins of its name, there have always been certain inalienable traditions in Hell's Kitchen, traditions that grew out of the neighborhood's reputation as a cauldron of urban activity. At their best, these traditions have produced the cream of a proud and thriving metropolis. Doctors, priests, politicians, scientists, judges, athletes. People who used their working-class roots as the foundation for a life of compassion, service, and achievement.

But over the decades, as Hell's Kitchen was buffeted by forces that would shape and reshape the city, the neighborhood became known for another kind of tradition – a tradition of gangsterism. This was the tradition inherited by Jimmy Coonan, Mickey Spillane and the others who now found themselves caught up in the Coonan/Spillane Wars. It was a rich tradition, proudly cultivated by successive generations of tough guys, with a lineage rooted deep in the soil of New York City's past.

At the turn of the century, the area was largely an Irish and German enclave. Its most dominant physical features were the noisy 9th Avenue elevated railway, which carried more passengers than any railway line in the city, and the Hudson River Railroad, which carried freight and livestock along 11th Avenue, or 'Death Avenue' as it was known to most West Siders because of the dust, congestion, and dangerous rail traffic.

In 1910, a privately funded report by a group of social workers painted a graphic picture of the area at its most wretched. Hell's Kitchen, they wrote, is characterized by 'dull, square, monotonous ugliness, much dirt, and a great deal of despair.' Their account included a description of what life was like for young kids, who spent most of their time on the bustling cobblestoned streets hawking newspapers, fighting, picking pockets, swimming in the Hudson River, or flying pigeons from tenement roofs.

There was a closeness within the community, however, that evaded the social workers. Because of their proximity to the docks and railroad lines, the people of Hell's Kitchen felt as if they were constantly under siege from transient forces, and they reacted accordingly. Those who stayed put cultivated a fierce loyalty to the neighborhood as protection against the outside world. The area's most prominent social institutions – the church, the political clubhouse, the neighborhood saloon – were more than just gathering places. They were fortresses of stability in the midst of what was largely a migrant community.

Throughout the early years of the twentieth century, by

49

far the most common form of activity for a young male was involvement in some sort of gang. Of all the gangs in the city, those on the West Side of Manhattan were known to be the most audacious. At night, local cops had to walk the beat in 'strong-arm squads' of four or five to avoid being bushwhacked by hoodlums. Street gangs like the Parlor Mob, the Gorillas, and the Tenth Avenue Gang flourished amongst the poverty and urban squalor so characteristic of the neighborhood.

The most powerful of the early Hell's Kitchen gangs was the Gophers, so named because they usually met in tenement basements. At their peak in 1907, they were believed to have as many as 500 members. Primarily an Irish gang, they burglarized shops along the gaslit streets at night, ruled the saloons and pool halls, and staged frequent raids on the docks and the Hudson River Railroad, later renamed the New York Central Railroad.

The Gophers were themselves a throwback to an earlier era of gangsterism when, in the late nineteenth century, New York City was at the mercy of nearly a dozen ruthless street gangs concentrated in the notorious Five Points area of lower Manhattan. Comprised largely of Irish immigrants who had fled their homeland during and after the Great Potato Famine, the Five Points gangs staged outlandish daytime robberies, engaged in nighttime gang wars and remained the bane of law enforcement throughout the latter part of the late 1800s. The Dead Rabbits, the Plug Uglies, and the Kerryonians were known and feared, but the most violent of all were the Whyos, led by the likes of Red Rocks Farrell, Googy Corcoran, and Baboon Connolly.

Neither the Five Points gangs nor the Gophers engaged in what would later be commonly referred to as organized crime. The turn-of-the-century gangs were undisciplined and relatively disorganized. There were none of the lucrative rackets that would come later in the Twenties with the passing of the 18th Amendment, otherwise known as Prohibition. Occasionally the Gophers could rent themselves out as bullyboys or enforcers for various political candidates, but much of their time was spent fighting among themselves – an Irish proclivity which amazed and appalled the less violent Dutch and German settlers of the era.

The Gophers were to continue in the tradition of the Five Points gangs, reigning over Hell's Kitchen for twenty-odd years in all manner of professional mayhem. Although no single member was as powerful or well known as Monk Eastman, the most prominent gangster of the era, they nonetheless established a pantheon of memorable psychopaths.

There was Happy Jack Mullraney, who had a partial paralysis of his facial muscles that made it appear he was always laughing. Mullraney was known to be very sensitive about his disfigurement. One night he was in a saloon on 10th Avenue and he said something that irked Paddy the Priest, the saloon's owner and a longtime friend of Mullraney's. Paddy sneered, 'Why don't you try laughing out of the other side of your face, Happy Jack?' Mullraney pulled out a revolver and put a bullet in Paddy's skull.

There was One Lung Curran, known for his occasional withdrawals to a tubercular ward at Bellevue Hospital.

Curran's girlfriend once complained she didn't have a warm coat for the winter, so One Lung promptly went out, blackjacked a policeman and relieved him of his jacket. After Curran's girlfriend had it tailored, other women in the neighborhood expressed envy. Their boyfriends reacted accordingly, and before long the streets of Hell's Kitchen were populated with coatless policemen.

The Gophers were known to be so turbulent and so fickle that very few of their leaders held that distinction for more than a few months. Nonetheless, they remained a force to be reckoned with until 1910, when the New York Central Railroad organized a special security contingent to take action against them. Many of the railroad's recruits were former policemen who had taken beatings at the hands of the Gophers and were now looking to get even.

The Railroad staged a week-long assault on the gang, beating and harassing known members, drastically depleting their forces, and effectively establishing the railway yards on 60th and 30th streets as off limits. Thus weakened, the Gophers spent more time defending themselves against rival gangs like the Hudson Dusters than they did bothering the law.

During the Prohibition years, what was left of the Gophers was resurrected by the infamous Owney 'the Killer' Madden. Born in Liverpool of Irish parentage, Madden made it through his turbulent youth (five arrests for murder by the time he was twenty-three) to become a gangster of distinction. He amassed his power through control of the bootleg liquor and rum-running trade, which became a booming enterprise in Hell's Kitchen. Speakeasies abounded throughout the district, and any late-night convoy of trucks loaded with booze inevitably made its way up 10th Avenue towards one of the many West Side warehouses.

Unlike the earlier generation of Gophers, who were mainly back-alley toughs who preferred to stay that way, Madden aspired to the highest levels of New York society. His nights were usually spent making the rounds at local speakeasies and clubs, where he was known as the Duke of the West Side. An average evening might be spent at his own Winona Club, or at one of the swankier West Side dance halls like the Eldorado or the Hotsy Totsy Club, owned by Jack 'Legs' Diamond.

Madden was the first gangster to come out of Hell's Kitchen with anything approximating a business sense. In fact, he seemed to have his fingers in everything – bootleg liquor, breweries, nightclubs, taxicabs, laundries, and cloak and cigarette concessions. Eventually, he owned a controlling interest in the highly prosperous Cotton Club in Harlem and a piece of the prizefighter Primo Carnera, who won the heavyweight crown in 1933.

With such a lucrative base of income, it was only a matter of time before Madden's reign would be challenged. For years, he'd been able to amicably share his bootleg liquor business with an uptown operator named Arthur Flegenheimer, better known as Dutch Schultz. But he didn't seem to have as much luck with some of his own Irish underlings.

Once, Little Patsy Doyle sought to take over Madden's operation while Madden was convalescing in the hospital following a late-night shooting at the Arbor Dance Hall on West 52nd Street. When Madden was discharged, he decided to use Patsy as an example. At Madden's insistence, Doyle's girlfriend lured him to a saloon at 41st Street and 8th Avenue, where Patsy was shot three times, stumbled through the swinging doors, and died in the gutter outside.

There were other, far more substantial threats. The biggest challenge of all came from yet another Hell's Kitchen Irishman with a thick mane of red hair and an engaging – some would say 'goofy' – smile. If Madden was the very model of the gentleman gangster, a shining example of a Hell's Kitchen street tough who had risen above his station, then Vincent Coll was his antithesis. Known in the underworld as the Mad Mick and later by the press as the Mad Dog, Coll was a throwback to the earliest days of the Gophers, when gangsters were doomed to die in the very streets that spawned them.

Born in County Donegal, Coll was brought to New York at an early age and raised in a cold-water flat in the Bronx by his mother; she died of pneumonia when he was seven. After a prolonged stay at the infamous Mt Loretto orphanage in Staten Island, Coll went to work for Dutch Schultz before he was even old enough to shave.

At first, Coll's gleeful ruthlessness made him a valued enforcer. He was nineteen when police charged him with having killed a speakeasy owner who refused to buy Schultz's booze. He was eventually acquitted of the charge, probably through Schultz's influence.

Before long, the Dutchman started to realize Coll was more trouble than he was worth. After Coll pulled a robbery at the Sheffield Farms dairy in the Bronx without his authorization, Schultz upbraided the young gangster. Rather than back down, as might have been expected, Coll had the audacity to demand that Schultz cut him in as an equal partner.

'I don't take in nobody as partners with me,' Schultz said. 'You're an ambitious punk, but you take a salary or nothin'. Take it or leave it.'

'Okay,' said Coll, with his customary toothy grin. 'I'm leaving it.'

Over the following months, Coll proceeded to make himself a major pain in the ass to both Schultz and Madden, hiring out as a freelance assassin and trying to muscle in on everybody's territory. On June 15, 1931, he kidnapped Madden's closest associate, Big Frenchie de Mange, in front of the Club Argonaut on West 50th Street. Then, in July, just weeks after Madden paid Coll a $35,000 ransom for de Mange, Coll was threatening to kidnap Madden himself.

At the same time, Coll was waging war against Schultz – hijacking beer trucks, trashing speakeasies, and moving in on the Harlem policy games, one of Schultz's most lucrative rackets. As his coup de grace, Coll targeted Joey Rao, Schultz's prime mover in East Harlem, for execution.

On the afternoon of July 28, 1931, Rao was lounging in front of his headquarters, the Helmar Social Club on East 107th Street. Accompanied by two bodyguards, Rao had a pocketful of pennies which he was distributing to a group of neighborhood children who had gathered. A touring car came around the corner and opened fire on

Rao, his protectors, and the children. When the fusillade was over, a five-year-old kid lay dead on the sidewalk and four other children had been wounded. Rao and his bodyguards escaped without a scratch.

Everyone in town knew Coll was behind the shooting. Newspaper headlines the next day christened him 'the Baby Killer.' People on both sides of the law were calling for retribution. Both Madden and Schultz put out a $25,000 contract on Coll, the psychotic 'Mad Dog' who was giving the underworld a bad name. Columnist Walter Winchell reported that, 'Five planes brought dozens of machine guns from Chicago Friday . . . Local banditti have made one hotel a virtual arsenal and several hot spots are ditto because Master Coll is giving them the headache.'

Finally, on the night of February 8, 1932, the inevitable came to pass. At a drugstore on West 23rd Street near 8th Avenue, Coll was in a phone booth carrying on a protracted conversation. An automobile with four men pulled up to the curb outside. Three of the men deployed themselves around the drugstore entrance, while the fourth, carrying a Thompson submachine gun, entered the store. Coll was still jabbering away when the gunman raised his tommy gun and let loose with a short burst of fire through the glass. After correcting his aim, the gunman fired another short burst, then another. He looked in the booth, where baby-faced Mad Dog Coll lay nearly sawed in half amidst blood and shattered glass. Then he strolled out of the drugstore.

It was Owney Madden who Coll had been talking to on the phone. Later reports suggested that the elder gangster held Coll on the line until the gunmen were able to arrive. If this was true, it was not the first time, nor would it be the last, that one child of Hell's Kitchen would eliminate another as part of a bloody battle for control of the neighborhood's bounty.

With Coll out of the picture, things quieted down on the West Side. But by this time, it hardly mattered. The Twenty-first Amendment was passed in 1933, repealing Prohibition. The speakeasies were all closing down and the big dance halls were soon to follow. Within a few months of Coll's shooting, Madden was imprisoned on a parole violation, where he would languish for twelve months even though newspaper stories claimed he had offered a million-dollar bribe to the state parole board. Upon release, he retired to Hot Springs, Arkansas, where he married the postmaster's daughter and ran what amounted to a resort town for mobsters on the lam.

Before Madden left New York, however, in the waning days of Prohibition he was to form one last alliance. In 1931, a young Sicilian immigrant named Charles 'Lucky' Luciano was in the process of forming an organized crime 'commission.' In a radical departure from the usual closed-door policy of the Italian crime syndicate, it was Luciano's intention to allow other ethnic mobsters to take part in a nationwide ruling body. Madden had been included as a personal friend of Luciano's and as a representative of New York's Irish Mob.

At the time, Madden's reign as Duke of the West Side had already peaked, so his inclusion might have seemed like an afterthought. But with this alliance, a relationship was begun between Italian and Irish racketeers on the West Side. It was a relationship that would sustain the area's criminal interests through the lean years of the Depression, and establish a partnership that would shape the lives of countless gangsters that followed.

2

LAST OF A DYING BREED

On Saturday afternoon, August 27, 1960, many of Hell's Kitchen's most distinguished citizens began to arrive at the Church of the Sacred Heart on West 51st Street just off 10th Avenue. It was a beautiful day, with temperatures in the mid-nineties, and the people – over 200 in number – were dressed in their Sunday best. There was a festive atmosphere, with everyone cheerfully greeting one another and exhibiting a communal pride commensurate with the occasion. After all, as any self-respecting West Sider would have known, this was not just *any* gathering. This was a gathering in honor of Michael John Spillane.

With his wavy black hair and dashing good looks, Spillane, then twenty-six years old, was especially well liked by the neighborhood's older residents. Though his exploits as a gangster were known to many, Spillane himself was rarely associated with these acts. Much of it had to do with his abundant personal charms. As they would say long after he was gone, nobody knew how to work the room like Mickey Spillane. And 'the room,' in this case, was most of Hell's Kitchen.

Spillane first began to make a name for himself at a

tender age in the late 1950s. Dressed in fine thousand-dollar suits, he frequently made the rounds bestowing favors in shops and saloons along 9th and 10th avenues. When he heard a neighbor had landed in the hospital, he usually sent flowers. On Thanksgiving, turkeys went out to families in need. He was especially popular with the nuns at Mount Carmel Convent on West 54th Street, to whom he made annual donations.

Behind this appealing facade was an extensive criminal past. Spillane's first brush with the law had come in 1950 at the age of sixteen, when he was shot and then arrested by a patrolman while robbing a Manhattan movie theater. There would be twenty-four more arrests over the years on an assortment of charges including burglary, assault, gun possession, criminal contempt, and the crime he was most often associated with, gambling.

Mickey Spillane's criminal record, however, was of no great consequence to those who gathered at the Church of the Sacred Heart in August of 1960. Instead, they had come to pay their respects to Spillane on the occasion of his marriage, and no talk of violence or gangsterism would spoil this fine day.

Only Sacred Heart Church could possibly provide the proper backdrop for such an illustrious event. The building itself had first been dedicated in 1885 by Archbishop Michael Corrigan, and it had since become one of the community's most enduring symbols. As late as 1920, an overwhelming number of parishioners at Sacred Heart were of Irish extraction. Eventually, more and more Italian surnames began to appear on the official list of subscribers. Even so, intermarriage between ethnic groups was rarely encouraged. Once, in the late 1930s, an Irish father had even threatened to shoot the Reverend William Scully for marrying his daughter to an Italian.

In later years, as the neighborhood's Catholic population became more and more Spanish-speaking, Sacred Heart's congregation was still disproportionately Irish. Those Irish who had remained rallied around this modest Venetian Gothic structure with its bright-red doors as if it were the last remaining link to their proud and embattled past.

On this particular afternoon, a soft light cascaded down from the cathedral's elegant clerestory windows as Spillane, dressed in an impeccably tailored black tuxedo, strolled down the aisle past the assemblage. In keeping with his image, he winked at those he knew and smiled politely at those he didn't.

Spillane's bride-to-be, the lovely Maureen McManus, was led down the aisle by her father. Dressed in a flowing white gown, her resplendent reddish-brown hair tumbling to her shoulders, she was flush with excitement. Following behind her was her good friend and bridesmaid, Eileen Farrell, and Mickey's best man and twin brother, Charlie Spillane.

As Spillane and Maureen McManus stood before the Reverend J. M. Brown, backed by a majestic fifteen-foot-high marble altar, the older guests could hardly contain their pride. Together, this distinguished couple represented two of the neighborhood's most formidable traditions.

Since 1905, the McManus family, affectionately known in the neighborhood as 'the McMani,' had controlled the political fate of the district through their leadership of the Midtown Democratic Club. In the beginning, there was Thomas J. 'The' McManus, who first wrested control of the district leadership from George Washington Plunkitt, one of the most powerful bosses of the infamous New York political organization known as Tammany Hall. Following his election, McManus himself became a practitioner of Tammany Hall politics, using his position to bequeath patronage jobs and welcome new immigrants with voter registration forms.

When McManus dropped dead unexpectedly of a heart attack, it was treated like the passing of a monarch. Some 500 floral pieces filled the back room of the Midtown Democratic Club, where the wake was held. Days later, New York Governor Al Smith led the funeral march of 100 policemen and 300 carloads of mourners.

In 1945, Maureen's father, Eugene, nephew of 'The' McManus and proprietor of a funeral home on West 51st Street, became district leader. But by the time of his daughter's wedding in 1960, Eugene was in ailing health. It was rumored that he would soon be turning the district leadership over to his son, James, Maureen's brother.

Successive generations of immigrants, Irish and otherwise, had turned to Maureen's great-uncle and her father, and soon would turn to her brother; the McMani represented something solid and reliable in a neighborhood constantly in a state of flux. Mickey Spillane, on the other hand, represented quite a different tradition. Much had happened since the days of Owney Madden and the Prohibition rackets. What had seemed like an indestructible criminal empire had been dismantled and forced underground. But the stories and traditions still remained, and even flourished – in somewhat altered forms – during the years of Spillane's youth.

In the postwar years of the Forties and Fifties, when Mickey was a teenager, Hell's Kitchen, like so much of New York City, was in the throes of 'development.' Long gone was the 9th Avenue El train and the noise and dirt that went with it. As part of the West Side Improvement Project, the New York Central Railroad had lowered its tracks below street level, out of sight and out of mind. And construction of the Lincoln Tunnel, running under the Hudson River to New Jersey, had devastated the area just south of 39th Street. All told, to make way for the tunnel, ninety-one tenements disappeared, as did 'Paddy's Market,' an outdoor bazaar that had been a neighborhood institution since the turn of the century.

The ethnic makeup of the neighborhood was also changing. Hell's Kitchen had always been a melting pot. First it was the Irish and the Germans. Then the Italians, Greeks, and eastern Europeans (mostly Poles and Yugoslavians). And in the decade following the war, there was a huge influx of new migrants, mostly Puerto Ricans and Southern blacks. The reasons were not hard to fathom. In 1944, as part of the Fair Labor Standards Act, the federal government increased the minimum wage to thirty cents an hour. In Puerto Rico, the *maximum* wage for the most skilled worker was twenty-five cents an hour. As for Southern blacks, the postwar period had seen the mechanization of the cotton industry, leaving thousands without employment. Enticed by the prospect of jobs and better wages, they headed north.

Yet, unlike many parts of New York, where changing neighborhoods had brought about considerable white flight, Hell's Kitchen was slower to change. The embattled Irish and Italians of an earlier generation were still firmly ensconced in the community's religious, political, and economic institutions, and they weren't anxious to relinquish their hard-won positions. As a result, even as racial tensions flared in the saloons and on the avenues, the power structure, both legitimate and criminal, remained remarkably intact.

In the legitimate world, the most visible example of Irish entrenchment was the Midtown Democratic Club. In the illegitimate world, it was the shylocks, gamblers, shakedown artists, hijackers and assorted strong-arm men who prospered along the waterfront during the second most lucrative era for organized crime in New York City.

Racketeers on the West Side were in an ideal position to reap the benefits of the Port of New York's booming postwar trade. Longshoremen seeking work in Manhattan were still under the thumb of a ruthless 'shape-up' system, which had existed from time immemorial. Each morning, a group of prospective workers gathered at the piers, where a hiring foreman selected who would work that day. At many piers the procedure grew into hiring a crew or gang as a unit.

A common result of the shape-up system was the kickback racket. A crew expecting to receive favorable attention from a hiring foreman was required to kick back 10 or 20 percent of its members' wages. In order to be able to afford such a kickback, many workers were forced to turn to loansharks, or 'shylocks,' who were always readily available to loan money at usurious rates.

With the Hell's Kitchen docks as its base, it was no surprise that Local 824 of the International Longshoremen's Association (ILA) soon became one of the union's most powerful. Harold Bowers was a neighborhood delegate to Local 824, commonly known as the 'Pistol Loçal' because its membership was made up of so many convicted felons. But the real power behind Local 824 was Bowers's cousin, Mickey, whose police record showed thirteen arrests between 1920 and 1940. Mickey Bowers was believed to be behind the death of, among others, Tommy Gleason, a rival for control of the Pistol Local who was gunned down in a 10th Avenue funeral parlor – a convenient spot for a mob hit if ever there was one.

Of all the Irish racketeers during the Forties and Fifties, the most powerful of all was red-haired Edward J. 'Eddie' McGrath. McGrath was a former whiskey baron from Prohibition days who'd made a successful transition to the waterfront rackets. One of an elite group of underworld figures with ties to some of the city's most influential politicians, he'd been appointed an ILA 'organizer at large' by the union's president, Joseph P. Ryan. At the time, McGrath's extensive criminal record included arrests ranging from burglary to murder, and he'd once done a long stretch in Sing Sing.

McGrath's main 'muscle' on the piers was his brother-in-law, John 'Cockeye' Dunn, a vicious convicted murderer, and Andrew 'Squint' Sheridan, another ex-con who'd once been a triggerman for Dutch Schultz.

With Cockeye Dunn and Squint Sheridan as his partners, McGrath controlled the lucrative numbers game throughout the Port of New York and was on intimate terms with many of the most powerful organized crime figures of his day. Meyer Lansky was a long-time companion, as was Moe Dalitz, head of the Cleveland syndicate that owned the Desert Inn gambling casino in Las Vegas, Nevada. And in 1950, McGrath shared a suite at the Arlington Hotel in Hot Springs, Arkansas, with Brooklyn-based syndicate boss Joe Adonis. While there, they were entertained by none other than Owney Madden, the former Duke of the West Side, for whom McGrath had driven a beer truck during the glory days of Prohibition.

On a slightly smaller scale, Hell's Kitchen had operators like Hughie Mulligan. For every Eddie McGrath, there were a dozen guys like Mulligan – localized numbers runners, strong-arm men, bookmakers, and all-purpose gofers. It was Mulligan who first saw the potential in a likable young neighborhood gambler named Mickey Spillane, who he immediately put to work as a 'runner' in the neighborhood's ever-expanding numbers racket.

Short and jowly, with thick black-rimmed eyeglasses, Mulligan himself served as a bookmaker for McGrath and a go-between for the neighborhood's various ethnic factions – including the cops. At the time, the New York City Police Department was still an Irish institution, and some cops didn't fancy dealing with Italian gangsters. Mulligan made sure the police got their cut. He liked to call himself a 'facilitator,' but most everyone else thought of him as a 'bagman.'

Even with his reputation as a pacifier, Mulligan's attitudes were no less insular than many West Siders'. Once, during an investigation of police corruption, detectives hid a recording device in his car as he made the rounds from pier to pier collecting tribute. Mulligan was overheard lamenting the changing ethnic makeup of the workers.

'Look at that over there,' he said, referring to a crew of longshoremen who had gathered. 'There ain't a white man in the bunch. Not a single fuckin' white man.'

The crew he was referring to was almost completely Italian.

Throughout the era of McGrath and Mulligan, criminal profits from the various rackets along the waterfront were staggering. In 1948 alone, the Grace Steamship Line reported losses of $3 million in pilfered goods, of which 80 percent occurred on its New York piers. Along with losses on the docks, many trucks moving cargo between the piers and inland freight terminals were hijacked by armed robbers. Payroll padding, no-show jobs, organized rip-offs, kickbacks, gambling concessions, and loansharking flourished as never before, and any organized crime group worth its salt had contacts in the ILA.

With so many different operators feeding off the waterfront rackets on so many different levels, no doubt the mob would sooner or later have begun to choke on its own gluttony, leading to the inevitable gang wars. Luckily for many mobsters, the United States government, in the persons of Senator Estes Kefauver and New York Governor Thomas E. Dewey, saw to it that it never happened. It was the 1951 Kefauver Committee that first declared that racketeers were 'firmly entrenched along New York City's waterfront.' That was followed by Governor Dewey's New York Crime Commission hearings, which spent most of 1952 investigating the activities of the ILA.

Ironically, at the same time various government commissions began to purge the New York waterfront of its criminal elements, the industry itself began to wane. In July of 1956, the *Andrea Doria* sank off Nantucket, signaling the beginning of the end for cruise liners, always a staple on the West Side docks. By 1959, airplanes carried nearly two-thirds of all transatlantic passengers.

The decline of New York's waterfront wasn't as dramatic or rapid as the end of Prohibition: the Twenty-first Amendment eliminated the underworld's business overnight. But the effect on Hell's Kitchen was immediate. The most reliable source of employment the neighborhood had ever seen was dying. As a result, the railyards went bankrupt. Housing conditions deteriorated. And the area's middle class, which held strong throughout the 1950s, finally began to erode.

The gangsters went their separate ways. Hughie Mulligan moved his 300-pound girth and his family to a respectable middle-income abode in Queens Village. Squint Sheridan was given a life sentence for the murder of a hiring stevedore in Greenwich Village. For his role in the same murder, Cockeye Dunn was given 2,000 volts to the cerebellum, courtesy of New York State.

In 1959, the granddaddy of them all, Eddie McGrath, took a plane ride to Florida. As king of the West Side waterfront rackets, he had presided over the most prosperous period for organized crime in New York since Prohibition. He was lucky. He had not only stayed alive but had come through all the various investigative committees without so much as an indictment. Now all he wanted to do was retreat to a warmer climate, just like the handful of other gangsters he knew who'd been fortunate enough to survive till retirement.

As the most influential gangster left in Hell's Kitchen in 1960, Mickey Spillane inherited what was left of the neighborhood rackets. They were troubled times for Hell's Kitchen and the city in general, with the relatively prosperous Fifties about to give way to the social and economic uncertainty of the Sixties. For the Irish, who had ruled the political clubhouses and gambling dens of the neighborhood throughout the century, it was a time of reckoning.

Within months of Mickey Spillane's marriage to Maureen McManus in August of 1960, John Fitzgerald Kennedy was sworn in as the thirty-sixth President of the United States. For millions of Irish Americans, it marked a point of no return. The children and grandchildren of Irish immigrants, whose ancestors had fled political persecution in their own land and overcome violent discrimination in the States, were now, proudly and unequivocally, American.

What that meant in the mind of many second- and third-generation Irish-American families was that they were now free to move to the suburbs in pursuit of the postwar American dream. No longer an immigrant class, middle-income Irish Catholics assimilated – with a vengeance.

But in some predominantly working-class neighborhoods

like South Boston, Chicago's Southwest Side, and Hell's Kitchen, the transition was slower. To the Roman Catholic poor of these communities John F. Kennedy's election was an empty promise. Their lives were a far cry from the Kennedys' lavish summer estates and expensive Harvard educations. What's more, the upper crust, known as the 'lace-curtain' Irish, looked on these 'shanty' Irish as a hopeless and disdainful breed, a reminder perhaps of what they had left behind in their frantic climb to the top of the social register.

While most of Irish America took advantage of their newfound status in the wake of Kennedy's election and headed for suburbia, there remained in Hell's Kitchen a small, hard-core community who had neither the means nor the inclination to leave. With the area now entering its newest phase of economic decline, these embattled Irish held tight – for better or for worse – to the traditions established by their forebears. It was this group who turned to Mickey Spillane, whose polite manner and handsome black-Irish features made him something of a Kennedyesque figure in his own right.

By the mid-1960s, what remained of the West Side rackets were now evenly divided between Spillane's crew, known simply as the Hell's Kitchen Irish Mob, and various Italian interests. The Italians still played a major role on the docks and at Madison Square Garden, the city's premier sports arena, then located at 50th Street and 8th Avenue. At the Garden the labor force was controlled equally by the Gambino crime family in Brooklyn, by Vincent 'the Chin' Gigante's Genovese family crew, and by Spillane's Irish Mob.

The prize New York Coliseum, which opened in 1956 at 59th Street and 8th Avenue, was also split among numerous criminal factions. Ensuring that everyone got a piece of the action, as many as fourteen different unions got involved, many of them acting as brokers between individual contractors, management, and the mob.

Spillane's alliance with the Mafia was always tenuous. He had inherited the relationship from his former boss, Hughie Mulligan, who had himself inherited a tradition going all the way back to Owney Madden. Since Madden first joined Lucky Luciano's Organized Crime Commission in 1931, the Italians had far outstripped the Irish in every facet of organized crime. As J. Edgar Hoover chased Communists and denied the existence of the Mafia, the Italians constructed an impressive national network controlled mainly by the 'Five Families' of New York City. Local neighborhood mobs like the Hell's Kitchen Irish were allowed to operate, but only as long as the Italians got their cut.

Along with having to walk a fine line between being a partner and a competitor, Spillane resented the fact that *La Cosa Nostra*, as the Mafia was now commonly known, was able to muscle in on his territory. Since he wasn't interested in seeing what he could get out of the 'partnership' by branching out into non-neighborhood activities, to Spillane the arrangement seemed like a one-way street – a shakedown, in fact. About the only thing he got in return for his cooperation was a guarantee he wouldn't be fucked with.

There was always a degree of mutual distrust, and things no doubt took a turn for the worse when Spillane snatched Eli Zicardi, who ran the policy games for Anthony 'Fat Tony' Salerno, head of the Genovese family. While he no longer nabbed neighborhood folks, Spillane still occasionally kidnapped wiseguys, holding them for ransom and then letting them go once he got paid. It was a peculiar aspect of his relationship with the Italians. They often knew Spillane was the one who had done it, but they were willing to tolerate it as long as nobody got hurt and the ransom never exceeded the $10,000 to $15,000 range.

But something went wrong with the Zicardi kidnapping. The ransom was delivered. Zicardi, however, disappeared from the face of the earth.

There were no immediate repercussions. But people wondered just how long Spillane would be able to get away with harassing bigshots like Fat Tony Salerno before it all came home to roost.

In the meantime, Spillane kept his control over Hell's Kitchen's 'ground-level' rackets. The numbers game was the most lucrative. Each day, Mickey had a dozen or more runners out collecting three-digit numbers and bets to go with them. Since the winning bet often paid extremely high dividends – sometimes as much as 600 to 1 – even nongamblers liked to play, betting anywhere between $1 and $1,000.

The number was determined by that day's 'total mutual handle,' or betting totals at the track, which were published in the daily newspapers. The last three digits of the total were the number for the day. Some days there was more than one winner; some days there were none – in which case the entire pot wound up in Spillane's pocket.

Along with the numbers racket, Spillane owned a piece of most of the gambling dens in Hell's Kitchen. There were at least a half-dozen all-night clubs on 10th Avenue, known simply as 'the Avenue' to most West Siders. Spillane himself was an avid dice and card player, and almost any night of the week he could be found at Tommy Collins's social club, a first floor walk-up at 722 10th Avenue, or at 694 10th Avenue, another frequent gambling spot.

When he wasn't gambling or tending to his rackets, Spillane spent a considerable amount of time shoring up his reputation as a man of influence in the community. His marriage to Maureen McManus, of course, was his biggest coup. Among other things, it reinforced the symbiotic relationship that had always existed between the neighborhood's various spheres of influence. To the old-time residents of Hell's Kitchen, the coupling of Spillane and McManus evoked nostalgia for those days when the gangster and the politician walked hand in hand, and the Irish ruled the roost. Current reality was quite different.

Since the turn of the century reign of the McMani and before, outside commentators had been accusing Hell's Kitchen pols of being under the influence of local gangsters. To a large extent, it was true, though anyone with a knowledge of New York City politics shouldn't have been surprised. Hell's Kitchen was far from unique in this regard. From the earliest days of Boss Tweed's Tammany machine, a local district leader's influence was based on his ability to deliver services and exert control in his community. In the Twenties and Thirties, that included unleashing gangsters on election day to make sure voters pulled the right levers – even if they had to do so with ten broken fingers. In return, a district leader was able to exert influence over a cop or a county judge when one of the local lads got busted.

By the 1960s, however, years of political reform altered the relationship between politics and crime in the neighborhoods. It became a lot less binding on both sides. Yes, Mickey Spillane still controlled a certain number of jobs in Hell's Kitchen, which were in turn parceled out through the Midtown Democratic Club as political favors. And Spillane would still, at the behest of the district leadership, extend loans to local merchants unable to get credit from the banks. But long gone were the days when a local gangster could control enough votes to swing an election, or a local district leader have enough sway to keep his constituents out of jail.

Throughout the mid and late Sixties, the neighborhood continued its slippery slide towards ghettoization. Funds for low-income housing, always a staple in Hell's Kitchen, dried up; older buildings stood empty and gutted. Drugs began to be a factor. The streets looked deserted a lot of the time, and there were random muggings, stickups, and harassment from landlords. It was getting so longstanding neighborhood folk couldn't walk around anymore and feel safe.

At the White House Bar on 45th Street and 10th Avenue, Spillane heard these and other complaints. Usually he was surrounded by his underlings – an up and coming young kid named Billy Beattie, older friends like Tom Devaney, Tom 'the Greek' Kapatos, the avuncular Tommy Collins, and Eddie Cummiskey. Old-time neighborhood residents came into the bar looking for a favor. Mickey took them off to the side or maybe into a back room and listened while they poured out their hearts. Maybe the guy had a business venture he thought Spillane might want to invest in. Maybe he'd been robbed by a local Puerto Rican kid and wanted to even the score. Maybe his wife or daughter had just gone into the hospital and he needed a loan to cover the bills.

Mickey listened quietly and did what he could. 'Thank you, Mr Spillane,' they would say. 'God be with you.' Sometimes there were hugs and even tears as they reminisced about those long-gone days when the rackets were thriving and the neighborhood was all theirs. Spillane seemed to cherish these encounters. It made him feel like he was doing something for the community. It made him feel like he had respect.

Meanwhile, outside in the streets, there was something brewing that the courtly Spillane did not fully comprehend. In the late 1960s, kids all across America were questioning authority, with many traditions and conventions being swept aside. Respect itself was becoming outdated as an entire generation embraced the politics of upheaval.

To the aspiring young gangsters of Hell's Kitchen it was as good a reason as any to let off a little steam. In the spirit of the times, they danced to the beat of a different drummer. For them Mickey Spillane was an antique, and his adherence to old-world neighborhood values was all phony bullshit. Even Spillane's reputation as a high-roller and a fancy dresser, as far as they were concerned, was crap. Everybody knew he bought his so-called thousand-dollar suits for almost nothing at Tassiello's 'swag' (stolen merchandise) shop on 9th Avenue.

What's more, the word on the street was that Spillane 'didn't have the balls' anymore. He was always getting other people to pull the trigger for him, just so he could stay clean in the eyes of the legitimate folk. There was even a story making the rounds that Spillane had agreed to pay a neighborhood kid, Alfred Scott, $5,000 to do a shooting for him. When Scott did it, Spillane reneged on the deal and the kid had to go on the lam in Arizona without a cent to his name.

True or not, that didn't wash anymore. There was a new breed now, more restless and violent than their immediate predecessors. If the working-class Irish of Hell's Kitchen had become something of a lost tribe in the 1960s, then this younger generation were the children of that lost tribe. The most dominant symbol of their lives was not J.F.K. riding proudly along Pennsylvania Avenue on Inauguration Day, but J.F.K. slumped over in the backseat of a limousine in Dallas, his brains splattered all over his wife Jackie's dress.

It was only a matter of time before one of these Young Turks stepped forward to lay claim to his generation's inheritance. Since the earliest days of gangsterism in Hell's Kitchen it had always happened that way, youth rising up to exert its physical authority. The only question was whether this person would have the *cojones* to take on someone as popular as Mickey Spillane, and once he'd done that, whether he'd be able to instill discipline into this increasingly wanton younger generation.

It was a daunting proposition. But before long a nineteen-year-old neighborhood kid with golden hair and a broad smile began to make his moves. Not since the days of the goofy and homicidal Mad Dog Coll would Hell's Kitchen see someone make their presence felt with such youthful audacity, such ambition, such brutal panache. This kid had all the makings of a serious challenger: he was manipulative, physically impressive, and he had a personal vendetta against Spillane he'd been harboring for years.

The year was 1966. The kid's name was James Michael Coonan.

Coonan.

3

JIMMY SOWS HIS OATS

'It's this fuckin' Mike Spillane,' said Eddie Sullivan. 'We wanna take him out.'

Sullivan looked like he hadn't slept in days. He was sporting a five-day stubble on his chin, his eyes were bloodshot, and he was chain-smoking cigarettes like they were the only thing keeping his lungs going. It was March 1966 and Sullivan was seated in a Naugahyde booth in the back of Tony's Cafe, a nondescript little bar on West 72nd Street in upper Manhattan, speaking to his old friend and criminal partner, Bobby Huggard. Huggard was accompanied by Georgie Saflita, *his* criminal partner. Rounding out this ragged ensemble was young Jimmy Coonan and his older brother, Jackie.

Built like a bull, with bulging forearms and a vacant, steely look in his eyes, Bobby Huggard was a hard-core criminal. Though only twenty-one, he'd already been charged a half-dozen times with an assortment of violent crimes, including numerous counts of felonious assault, his specialty. Even in jail Huggard was known as a mean dude. In other words, not a bad guy to have at your side if you were planning to engage in an all-out gang war.

Huggard knew all about Mickey Spillane. Recently, he'd moved from Queens to the West Side of Manhattan, where he rented a small apartment on 43rd Street, just a few blocks from Spillane's White House Bar. Huggard had a cousin who regularly placed bets with Spillane. One afternoon, his cousin had introduced him to Spillane, Eddie Cummiskey, and some of the others who hung out regularly at the White House.

Huggard didn't really give a fuck about Spillane one way or the other. He'd met him, that was all In fact, once he got a look at Spillane, he couldn't really figure out how he'd gotten to be such a power on the West Side. Spillane was about forty pounds lighter than Huggard and dressed in a suit and tie. The way Huggard saw it, he didn't seem like a tough guy at all; just a high liver.

While Huggard demurred, Eddie Sullivan sipped on his beer and lit up another cigarette. 'What we wanna know, Bobby, is are you with us on this thing or not.'

Huggard shrugged. It wasn't the best offer he'd ever had, but it was something to do. 'Sure, Eddie. You know you can count on me.'

For the next thirty minutes, Eddie Sullivan explained how they were going to build an arsenal to take on Spillane. But before they did that, he said, they would need cash. And to get cash they would have to pull a robbery. Sullivan knew a bar in the Bronx he felt would be a pushover. That would be their first target.

Bobby Huggard listened as Eddie Sullivan babbled away. Some of it made sense; some of it made no sense at all. Occasionally Jackie Coonan jumped in with a comment. Nineteen-year-old Jimmy Coonan, by far the

79

youngest person at the table, hardly spoke at all.

To Huggard, this was intriguing. He knew all about Jimmy Coonan's feud with Spillane. From what he'd heard, Spillane once pistol-whipped Coonan's old man and Jimmy had turned vengeance into a personal crusade. There was definitely something about this kid, thought Huggard. Even as the others did all the talking here at Tony's Bar – with the elder Eddie Sullivan assuming the role of leader – Huggard could tell the person really behind the move on Spillane was this intense little blond-haired kid, Jimmy Coonan.

Unlike a lot of Irish kids in Hell's Kitchen who fell prey to the neighborhood's 'glorious' tradition of gangsterism, Jimmy Coonan had come from a respectable middle-class background. His father, John Coonan, was a certified public accountant. Coonan's Tax Service at 369 West 50th Street was no great threat to E. F. Hutton, but it was steady employment. Coonan's mother, Anna, who was of part German extraction, also worked there.

Born on December 21, 1946, Jimmy was the second of John's and Anna's four children. Their residence was a five-room walk-up at 434 West 49th, between 9th and 10th avenues. As a teenager, Jimmy was only five-foot-seven-inches tall, but stocky, with a thick neck and broad shoulders. He showed a lot of promise as a boxer, a skill he would later hone at Elmira Reformatory. Although he was a reasonably affable youngster, he was known to have an explosive temper. Once, at the age of seventeen, he got in a fight with a neighborhood kid. The kid wound up in a local hospital with nearly sixty lacerations on his face and body.

It was also at the age of seventeen that Coonan dropped out of high school and began running with the neighborhood's professional criminal element. Because of his boxer's physique, it was always assumed Coonan would be one of a dozen strong-arm types, the kind of kid a more established racketeer might use to do the dirty work for him. But Jimmy showed early on that he had higher aspirations, and he was smart, always looking to form alliances that might strengthen his position in the neighborhood.

One of the first partnerships Coonan formed was with brawny, brown-haired Eddie Sullivan, a small-time burglar and bank robber who was nearly fifteen years his senior. Sullivan was a freelance criminal, not attached to any gang, who often hung out in West Side saloons looking to borrow money or drum up business.

Mickey Spillane, for one, never liked Sullivan. Not only was he not from Hell's Kitchen, but he was a drunk and a troublemaker who seemed to have designs on the neighborhood rackets. One time, in the back of the White House Bar, Spillane and his brother even had to give Sullivan a beating just so he'd stop coming around the neighborhood.

To young Jimmy Coonan, Sullivan was useful. For one thing, ever since the Spillane brothers smacked him around, Sullivan had been saying he was going to make a move on Mickey Spillane whether Coonan was with him or not. Jimmy knew Sullivan was crazy enough to do it, and that if he used Sullivan properly, Coonan would be the prime beneficiary.

The other thing was that Sullivan had a lot of criminal

contacts from his many years in prison. If Coonan was going to make a serious move on Spillane, he knew he'd need an arsenal and a few helping hands. At the moment, it was only himself, Sullivan, and his twenty-two-year-old brother, Jackie, against the Spillane twins and at least a dozen other guys who'd come to Spillane's defense.

It was Sullivan who reached out to Bobby Huggard, who he'd once done stickups with. That's how they'd all wound up at Tony's Bar on West 72nd Street this sunny March afternoon. They were a ragtag collection of criminal misfits, an unlikely crew to take on someone as powerful and well-liked as Mickey Spillane. But with Sullivan's know-how, Huggard's brawn, and, most of all, Jimmy Coonan's desire, they were determined to follow this thing through to its logical – or even illogical – conclusion.

Within days of the meeting at Tony's Bar, developments on the West Side were threatening to overtake Coonan, Sullivan, and their makeshift crew. For one thing, the Bobby Lagville killing went down. Lagville was the guy who was sent by Spillane to kill Eddie Sullivan. But Lagville had been found out by Coonan & Company, taken out to Long Island City, and turned into a receptacle for an assortment of large-caliber bullets.

Detectives from the 108th Precinct in Queens were asking questions up and down 10th Avenue trying to find out who might have had a motive for killing Little Bobby Lagville, a known Hell's Kitchen gangster. In keeping with the West Side Code, nobody knew nothin'.

One person the cops questioned was Julius 'Dutch' Grote, a strapping ex-con and neighborhood gambler who worked behind the bar at Pearlie's, a saloon on 9th Avenue between 48th and 49th streets. Grote told the police he knew Lagville because they'd worked together in the Metal Lathers union. But that was all he had to say.

What he didn't tell the cops was that on March 22, 1966, the night Lagville disappeared, he'd stopped by Pearlie's for a drink. Lagville told Grote he'd been called to a meeting with Sullivan, Jimmy and Jackie Coonan. Grote had been with Spillane and Tommy Collins when Jimmy Coonan sprayed them with machine-gun fire from a West 46th Street rooftop. So he knew there was a gang war going on. He asked Lagville, 'Do you think that's a good idea?'

'I got no choice, Dutch,' Bobby replied. 'They called me, I gotta go.'

Now the cops were telling Grote that Bobby Lagville had been shot seven or eight times, stabbed repeatedly, then run over by a car.

Only the car was an exaggeration.

Not long after the Lagville murder, Jimmy, Jackie, and Eddie Sullivan stumbled into Pearlie's. They looked demented, as if they'd been up for weeks without sleep. Dutch Grote knew they'd been hunting around the neighborhood for Mickey Spillane the last few days, and that Spillane had gone into hiding.

Sullivan, his thick features frozen in some permanent, sinister expression of paranoia, had a long gray overcoat on. Underneath the coat he was holding a glistening chrome-colored submachine gun.

'Where the fuck's Spillane?' Sullivan asked Dutch Grote.

Like a lot of people in Hell's Kitchen at the time, Dutch had been trying to remain neutral during the Coonan/Spillane Wars. He'd gambled with Spillane a lot and thought of him as a godfather. But he knew the Coonans, too. In fact, John Coonan, Jimmy's and Jackie's father, had been the best man at his wedding. So he wasn't about to take sides.

'He was in here this morning,' said Grote, 'but I ain't seen him since.'

'You sure?'

'Sure I'm sure.'

'Hey, Dutch,' asked Jackie Coonan. 'Whose side you on anyway?'

'I'm on nobody's side, Jackie; you know that. I walk right down the middle.'

There was some mumbling among the three of them as they looked around the bar. Grote thought he heard Jackie say, 'He's a fuckin' liar and we oughta get rid of him.' To which Jimmy said, 'No, he's neighborhood. He's good people.' Then they left.

A few days later, Jimmy, Jackie, and Eddie Sullivan met again with Bobby Huggard and Georgie Saflita uptown at Tony's Bar. They were all in a surly mood, chain-smoking cigarettes and swigging beer. While they'd been looking for Spillane, there were all kinds of rumors surfacing about hired gunmen being flown in from Texas and Boston to blow them away. The Coonan/Spillane Wars had become like a runaway train. There wasn't much time, they figured. They'd have to pull the Bronx stickup immediately.

That night at around 12 A.M. they all piled into Eddie

Sullivan's girlfriend's rented car. They drove to a small bar near Westchester Square in the Bronx, underneath the elevated railway. All five of them went into the bar. The take wasn't much, but it was the easiest $800 any of them had made in a long time. They didn't even have to fire a shot.

From there, they drove through the night to Bennington, Vermont, where they had no trouble buying four handguns – two .38-caliber automatics, a .45, and a .25 Beretta. They slept the next morning at a hotel in Bennington, then headed to Georgie Saflita's apartment in New Jersey.

At Georgie's place, the boys patted themselves on the back. So far, things were going swell. Eddie Sullivan said he knew of a numbers joint in Greenwich Village they should hit next, and everybody agreed that was a good idea. In the meantime, with Spillane's alleged hit men after them, they decided to split up and reconvene back at Georgie's apartment in a few days. Georgie stayed put with his wife, Jimmy and Eddie Sullivan went to stay at a friend's apartment in Manhattan, and Jackie and Bobby Huggard headed for Brooklyn. It was April Fools' Day, 1966.

In Brooklyn, Jackie and Bobby immediately went to a bar where Huggard used to hang out when he lived on Kent Avenue in Greenpoint. They planned to spend the night at Huggard's ex-wife's apartment, but first they would have a few drinks and relax. They were both carrying weapons from the buy in Vermont, Jackie a .45 and Huggard a .38.

Huggard liked Jackie. He was about the same size as his younger brother Jimmy – five-nine and 175 pounds

– and he liked to grease his sandy-blond hair straight back in a vintage 1950s ducktail. He seemed a lot more talkative and easygoing than his brother, who was about the most serious nineteen-year-old Huggard had ever met.

Huggard and Jackie sat for a few hours, telling jokes and getting quietly stewed. Then Jackie said he had to go outside for a while and would be right back.

It was now about 2:30 A.M. Huggard sat in the bar for at least an hour asking himself, 'Where the fuck is Jackie?' Finally, the bartender told him he had to close up the joint. Huggard left the bar and walked a couple of blocks to Greenpoint Avenue. Two blocks to the north, at the intersection of Greenpoint and Manhattan avenues, Huggard saw two or three squad cars gathered around a corner saloon with their lights flashing. There were cops everywhere.

Nervously, Huggard sidled up to the bar to find out what was going on. He peeked through a window.

Inside the bar, spread-eagle on the floor, was Jackie Coonan. Standing over him were two cops with their revolvers pointed at his head.

Huggard got the hell out of there as fast as he could. The next day, from his ex-wife's place, he called Coonan's father to find out what had happened. It turned out Jackie had tried to rob the bar on Greenpoint Avenue, and the bartender had jumped over the counter after him.

So Jackie shot him dead.

Huggard knew there was bound to be some kind of investigation. He got together what money he could and immediately got the fuck out of New York City.

In the meantime, Jimmy Coonan and Eddie Sullivan heard what happened and stayed put at their friend Billy Murtha's apartment. They were pissed off. Things had been building nicely towards a showdown with Spillane, and now Jackie had to screw it all up by killing a bartender in Brooklyn for no good reason. It would really be hot on the West Side now; they would have to be on their toes even more than usual.

A few days later, Charles Canelstein and Jerry Morales walked into the Pussycat Lounge and bumped into a very paranoid Eddie Sullivan. Hours later, in a vacant lot across from Calvary Cemetery in Queens, they were both riddled with lead and left to die. Unfortunately for Coonan and the boys, it was a sloppy hit and Canelstein lived. (Unfortunately for Jerry Morales, it wasn't *that* sloppy. He was dead by the time the cops arrived.)

On May 12, 1966 – thirty-seven days after the shooting – Charles Canelstein was wheeled into the Queens County criminal courthouse on a gurney. Before a grand jury, he identified Eddie Sullivan as the triggerman and Jimmy Coonan and the others as his accomplices. What he remembered most vividly was the noise coming from his assailants after he was shot.

'I heard footsteps going back to the car,' he said. 'I heard the doors shut and I heard a hysterical kind of laughter. It wasn't like somebody told a joke, it was almost an animalistic kind of laughter coming from the car.'

All four were indicted. Eddie Sullivan, a three-time loser, was convicted and given a life sentence.

Jimmy Coonan plea-bargained and wound up getting five to ten for felonious assault. He served his time quietly at an assortment of penal facilities, including Sing Sing, where he was reunited with his brother Jackie.

In the meantime, the Coonan/Spillane Wars were put on hold.

At the same time Jimmy Coonan was waging war with Mickey Spillane, Francis Featherstone was passing through adolescence. He'd been born and raised in an apartment at 45th Street and 10th Avenue, just six blocks from Coonan, and later moved to 501½ West 43rd Street. The last of nine children, Mickey, as he was known to family and friends, was two years younger than Jimmy. By 1966, the two Hell's Kitchen Irishmen had heard of each other, but they traveled in different circles. Mickey was a baby-faced kid who nobody payed much attention to, Jimmy a young gangster on the make.

On April 27, 1966, just three weeks after Coonan's arrest for the Canelstein/Morales shooting, seventeen-year-old Mickey Featherstone enlisted in the army. Ultimate destination: Vietnam. While Jimmy Coonan put down his guns and readied himself for a prison sentence, Featherstone was being issued a weapon by the United States government. By November, they would be in opposite corners of the earth – Coonan in prison in upstate New York, Featherstone on his way to Saigon.

In the autumn of 1969, the New York Mets shocked the sports world by beating the heavily favored Baltimore Orioles four games to one in the World Series. After years of being the ugly ducklings of baseball, the Amazin' Mets became the pride of New York City almost overnight.

For Mickey Spillane and other bookmakers throughout the city, however, the World Series was a disaster. The Las Vegas odds-makers had the Mets as 7 to 1 underdogs, and when outfielder Cleon Jones caught the fly ball that ended it all, the city's bookmakers took a beating. Every sentimental slob in the five boroughs who had put down a few bucks on the Mets had a big payday. As the rest of the city rejoiced with parties and a ticker-tape parade, operators like Mickey Spillane counted their losses. Such were the vagaries of being a neighborhood racketeer.

A few months later, Spillane had even more serious problems. Both he and 300-pound Hughie Mulligan, his criminal 'rabbi,' had been called before a grand jury investigating allegations of police corruption. Mulligan had already refused to answer questions, even though he was offered immunity from prosecution. Eventually, he would be cited for criminal contempt.

Spillane took the stand in the fall of 1970 and also refused to talk. Among the questions he was asked by an assistant district attorney were: 'Have you ever assaulted anyone in an attempt to collect a usurious loan for anyone?' and 'Were you present on certain occasions when Hughie Mulligan paid bribes to police officers?' Other questions concerned an alleged conversation between Mulligan and Spillane, recorded by the police, in which Spillane was said to have sanctioned the murder of a government witness.

After Spillane had refused to answer questions throughout his afternoon on the stand, an exasperated assistant D.A. finally asked, 'Well, can you tell me this: Are you related to the other Mickey Spillane?' – the well-known pulp-fiction writer. After a momentary pause, Mickey smiled and leaned over to the microphone. 'No. But I'd be happy to change places with him at the moment.'

Everybody laughed, but Spillane's refusal to talk still cost him sixty days on Rikers Island.

Also in the autumn of 1970, Jimmy Coonan got an early parole from prison and returned to Hell's Kitchen. As with most young adults who do time behind bars, he'd developed a slightly harder and leaner look, his physique enhanced by hours in the prison weight room. In certain circles, as a result of his time inside, he had also enhanced his reputation as a tough guy.

Nonetheless, Spillane was still ruler of the West Side rackets, and Coonan, if anything, was in a worse position than before. His pal, Eddie Sullivan, was behind bars for good. His brother Jackie was still serving time for the murder of the bartender in Greenpoint. And Bobby Huggard had fled New York City. It was just Jimmy now, and it looked like he'd have to start all over again from scratch.

It had always been Coonan's ambition to move into more stable rackets like loansharking. In the pantheon of organized crime, loansharking was a halfway respectable endeavor. You always knew who your customers were, and if violence was needed, as far as the loanshark was concerned there was a built-in justification. After all, the customer knows who he's borrowing from to begin with. And he knows exactly what's supposed to happen if he doesn't make his payments.

To start a loanshark operation, however, you need capital, of which Coonan had very little. Once again, he had to start at the bottom pulling together contacts and engaging in assorted quick-cash schemes. He never lost sight of his goal of getting enough power to be able to challenge Spillane.

For a few months in early '71, Coonan worked as a carpet installer in lower Manhattan. But the rigors of a nine to five job were not only boring, they were a time-consuming impediment to his criminal aspirations. Before long, Coonan was back on the streets hijacking warehouses, sticking up liquor stores and – taking a page from Mickey Spillane – kidnapping local merchants.

His most ambitious crime during this period was the kidnapping of a taxi broker from Staten Island who was supposed to be 'mobbed up.' But that job took a sudden and disastrous turn when the kidnapee escaped from the back of a car he was being transported in. With his hands still in cuffs, the guy fled on foot through Times Square until he found a cop. Coonan had to go into hiding for a few months to escape arrest.

When he returned to the neighborhood, Jimmy was immediately charged with the kidnapping. In February of 1972, there were grand jury proceedings. But the district attorney's office in Richmond County had trouble finding witnesses. Even the victim was now reluctant to take the stand. Eventually the case was dismissed on 'speedy-trial' grounds.

Coonan had gotten lucky with that one, and he knew it. He also knew his luck wasn't going to last forever. Here he was, just twenty-five years old and already he'd chalked up one homicide the authorities hadn't gotten him on and one they had. He'd spent four years of his young life in prison and six or seven months on the lam. Now, he'd just barely missed a kidnapping indictment.

It was definitely time to lead a more careful existence.

In early 1973, a venture came Coonan's way that was to give him some breathing room and lay the foundation for all that would come later. Using what little capital he'd been able to muster, he bought into a saloon once known as McCoy's, now known as the 596 Club because of its location at 596 10th Avenue. Since Coonan was a convicted felon and prohibited from owning an establishment where liquor was sold, the ownership was in his brother-in-law's name. But everyone knew it was Jimmy's bar, and it quickly became his base of operation.

With its old brick facade and two tiny front windows covered by cast-iron bars, from the outside the 596 Club looked like a World War I bunker. On the inside, it looked like a typical Hell's Kitchen gin mill. As you entered, the bar was to the left, running about twenty feet back towards a doorway that led into a small kitchen. To the right of that was an elevated area that looked like a small stage. Beyond that was a doorway leading to the restrooms.

In the early 1970s, the younger neighborhood criminals started hanging out at the 596 Club. On any given night of the week you might find Patrick 'Paddy' Dugan, Denis Curley, Richie Ryan, Tommy Hess, James 'Jimmy Mac' McElroy and a dozen others drinking into the early hours of the morning. Many of these guys had known each other since they were kids. They'd played hockey together at Hell's Kitchen park just up the Avenue, or maybe they'd boxed together on the local Boys Club boxing team.

Eventually, they had gone into crime together, pulling burglaries in the commercial buildings to the east and stealing cargo from the warehouses to the west.

They were high school dropouts, mostly, known more for their nerve than their brains. Their existence seemed predicated on three simple maxims: You don't rat, you don't kill a cop, and you don't smack your woman – at least not in public. At the time, there was little indication that they would eventually form the nucleus of the wild and fearsome Westies, who prosecutors called 'the most savage organization in the long history of New York City gangs.'

Before long the 596 Club was seen as a rival headquarters to Spillane's White House Bar, which was located only two blocks north. That was where the older generation held court and the gangsters loyal to Spillane cursed the recklessness of this new breed. The kids seemed motivated only by a desire for profit, not by any fidelity or respect for the neighborhood where they'd grown up.

One local tough guy who moved easily between the two saloons was Edward 'Eddie' Cummiskey. With his curly black hair, piercing blue eyes, and the cockiness of a bantam rooster, Cummiskey looked and sounded like a gangster from the 1920s. At thirty-nine, he'd already done a long stretch in Attica on an assault and robbery conviction and was there during the infamous Attica riot of 1971. He'd also once spent the better part of a year on the lam after hopping an ILA freighter to Brazil in order to avoid a murder rap. Even by Hell's Kitchen standards, Cummiskey's life as a gangster had been an unusually eventful one.

Maybe it was because Coonan knew that Cummiskey was Spillane's 'muscle.' Or maybe it was just Cummiskey's 'innate charms.' But in the months following his takeover of the 596 Club, Coonan spent a good deal of time cultivating a friendship with the elder gangster. They were often seen together sitting in the back of the bar, drinking and discussing business. Sometimes Cummiskey would come forward to tell the other kids stories from his violent past, stories that usually left everybody in stitches.

One of Eddie's most infamous homicides had taken place just up the street at the Sunbrite Bar, located at 736 10th Avenue. As Cummiskey would tell it, he'd been walking by the bar one afternoon when a young neighborhood woman came out the front door in tears. Cummiskey asked her what was wrong. She told him the bartender inside had insulted her.

Eddie knew the bartender, so he walked inside and confronted him. When the bartender told him he had indeed insulted the woman and it was none of Cummiskey's business, Eddie hauled off and belted him. The bartender was quite a bit huskier than the diminutive Cummiskey, so the punch barely fazed him.

'You punch like a little girl,' snarled the bartender.

Cummiskey pulled a .38 from inside his jacket, pointed it at the bartender.

'Oh yeah?' he asked. 'Well, do I shoot like a little girl?' He pulled the trigger twice, striking the barman in the chest and the head. Then he climbed over the bar and shot him again.

There was another murder Cummiskey was telling people he'd done that the cops didn't even know about.

In 1971, Mike 'the Yugo' Yelovich disappeared from the neighborhood, never to be seen again. Cummiskey was claiming he'd had to kill Mike the Yugo for accidentally shooting him in the shinbone with a rifle. After he'd dispatched Mike, Cummiskey said, he cut up the body and put it in plastic bags. When he was loading the bags into the trunk of his car, one of the legs fell out just as a police car was driving by. Cummiskey figured the cops must have thought it was a mannequin's leg, because they just smiled, waved, and kept on driving.

Cummiskey used to laugh like hell when he told these stories, so people never knew quite what to make of them. But it was known that while at Attica, Cummiskey had trained to be a butcher. So that's what they nicknamed him – Eddie 'the Butcher' Cummiskey.

Another gangster from Spillane's generation that Coonan was beginning to be seen with a lot was Anton 'Tony' Lucich. Born in 1919, Lucich was now a retiree with a reputation as a shrewd businessman. At five-feet-nine-inches tall, with a barrel chest and a broad midriff, Lucich looked like somebody who might have been a tough guy years ago. In fact, he never was. Unlike Eddie Cummiskey, Tony was the kind of guy who always let somebody else pull the trigger. That, he felt, was the secret of his longevity.

Back when he had lived in an apartment on West 47th Street, Lucich was a well-known loanshark in Hell's Kitchen. In the years following World War II, loansharking was a relatively common way for a neighborhood kid to supplement his income. Lucich had begun lending out money while he was working the docks as a shipfitter's helper, then as a welder, and later when he became an asbestos installer.

The first time he ever shylocked was when a fellow dockworker suggested that if he lent him twenty bucks, he would pay him back twenty-four the following week. Something clicked; Lucich saw it as the easiest four bucks he'd ever made. After that, he started lending out small amounts to bartenders, cabbies, neighborhood shop-owners, and gas station attendants. He even started lending to an elderly woman on 10th Avenue who would hang a towel from her tenement window if she needed money that week. Unlike most customers, she always paid her debt off in one lump sum.

Along with loansharking, Lucich became adept at the various other low-level rackets that flourished in Hell's Kitchen throughout the early 1950s. A man of temperate habits, he was able to parlay his modest criminal enterprises into a substantial savings, which allowed him to put down a mortgage on a home in Valley Stream, Long Island. But the rackets in Valley Stream were not quite as lucrative as those in Hell's Kitchen. So before long, Lucich was sniffing around the old neighborhood looking for an investment.

That's where Jimmy Coonan came in. Lucich knew that in the early 1970s, the kindly neighborhood loan-shark was a thing of the past. Lucich was fifty-three, with a heart condition. He was a threat to no one. What he needed now was a strong-arm man, someone a lot younger than himself. Someone like Coonan, whose well-deserved reputation for violence would make collecting outstanding debts a hell of a lot easier.

So one afternoon, sometime in late '73 or '74, Lucich said to Coonan, 'Jimmy, you're a good kid; a smart kid. This cowboy shit is beneath you. Why don't you go in with me? Partners. We front the same amount. I teach you the ropes, share my wisdom. All you gotta do is provide the protection.'

It was the kind of arrangement Coonan had been looking for for years.

Together with Charlie Krueger, a bartender at the 596 Club, they all kicked in $1,000 to get things started. It was agreed they would have their own customers, but once a week, on Friday afternoons, they would meet at the bar and pool their resources. The idea was to keep the cash flowing. Once it came in, it went back out on the street immediately.

Over the next few months, Coonan learned a lot from Tony Lucich. They started out shylocking in increments of $50, $150, or $250. Interest could be anywhere from 2 to 5 points a week, meaning if they lent $100 to somebody, the person had to pay between $102 and $105 the following week. A person could pay back the whole sum, or they could pay just the interest, or 'vigorish,' without touching the principal.

If a customer went weeks without paying his debt, the 'vig' or 'juice' could add up pretty quick, causing the inevitable friction between lender and borrower. With Coonan's reputation, though, it rarely came to that.

Not long after they started, Charlie Krueger dropped out, but Jimmy and Tony were doing better than ever. Their operation followed the usual progression from street-level gamblers and drinkers to more sophisticated borrowers. Soon neighborhood merchants, union members, and sometimes even other shylocks were seen coming to and from the 596 Club, picking up and dropping off cash. Since neither Lucich nor Coonan were heavy bettors or boozers themselves, they were able to keep it moving without touching their initial outlay. The juice alone was enough to live on.

For Coonan, it was the beginning of what he hoped would be a growing enterprise. He told Lucich he wanted to start up a numbers racket, and after that maybe his own bookmaking operation. Coonan proved to be a good businessman with a nose for the bottom line and expansion opportunities. He'd been lending out money to some of the other guys in the bar who were using it to finance their own racketeering schemes. It was the beginnings of a group, or crew, that was increasingly beholden to Coonan. Slowly but surely, as the debts piled up, they were starting to see him as their 'boss.'

In the midst of his burgeoning business ventures, Jimmy Coonan got an unexpected visit from Cupid. He'd been hanging out with a neighborhood woman named Edna Fitzgerald who'd just recently broken up with her boyfriend. Before that she had been married to a cop named Frank Fitzgerald. Fitzgerald had died suddenly of an overdose, leaving her with two children.

Edna was a tough cookie. Born Julia Edna Crotty in 1942, she was orphaned at the age of fourteen and bounced from relative to relative before marrying Fitzgerald in 1962. She was five-foot-three, with dark hair, a plump figure, and her travails as a young widowed

98

mother with little or no means of support had given her a hard, bitter edge. But Jimmy liked her.

Coonan had never been much of a womanizer and wasn't really one for elaborate courtships. Not long after he started seeing Edna, who was four years his senior, they made plans to get married. But first Jimmy wanted to meet with her old boyfriend, Billy Beattie, to make sure the coast was clear. Through a mutual friend of theirs, he arranged a get-together at Sonny's Cafe on 9th Avenue.

Coonan and Billy Beattie were roughly the same age and well aware of each other's reputations, though they'd never been formally introduced. Beattie, who was tall and gangly with curly black hair, had gotten his start with Mickey Spillane. At the age of nineteen, he'd been given a maintenance job at Madison Square Garden, where he began his life of crime by stealing coin change from the pay toilets. After that, he stopped showing up for work altogether – except to pick up his weekly paycheck.

Eventually, Beattie graduated to the art of auto theft. It was his job to steal the cars that Spillane and his crew used for their burglaries and bank heists.

At Sonny's Cafe, Coonan gave the appearance of being less interested in Beattie's criminal career than he was in his romantic predilections. He asked Beattie what his current status was with Edna Fitzgerald.

'I ain't seen her in about a month,' said Billy. 'Far as I'm concerned, it's over and done with.'

'That's good,' replied Jimmy. 'That's what I was hopin' to hear. I been hangin' out with her myself.'

'Hey, knock yourself out. She's all yours.'

The two of them relaxed, had a few drinks, talked

about the neighborhood and other neutral topics. It was a seemingly innocuous conversation, but like so many of Coonan's liaisons during this period, there was an ulterior motive. Within weeks, he hired Beattie as a bartender at the 596 Club, and Billy became the first of many neighborhood tough guys to openly shift his allegiance from Spillane to Coonan.

With his marriage to Edna on July 28, 1974, Coonan's life looked more stable than ever before. He even talked about buying a nice middle-class home in New Jersey, a display of upward mobility that would have been financially impossible just six months earlier. On the professional front, he had the 596 Club and his thriving loanshark operation with Tony Lucich. At twenty-eight, with his well-deserved reputation as a tough guy *and* a smart businessman, Coonan had everything to look forward to.

All of which made it even more aggravating for him when he finally fucked up . . .

It was stupid, really. A little shooting out on the avenue. A few folks from Harlem had been making their way uptown after spending an evening on the Circle Line, a sightseeing cruise boat docked at West 42nd Street. It was June 22, 1975, a warm summer evening. Around 12 A.M., Vanderbilt Evans, black, twenty-nine years old and a strapping six-feet-five-inches tall, went looking for a cab in front of the 596 Club. He was accompanied by two ladies and two male friends, both of whom were about his size.

John Reid, a nineteen-year-old neighborhood kid, was

pulling his car into a parking lot just north of the bar. Evans and his entourage made no great effort to get out of the way. Reid, who was a good ten inches shorter and 100 pounds lighter than Evans, stepped out of his car. He and Evans exchanged angry words, then Reid challenged the Harlem folks to a fight. Evans and his friends looked at this little kid and smiled.

'Oh, you think it's funny, do you?' asked Reid. 'Why don't you wait right here?'

Reid disappeared into the 596 Club. A few seconds later Evans and his friends heard a commotion and turned around. Behind them was a group of five or six white folks charging from the bar. Some of them were carrying sticks and baseball bats. At the front of the pack was the bar owner and rising neighborhood leader, Jimmy Coonan.

Two cops from the Midtown North Precinct's anti-crime unit happened to be sitting in an undercover taxi waiting at a red light. The whole thing was unfolding right before their eyes. As the mob advanced, they got out of the cab and approached. At precisely that moment, Evans, who was standing near some street construction on 10th Avenue, picked up a metal Con Edison sign to use as a weapon.

That's when Coonan pulled a .38-caliber Colt Special from his pocket. Amidst the yelling and confusion, Coonan fired, hitting Vanderbilt Evans once in the right shoulder, just inches from his heart.

The cops charged. 'Halt! Halt!' they shouted, grabbing Coonan and wrestling him to the ground.

At the precinct house, Jimmy claimed that someone

else pulled the gun and he'd only picked it up after it was dropped. As for the shot that was fired? Yes, sir, he'd heard it, but it must have been somebody else.

The Vanderbilt Evans shooting was a complete pain in the ass, as far as Coonan was concerned. He was let out on bail, but there was sure to be a grand jury investigation. Not only that, but the cops had found him with $1,500 in his pocket, which they were saying they knew was part of his loansharking operation.

In July and August of '75, Jimmy spent a good deal of time trying to get his witnesses together. At one point he assembled a group of neighborhood people, including fellow loanshark Tony Lucich, at Eddie White's apartment at 501 West 43rd Street, across from the 596 Club on the northwest corner of 10th Avenue. 'Eddie,' Jimmy Coonan told White, 'remember how you seen this thing. You seen it plain as could be from your window. And Jimmy Coonan didn't pull no gun on nobody.' Lucich, who was best man at Coonan's wedding and a stand-up guy, was going to back up Eddie White's version, even though he'd been playing cards somewhere else on the night of the shooting.

It was Coonan's hope that he could confuse the issue enough that he wouldn't get indicted. But with two cops as witnesses against him, he knew it was a long shot.

Even if he was able to finagle his way out of this one, Jimmy knew this Wild West shit had to stop. Sure, it served a purpose, in a way. In Hell's Kitchen these types of incidents tended to enhance a guy's reputation, make him seem like someone who was quick with a gun, someone who had to be taken seriously. Also, John Reid had been in trouble with these menacing black dudes from Harlem and Jimmy had come to his defense. That was admirable.

But Coonan knew that with his criminal record and his new business ventures at stake, it just wasn't worth the risk.

What he needed now was someone to share the violence with him. In racketeering circles, it is an acknowledged fact that a boss or crew chief has to have a right-hand man. Someone who'll stand over a union official, a shopowner, or a loanshark customer and say, 'Listen, friend, you best come up with the money. My boss here, he's too nice, but not me. Me, I'll break your fuckin' legs.'

In the old days, Eddie McGrath had his Cockeye Dunn and Squint Sheridan. Mickey Spillane had his Eddie Cummiskey. Hell, the Italians had whole crews for this sort of thing. Why not me? reasoned Coonan. For appearances' sake, if nothing else.

Before long, Jimmy found a kid who fit the bill – Mickey Featherstone had returned from Vietnam. Featherstone was not a gangster – not yet, anyway. His violent actions had nothing to do with profit motive. They had nothing to do with anything, really, other than the kid's own personal demons.

Everybody knew Featherstone because his family had been in the neighborhood for years. He'd had brothers and sisters who came before him. But they weren't like Mickey. Nobody was. Jimmy had been told stories about this kid and he liked what he heard. Featherstone had potential.

Later, they would form an alliance that was as terrifying

as anything any West Sider had seen since the days of the Gophers. But for now, they had slightly different priorities. For Coonan, the early Seventies had been days of planning and hustling and laying the foundation for a time when he could resume his war with Spillane.

For Featherstone, they were days of random violence and self-hatred.

4

MICKEY

When Mickey Featherstone walked into the Leprechaun Bar with two friends early on the morning of September 30, 1970, he had every reason to believe there might be trouble. Just forty-eight hours earlier, across the street from the bar on the northwest corner of 9th Avenue and 44th Street, there had been an altercation. A bunch of female impersonators were beating up a neighborhood kid and Mickey had done his bit.

A fight between someone from the neighborhood and a group of 'fags in drag' was not an altogether uncommon sight in Hell's Kitchen. Especially on 9th Avenue, just a few blocks from the heart of Times Square, prostitutes, transvestites, and other creatures of the night often made the rounds looking for business, drugs, or just plain companionship. It was Frank McCarthy, a neighborhood kid in his early twenties, who had been walking home with his girlfriend when he came across three men dressed as women cruising along West 42nd Street. Various insults were hurled back and forth; then McCarthy and his girlfriend headed north. The drag queens followed. A scuffle broke out across the street from the Leprechaun Bar,

105

located at 608 9th Avenue. When Featherstone arrived, he did what any self-respecting West Sider would have done. He dove right in, no questions asked.

Before Mickey even had a chance to land a punch, a huge black guy who identified himself as a police officer intervened. The guy moved and spoke with a certain authority, so his claim seemed plausible enough. He was also carrying a police billyclub, which he used to force Featherstone and McCarthy up against the wall.

When a squad car from the Midtown North Precinct pulled up, much to Mickey's surprise the black dude and the drag queens scattered.

'What the fuck's going on here?' asked one of the patrolmen as he stepped out of the car and approached.

By this time Mickey realized the guy who had said he was a cop wasn't really a cop at all. He and McCarthy told the patrolmen what had happened – that the three transvestites had jumped McCarthy and his girlfriend, and that a big black guy with a billyclub had pretended he was a cop and tried to shake them down. The patrolmen didn't seem too concerned; and since no one was willing to press charges, McCarthy, his girlfriend, and the cops went on about their business.

Mickey would have let it slide, too, if he hadn't walked into the Leprechaun Bar two nights later to find the asshole who had pretended to be a cop, billyclub and all.

The Leprechaun Bar was another typical Hell's Kitchen bistro. To the right, as you entered, were four booths against the wall. In the middle of the room there was enough space for three or four tables. To the left, running nearly the length of the wall, was a counter flanked by a half-dozen stools. There was a cigarette machine near the front door and a jukebox in the back. The rest of the room was cluttered with empty beer kegs, cases of booze, and cardboard boxes that lined the walls leading down a hallway to the restrooms.

Mickey was with two neighborhood acquaintances, Jimmy Russell and Kevin Kerr. They ordered a few drinks; then Featherstone asked the old Greek bartender, 'Who's the dude with the billyclub?'

The Greek looked to see who Mickey was talking about, then answered: 'That's Milton. Security.'

Oh shit, thought Mickey, this fucking guy's a bouncer!?

The last thing he and his companions needed was trouble. Jimmy Russell was a small-time criminal with an assault charge pending. He was also a heroin addict. Kevin Kerr had no criminal record, but he had been seen hanging out with neighborhood crooks so often that the cops had his name right up there with all the others. And Featherstone . . . well, twenty-one-year-old Mickey Featherstone had the kind of criminal record that would make a parole officer blanch. Not one but *two* homicides, numerous arrests for assault, and one outstanding charge for possession of an unregistered weapon – all in the last eighteen months.

Not only that, but right this moment, as he sat in this bar with the music blaring and the cigarette smoke billowing and intimations of violence beginning to swirl in his head, Mickey Featherstone was an escapee from the psychiatric ward of a veteran's hospital. 'A passive-aggressive personality with an acute impulse disorder,' is how doctors had described him just days before he snuck away from their fine upstate New York facility.

Before Featherstone and his friends even had a chance to assess the situation, one of the guys who'd been talking to Milton the bouncer started to move towards them. He was a big, lumbering white guy, about six-one and 190 pounds, with blond hair and a thug's face. They could see by the way he moved and the look in his eyes that he'd been drinking. They could also see he was spoiling for a fight. Later, they would learn his name was Linwood Willis.

'Why you lookin' at me?' Willis demanded in a loud Southern accent. 'Y'all tryin' to be smarties or somethin'?'

Russell looked at Kerr; Kerr looked at Russell; they both looked at Featherstone. What had they done to deserve *this* shit!?

'Buy me a drink,' insisted Willis. 'Buy me a drink or I'll cut all three of you.'

Mickey Featherstone was beginning to get annoyed. Russell and Kerr tried to calm him down, but Mickey glared at Milton the bouncer, who had listened to the whole thing and was laughing. Then he glared at this Southern hick, Willis, who was still cursing them for no good reason. Something sinister was going on here, he thought, and he didn't like it one bit. At five-nine and 138 pounds, Mickey was a little guy, and his friends weren't much bigger. Willis was over six feet and Milton the bouncer maybe six-two and 260 pounds.

Featherstone could see right away that what he and his friends needed was an equalizer – a .38, maybe, or anything else that would stop these two fat fucks in their tracks. He told Russell and Kerr to sit tight.

It was now about 3 A.M. The streets were quiet and there was an early autumn chill in the air as Featherstone went looking for a gun. Ever since his discharge from the army over a year ago, Mickey had been certain that people were out to fuck him over. Tonight, he felt, was another one of those nights. When he went into that bar with his friends, all he wanted was a peaceful drink, and a complete stranger had harassed him. Why did it always have to end like this?

Sometimes he was sure it was a conspiracy of some kind, people he knew from 'Nam trying to get back at him. Sometimes he thought it was the Communists.

The doctors said he was crazy, and a lot of other people did too. Mickey could live with that. He knew that for the last few years of his life he had been on some wild self-destructive course. There had been violent nightmares, shootings, and dozens of rumbles. Of course something was wrong. But every time he got away from the hospital, whether it was on a furlough, or, like this time, an escape, he would go into a bar and somebody would show him disrespect, somebody he'd never even messed with. Then there would be trouble. Sometimes people would even get killed; and Mickey would wind up back in the hospital, and he'd say, 'See, you people always tell me I'm paranoid, but I was right. Always, there's somebody out to get me.'

Jimmy Coonan didn't usually spend his nights drinking late in neighborhood saloons, so Mickey was surprised when he spotted him sitting in a booth near the back of

Sonny's Cafe, at 47th Street and 9th Avenue. Coonan was with a few people Featherstone didn't know, so he motioned for him to come into the men's room.

'What's wrong?' asked Coonan, as they crowded into the small lavatory at Sonny's.

Mickey had known Jimmy on a casual basis almost all his life. He knew his older brother Jackie a lot better, but, like everyone else in the neighborhood, he was familiar with Jimmy's story. Ever since his return from the service, Mickey had been hearing about Coonan's feud with Spillane. He'd always sort of admired Coonan, and figured one day, if things worked out, he and Jimmy might even be able to make some money together.

But all that meant nothing at the moment; what he needed right now was a gun, no questions asked, and that's exactly how he put it to Coonan.

With no hesitation at all, Coonan produced a handgun – a .25-caliber semiautomatic – which he kept in his belt in the small of his back, covered by his jacket.

'Mickey, you need any help?' asked Jimmy.

'No,' replied Featherstone. 'This is somethin' I gotta take care of myself.'

With that, Featherstone split the scene. As he headed south on 9th Avenue towards the Leprechaun, he felt an overwhelming sense of gratitude towards Jimmy Coonan. Here was a guy who would be there when you needed him; a guy who could be trusted to do the right thing. Some people would have given a bullshit answer, tried to pretend they didn't know anything about guns. Some might even have been scared. But Jimmy didn't bat an eye; just turned over his piece like Mickey was his own brother.

To Featherstone, it was the ultimate act of friendship, and he would remember Coonan having come through in the pinch long after the other events of September 30, 1970, had become a hazy, troublesome memory.

Back at the Leprechaun, Linwood Willis was still holding court, drunkenly oblivious to the fate that awaited him. When Featherstone walked in, Willis immediately started shouting insults at him; words that were heard clearly by the bartender, the barmaid, and everyone else in the bar. Finally, Willis stepped out the front door, telling Featherstone and his friends he was going to wait for them outside. Mickey said to his buddies, 'You guys stay here. I'll take care of this.'

The barmaid at the Leprechaun sidled over to the window to watch the show. What she saw, and heard, was this:

When Featherstone and Willis got outside, the big Southerner pushed the Irish kid from behind. Mickey circled around so he was now standing opposite Willis, facing north.

'So you're a tough guy?' Featherstone asked as Willis stumbled towards him. 'You got your gun?'

'Yeah,' snarled Willis, reaching inside his jacket.

Mickey pulled the Beretta from his right coat pocket and fired twice, hitting his target once directly in the heart and again a quarter of an inch below. The body immediately dropped to the pavement.

Mickey froze for a moment, the sound of gunfire still echoing in his ears. Then he went over to look at what

111

he'd done. Blood had already begun to run from Willis's chest towards the curb.

Featherstone got a nasty surprise when he flipped open Willis's jacket. There was no gun. The corpse was totally unarmed. His heart pounding and his temples beginning to throb, Mickey quickly headed west on 43rd Street.

A few minutes later, on 10th Avenue at 45th Street, he was confronted by a patrol car from Midtown North. Using the car as a shield, Sergeant John Hanno and Patrolman Robert Erben drew their revolvers and directed Featherstone to drop the gun which he'd been holding in his hand for all the world to see. Standing in the car's headlights, looking dazed and disoriented, Mickey did what they asked. Then he put his hands out, waiting for the cops to slap on the cuffs.

At the precinct house on West 54th Street, three or four detectives interrogated the suspect. His hands and legs trembling uncontrollably, Mickey first claimed that Willis had pulled a gun on him and that he'd used his military expertise to disarm him. But nobody believed that. Eventually, as the darkness outside the squad room gave way to the soothing lightness of dawn, Mickey cut the bullshit.

'He was hasslin' me for no reason,' said Featherstone. 'That was the first mistake he made.'

In October 1970, within weeks of the Linwood Willis shooting, Featherstone landed in the third floor Mental Observation Unit of Rikers Island Hospital. It hadn't taken a grand jury long to pass down an indictment for murder and criminal possession of a dangerous weapon. With Featherstone's past, there was never much question whether or not he committed the act – and he wasn't denying he had. The only real question was whether he would be found psychologically sound to stand trial.

Since Mickey's return from a twelve month tour of duty in Vietnam, all of Hell's Kitchen had been witnessing his violent transformation from a shy, anonymous neighborhood kid into a stone-cold killer. At first, everybody figured Featherstone was just letting off steam and that once he readjusted to civilian life he'd be okay. But the violence kept getting worse and worse, until finally it was too late. Some people felt if he'd only gotten out of the neighborhood things could have been different.

In April of 1966, when he first left high school at the age of seventeen to enlist in the army, Featherstone might have agreed. The drugs and street violence that were then becoming so common in the neighborhood made the service seem like an attractive escape route. At the time, the war in Southeast Asia was still something of a mystery. It was pre-Tet Offensive. Pre-My Lai Massacre. There was no stigma attached to following in John Wayne's footsteps, and even if there had been it wouldn't have applied in Hell's Kitchen. Joining the service was another of the neighborhood's glorious traditions, dating back to World War I and the widely heralded 'Fighting 69th' Regiment, known in the neighborhood as 'Hell's Kitchen's own.' The tradition was continued in World War II with the 165th Infantry, another regiment made up mostly of Hell's Kitchen natives.

Like many volunteers, Featherstone entered the service with a gung-ho attitude. He had every reason to believe this would be his calling. His father had served in the army for eight years and seen action in Korea. His brothers Bobby and Henry had enlisted a few years before him, and another brother, Joseph, had joined the same day he had as part of the army's 'buddy plan' and been assigned to the 173rd Airborne Division.

Within weeks after he completed basic training, Mickey was assigned to the Nhatrang headquarters of Special Forces, the elite commando unit commonly known as the Green Berets. Casualties were high among the Green Berets in 1966–67, and as a result, regular army personnel were often assigned to Special Forces compounds to serve in menial capacities. Featherstone had not gone through Green Beret training, nor would he be going on combat missions with specialized guerrilla units. But technically, he could now call himself a Green Beret.

At first, his Special Forces designation was a source of great pride. Like other kids in his neighborhood, he'd fantasized about being a member of America's most glamorous fighting force. He and his teenage friends spent lots of time hanging out on stoops and streetcorners along 9th and 10th avenues singing the words to the 'Ballad of the Green Berets':

> Fighting soldiers from the sky,
> Fearless men who jump and die.
> Men who mean just what they say,
> The brave men of the Green Beret.

Silver wings upon their chests,
These are men, America's best,
One hundred men we'll test today,
But only three win the Green Beret.

In 'Nam, however, far from the stoops of Hell's Kitchen, it didn't take Featherstone long to realize his situation was not all it was cracked up to be. In Nhatrang he served as an ordnance supply specialist, spending most of his day cooped up in a warehouse or drinking at the local Playboy Club in town. Within the army's rigid caste system, Private Featherstone was squarely at the bottom, and those higher in rank never let him forget it. 'The ash and trash' was the name officers and soldiers in the field used for guys like Featherstone, stock clerks and mess-hall officers who lounged around the compound all day while the real soldiers got their asses shot off.

Featherstone hated his assignment. He was embarrassed that he had come this far only to work as a clerk in a warehouse. In tape-recorded letters he sent home to his mother, he was vocal about his dissatisfaction. He was bored and lonely, he said. Throughout his young life he had rarely been outside his own neighborhood, much less stationed in some far-off land with strange terrain and even stranger people. On the recordings, his voice was full of paranoia and bitterness, and his mother was so disturbed by what she heard that she would later destroy the tapes in a fit of anguish.

Mickey's spirits rose somewhat in early 1967 when he was reassigned to D Company, 5th Special Forces Group, then based along the Mekong Delta in Cantho Province. The Delta was hot in '67, and Featherstone was sure he'd finally get to see some action.

In Cantho, however, his situation only got worse. Once again he was assigned to the stockroom and later to the mail room. Much of his day was spent drinking at the Alamo Lounge, the base saloon, while Mobile Guerrilla Teams fought the war he'd hoped to fight out in the bush.

Occasionally, he got to go on chopper 'milk runs' delivering mail to A and B teams out in the field. Sometimes mail got sent back with envelopes marked SEARCH, usually meaning the person had been killed in action. Featherstone would read the names on the envelopes and sometimes ask himself, Why them? Why not me?

As his tour of duty wore on, Featherstone's sense of guilt and displacement deepened. He drank almost every day. Sometimes, he would get so fucked-up he would have blackouts and hardly remember what had happened the night before.

On one such occasion he was out drinking with a group of orderlies from the base hospital. 'Hey,' said one of the orderlies, pointing towards Mickey. 'Whaddya say we give this cherry a circumcision? He ain't been initiated yet.'

Barely conscious of what was happening, Featherstone was taken to his hootch and operated on by a drunken medic. He woke up the next morning with his prick wrapped in gauze and covered with adhesive tape.

A few days later, Mickey's brother Joseph got a weekend pass from the Airborne Rangers and came to see him in Cantho. They hadn't been together since basic training, so they immediately went into the city to celebrate. After a night of drinking they wound up at a local whorehouse. Mickey was led into a makeshift bedroom. When he got a hard-on he experienced incredible pain. He pulled down his pants and saw that his incision had ripped open – his prick was covered with blood.

Featherstone felt like crying. The frustration and humiliation of his entire tour of duty welled up inside him. He came to 'Nam to be a war hero, to follow in his father's footsteps as a dedicated soldier. But the whole thing was a bust. Not only was he treated like shit and given bullshit duties, but now here he was in some two-bit blow-job joint in Cantho with a dick that would probably be scarred for life.

After that, Mickey didn't seem to give a shit. He had frequent disciplinary problems. Once, he stole a jeep from the compound and drove into town for a night of debauchery, missing the next morning's flag-raising ceremony. The company commander docked his pay and reduced his rank, but it was all perfunctory. No one seemed to care much. It wasn't like Mickey was one of the army's most prized commodities. On the contrary. Private Featherstone was just one of the faceless thousands in 'Nam who got stuck in the most menial of jobs, had friends die in combat, was harangued and humiliated by supervisors, then abruptly released stateside to sort it all out.

* * *

Long before he gunned down Linwood Willis in front of the Leprechaun Bar in September of 1970, Mickey's life had degenerated into a succession of violent, drunken episodes. Ever since his return to Hell's Kitchen, he'd fallen into a routine of sleeping during the day and drinking through the night and into the early hours of the next morning. He seemed to have no interests, no personality, no ambition. He withdrew from his family and friends.

In the neighborhood saloons, Mickey usually sat at the end of the bar and drank alone. He viewed everyone with suspicion. Of the barflies he spent most of his time boozing with, he used to say, 'I hate the people. They hang on you with their faces.' He took any imagined slight as a full-fledged insult, and he'd lash out with a pent-up fury that shocked people who'd known him as a kid.

Not that Mickey was any saint before he joined the service. Like any kid growing up in Hell's Kitchen, he'd seen his share of violence. At age ten he threw his chair at a teacher who smacked him in the head for sleeping in class. Young Featherstone was dragged into Children's Court, but the charges were eventually dropped. As punishment, he was assigned to a '600' school for kids with discipline problems. But those who knew him best – his family and close personal friends – remembered Mickey as a shy, slightly skittish kid with a quiet disposition.

There was, however, a lack of supervision around the Featherstone household that made it possible for Mickey and his brothers to roam the streets at all hours of the day and night. Many people figured it was only a matter of time before Mickey started to get into trouble, just like so many other kids who roamed these same streets before him.

Some folks looked at Mickey's mother, Dorothy Boyle, and figured the Featherstone kids never had a chance. Dottie, as she was known to her friends, had married Charlie Featherstone in the late 1930s. By most accounts, the elder Featherstone, who sometimes worked as a longshoreman, was a drunk and a louse who beat his wife regularly. Eventually he deserted Dottie, leaving her with little or no money and six children to raise.

She then struck up a relationship with Charlie Boyle, a military man. They were unable to find Featherstone, who was still her legal husband, so proper divorce papers were never filed. Dottie and Charlie Boyle entered into a common-law marriage and had three children of their own, the youngest of whom was Mickey.

Boyle was a mild-mannered presence around the house, at the time a modest five-room railroad flat located at 43rd Street and 10th Avenue. Along with working long hours at his job as a guard in a veterans' hospital in the Bronx, there was the strain of trying to raise nine children while not even legally married. Often Boyle withdrew into himself, leaving the disciplining of the children to their mother.

The fact that they had to keep the Featherstone name while their actual father's name was Boyle always bothered Mickey and his two older brothers, Henry and Joseph. That, along with the fact they often had to wear hand-me-down clothes, made for a lot of teasing at school and in the neighborhood. They fought a lot with

119

neighborhood kids and with their various half-brothers and half-sisters. Mickey, it seemed, was always running away from these skirmishes, leaving his brothers to fight his neighborhood battles for him.

That was one of the first things everybody noticed about Mickey when he came back from 'Nam. He didn't run from fights anymore.

His first major altercation took place within days of his return from overseas duty. Four guys jumped him after an argument in a bar on 9th Avenue. One of them used a baseball bat to break his nose and knock a few of his teeth out.

One month later, again on 9th Avenue, a would-be robber confronted him with a .22-caliber target pistol. Rather than give up what little change he had, Mickey defended himself with a garbage-can lid. The robber fired and hit him in the arm. The next day Mickey was discharged from the hospital with the bullet still embedded near his left elbow.

Featherstone was small but not stupid; he quickly learned from these and other scuffles that it didn't make much sense to hang out in Hell's Kitchen without some kind of protection. In most street battles where it was one-on-one, Mickey was able to hold his own, even though he was almost always smaller and lighter than his opponent. But since few neighborhood fights were one-on-one (there were usually friends or relatives involved), an 'equalizer' was often called for.

The first time Featherstone used a gun in a neighborhood altercation was on the night of September 26, 1968. He had been drinking at the Market Diner on 43rd Street and 11th Avenue, just down the block from his parents' apartment building. A kid from New Jersey named John Riley, his brother Jimmy Riley, and a friend of theirs came into the bar section of the diner.

'Got a cigarette?' John Riley asked Featherstone.

Mickey had seen the Riley brothers around the neighborhood before. They were big, muscular guys who were always trying to intimidate people. He hated their swagger and their loud Jersey accents.

'Nah,' replied Mickey. 'Not for you.'

'Whaddya call those?' said Riley, pointing towards a pack of Kools Mickey had resting on the bar.

'Those is New York cigarettes,' shrugged Mickey, 'not Jersey cigarettes.'

A few neighborhood onlookers laughed. Riley reached over and slapped Featherstone across the face.

Mickey's brother Henry and a neighborhood kid named Tommy McElroy – Jimmy Mac's cousin – were also in the bar. When the fight began, they helped move it outside to the parking lot, where it was now going to be the Riley brothers and their friend against the Featherstone brothers and Tommy McElroy. Just as the rumble got started, the cops arrived and broke things up. They escorted the Riley brothers to the Lincoln Tunnel, where they were told to take their white Cadillac home to New Jersey.

Thirty minutes later the Rileys returned to the Market Diner and the whole scene was replayed. This time, as the cops led them to their Caddy, John Riley told Featherstone they were going to be back again – with weapons.

Everyone told Mickey to go home. As a U.S. soldier out

on a weekend pass, he had the most to lose if someone got arrested.

Featherstone lay on the couch at his parents' apartment and wondered if he'd done the right thing. There was probably going to be a fight, he thought, and it would be disgraceful if people knew he'd walked away from it. Plus, it was the Riley brothers, who had been bullying people in his neighborhood for months.

His head was spinning from the booze he'd drunk that night and from all of the bad thoughts that kept passing through his mind, causing the usual agitation and paranoia. Then the phone rang.

'Mickey,' said a voice on the line. 'The Rileys are back with a tire iron, an ax, and every fuckin' thing.'

Featherstone grabbed a hunting rifle that his father had in a closet, headed out the door and down West 43rd Street.

When he got to the diner, he hid in a grassy area that straddled the parking lot. There was an old-fashioned Western showdown going on. He saw Tommy McElroy, his brother Henry, and his half-brother Bobby. In front of them was John Riley holding a tire jack, standing under a streetlight. The other Riley, Jimmy, was holding the jack handle. Another guy was standing behind him with an ax handle.

Mickey fired once and hit the Rileys' car. He fired a second time and hit John Riley in the arm.

With his rifle pointed at the New Jersey boys, Featherstone rose from the ground and approached. He walked over to John Riley, who had been hit but was still standing, and smacked him across the face with the butt of the rifle. After Riley went down, Tommy McElroy picked up the tire jack and started hitting Riley on the head with it. Henry walked over to the other Riley and punched him in the face. 'Don't ever fuck with a Featherstone,' he said.

McElroy was still whacking away at John Riley, like the jack was a golf club and Riley's head the ball. Bobby Featherstone had to come over and punch McElroy in the face just to keep him from murdering the guy.

By the time the cops arrived a sizable crowd had gathered and Riley was covered with blood. Mickey and his brother Henry were handcuffed to a No Parking sign.

The next day, September 27, 1968, Mickey and Tommy McElroy were charged with aggravated assault. They were held at Rikers Island for a week until they were able to secure bail. The same day they were released, John Riley was discharged from the hospital. On his way out the door, he dropped dead from the head injury. The charge against Featherstone and McElroy was upgraded to manslaughter.

After the Riley shooting, Mickey's mom was hysterical. On top of everything else, she'd heard that weeks earlier Mickey had applied for another tour of duty in Vietnam. She immediately contacted Fort Dix and told Mickey's commanding officer that there was no way her son should be allowed to go overseas again.

No need to worry, she was told, the military didn't want him. As part of Mickey's request, he'd had to agree to a psychosocial evaluation by a staff psychiatrist. After a few days of interviews and tests, Featherstone was diagnosed as suffering from a nervous condition which manifested itself in severe nightmares, heavy drinking, an inability to sleep, and withdrawal from the outside world. The report concluded '. . . the assigning of EM [emergency medical] back to a combat area will probably bring back the difficulties that it previously created and probably with much more intensification. The experiences the young man went through while serving his one year appear to be too traumatic for even a mature, well-adjusted individual to cope with.'

Featherstone's request for another tour of duty was denied. While he was out on bail, what remained of his three-year military commitment was completed at Fort Hamilton in Brooklyn, where he served as a driver and a mail clerk. On May 13, 1969, he was given an honorable discharge.

At the same time Mickey Featherstone was finishing his military career, the neighborhood rackets had begun to stagnate. Jimmy Coonan was currently in Sing Sing, serving time for the Canelstein/Morales shooting. Many other young gangsters were either doing time in prison or in Vietnam. Mickey Spillane was still out and about, but, in general, it was not a particularly lucrative time for Hell's Kitchen's criminal element. Compared to the years of the Coonan/Spillane Wars, it was relatively calm – except, of course, for the presence of Featherstone, who was fast becoming a one-man crime wave.

In July 1969, just two months after his official discharge from the service, Mickey married a young girl from the neighborhood named Juanita Arturo. Nobody came to their wedding because just about everyone thought the marriage was a bad idea. Some of Mickey's family didn't like the idea of his marrying a Puerto Rican. Some thought he was too volatile and immature for marriage. Others felt Juanita wasn't the right girl, she was too 'square,' too sedentary.

Juanita was a strict Catholic who went to church every Sunday. Since Mickey was also Catholic, it was her hope that she could get him to pay more attention to his faith. This annoyed Featherstone, and it quickly became a source of contention.

There were other difficulties, not the least of which were Juanita's sexual hang-ups, which had been a problem since the day they were married. It was on their honeymoon that Featherstone first called his half-sister, Joan, to tell her that his new bride was terrified at the thought of having sex with him.

'Sis,' said Mickey, 'I don't ever want you to tell anyone about this, but please get on the phone with Juanita. She's afraid.'

Joan was flabbergasted. The idea of someone calling from a honeymoon asking for sexual advice seemed pretty damned strange. She heard Mickey in the background talking to Juanita. 'Go ahead,' he was saying, 'my sister will talk to you. Don't be embarrassed.' Then Mickey got back on the line, giggling nervously. 'She really needs your help, Sis.'

Joan did what she could. But it was obvious from talking to Juanita that she was scared to death.

It all came crashing down just a few months after the wedding. On one of those rare occasions when Mickey came home to spend the night, he awoke from a terrible nightmare and tried to strangle Juanita in their bed. She moved out the next day, taking most of the furniture with her. Later, Mickey told doctors he'd been having a bad dream about the war, and he awoke thinking the person in bed next to him was a Vietnamese agent.

After Juanita left him in the fall of '69, Featherstone, now twenty-one, became increasingly despondent. He moved back in with his parents. Whatever money he had came from Charlie Boyle, his father, and most of that was spent on whiskey. Mostly, he hung out in places where he could drink for free – places like the American Legion post on West 43rd Street, which was run by his father and his brother Henry. Mickey could be found there almost any night getting sloshed while watching TV. His favorites were old horror movies like *Frankenstein* and *Dracula*.

No doubt his life would have continued this way were it not for a quirk of fate. Not long after Juanita left him, Mickey developed an abscess on his neck. He'd tried numerous home remedies, but they only made things worse. So he went for treatment to the Bronx Veterans Administration Hospital on Kingsbridge Road, the same hospital where his father now worked as supervisor of security.

While he was there, the doctors noticed Featherstone's extreme nervousness and agitation. They treated his abscess and referred him to the psychiatric division, where he was described as anxious and hallucinatory with 'suicidal and homicidal ideations.' They suggested he stick around.

126

Mickey knew he was fucked up, so his parents didn't have too much trouble convincing him that the hospital was the best place for him to be. Also, as long as he was in a psychiatric facility his homicide indictment for the Riley shooting would be kept 'off calendar,' meaning a court date could not be set.

At the Bronx V. A. hospital Featherstone was diagnosed as a 'paranoid schizophrenic' with an alcohol addiction and something they called Traumatic War Neurosis. They kept him on the psychiatric ward and tranquilized him daily. Charlie Boyle often came by to see how his son was doing. Usually, Mickey was under heavy sedation and totally incapable of conversation.

Although numerous tests and interviews were done to determine the extent of Featherstone's illness, there was very little done to actually treat his condition. Doctors listened carefully as Mickey enumerated the nightmares from his past. He'd had to execute Cambodian spies in the war, he said, and this had caused him to resent authority. He'd witnessed other atrocities as well – soldiers being decapitated, friends being killed, prisoners tortured. Of course, there was nothing in Mickey's military record to suggest any of this was true. But as he told these stories over and over, after a while it hardly mattered. In Mickey's own mind they *became* true. The delusions became his reality.

Physician after physician listened to these stories and filed remarkably similar reports. Certainly Mickey Featherstone was ill, they wrote. Certainly he was paranoid. Then they'd prescribe a daily dosage of antipsychotic tranquilizers – known in the trade as a 'liquid straitjacket'

– and suggest the patient be kept under observation. The idea was to shuffle him along to the next doctor and keep him off the street.

In April 1970, however, a few months after his admission, Featherstone was declared healthy enough to be given an indefinite furlough. A steady diet of drugs had deadened his senses, and it was hoped his paranoid and aggressive tendencies had abated. After all, he'd conducted himself admirably while confined to his hospital room. He hadn't attacked anyone at all.

Unfortunately, Hell's Kitchen was a long way from the V.A. hospital. Two weeks after his discharge, on April 23rd, Featherstone walked into a bar on 10th Avenue and killed again.

This time he hardly knew what was going on, even as it unfolded right before his eyes. It was at the Sunbrite Saloon at 736 10th Avenue. The place was packed, the music loud. Mickey had been drinking for hours. Suddenly there was a lot of commotion. A gun was being passed around the bar, over everybody's head.

The next thing Featherstone knew it was in his hand. Or it looked like his hand. Was it his hand? The music blared, people were shouting. In front of Mickey was a guy he recognized named Emilio Rettagliatta, although he knew him as Mio. It was Mio's gun, they said. Mio had pulled a gun on someone in the bar. Shoot Mio! they said. Mio made a move for the gun and Mickey fired, hitting him in the stomach. He looked in Mio's eyes. He knew that look. It meant Mio was dead.

At the sound of gunfire, everyone stampeded for the

door. The body was taken outside and dumped in the street so the bar wouldn't be held accountable. Mickey was hustled into the backseat of somebody's car and taken to 414 West 46th Street, Johnny Diaz's place. 'Sit tight,' a voice commanded. 'Don't fuckin' move. Just wait till things blow over.'

But Mickey couldn't wait. He'd heard in the car on the way over that the guy he'd shot was Mickey Spillane's numbers runner. It didn't take a genius to know that meant trouble. Mickey knew Spillane – everybody in the neighborhood did. He'd never had any beefs with him or his people. But this was different. Mickey knew what he had to do. He had to get Spillane before Spillane got him.

Featherstone grabbed a .22-caliber pistol he knew Johnny Diaz kept stashed away in his closet. He stuck the gun in his pants and headed into the night, running south on 9th Avenue and west on 45th Street until he came to the White House Bar. It was now around 4 A.M. It looked like the bar was closed. Mickey peered in the front window and saw Spillane seated with a few other guys at a table. He knocked on the window and motioned for Spillane to come out.

While he was running down the avenue, Mickey had decided he was going to try to explain things to Spillane first. Maybe Spillane would be understanding about it, and he wouldn't have to shoot him. Because if he had to shoot Spillane, Featherstone knew his life probably wouldn't last very long after that.

Spillane came out of the bar dressed, as always, sharp as a tack. Mickey was in a T-shirt and blue jeans and he was shaking like a leaf.

'Mr Spillane, I just want you to know it couldn't be helped . . .'

'Mickey . . .'

'I know he was your guy and all, but he pulled a gun . . .'

'Mickey, don't worry about it.'

'Huh?'

'I already heard. I know what went down, so don't worry. You already got enough problems of your own.'

Featherstone liked what he was hearing. Spillane was being a real gentleman about it. But then he saw a cop car slowly cruising up 10th Avenue. He looked at Spillane, then at the cops. Maybe this was some kind of setup, he thought. Maybe Spillane was just stalling.

He didn't wait around to find out. He bolted down 45th Street towards the river, leaving Spillane standing on the sidewalk. When he got to the Hudson, he tossed the .22 into the water. Then he got on a subway and headed up to the Bronx, where he stayed at his parents' new apartment on Webb Avenue.

Two weeks later he called Johnny Diaz on West 46th Street. 'Mickey,' Johnny told him, 'the fuckin' neighborhood's crawlin' with cops. They know you was the shooter.'

Mickey saw the writing on the wall. He took a subway down to Johnny's place, called Midtown North, and turned himself in.

After that, everything was a blur. He remembered being sent to the Manhattan Detention Center for Men, otherwise known as 'the Tombs,' a prison adjacent to the courthouse in downtown Manhattan. Although the

130

bar had been packed the night of the Mio shooting, few witnesses came forth, and even those who testified said there was so much confusion they didn't really see what happened. A 'justifiable homicide' is what the grand jury wound up calling it. They wouldn't indict for murder, only for possession of an unregistered weapon.

From the Tombs, Featherstone was sent back to the Bronx V.A. and pumped with 500 milligrams of Thorazine, the same antipsychotic drug he'd been taking since he first entered the hospital. It didn't seem to help. He was more paranoid and unruly than ever. There were concerns that he would try to escape, so he was bound and shackled and transferred to another veterans' hospital in Montrose, New York, known for its tight security.

Four days later he was considered well enough to receive visitors. His wife, Juanita, came by with a psychiatrist. She was filing for divorce, she said, citing 'extreme cruelty,' and she'd brought the doctor along to offer his diagnosis. Mickey paid little attention. The only time he spoke was to ask if he could borrow some money. When Juanita and the doctor had left, he escaped by walking past the guards and out the front door. Still dressed in his army-green hospital garb, he hitchhiked to a local train station and used the money he'd borrowed to buy a one-way ticket to New York City.

On the train on the way back to his hometown, Mickey stared out the window at the passing terrain. So much had been happening in his life, so many crazy things. I gotta slow down, he thought to himself. I gotta stop letting people get to me.

When he got back to the neighborhood he crashed at his brother's apartment on West 43rd Street. A week later, he walked into the Leprechaun Bar and came face to face with a loud, drunken Southerner named Linwood Willis.

5

POETIC JUSTICE

Attorney Lawrence Hochheiser sat in his small Brooklyn office sipping on a cup of coffee and asked himself: *Why do I always get stuck with cases like this?* At thirty-one, he'd only recently left the Manhattan District Attorney's office, where he'd worked in the Complaints Bureau, the Appeals Bureau, and finally the Rackets Bureau. Over the years, he'd seen it all, especially those twelve months he'd spent in downtown Manhattan working night court, where justice is a carnival. Three hundred cases in a twelve-hour period; a judge in one ear, a cop in the other, and a deranged Legal Aid attorney in front of you. Hochheiser loved it, but the pace was too much. He'd been lucky enough to land a job in private practice and get out with his sanity intact – relatively speaking.

So now here he was with the respected criminal defense firm of Evseroff, Newman, and Sonenshine and he still always seemed to be dealing with society's misfits, the little guy with no money and a rap sheet you could stretch from here to Hoboken and back.

Part of the problem was the Bishop, a man Hochheiser could not say no to. Known as Salvatore Cella to the rest of the world, the Bishop was a seventy-year-old former New York City cop who'd served as Hochheiser's mentor from his earliest days in the Brooklyn D.A.'s office. A veteran of over thirty years on the force who spoke fluent Sicilian, the Bishop had an uncanny knack for coming up with eyewitnesses to crimes. Many times when Hochheiser had needed a corroborating witness, the Bishop would produce some old Italian woman who just happened to be sitting at her front window overlooking the street when the crime took place. Invariably, she would have seen it just the way Hochheiser had hoped she would to benefit his side of the case.

Now that Hochheiser was in private practice, the Bishop had occasionally called in his chits. That's how Hochheiser wound up with this latest client, Francis Featherstone. The way he heard it, the Bishop had been asked to help find Featherstone an attorney through one of his in-laws. A barrel-chested, physically imposing man with a kindly manner, the Bishop had told Hochheiser from the start, 'Larry, the kid's a complete loony-bird. There probably ain't much of a case and God knows there won't be much money. But you'd be doin' me a big favor.'

The young attorney didn't know much about Featherstone, but he was reasonably certain of one thing: Whatever he got paid, it wasn't going to be much. And a good portion of that would probably go to the Bishop.

Hochheiser met Featherstone for the first time in the Tombs in the fall of '71, nearly one year after the Linwood Willis killing. Mickey had been transferred there from the Fishkill Correctional Facility in upstate New York after being declared 'no longer in a state of idiocy' – and therefore fit to stand trial.

Conditions in the Tombs had recently been deemed inhumane by a U.S. judge for the Southern District of New York, who found the facility to be overcrowded and inadequately supervised. Built thirty years earlier, in 1941, on the same site as Manhattan's first detention center for men (which had been designed to look like an ancient Egyptian tomb), the current structure sported a decaying institutional look. Prisoners were packed three to a cell, many of the toilets were broken, and recreational areas were breeding grounds for rodents and roaches. In December of '74, the Tombs would be closed by court order and completely renovated, but right now it was a cesspool.

When Hochheiser arrived in the prison's bullpen area to meet with Featherstone, he was slightly taken aback. With Mickey's military background and violent criminal record, he'd expected to find a loud, physically imposing figure – the toughest kid on the block. Instead, Mickey seemed like exactly the type neighborhood bullies always pick on. He was a nervous, soft-spoken kid who looked a lot younger than he really was. A street urchin.

The young attorney listened as Featherstone tried to explain what had been happening in his life in recent years. Mickey was still on medication, so he talked in a rambling, colloquial manner that wasn't entirely coherent. But Hochheiser liked what he heard. He respected the fact that none of Mickey's crimes were for profit or vengeance. There seemed to be a principle behind Featherstone's actions, though obviously, thought

Hochheiser, somewhere along the line the kid had lost the ability to differentiate a real threat from an imagined one.

The homicide Hochheiser wanted to hear about was the most recent one, the shooting of Linwood Willis, which would be the first to go to trial. Hochheiser listened as Featherstone gave his version of what happened on September 30, 1970, in front of the Leprechaun Bar. Mickey admitted he'd been drinking that night and had gone without his medication for a few days. The events weren't very clear in his head. About the only thing he really remembered was that Willis had threatened to 'blow his brains out.'

Hochheiser wasn't surprised to hear Featherstone say he thought the best way to fight the case would be to plead self-defense, but the attorney knew that wouldn't wash with a jury. From what he'd heard about Featherstone, Hochheiser knew there was only one way to go.

'Mickey,' he said, pausing to let the words sink in, 'there's only one way to fight this case, and that's with an insanity defense.'

Featherstone eyed Hochheiser with skepticism and anxiety. It was his half-sister's family who'd found the attorney, so he hadn't really known what to expect. He didn't have much experience with lawyers, and those he had dealt with seemed far removed from life on the streets. Mickey had to admit it though, Hochheiser seemed different. For one thing, his unruly mane of curly brown hair, droopy mustache, and cowboy boots made him look kind of wild. And Mickey liked the fact that he spoke in a language any streetwise hustler could understand.

Eventually, Hochheiser convinced his client. The clincher came when he told Featherstone if they were able to beat this case with an insanity defense, it would lay the foundation for all his future cases. To Mickey, that was good planning.

What Hochheiser *didn't* tell Featherstone was that nobody had beaten a murder rap on an insanity defense in New York County in more than fifteen years. It was definitely a long shot.

As soon as Hochheiser went to work on *The People of New York v. Francis Featherstone*, he could see there was a lot more to it than he'd originally anticipated. Granted, since even the Bishop thought the kid was nuts, his expectations had been outrageously low. Yet the more Hochheiser delved into Featherstone's past, the more he liked what he saw. Yes, there was violence. But there was also pathos. He could work with it.

The Vietnam War, of course, would have to be a factor. By 1972, the war was reaching its ignominious conclusion, and even many of the hard hats and middle-Americans who had supported it were admitting it had been a mistake. There was a growing awareness of the atrocities some American soldiers had witnessed or taken part in, and a sensitivity to the psychological problems they experienced when they got home. Based on the war stories Mickey had been telling doctors over the last few years – stories that Hochheiser had no reason to believe were untrue – the attorney thought there was a good chance they could find a sympathetic juror or two.

The war, however, was an abstraction to most people. Hochheiser knew his testimony also had to address more specific issues. Therefore, to explain the nature of Featherstone's mental instability in technical terms, he would need to call some of the many psychiatrists who'd examined Mickey in recent years. And to describe the kind of person Mickey had become in *human* terms, he would need to call Featherstone's family.

The latter was a risky proposition. There wasn't a juror alive who would believe the family was objective. If the jury thought Hochheiser was being unduly manipulative, he could lose the case right there. But when the attorney met Featherstone's mother and father, his brother Henry, and his two half-sisters Doris and Joan, he instinctively knew they had to be subpoenaed. Although none of them had much formal education, when Hochheiser listened to what they had to say about Mickey he was genuinely moved. As a middle-class Jewish kid born and raised on Long Island, Hochheiser was from a different world. But it was obvious that their anguish was real. And in their own way, they articulated their emotions clearly and powerfully.

Along with getting his witnesses together, Hochheiser spent a good deal of time preparing his client for trial, and it was proving to be a delicate situation. The attorney didn't doubt for a minute that Mickey was indeed 'troubled.' But he knew that Mickey believed it was all a charade, that he had once been crazy but was now better, and that the insanity defense was in fact a scam.

Hochheiser played along. 'Remember, Mickey,' he told Featherstone on one of their many meetings in the visiting room at the Tombs, 'you're supposed to be crazy. When we get into that courtroom, I don't want you doing anything that might lead the jury to believe otherwise.'

Often, after these encounters, Hochheiser would shake his head in disbelief. Here he was asking someone *he knew* was crazy to *pretend* he was crazy so they could beat a murder rap with an insanity defense. It was a strategy he didn't recall ever being mentioned in law school.

Mickey, for his part, was only vaguely aware of what was going on. The prison doctors had him on a high dosage of Thorazine, and he spent most of his days in a near comatose state. At times, he would revive himself and take an active interest in the case. He seemed especially fascinated by all the documentation – police, prison, and psychiatric reports – that had been gathered. But he usually didn't remain clearheaded for long. Throughout the early pre-trial stages of the case, Mickey was just along for the ride, totally dependent on his hip, young, and relatively inexperienced attorney, Larry Hochheiser.

Most of what Hochheiser had learned about criminal law since he left the Manhattan D.A.'s office had come from Jack Evseroff, the senior partner of Evseroff, Newman, and Sonenshine. Ever since he'd moved into Evseroff's seedy little office at 186 Joralemon Street in downtown Brooklyn, Hochheiser had been enamored of the wily veteran attorney, who was fifteen years his senior. Tall and lean, with a strong Brooklyn accent, Evseroff was a bit of a dandy. He wouldn't think twice about going shopping on an afternoon off and dropping $40 on stuff that would make him smell good.

Underneath Evseroff's smooth exterior was an equally smooth courtroom instinct; above all, he was known as a masterful cross-examiner. In fact, Jack Evseroff was the most recent lawyer in the New York area to beat a murder charge with an insanity defense. In the late 1960s, in Nassau County out on Long Island, he'd successfully defended a cop who shot his wife and daughter. Evseroff beat the charge by focusing his case on the pressures of police work, and by decimating the prosecution's 'expert' psychiatric witness, who tried to claim the cop was mentally competent.

It was Evseroff's handling of the government psychiatrist in that case that most interested Larry Hochheiser. Ever since he'd begun working on the Linwood Willis murder case, Hochheiser had been trying to pin Evseroff down, hoping to glean some of his wisdom. As a relative newcomer to the criminal defense game, Hochheiser didn't know shit about psychiatry. Evseroff had promised he would give him some pointers on how to cross-examine a psychiatrist. But whenever Hochheiser approached his busy senior associate, he was told, 'Not now, not now.'

In September of '72, as jury selection began and the trial date approached, Hochheiser felt he could wait no longer. The government had let it be known that they were going to call Dr Stanley Portnow, a psychiatrist who'd examined Featherstone at Bellevue Hospital. Hochheiser knew that Portnow would be used to refute claims made by other psychiatric witnesses that Featherstone was insane. His cross-examination of Portnow, Hochheiser felt, might be the single most important event of the trial.

Late one evening, after nearly everyone else had left the normally hectic offices of Evseroff, Newman, and Sonenshine, Hochheiser stopped by Jack Evseroff's office.

Evseroff was seated at his desk, feet up, schmoozing with his girlfriend on the telephone. In the two or three years Hochheiser had known Evseroff, the forty-four-year-old attorney had been through two wives. He always seemed to be in the process of finalizing a divorce while at the same time grooming his latest flame for marriage.

Hochheiser sat down quietly in a sunken green leather couch across from Evseroff's desk. As he waited patiently, Evseroff continued whispering sweet nothings into the phone. Finally, Hochheiser loudly cleared his throat. Evseroff looked up, as if noticing Hochheiser for the first time, then put his hand over the receiver.

'What is it, boobie?' he asked. Evseroff called everyone he knew 'boobie.'

'Jack,' pleaded Hochheiser. 'You told me some time ago that you were gonna teach me how to cross-examine a psychiatrist. Now weeks have gone by and I'm gonna have to do this in a matter of days. There really isn't any more time. I was hoping we could go over this tonight.'

Evseroff looked mildly annoyed. 'Okay, boobie.' Speaking into the mouthpiece, he told his girlfriend, 'Honey, can you hold on just a minute?'

With his hand again over the receiver, Evseroff turned his attention back to Hochheiser. 'Alright, boobie, so you wanna know how to cross-examine a psychiatrist.'

'Right. Exactly.'

'Alright, you ready?'

Hochheiser fumbled to get a pen and notepad out of his coat jacket. 'Yeah, I'm ready.'

Evseroff furrowed his brow. 'Okay, this is it. Listen carefully . . .

'Don't ask him nothin' about psychiatry.'

Hochheiser sat in silence for a good four or five seconds, his pen still poised.

'That's it, boobie,' said Evseroff, looking at the junior attorney as if he couldn't understand why he was still there.

'Uh,' stammered Hochheiser, 'I mean . . . you mean, that's all?'

'Yeah, that's it. Goodnight boobie.' Then Evseroff went back to schmoozing with his girlfriend.

All that night and into the next day Hochheiser pondered Evseroff's words as if they'd been delivered by some guru on a mountaintop. 'Don't ask him nothin' about psychiatry,' Hochheiser kept mumbling to himself over and over. He thought it might just be the most brilliant thing he'd ever heard, but he wasn't sure.

Eventually, he stored it away in the back of his mind. As with much of the advice Evseroff had given him in recent months, it was one of those statements the meaning of which remained elusive, until it finally made perfect sense weeks later in court, usually in the heat of battle.

Throughout 1972, as Hochheiser readied himself for the Linwood Willis murder trial, events outside the courthouse provided an emotional undercurrent to the case. Antiwar protests raged throughout the country that spring and summer. In New York City, on April 30th, twelve Catholic nuns, some wearing white sheets with the legend 'One more person dead in Indochina,' lay down in the aisles of St Patrick's Cathedral during Sunday mass.

As the presidential election campaigns heated up in

October, President Richard M. Nixon promised that 'peace with honor' was imminent. Hoping that Nixon and his national security advisor, Henry Kissinger, were onto something, American voters were about to resoundingly reject the Democratic challenger, George McGovern. But even with Nixon's reelection a certainty, the American public had made it clear in the streets and in poll after poll throughout '72 that the war in Vietnam was never more unpopular.

With these events as a backdrop, the Willis trial got underway on October 6th, two years and seven days after the shooting actually occurred. The trial took place in the courtroom of Judge John M. Murtaugh in the criminal courts building at 100 Centre Street in lower Manhattan.

By the time Hochheiser came forward to present his case, the events surrounding the death of Willis had been thoroughly outlined by the prosecution. Witnesses had been called; charts of the Leprechaun Bar had been displayed; ballistics evidence had been presented. Since Hochheiser was not denying that Featherstone had in fact shot and killed Linwood Willis, he was free to mount a totally separate defense – one that focused not on the act itself, but on whether or not his client, as he would say time and time again, had the capacity to 'know and appreciate the nature and quality of his actions.'

Hochheiser called a number of psychiatrists, including Dr Stephen Teich, who was in charge of the tenth floor Mental Observation Unit at the Tombs. Among other things, Teich described an incident where Featherstone was found with his wrists cut in what appeared to be a suicide attempt. When Teich talked to Mickey about this, Featherstone told him he'd been hearing voices and having Vietnam flashbacks. 'These events have played a major role in his illness,' said the doctor, in reference to Featherstone's war experiences. 'And when these memories come up, or when something brings up the emotions connected with them, his ability to reason and operate in a rational manner is destroyed.'

After Teich and the other psychiatrists, it was time for Featherstone's family to take the stand. As he watched from the defense table, Mickey couldn't help but feel nervous and uncomfortable. All these doctors talking about how crazy he was had been disturbing enough, but now he would have to sit through his own family's digging up events from his past. His brother Henry and his father were up first. Then came his mother.

Over the years, Mickey had developed strong, conflicting emotions about his mother. In his many talks with psychiatrists leading up to the trial, he'd been quick to blame her for his problems. One of the things that bothered him the most was how she never told him about his name. He'd been raised thinking his first name was Matthew, which is how he got the nickname Mickey. But when he went to get his birth certificate to join the service, he found out that his legal name was Francis. Mickey hated Francis; he thought it was a sissy name. When he asked his mother about it, she acted strange and said she didn't know anything. The hospital must have made a mistake, she said.

First it was his last name, which was really Boyle, not Featherstone. Now his first name, which was really

Francis, not Matthew. Sometimes Mickey felt his mother must have *wanted* him to have an identity problem.

There were other things, too – the beatings she gave him as a kid and the fact she always blamed him for her ailments. Mickey could hardly look at her without getting knots in his stomach.

The courtroom was silent as Dorothy Boyle took the stand. A small, frail woman with an equally frail voice, she described Mickey as a happy, pleasant child. Then he came back from Vietnam and the nightmares started. He would toss and turn and scream out in his sleep.

'When you say "nightmares,"' Hochheiser interjected, 'can you describe what you observed with regard to Mickey having an apparent nightmare?'

'Can I give you an example of one?'

'Please do.'

'I had to buy a second television set because Mickey would sit up all night and watch television after he'd come home, because he couldn't sleep at night. So I bought a portable television and I put it in the kitchen. So Mickey was sleeping in the day, and it was, I'll say, about six o'clock . . .'

'Six o'clock P.M.?'

'Yes, sir. So I had the news on, and my dog, he went "Woo-woooo," you know, whining like. I looked in the room and the dog was backing up, and then when he came out further I seen my son was on his stomach crawling like a snake. The dog's hair was up on his back. I run to the sink and I threw the towel in the sink and got water on it. I threw it at Mickey and run out of the house. And

145

then I heard the dog bark, and Mickey was laughing. I went in the house, and he had the wet towel and he was playing with the dog, and he . . .'

Mrs Boyle's voice had been rising steadily. Now it began to crack. There were tears in her eyes.

'Mrs Boyle, just relax for a moment,' said Hochheiser in a soothing tone.

Still sobbing, she continued. 'And he said to me, "Momma, what happened?" And I told him. I said, "You come out of your room like this . . ."'

'Indicating moving the elbows as in crawling.'

'Yes, on his stomach. Then he looked at me like he didn't even see me. He was looking right . . . right through me. So he said to me, "Momma, I didn't hurt you, did I?" I said, "No, you didn't hurt me."'

'So I put him back into bed and he cried for over two hours. Then he . . . then he went to sleep.'

There was utter silence in the courtroom. Many of the jurors had tears in their eyes, and Hochheiser thought he'd even seen a touch of moisture in the eyes of crusty old Judge Murtaugh. After Dorothy Boyle there would be other witnesses. Dr Stanley Portnow, the government psychiatrist, was finally called as part of the prosecution's rebuttal. In keeping with Jack Evseroff's advice, Hochheiser didn't ask him nothin' about psychiatry. He asked him about his fees, his practice, when he had time to read the background material on Featherstone. Certain that his expertise was being trivialized, Portnow became unglued. As Evseroff put it to Hochheiser later, 'You left him for dead, boobie.'

But the real clincher had been the sight of Mickey's

mother, broken and distraught. For all intents and purposes, the trial was over right there.

On October 28th, the jury delivered its verdict. Featherstone was convicted of possession of an unregistered weapon but found not guilty of murder by reason of 'mental defect.'

Mickey's family was ecstatic, and so was Hochheiser.

As for Featherstone, after his mother cried some more and he'd wished his father well, he was led back to the Tombs, where he stared at the blank walls of his cell. At the moment, it was hard for him to feel much joy. He still had to be sentenced on the gun possession charge; then there were his other cases. With all this still ahead, Featherstone figured it was a hollow, short-term victory.

Neither he nor Hochheiser had any idea that what had just gone down in Manhattan criminal court would later be seen by the city's cops, judges, journalists, and lawyers as the genesis of the Featherstone legend.

At the same time Mickey Featherstone was scoring his first courtroom victory, a young, inexperienced cop was making his bones on the streets of New York. His name was Richard Egan, though everyone knew him as Richie. Born in 1946 – the same year as Jimmy Coonan – Egan stood five-foot-eight, weighed 160 pounds dripping wet, and had a boyish smile and charm. He looked a bit like the comic book character Dennis the Menace, which was funny, since Egan was a menace to no one. To most cops who knew him, Richie was Mr Nice Guy.

Like many of the gangsters in Hell's Kitchen, Egan was Irish-American. He'd grown up in Elmhurst, Queens, at that time a relatively placid working-class neighborhood, mainly Irish, German, and Italian. Unlike most of the gangsters in Hell's Kitchen, Egan came from a stable family background. His parents were both Irish-born, and Richie was their only child. By the time Egan's father retired in the mid-Seventies, he'd worked forty-five years as a subway motorman.

When Egan graduated from Archbishop Molloy High School in 1962, like many Catholic working-class boys in the city, he saw himself as having three choices. He could go into the service; he could join the priesthood; or he could take a shot at the police training program. Ever since he could remember, Richie had dreamed of being a New York City cop. He took the entrance exam and wound up among the first 100 who were picked.

He joined the force in 1968 and spent the next four years on the streets of Spanish Harlem in upper Manhattan. In '72, just months before Mickey Featherstone's acquittal at the Linwood Willis murder trial, the twenty-six-year-old Egan was offered a chance to join the Intelligence Division.

Even as a young cop, Egan had a passion for information – gathering it, evaluating it, and following wherever it might lead. Making arrests interested him a lot less than formulating investigations. The Intelligence Division was perfect. Here, he was certain, he would find his calling – so he jumped at the chance to join.

It was a choice that would prove prophetic for Officer Egan, though he didn't know it at the time.

In the following months, as Egan learned the basics of intelligence work, Mickey Featherstone would take up residence at Matteawan State Hospital for the criminally insane. Jimmy Coonan was establishing a name for himself in local criminal circles. And Hell's Kitchen remained a product of its history – a history that would continue to be written in blood.

PART TWO

PART TWO

6

NO CORPUS DELICTI,
NO INVESTIGATION

In the summer of 1975, Patrick 'Paddy' Dugan murdered his best friend Denis Curley and the whole neighborhood got depressed about it.

It started as a barroom joke at the 596 Club, Jimmy Coonan's saloon, the site two months earlier of the Vanderbilt Evans shooting. With a bunch of people watching, Curley aimed an unloaded pistol at Dugan. But Dugan didn't know it was unloaded. 'You pointed a fuckin' gun at me!?' he asked his friend incredulously. The next thing people knew Dugan was going over the table, trying to get at Curley. A couple of guys held him back, but it only got worse after that.

It ended an hour later, on August 25, 1975, in front of Denis Curley's apartment building at 444 West 48th Street. Before numerous onlookers, Dugan put a single .38-caliber bullet into his friend's temple and fled. Curley died right there, the bullet lodged in his brain, a trickle of blood running across the pavement, over the curb, and into the street.

For weeks after the Denis Curley shooting, the

neighborhood was gripped by a wave of near hysteria. Everyone knew that Paddy Dugan and Denis Curley were best friends. They'd practically grown up together. Hell's Kitchen had always been a violent place, but the idea that someone would shoot his best friend because of a barroom argument was horrifying to a lot of people. It represented a new kind of violence, where the traditions of loyalty and friendship no longer seemed to mean much.

Those in the know figured drugs had something to do with it. In the early and mid Seventies, a huge influx of street-level narcotics, including heroin, was being sold along 9th and 10th avenues. It was nickel and dime stuff, mostly, and the primary users were the poorer black and Hispanic residents. But many of the white kids were into it too. It was the new kick, the new high.

The professional criminals, of course, wouldn't go near it. Not yet, anyway. Most of the Italians were still a few years away from the full-scale distribution of drugs. Local Irish gangsters like Mickey Spillane had no interest in it. Spillane didn't use it and didn't allow any of his inner circle to, either. He was against the sale of narcotics, even marijuana, on principle. But that didn't stop a lot of the neighborhood kids from getting involved. Both Curley and Dugan were known junkies, and so were some of the other up-and-coming neighborhood criminals.

Supposedly, Paddy Dugan felt terrible about what he'd done to Denis Curley. Billy Beattie, who was bartending at the 596 Club the night it happened, asked Paddy about it. It was the morning after, and Beattie woke Dugan up from a deep sleep at 452 West 50th Street, a 'flophouse' apartment they shared.

'Why'd you do it?' asked Beattie. 'Why'd you kill your best friend?'

Dugan was hung over and looked grief-stricken. 'I don't know,' was all he could say, 'I really don't know.' A few days later, in front of two dozen people at Curley's wake, Paddy cried like a baby.

To most people, though, Dugan's remorse just wasn't good enough. Retribution became the talk of the day. The notorious Eddie 'the Butcher' Cummiskey, for one, had been a close friend of Denis Curley's. Cummiskey used to call Curley the Rhinestone Cowboy because he and Denis drank together at the Sunbrite Bar and sang along with the Glen Campbell song 'Rhinestone Cowboy' as it played over and over on the jukebox. Cummiskey was fifteen years older than Curley and thought of him as a younger brother. Not long after the shooting, he let it be known that he took Curley's death as a personal insult.

One afternoon he strolled into the Sunbrite Bar and there stood Paddy Dugan, stoned out of his mind. Cummiskey, the bantam rooster, walked right up to him and said: 'What kind of a scumbag kills his own friend?'

'Go ahead,' replied Dugan, taking a pistol out of his jacket and placing it on the bar. 'Go ahead. You can't make me feel any worse. Blow my fuckin' head off.'

'Oh, no,' said Cummiskey. 'No way. You're not gettin' off that easy.'

Not everyone got as worked up about it as Cummiskey. Mickey Featherstone, who'd just gotten out of prison after serving time for his gun possession conviction in the Linwood Willis killing, was at the 596 Club the night Denis Curley got killed. He thought what Dugan had done to Curley was wrong, but he felt a lot of people were responsible for what happened that night, not just Paddy. When he heard that Mike Ryan, a neighborhood kid, had talked to some detectives who were snooping around after the shooting, he found the kid and gave him a beating. 'People don't rat in this neighborhood,' he told Ryan. 'And they especially don't rat against my friends.'

James Coonan was not at the 596 Club on the night of the shooting, but he heard all about it. He knew that Cummiskey and Curley had been tight, and that Cummiskey would be looking to even the score. He knew this, and he began to think. It was a fact of life in the criminal underworld that most alliances are born out of other people's anger and misfortune. For years Coonan had been looking for an event that might lure the dreaded Eddie Cummiskey totally over to his side. The death of Denis Curley might just do the trick, thought Jimmy. And Paddy Dugan might just be the sacrificial bait.

The last few years had been good to Jimmy Coonan. Since his marriage to Edna Fitzgerald a year ago, in 1974, he'd moved out of the neighborhood to a modest, two-story house just across the river in Keansburg, New Jersey, a quiet, lily-white middle-class suburb. They had the two children from Edna's first marriage, and they'd quickly added one of their own. Jimmy owned a big black Buick four-door which he frequently drove into the old neighborhood, where he still did his daily business. Usually, there were messages and payments waiting for him at the 596 Club.

Not only had Coonan's loansharking operation improved in recent years, but he'd established a relationship with a dapper, old-time gangster named Charles 'Ruby' Stein. An exceedingly vain man with slicked-back hair and a formal manner, Stein, then sixty-two years old, was known in the trade as a 'shylock's shylock.' Indeed, he was one of the most successful loansharks the city of New York had ever seen, with a customer list that included big-time businessmen, politicians, and bank presidents. Lately, he had aligned himself with Fat Tony Salerno's Genovese family. Cops and syndicate insiders usually referred to Stein as 'Fat Tony's Meyer Lansky,' a reference to the legendary underworld financier.

In early 1975, Coonan had met Stein, strangely enough, by way of Mickey Spillane. Since the late 1950s, Spillane had borrowed upwards of a million dollars from Ruby, some of which he used to finance his criminal operations and some of which he used to satisfy his own insatiable gambling habit. Because of Spillane, all West Side racketeers – not just Spillane's crowd – were always welcome at the Aeon Club, Ruby's posh gambling den at 76th Street and Broadway, where Spillane was often allowed to run his own table. It was there that Coonan and Stein first shook hands.

Stein took a liking to Coonan, even though he'd been warned by Fat Tony to stay away from the Irish Mob. They were 'crazy' and undisciplined, Fat Tony used to tell Ruby, remembering no doubt Spillane's Eli Zicardi kidnapping fiasco. But Stein didn't listen; he felt Coonan was a step above the average thug. For one thing, Jimmy was polite and exceedingly deferential towards Stein. Also, he'd expressed a genuine interest in learning more

157

about big-time loansharking from 'the man who knows it best.' With Ruby, flattery always worked.

Of course, the fact that Coonan was built like a long-shoreman didn't hurt either. Stein immediately put him to work as a part-time driver, bodyguard, and all-purpose gofer.

Now that Coonan was dealing with serious racketeers like Ruby Stein, it was more important than ever that he show the big boys just how feared he was. For years now he'd been establishing himself as the likely succes-sor to Spillane. Slowly but surely he had been acquiring a crew of faithful young toughs like Richie Ryan, Jimmy McElroy, Tommy Hess, and, most recently, Billy Beattie, Edna's former boyfriend, now a loanshark and a part-time bartender at the 596 Club. Even some of the old Spillane stalwarts like Cummiskey, Tom Devaney, and Walter Curich were now doing business with Coonan, not so much out of allegiance, but because anybody with any brains could see Jimmy was a man on the make. To align yourself with him now would put you in a 'respectable' position in the event he did, through some sudden means, become boss of the entire neighborhood.

After Dugan killed Curley in August '75, Coonan knew it was time to make his move. With the influence of drugs, the neighborhood seemed to be on the brink of tearing itself apart. The violence just kept getting crazier and crazier. If he could somehow harness that, somehow make it beholden to him and him alone, he would have the most feared gang the West Side of Manhattan had ever seen.

That's where Paddy Dugan came in.

Ironically, Dugan had always been tight with Coonan. In fact, a few months earlier, when Jimmy was having trouble with Charlie Krueger, another part-time bartender at the 596 Club, he turned to Dugan. Coonan heard that Krueger had been freelancing on the 'business' they had with Tony Lucich, loansharking out in Queens and Brooklyn, using Jimmy's name to get people to pay and not giving him a cut. When he first got the news, Coonan was mad enough to kill Charlie Krueger. But he had a better idea.

He arranged for Paddy Dugan and Billy Beattie to lure Krueger down to the 596 Club late one night on the pretense that they wanted to borrow money. When Krueger got there, they proceeded to strap him to a chair and beat the shit out of him. He could barely talk from the pistol whipping they gave him. Dugan and Beattie told Krueger they'd kill him unless he called Jimmy Coonan and demanded a $5,000 ransom. This had all been prearranged, of course, without Krueger's knowledge.

In an extreme state of desperation, Krueger called Coonan and mumbled his predicament into the phone. When Coonan told him he'd be glad to loan him the $5,000 at 5 points – a relatively high rate of interest – Krueger was not only relieved, he felt indebted to Coonan. He thought Jimmy had saved his life.

Coonan paid Dugan and Beattie $1,000 apiece for their night's work, and told them not to bother Charlie Krueger anymore.

Only problem was, Paddy Dugan was a junkie who couldn't leave well enough alone. In November, three months after he'd killed Curley, Dugan nabbed Charlie

159

Krueger again, this time without Jimmy's authorization. He had Krueger call Coonan and make the same demand as before.

Coonan was beside himself. That night he called Billy Beattie. 'Do you know what that jerk buddy of yours did?' he screamed into the phone.

'What?'

'He's got that fat bastard Krueger down at the club. He's holdin' him for ransom!'

'Oh, shit. Well, I hope you know I had nothin' to do with it.'

'Yeah, he told me he was on his own. Billy, I'm glad you ain't got a piece of that, you know. I warned the son of a bitch.'

The very next day, on November 17, 1975, Paddy Dugan disappeared. The last anybody saw of him he was headed for his bachelor pad at 452 West 50th Street . . .

On the night Paddy disappeared, Alberta Sachs, Jimmy Coonan's niece, was asleep in her mother's apartment at 442 West 50th Street, just four buildings over from Paddy's. She heard a knock at the door. It was her Uncle Jimmy and Eddie Cummiskey. They wanted to borrow some kitchen knives. They took three or four of the sharpest ones, gave Alberta $20, and left.

Alberta went back to sleep on the couch. About an hour later, she heard a noise out in the hallway. When she opened the door, she saw Coonan and Cummiskey again. This time Jimmy was holding a green plastic bag that had something round in it. Something about the size of a basketball.

It was dripping blood.

'What the hell is that?' asked Jimmy Coonan's thirteen-year-old niece.

'It's Paddy Dugan's head,' replied Cummiskey.

Coonan told her they were going down to the boiler room and they wanted her to clean up the hallway after them. Then they disappeared into the dark stairwell.

Alberta did as she was told. Then she lay down on the couch and pulled the covers up to her neck . . .

The following morning, a number of neighborhood people saw Coonan and Eddie Cummiskey at the Sunbrite Bar on 10th Avenue. They looked exhausted and demented, as if they'd been up all night drinking. Coonan had a big shit-eating grin on his face. Cummiskey had a mischievous glint in his baby blues. He was singing along with the juke box at the top of his lungs. The song he was singing was 'Rhinestone Cowboy.'

When Billy Beattie and Tommy Hess came into the bar, Jimmy instructed them to go over to Paddy's apartment, open the refrigerator, get a milk carton that was in there, and bring it back down to the bar.

Tall, gangly Billy Beattie did exactly as he was told. As he was heading north on 10th Avenue, back towards the Sunbrite, he noticed the milk carton had something loose inside that definitely wasn't milk. He peeked through the opening in the top of the carton. It was hard to tell, but he had a pretty good idea what it was: Paddy Dugan's private parts.

As soon as he stepped inside the bar, Eddie Cummiskey grabbed the carton. He was being loud and rowdy. 'Let's take it and dump it right on the fuckin' stoop. Right where the bastard killed Denis.'

Coonan got suddenly serious. 'Can't let you do that, you crazy bastard. That's gonna bring the heat. It's part of him, for Chrissake!'

Cummiskey held the carton aloft like it was a trophy. Finally, Coonan grabbed it and gave it back to Beattie. 'Here,' he said under his breath, 'take this and get rid of it.'

Beattie took the carton back to 452 West 50th Street and flushed the contents down the toilet.

For days afterwards, Paddy's demise became the talk of the neighborhood. Some people were saying his genitalia were in a pickle jar behind the bar at the Sunbrite. Others were saying they had seen Eddie Cummiskey walking along 10th Avenue at dawn holding Paddy's severed head by the hair. Still others said they'd seen Cummiskey walk right into the Sunbrite with Paddy's head and roll it down the bar.

They were *crazy* stories, of course. Outrageous. Unbelievable.

But the facts were the facts. Denis Curley's killer was gone. Jimmy Coonan and Eddie Cummiskey had a motive. And Paddy Dugan's genitalia didn't wind up in a milk carton by accident.

Mickey Featherstone was not in the neighborhood at the time of Dugan's murder. He was in Sing Sing finishing off a short two-month stint for a parole violation. Both he and Jackie Coonan had violated the terms of their parole by consorting with known felons – each other. They were held in prison until they were able to secure

162

a hearing before the state parole board, at which time a half-dozen neighborhood people showed up to vouch for them. The neighborhood people perjured themselves by telling the parole board that Mickey and Jackie had not been together, when in fact they had. One of the people who'd lied on their behalf was Paddy Dugan.

While Featherstone was in Sing Sing, he heard about Paddy's demise. The thing that pissed him off the most was that Billy Beattie, who was supposed to be Paddy Dugan's good friend, was the person who set him up to be killed – or at least that's what Featherstone had heard.

On the day of his release from Sing Sing – a chilly afternoon in early December 1975 – Featherstone made a bee-line for the 596 Club.

'Hey, Billy,' he said, walking in the front door, 'let's go for a stroll.'

Billy Beattie was tending bar at the time. He seemed surprised to see Featherstone. 'Mickey. I didn't even know you was back.'

'Never mind that. We got some talkin' to do.'

'I'm kinda busy right now.'

'So take a break.'

Beattie nodded and threw down his bar towel.

Once outside, they headed west on 43rd Street past the tenement where Featherstone had grown up; past the old New York Central Railroad tracks; past Engine Company 2, the red-brick firehouse where Mickey used to play as a kid. It was so cold that steam came from their mouths as they spoke.

'Billy, I heard somethin' I gotta ask you. Why'd you sell Paddy out?'

163

'Mickey, wait a minute . . .'

'I wanna know why you sold your fuckin' partner down the river.'

'I had no choice, Mickey. Had no fuckin' choice. They caught me when I was takin' a shower, man. Put guns to my fuckin' head and forced me to call him, forced me to set him up.'

'Who's they? Who the fuck is they?'

'Jimmy and Eddie.'

As Featherstone and Beattie spoke, Jimmy Coonan came up the block behind them.

'Hey, Mickey, don't blame Billy,' said Coonan. 'Ain't his fault. We forced him to do it, okay? He had no choice.'

Mickey was upset. 'Why Paddy, man? What'd he do to you?'

'Mickey, that little cocksucker kidnapped my bartender; he kidnapped Charlie Krueger. Then he calls me on my home phone, *my home fuckin' phone* and tells me he's holdin' him for ransom. In my bar. Holdin' him in my fuckin' bar!'

'Paddy did that?'

'Yeah, Paddy did that. Fuckin' junkie. He was outta control, man. Had it comin'. And that's not even mentioning the Denis Curley thing.'

Mickey let out a deep sigh and looked at Billy, who shrugged and stared down at his feet to avoid eye contact.

'Mickey,' said Coonan, 'c'mon back to the bar. It's friggin' freezin' out here. C'mon. I'll tell you all about it.'

Back at the 596 Club, Coonan and Featherstone sat in the rear, and Jimmy explained what happened with

Paddy Dugan. He'd been home that night with his family, he said, and Paddy kept calling him to say he was going to kill Charlie Krueger. Jimmy would hang up and Paddy would call again ten minutes later. It got very annoying. So Jimmy drove into town and got hold of Eddie Cummiskey, who he knew was after Dugan for the Denis Curley thing. Coonan and Cummiskey went to Billy Beattie's apartment and forced him to lure Paddy there. That's when Cummiskey nailed him with a .32.

It was an old apartment, with the bathtub in the kitchen. So they dragged Dugan's dead body in there and threw it in the tub. Then they went through Dugan's clothes and took all his money. After that, they stripped the body naked and Eddie and Jimmy began cutting it up.

'You did what?' asked Featherstone.

'We got rid of the body.'

'What the fuck for?'

Coonan shrugged. 'It's the only way to go, my man. No corpus delicti, no investigation.'

After they finished dicing up the body, they put Paddy's head in a plastic garbage bag and went up to the rooftop of 452 West 50th. They made their way through the moonlit night, over the rooftops of three tenement buildings, until they came to 442 West 50th, Coonan's sister-in-law's building. It was on the way down to the boiler room to incinerate Paddy's head that they ran into Jimmy's niece.

Featherstone, of course, had heard about Cummiskey's dismemberment routine before. But he didn't know Coonan was into it. It was Cummiskey who had trained to be a butcher at Attica. Mickey figured Cummiskey must have passed his skills along to Jimmy.

Coonan went on to explain to Mickey all that had been happening in the nearly five years he'd been away from the neighborhood. In that time, said Jimmy, he'd learned the loansharking business from Tony Lucich and hooked up with Ruby Stein. He was now pushing more money than anybody on the West Side, including Spillane.

'Spillane's a punk,' he said. 'A small-timer. His days are over.'

Featherstone had heard most of what Jimmy had to say before, but he let him go on anyway. He liked hearing about the Coonan/Spillane Wars and about how Jimmy had been making a name for himself. Sure, he'd been mad at Coonan about the Paddy Dugan murder, but he didn't know Paddy had kidnapped Krueger and held him for ransom. That was wrong, thought Mickey. And stupid. It put everything in a new light.

'You know, Mickey,' said Coonan, 'there ain't no reason with all that's goin' on here why you shouldn't be in on this.'

'Yeah?'

'Yeah. I mean, you been to prison for crazy stuff, stuff you don't make no money on. You come in with me, you make money. This way, you ever go back to the joint, least you went there tryin' to make a buck. Right?'

Featherstone could see the logic in what Coonan was saying. In fact, he'd thought of it himself before. Ever since Coonan had given him that gun years ago when he needed it to shoot Linwood Willis outside the Leprechaun Bar, Featherstone had felt a debt of gratitude to Jimmy. If Coonan ever needed him, he'd told himself many times, he'd be there. But Coonan seemed to be doing fine at the moment. He didn't really need Mickey. It was just an offer, an offer from one friend to another.

Featherstone told Coonan thanks, but no thanks. He'd just gotten back from prison and he wasn't ready yet for any big-time shit. 'But if you ever need me, Jimmy, for anything, you know I'll be there.'

Jimmy said thanks, he appreciated it, and that's where they left it.

Over the months that followed, Featherstone thought about Coonan's offer every now and then. The only money he had coming in were his $150-a-week veteran's benefits (he'd been declared 100 percent disabled) and social security. At the moment, he was living with his half-brother Bobby and not paying rent, so he didn't have many expenses. But he knew he was going to need some steady bread somewhere along the line. A straight job was out of the question, of course, even if he had been able to get one with his prison record, which was doubtful. He'd tried a few quick-cash schemes, but nothing seemed to add up to much. All roads kept leading back to Jimmy Coonan's offer . . .

One thing was sure: If Mickey Featherstone wanted to get involved in organized crime, he wouldn't have to spend much time establishing a reputation. Since beating his murder rap on an insanity plea, he'd served just under five years (including his pre-trial incarceration) for possession of an unregistered weapon in the Willis shooting. After being sentenced in early '73, he'd bounced from facility to facility. First it was the Bronx State Hospital for eight months, then Sing Sing for a month, then Comstock for nine months, Matteawan for two months, Great Meadow for eight months, Attica for a few weeks, then back to Matteawan for the remainder of his 'bit.'

Unlike Coonan, who'd done his time for the Canelstein/Morales shooting without incident, Featherstone's five years had been a horror show. He kept getting relocated from psychiatric wings to general population, where he'd get into fights and be sent back to the nuthouse.

When he was finally released in May of 1975, his attorney, Larry Hochheiser, plea-bargained on the remaining charges. Manhattan district Judge Harold Rothwax gave Featherstone five years' probation for both the John Riley homicide and possession of a weapon in the shooting death of Emilio 'Mio' Rattagliatti. Soon he was back on the West Side.

When he returned, those who knew Featherstone detected a slight difference. He seemed somewhat less agitated than before and a little more outgoing. His years in prison had helped bring his anger into focus, making him less wantonly dangerous, though harder and more calculating. Before prison, Mickey didn't have a concrete identity. Now, emboldened by his experiences, he saw himself as a survivor. He'd never allow himself to be 'victimized' again like those years after 'Nam.

Despite the personality changes, as he settled back into the neighborhood the end result was largely the same: Mickey found trouble at every turn. Along with the police, who he was sure were out to get him, there were the folks in the neighborhood saloons. With his Vietnam background, numerous homicides, dozens of barroom brawls, and ex-con status, he was already a legend in

Hell's Kitchen. When people met him, they were often surprised by how small and unassuming he looked. Some fools figured it would enhance their reputation if they kicked his ass, just so they could tell their friends they'd made a punk out of Mickey Featherstone.

On one such occasion Mickey was drinking in the 596 Club in the middle of the afternoon. A guy who wasn't even from the neighborhood was there with his girlfriend giving Mickey a hard time. He was bragging about being some kind of karate expert. After numerous insults were hurled back and forth, the guy asked, 'You think you're a motherfuckin' war hero? Is that it? You think you got balls? Well, I got more balls than the balls you got.'

Eventually he and Featherstone faced each other down. When the so-called karate expert went into his kung fu stance, Mickey, without even putting his drink down, belted him once in the face. The karate expert fell to the floor, whereupon Mickey grabbed a barstool and set it on the floor over the guy, pinning him helplessly to the ground. Then he made the guy's overweight girlfriend sit on the stool and have a drink.

'But I don't want no drink,' she said.

'So what,' said Featherstone. 'You're gonna sit there on that stool till you finish the drink, whether you like it or not.'

Sometimes it was so crazy Mickey just had to laugh. He'd gone from Hell's Kitchen to 'Nam to nuthouses to prisons. Now he was back in the environment he knew best. But he was beginning to think maybe this was the worst of all, and it was getting worse every day.

* * *

In December 1975, just days after his conversation with Billy Beattie and Jimmy Coonan about Paddy Dugan's demise, Featherstone's life took an unexpected turn. Once again, it began in a bar – this time in Amy's Pub, one of the neighborhood's more respectable saloons, located on 9th Avenue between 55th and 56th streets. Much of Amy's clientele came from the television and recording studios on West 57th Street, one of midtown Manhattan's busiest crosstown thoroughfares. The bar had a large picture window that overlooked 9th Avenue. The inside was always well lit and thick with plants and hanging ferns. They even had tablecloths at Amy's, an amenity unheard of at most of the places Featherstone frequented.

One evening, while Mickey was minding his own business, a group of local girls sauntered in and took a table near the back of the bar. He recognized a few of them, particularly a nicely built blonde he'd seen a few times since he got back from prison. He leaned over to the barman, who he knew, and asked about her.

'That's Sissy,' said the man behind the bar. 'Tommy Houlihan's sister.'

Mickey did a double take. 'That's Tommy Houlihan's sister? Man, she's grown.'

Featherstone vaguely remembered Sissy as a nondescript little girl from around the neighborhood. Now nineteen, eight years younger than Mickey, she was five-foot-three, had brown eyes, a sharp, slightly upturned nose, and sandy-blond hair just like his. She also fit nicely, very nicely, into a pair of jeans. He knew a little bit about her past; that her last name was actually Knell and that her mother had remarried. He'd heard something about one of her brothers overdosing and another being beaten and paralyzed for life. Naturally, he was intrigued.

He walked over to her table. 'Hey, how ya doin'? I'm Mickey Featherstone.'

'I know who you are,' she said in a tough, unmistakable Hell's Kitchen accent. 'So what?'

Mickey was taken aback. 'Hey, listen, I ain't gettin' smart with you or nothin'. I know your family and everything, so I was just sayin' hello.'

'So because you're Mickey Featherstone I'm supposed to talk to you? Is that it?'

'No. I was just tryin' to be friendly. Forget about it.'

Featherstone walked back over to the bar. After that, he couldn't take his eyes off her. He could see she was giggling and talking to her friends about him. Later, when there weren't as many people around, he went over to the table again. She was friendlier this time. He bought her a drink. They got up and danced.

After that, they started seeing each other regularly. They both came from broken families and violent backgrounds, so they had a lot in common. Since Mickey's first marriage had been such a disaster, he wasn't anxious to get involved in anything serious. But he and Sissy got along so well he couldn't believe it. She was pretty and streetwise; he was a tough guy. They fit each other's needs.

Soon they were hanging out late at night at her mother's apartment, sometimes making love on the floor by the light of the television. During the day, whenever Sissy got time off from her part-time job as an usherette at the nearby Broadway theaters, they'd go to Central Park. Sissy liked to go ice-skating. Mickey liked to watch her.

For Sissy, the relationship with Mickey brought stability to her life – a pretty good indication of just how screwed up she'd been. When Mickey came along, she was just beginning to get out from under a heroin habit she'd developed at the age of seventeen. That habit had led her to engage in purse snatching and wallet stealing. She'd known she was headed in a bad direction, but it wasn't until she saw two of her girlfriends reduced to hooking on 10th Avenue that she knew she had to pull herself out of it. Through her stepfather she'd landed a job as an usherette. Tentatively, she'd been putting the pieces back together when Mickey came along. The way she saw it, he was her reward for kicking her junk habit.

Eventually Mickey moved out of his brother Bobby's apartment and in with Sissy's family on West 51st Street, near Sacred Heart Church. It was crowded – there were maybe six or seven people living in a five-room flat most of the time – but they got by. Then they moved into their own place, a new apartment at 520 West 56th Street, on the fifteenth floor.

Featherstone tried to lead some semblance of a normal life, but it wasn't easy. For one thing, he was still drinking constantly, sometimes a quart of whiskey over the course of a day. He'd also gotten into smoking hash and marijuana. Whatever it took to deaden the senses, to get him to a place where he felt no pain – that was Featherstone's daily goal. Increasingly, his habits were leading to a need for more cash.

Undaunted by the state parole board, who'd warned

him and Jackie Coonan not to consort with one another, Mickey and Jackie opened an after-hours club on 44th Street between 9th and 10th avenues. Ostensibly, it was supposed to make Mickey and Jackie a few bucks and serve as a place where the neighborhood crowd could drink peaceably without being hassled. A nice idea. But given the company Mickey and Jackie kept, there was never much chance it would work out that way.

One night, Mickey was there with Eddie Cummiskey, Jimmy Coonan, and a group of Puerto Ricans from Brooklyn. There was a card game going on, but Mickey was hardly paying attention. He'd been drinking most of the day, and then later that night somebody brought in some Thai stick. Mickey smoked a few joints and was flying high. Everything was a blur. He moved slowly past the card game, past the pool table, into a back room to lie down.

The music was loud. Something in the back room was glowing in the dark, somewhere. Mickey closed his eyes and his head started to spin. He heard shouting and arguing in the distance. Maybe I should help, he thought to himself. Maybe they need me.

The next afternoon, he woke up in the same spot he'd crashed the night before. As he walked into the front room, his head was throbbing. The place looked like a tornado had hit it – chairs and ashtrays were turned over, glasses were broken, debris was scattered all around. It stank of stale whiskey and cheap cigars.

Standing by the pool table were Jimmy Coonan and Eddie Cummiskey. They looked haggard, as if they'd been up all night without sleep. Featherstone strained to see through his swollen, bloodshot eyes. He noticed that the smooth felt covering on the pool table was soiled with some dark liquid that looked like blood.

'What the fuck?' he asked, staring in disbelief. 'What happened?'

'You don't remember?' asked Cummiskey, a devious twinkle in his eyes. 'You knifed a fuckin' spic hustler last night. Cut the shit outta him. Killed the fucker.'

Featherstone was skeptical. 'Naaah. Where's the body then?'

Cummiskey smiled that twisted smile of his. 'We made it do the Houdini act.'

Mickey stared at Eddie and Jimmy, who were now laughing, then at the blood-stained pool table. He had no recollection of killing anybody that night, but anything was possible.

His head felt like shit and so did his stomach. 'You guys are full of it,' said Mickey, as he made for the toilet, his stomach beginning to heave.

Eddie and Jimmy just kept laughing. Mickey went into the bathroom and threw up in the sink.

A few days later, in January 1976, Mickey was to witness 'the Houdini act' in living color. This time the victim was a neighborhood guy known as Ugly Walter, and once again the perpetrators were Eddie and Jimmy.

Seeing Ugly Walter disappear piece by piece was a memory Mickey would spend the next ten years of his life trying to forget.

At the same time bodies began to disappear in Hell's Kitchen, Police Officer Richie Egan was assigned to the Syndicated Crime Unit of the NYPD's Intelligence Division. In 1974, he'd worked on OPERATION UNCOVER, a major narcotics investigation set in his old post in Spanish Harlem. After that, in '75, he'd tracked a big-time cocaine dealer named James Austin, a bogus M.D. who'd set up a distribution ring in the Riverdale section of the Bronx.

While working on these cases, Egan was acquiring expertise on organized crime in general. Part of his job was to update files on some of the biggest mobsters in New York, including Fat Tony Salerno, Vincent 'the Chin' Gigante, and Carlo Gambino, then boss of the powerful Gambino crime family. Much of his workday was spent following gangsters on their daily routines. In time, Egan came to know their habits: where they conducted business, how they communicated, where they buried the bodies.

He didn't know it yet, but his expertise would soon lead him to the most hazardous investigation of his career, one that would require he spend most of his waking hours in the diners, bars, and backalleys of the bloody and volatile West Side.

7

DOIN' BUSINESS

In the summer of 1976, Hell's Kitchen played an integral role in one of the most spectacular celebrations the city of New York had ever seen. On the Bicentennial, July 4th, an armada of sixteen tall ships from around the world and a parade of more than 225 sailing vessels made its way up the Hudson. A twenty-two-nation fleet of fifty-three naval units lined the river. The host ship of the review, the 79,000-ton aircraft carrier *Forrestal*, was moored at the West 46th Street pier. Among the 3,000 distinguished guests on board was President Gerald Ford, who reviewed the proceedings from a grandstand on the ship's flight deck.

The irony, of course, was that even as New York celebrated the nation's 200th birthday in high style, the city itself was dying. An economic crisis had put New York on a crash course with bankruptcy. For months, Mayor Abraham Beame had been imposing severe austerity measures, cutting back on all manner of city services. Poor and working-class neighborhoods were hit the hardest. Development ceased. The streets went unswept. The police patrolled in smaller and smaller numbers.

In Hell's Kitchen, the terrain began to look a lot like the South Bronx, the city's most notorious ghetto. Residents and small-shop owners pulled the gates down on their stores, locked them, and left in droves. Even in the best of times, the neighborhood often had a ramshackle, derelict air. But now, as the city's finances worsened, it seemed perched on the edge of total neglect.

On August 20, 1976, roughly six weeks after the Bicentennial, Eddie Cummiskey was drinking in the Sunbrite Bar at 1:30 in the afternoon. A car pulled up to the bar and double-parked. A lone man got out, went into the bar and put a gun to the back of Cummiskey's head. He fired one shot. The bullet entered Eddie's skull on the right side just below the ear, then lacerated upward through the right and left lobe until it finally lodged itself in the upper left hemisphere of the brain. Bleeding profusely, Cummiskey slumped over on the bar and immediately lapsed into a coma from which he never recovered.

The gunman calmly left the bar, got back in his car, and drove off.

A small crowd soon gathered in front of the bar, drawn by the wailing sirens from the ambulance and the police cars rushing up 10th Avenue. Mickey Featherstone was there. So was Tony Lucich. As Cummiskey's body was brought out on a stretcher, a nearby patrolman asked Lucich, 'That's Eddie Cummiskey, right?'

'Yep,' said Lucich. 'That *was* Eddie Cummiskey.'

Lucich remembered seeing Eddie just a few weeks earlier, on the 4th of July. They'd had a couple of drinks together, and when Eddie got up to leave he slapped

Lucich on the back and said, 'Well Tony, we'll have to do it again next centennial.'

That was the way Lucich was always going to remember Eddie Cummiskey.

After Cummiskey's death, Featherstone met with Jimmy Coonan in the bar of the Skyline Motor Inn, just across the avenue from the Sunbrite. Ever since it was first built in 1959, the Skyline had been a frequent gathering place for the neighborhood's criminal element. On Sunday mornings, Mickey Spillane and his crowd used to gather in the dining area so they could be seen by the dozens of neighborhood well-wishers who inevitably came by to pay their respects. Coonan preferred to do his business in the bar, where it was darker and less populated.

Jimmy was worried about the Eddie Cummiskey hit. Moments after Cummiskey was shot, Jackie Coonan had run over to his apartment and gotten an old photograph taken at Sing Sing Prison in 1969. In the picture were Jackie, Jimmy, and a few other people, including Joseph 'Mad Dog' Sullivan. Jackie had shown the photograph to the bartender at the Sunbrite, who was still in a state of shock from just having seen Cummiskey get half his head blown off. But he was able to identify Mad Dog Sullivan as the triggerman.

Joe Sullivan (no relation to Eddie Sullivan, Coonan's partner from the late Sixties) was a well-known freelance assassin from way back. His claim to fame was a prison break he'd made from the Attica Correctional Facility in April of '71. At the time, no one had ever escaped from Attica – a maximum-security, upstate New York prison – in its forty-year history. Sullivan, then thirty-two years old, had done so by hiding himself beneath some grain and feed sacks piled aboard a truck that left the prison in broad daylight. He was captured five weeks later strolling down a street in Greenwich Village.

Both in and out of prison, Sullivan was known as a trigger-happy gunman, frequently employed by *La Cosa Nostra*. In fact, it was long rumored in Hell's Kitchen that Sullivan, along with Anthony Provenzano and a few others, was behind the disappearance of Teamsters boss Jimmy Hoffa.

If Mad Dog Sullivan was the one who killed Cummiskey, then chances were it was a Mafia hit. And if it was a Mafia hit, Jimmy Coonan suspected something serious was going down, something he was not privy to.

Just a few weeks earlier, on July 20, 1976, Thomas Devaney, another neighborhood Irishman, had been gunned down in a similar fashion in a bar-and-grill on Lexington Avenue. Like Cummiskey, Devaney had been tight with Mickey Spillane. So it was possible, surmised Coonan, that these killings were somehow leading towards Spillane.

But it was also true that both Cummiskey and Devaney recently had been shifting their allegiances to Coonan. Cummiskey, in particular, had been spreading his time evenly between Spillane and Coonan, acting as a strong-arm man for both. So it was equally possible that these hits were, in fact, leading toward Jimmy.

Coonan wasn't sure just what the hell was going on, he told Featherstone at the Skyline Motor Inn, but he didn't like the looks of it. 'I don't know, Mick,' he said. 'With Cummiskey outta the picture, I'm gonna need somebody to watch my back.' Once again, Jimmy asked Mickey if he'd be willing to come in on his loanshark operation. This time he emphasized his need for 'protection,' telling Mickey his primary role would be as a bodyguard.

Featherstone interpreted it as an appeal for help, and he couldn't say no. Jimmy had been his friend. Now it was time to return that friendship. Of course, there was also the matter of $150 a week Coonan was willing to pay, plus the promise of a lot more down the line.

'Okay,' said Mickey. 'You can count on me.'

After that, they established a routine. Coonan would drive in from New Jersey on Wednesday afternoons, usually around one or two o'clock. He'd pick Mickey up at his place on West 56th Street and they'd go over to Tony Lucich's new apartment at 747 10th Avenue, between 52nd and 53rd. Lucich would be there, along with Andy Wheeler, a neighborhood racketeer who acted as their controller. Wheeler was another of the older breed who'd been slowly shifting his support from Spillane to Coonan. After the death of Cummiskey, Wheeler jumped ship entirely.

Sometimes Coonan liked to kid Wheeler about his previous affiliations. Once, in front of Featherstone and Lucich, he reminded Wheeler about a time when he and a few others had kidnapped Wheeler and held him for ransom. Coonan had strapped him to a chair and called Spillane. 'We got your controller,' he told Spillane. 'You don't come up with five grand we're gonna put air conditioning in this motherfucker's head.'

'Oh yeah?' said Spillane. 'Do what you gotta do.' Then he hung up.

Coonan would laugh his ass off when he told this story,

and so did Featherstone and Lucich when they heard it. 'There's your fuckin' buddy Mickey Spillane,' Coonan used to say to Wheeler, who always got red in the face with embarrassment.

In the apartment, Lucich would pass along a number of envelopes to Jimmy. 'This is my portion of the shylocking money,' he'd say. 'This is the numbers money. This is the pier money.' The loansharking and gambling money was always in cash. The money from the piers often came in the form of payroll checks from the International Longshoremen's Association.

Coonan and Lucich had been farming out money to other neighborhood shylocks for years now. But it was only recently that Coonan had taken over the lucrative numbers racket. Up until Cummiskey's death, it had been run by Spillane, Cummiskey, Lucich, and Wheeler. But when Cummiskey got whacked, Spillane got scared and wanted out.

'No problem,' Lucich told Spillane. 'You ain't shit without Cummiskey anyway.'

By that time, a principal of $10,000 had accrued. Lucich gave Spillane $2,500 and said good-bye. Coonan stepped in immediately.

As for the money from the piers, that was a little something Coonan had cooked up himself. At the time, the piers were not exactly booming with business. But Local 1909 of the ILA, whose headquarters were located at 48th Street and 12th Avenue, still had a sizable payroll. Through Walter Curich, another old-timer from Spillane's generation, Coonan had been able to extort a weekly tribute.

After picking up the envelopes at Lucich's apartment, Coonan and Featherstone would continue making the rounds collecting Jimmy's debts. If Coonan had driven into town, they'd use his car. If he had taken the bus in, they'd make their rounds on foot. The Market Diner, the 596 Club and the Sunbrite were all regular stops. So was Donald Mallay's candy store at 55th and 10th Avenue, William 'Whoopi' Meyers's auto garage on 46th Street between 11th and 12th Avenue, and one of Carl Mazzella's many produce stands around the neighborhood.

Usually an envelope was waiting for Coonan, filled with neat green currency. But sometimes there were problems. That's why he and Mickey both carried .25-caliber automatics everywhere they went.

Featherstone knew full well what his role was supposed to be in the event Coonan had to get rough with a customer. He'd gotten a crash course a few months earlier when he accompanied Jimmy, along with Tom Devaney and Tommy Hess, to a bar called Polly's Cage on 57th Street near 8th Avenue. There was a construction worker there who was looking to borrow money from Coonan. But Jimmy had been tipped off that the guy was a 'beat artist,' a person who borrows from shylocks and never pays his loans. So Jimmy had a message he wanted to deliver.

The four of them walked into the saloon. Tommy Hess and Featherstone went to the back of the bar and stood guard, while Tom Devaney and Coonan grabbed the construction worker and took him outside for a chat. When the bartender tried to follow, Tommy Hess – dark-haired, five-foot-ten and muscular – advised otherwise.

Featherstone sauntered up to the front of the bar and peeked out the window. He could see Tom Devaney with his gun wrapped in a newspaper, smacking the guy upside the head. 'You think you're gonna rob my friend?' he was saying. 'Huh? Huh?'

Jimmy was standing in front of the guy – who was now whimpering like a child – gesturing with his finger. 'If you think you're gonna get money off me, then rob me, I'll make you suffer. Do you follow what I'm bringing out?'

Weeks later, when it was just Coonan and Featherstone making the rounds, there were similar encounters. Bar owners, restaurant managers, and neighborhood gamblers were slapped and beaten. Sometimes the boys stuck loaded guns in their customers' mouths for added emphasis.

Mostly, though, both Jimmy and Mickey's reputation was enough to ensure payment. If not, a verbal threat often did the job. Like the time Jimmy told Whoopi Meyers in front of his garage on 46th Street, 'Just because your brother's a cop don't mean I won't hurt you. Got it?' They had no trouble with Whoopi after that.

Their midweek rounds almost always ended at the bar of the Skyline Motor Inn, where Jimmy met with his midlevel shylocks, the people he was lending money to so they could sustain their own loanshark operations. This group usually included Tommy Collins, who'd come over to Coonan from Spillane's side even though he'd once had to duck Jimmy's machine-gun fire, Billy Beattie, Paddy Dugan's former partner, Nick 'the Greek' Kagabines, and a few others. These were people who were close to Jimmy, members of his crew who often had large outstanding debts and endless stories to tell about how they were having trouble getting their own customers to pay up.

One time, Billy Beattie was bitching about Jimmy McElroy, the former boxer, neighborhood ladies' man, and a chronic late payer. 'I don't know what he does with his money. Where does it go? In his mouth, up his nose? I don't know what to say.'

'You havin' a problem with Jimmy Mac,' said Coonan, 'maybe it's time to tighten back or lay up.'

'Tighten back or lay up' was one of Jimmy's favorite phrases. It usually meant he was tired of hearing about it. Either *make* your customer pay, Jimmy was saying, or come up with the bread yourself.

Mickey Featherstone would listen to these and other conversations in total fascination. He had come back from prison with a thorough hatred of anything that represented the establishment. By extension, anything that represented a threat to the establishment was to be admired. Jimmy Coonan was the most sophisticated criminal he knew, a man who was brutal but also had foresight and organizational skills. To be near Jimmy gave Mickey a new identity, a feeling of self-worth. When he first started working with Jimmy, Mickey had always been quick to stress that he was doing it out of friendship. He still believed that. But as the weeks passed, Coonan's ways began to rub off on him. He began to take pleasure in that sudden look of fear he and Jimmy would get when they walked into a neighborhood saloon. He began to laugh at the way grown men groveled and quaked whenever his or Coonan's name was mentioned. You could see it in his walk, in the cockiness he began to exude . . .

Mickey Featherstone was becoming a gangster.

It wasn't anything he was ready to announce to the world, however. For months, even his girlfriend Sissy wouldn't know the full extent of his involvement with Coonan. She was smart enough to figure out a lot of it, of course, but she was also smart enough not to ask questions. Even after they became husband and wife on October 28, 1976, there were few conversations over the dinner table about Mickey's day at work. This was, after all, not 'Ozzie and Harriet.' This was Hell's Kitchen.

Throughout 1976 and into '77, Jimmy Coonan continued to consolidate his power. With the death of Eddie Cummiskey, Mickey Spillane had lost his 'muscle' and all but disappeared from the neighborhood. Coonan pretty much ran everything now; the policy games, loansharking, extortion – you name it.

There was no question in anyone's mind that Jimmy Coonan was ruthless. The Paddy Dugan murder was still a topic of conversation in neighborhood bars nearly two years after it had happened. Now, with Mickey Featherstone at his side, there wasn't a gangster in Hell's Kitchen who would have considered conducting criminal business without first making sure it had been okayed by 'Jimmy C.'

But for Coonan, this newfound power wasn't enough. In time, his interests began to extend beyond the roughly 150 square blocks that were the base of his budding empire. As the other neighborhood tough guys were beginning to find out, Jimmy was looking to forge some kind of alliance with the Italians that might take the rackets beyond the neighborhood.

Many, including Featherstone, wondered why. Unlike Jimmy, whose criminal ambitions had always been grandiose, they were content to spend the money they were making on booze, women and – increasingly – cocaine. As long as no one had designs on the local bounty, why should they want to go into business with a bunch of 'wiseguys'?

But Jimmy saw things differently. For one thing, he'd always admired the organizational structure of *La Cosa Nostra*. In the volatile world of organized crime, it was in the interest of those in power to have a strong system of accountability. Especially with his West Side Irish crew, known for their 'craziness,' Coonan stood to gain if he could align himself with a more stable, business-minded class of racketeer. Coonan, after all, had always seen himself that way. Even his instincts for violence, he believed, were always part of a larger plan.

But even more than that, as Jimmy had told his underlings time and time again, he wasn't sure just yet whether or not the Italians *did* have designs on the neighborhood rackets. 'You never know with the guineas,' Jimmy used to say. 'The bastards are always one step ahead of everybody.' It would be months before the Hell's Kitchen Mob would know who was behind the gangland killings of Tom Devaney and Eddie Cummiskey. In the meantime, Coonan sensed a restlessness on the part of *La Cosa Nostra*. Now that Spillane had, for all intents and purposes, been moved aside, it was more important than ever that the Italians know that Coonan & Company were in charge.

It was in this curious spirit of ambition *and* paranoia

that Coonan tentatively began to establish his 'Italian connection.' Through the late Eddie Cummiskey, who'd once worked at a sewage treatment plant on Ward's Island, Coonan had gotten to know Danny Grillo, a co-worker of Cummiskey's and a *soldato*, or soldier, in the powerful Gambino crime family. Grillo was connected with a notoriously violent crew based in the Canarsie section of Brooklyn headed by an up-and-coming *capo*, or crew chief, named Roy Demeo.

In the early months of 1977, Coonan began to trudge his underlings out to Ward's Island, a sizable island in the East River that, among other things, served as a foundation for the massive steel towers of the Triborough Bridge. In a small industrial trailer on the island's eastern flank, Coonan, Featherstone, McElroy, and Richie Ryan would meet a guy named Tony, who was a foreman at the sewage treatment plant. On most occasions, Danny Grillo and Roy Demeo were there as well.

As far as Coonan's underlings could tell, the meetings had little to do with 'serious' criminal business. Jimmy was just testing the waters. More than anything, it seemed like Coonan wanted to show off his crew in front of the powerful Roy Demeo and Danny Grillo.

'We can do business,' Jimmy once told Demeo.

Demeo nodded. 'I got no prejudice against nobody,' he replied, assuring Coonan that the fact he was Irish would not get in the way.

One of the last West Siders to be dragged out to 'Tony's island,' as it eventually became known to the Irish gang, was part-time bartender Billy Beattie. It was a brisk afternoon in May of 1977. He and Coonan had arrived by car, driving past the Manhattan State Hospital for the Insane, which occupied the western edge of the island in a series of connected brick buildings.

Beattie was introduced to Tony, the foreman at the sewage treatment plant, and to Danny Grillo. After thirty minutes of small talk in Tony's trailer, Beattie and Coonan were led to another trailer nearby, where they climbed some portable wooden steps and, inside, a black guy named Louie showed them a lathe where silencers were made.

Coonan took one of Louie's silencers, hot off the lathe, and screwed it onto a 9mm machine gun he'd brought with him. Then they all went outside, where cold gusts of wind swept off the East River and across the island. There were big piles of sand and gravel all over the place. Coonan fired the machine gun into one of the piles of sand and smiled like a little kid. Beattie was amazed. You couldn't hear a fucking thing.

Later that afternoon, Coonan and Beattie said good-bye to Tony and Danny Grillo. They were in Billy's car, heading south on the FDR Drive towards the Holland Tunnel, which would take them under the Hudson River to Coonan's home in Keansburg, New Jersey.

Coonan was in a talkative mood, explaining to Beattie the importance of doing business with the people he'd just been introduced to. Grillo, he said, was a professional triggerman who got $20,000 and up for a killing. Tony was a bomb expert who knew how to build bombs that could be detonated electronically.

'Hey,' said Beattie, smiling, 'that's what we'll call him – Tony the Bomb.'

Ever since Beattie had gone in with Coonan over a year ago, he'd been slightly nervous about where he stood. Beattie had gotten his start with Mickey Spillane, which he knew put him on shaky ground with Coonan. Then he'd dated Jimmy's wife, Edna, before Jimmy got to her. As far as Beattie was concerned, it was never serious. But who knew what Edna had told Jimmy about him?

Finally, there was the fact he was deeply in debt to Coonan. Jimmy had more or less financed his shylock operation. Billy had never been very good at collecting what was owed him, which made him equally erratic at paying what he owed.

Whatever the reasons, Beattie felt Coonan sometimes went out of his way to make sure that he, Billy, knew who was on top. Which is exactly what Jimmy was doing as they drove south on the FDR, past the enormous glass towers of lower Manhattan.

'You know,' said Jimmy, 'back there at Tony's island, that's where we finished off Paddy.'

Coonan knew the subject of Paddy Dugan's death was not a pleasant one for Beattie, who'd been forced to set up his former partner. But Coonan seemed to take particular pleasure rubbing it in. He explained to Beattie, in great detail, how they took what was left of Dugan's body out to Ward's Island and dumped it in the river.

In the old days, said Jimmy, Cummiskey used to work at the sewage plant along with Tony the Bomb and Danny Grillo. It was Cummiskey who first learned that the currents around the island were exceptionally strong. That's why the passageway on the east side of the island had been named Hell Gate. But Cummiskey had his own

189

name for it. He called it 'the burial grounds,' because it was where he'd been dumping the severed body parts of his murder victims for years.

As Coonan talked on and on about Paddy Dugan, the Italians, Spillane, and other subjects he'd become downright obsessive about in recent months, Beattie began to get the feeling he was building towards something. It was weird, he thought. One minute Jimmy was throwing an arm around you and letting you into his confidence – like he did with the trip to 'Tony's island' – and the next he was reminding you what happened to people who got on his bad side.

When they arrived at Coonan's modest, wood-framed house on Forest Avenue in Keansburg, they stood outside the car. A pleasant breeze whisked through the trees that lined the street, a street very different from the ones back in Hell's Kitchen where Jimmy and Billy had both grown up.

'Billy,' said Jimmy, reaching out to rest a hand on his right shoulder, 'I need you to pick me up tomorrow morning. We got a piece of work to do.'

Okay. Alright. At least Beattie now knew exactly what was up. 'A piece of work' was another of Coonan's pet phrases. It meant somebody was going to get whacked. Beattie knew enough not to ask a lot of questions – not yet, anyway. In time, he'd probably learn more than he wanted to know.

The following morning, on May 5, 1977, Beattie picked Coonan up in front of his house in Keansburg. The first thing they did was stop at a Food Town supermarket. Jimmy sent Beattie in to buy three boxes of plastic garbage bags – the jumbo size. Then they continued on through the Lincoln Tunnel to Manhattan, where they stopped at a hardware store on 9th Avenue, just south of 42nd Street. They went into the hardware store and Jimmy picked out an assortment of kitchen knives – one butcher knife, an eighteen-inch steak knife with a serrated edge, and a small filet knife.

'This one,' said Coonan, holding up the filet knife. 'You need this to take off tattoos, birthmarks, anything's gonna make it possible to identify the body.'

From the hardware store they went straight to the 596 Club at 43rd Street and 10th Avenue. Inside, Tommy Hess, dark-haired and muscular, was behind the bar. Richie Ryan, twenty-three years old, with curly brown hair and a soft Irish face, was playing pinball. After a few minutes, Danny Grillo, the professional hit man from Ward's Island, came out of the bathroom.

Hess, Ryan, and Beattie sat at one end of the bar while Coonan and Grillo went into a huddle at the other end. Beattie could hear Grillo saying he thought it would be best if he hid in the kitchen until 'the stiff' walked in the door. Then he'd come out and pull the trigger.

About thirty minutes passed before Jimmy said, 'Alright, let's get started.' He motioned for Beattie to go with him back outside to the car. As they walked into the small adjoining parking lot just north of the saloon, Jimmy told Billy they were going to the Aeon Club, Ruby Stein's gambling parlor at 76th and Broadway.

Beattie had met Ruby Stein through Coonan a few months earlier at the Aeon Club. He was introduced to Ruby as 'one of the okay guys,' which meant he would be free to gamble at the club and, if need be, borrow money through Stein or one of his many midlevel shylocks. Beattie didn't know a lot about Stein at the time. But he later learned that Ruby was one of the biggest loansharks on the East Coast.

The thought that Coonan was going to knock off Ruby made Beattie's mouth go dry. This was not like killing somebody from the neighborhood. Ruby Stein was bigtime, as big as they get.

In the car on the way uptown, Jimmy explained his reasoning. 'I got a feelin' this fuckin' Ruby Stein had somethin' to do with Devaney and Cummiskey bein' taken out – know what I'm sayin'?'

But even more pressing than the revenge motive, Jimmy admitted, was the fact he was now in debt to Stein to the tune of $70,000. Supposedly, Tommy Collins and a few other West Siders owed Stein similar amounts. So it was an opportunity to clear everyone's slate and maybe even take over Ruby's operation after he was gone.

Although Coonan wasn't saying it, Beattie knew there was one other reason Ruby was a goner. One way or another, Stein's death was going to attract a lot of attention from *La Cosa Nostra*. And that's just how Jimmy wanted it. By forcing his relationship with the Italians to the next stage, this was Jimmy's first big power play. And it was either going to get them all killed or make Coonan's crew a definite force to be reckoned with in the underworld.

Jimmy must have worked out some arrangement ahead of time to get Ruby out of the Aeon Club, because when they arrived he was waiting for them. Beattie drove, with Coonan in the passenger seat and Ruby in the back. First they went to Delsomma's restaurant, at 47th Street between 7th and 8th Avenue. Much to Beattie's surprise, they dropped Ruby off there and he and Jimmy headed back to the 596 Club. Something to do with setting up an alibi. They'd only been in the bar a few minutes when Jimmy took Billy's car keys and said, 'Be ready. I'll have him here in ten.'

Beattie stood to the right of the entrance, near a pay phone on the wall. It was his job to lock the door and pull the shades once Jimmy brought Ruby into the bar. Danny Grillo went into the kitchen. Tommy Hess was behind the bar and Richie Ryan was seated at a stool on the other side. As they waited, the tension overwhelmed whatever desire there may have been to make small talk. The only sound was an occasional squeaky barstool.

Finally, Coonan walked in the door with Ruby Stein right behind him. Beattie immediately pulled the shades and pretended he was using the pay phone. Then he locked the door. Hess and Ryan greeted Ruby, who walked into the middle of the bar. Jimmy told him to take a seat at the counter, he'd be right back. Sensing something was not right, Ruby hesitated.

'Go ahead,' said Jimmy, smiling like a cat with a secret, 'have a seat.'

Suddenly Danny Grillo burst out of the kitchen with a .32-caliber automatic aimed straight ahead. 'Oh my God!' gasped a startled Ruby Stein as Grillo fired six shots, hitting him in the chest, arms, and leg. The jolt lifted Ruby an inch or two off the ground and spun him completely around. He collapsed on the floor in the middle of the bar.

193

It was over just that fast. Tommy Hess stepped outside to stand guard. The others gathered around to look at Ruby's contorted body. There was a stunned silence. Then Coonan nodded towards Billy Beattie. 'Go ahead,' he said solemnly, 'put a bullet in him.'

Beattie wasn't about to ask questions. He removed a .22-caliber pistol with a silencer on it from inside his coat and fired a bullet into Ruby's face. The impact caused Ruby's head to twitch, but the rest of his body hardly moved. Then Coonan nodded towards Richie Ryan. Beattie handed the .22 to Ryan, who also fired a shot into Ruby's bullet-riddled corpse.

Jimmy Coonan smiled at this gesture of solidarity; they were all accomplices now. The emotions were so strong that Jimmy and Danny Grillo embraced, holding each other in a bear hug for three or four seconds as the others looked on.

Then they all went to work.

Several of the plastic bags that Beattie had bought at the supermarket that day were split down the seams and laid out flat like a sheet. As they were rolling Ruby's body onto the plastic bags, his shoe came off and a wad of bills fell out on the floor. Coonan picked it up, looked it over quickly and tossed it onto the bar. 'Whack it five ways,' he said to no one in particular. 'Looks to be about a grand.'

Once Ruby was completely laid out, they grabbed the plastic by the ends and dragged his body back to the ladies' room, where Coonan and Richie Ryan began stripping him naked. Coonan took Ruby's little black book, with the names and phone numbers of his loanshark customers in it, and tossed it to Beattie. 'Copy those numbers down,' he said. 'That's money in the bank, right there.'

When they had Ruby completely naked, Coonan took the eighteen-inch serrated knife he'd picked up at the hardware store and grabbed Ruby's bloody head by the hair. 'Come here,' he shouted to Richie Ryan as he put the knife to Stein's neck. 'I want you to feel how fuckin' heavy this head is. Feel that?'

Up to this point, Beattie had been watching. But he couldn't take any more. As he saw the knife begin to tear through Ruby's flesh, he walked over to the bar and poured himself a drink. He knew the reasoning behind all this – no corpus delicti, no investigation – but it still made him nauseous.

'Don't have the stomach for it, huh?' asked Grillo, who'd also walked over to the bar.

'No,' replied Billy. 'It's not my bag.'

'Yeah, me neither. I'm a shooter. I'll shoot anybody any fuckin' time. But I ain't into cuttin' 'em up.'

As Beattie and Grillo waited, Coonan showed Ryan, the aspiring young tough guy, the finer points of human butchery. Occasionally, he could be heard offering a word of professional advice: 'This here, the elbow, this is the toughest part.'

Finally, after about an hour, they were finished. The various body parts had been stuffed into six or seven bags. Whatever was left over in the way of excess flesh or gristle was flushed down the toilet. The walls were wiped clean, the floors mopped.

After that, Nick 'the Greek' Kagabines pulled his powder-blue Chevy Caprice up in front of the bar. They all helped load the bags into the trunk. From there, Kagabines was to go to 'the burial grounds' on Ward's Island and dump what was left of one of the most notorious loansharks in the history of New York into the East River.

Presumably, the bags would then follow the strong southerly flow of the river's currents, bobbing past the towering skyscrapers of lower Manhattan, past Governor's Island, past the Statue of Liberty, until the remains reached their final resting place amongst the bass, barracuda, crabs, and other creatures of the deep.

A few days after the murder, Mickey Featherstone was walking north on 10th Avenue when Coonan pulled over in his big black Buick and honked. When Jimmy got out of the car, Mickey could see right away he was steamed.

'Hey,' said Featherstone, 'what's goin' on?'

'It's fuckin' Ruby. They found part of Ruby.'

Featherstone had heard all about Ruby getting whacked and cut up. He wasn't surprised. In fact, at one time he and Jackie Coonan were supposed to kill Ruby Stein. They didn't want to do it, but Jimmy had insisted. So they hung around Ruby's club a few times to make it look like they were trying to find him.

Mickey had always liked Ruby. When Ruby had heard that his wife Sissy was going to have a baby, he told Mickey he was going to buy them a case of Dom Perignon. That was the last time Mickey talked to Ruby. When he heard he'd been whacked in the 596 Club it made him kind of sad.

Now, here was Jimmy Coonan screaming about how Ruby's bloated torso had washed ashore at Rockaway Beach in Queens. Although there was no head, arms, legs, or genitals, the medical examiner was able to identify it as Ruby's by a scar on his chest from a recent heart operation.

'I fucked up,' said Jimmy. 'Man, did I fuck up.'

'Yeah?'

'See, you gotta open 'em up. I was told this, but I didn't do it.'

'I don't get it.'

'The stomach, the lungs, they inflate. If you don't cut 'em open the torso floats, which is what happened with Ruby.'

There was sure to be an investigation now, said Coonan. Since he was one of the last people seen with Ruby before he disappeared, he'd already had a detective come out to his house in Jersey. Now they would be snooping around Hell's Kitchen asking a lot of questions.

'We got nothin' to worry about, right?' asked Jimmy.

'Of course not,' Mickey answered, backing him up.

Later, when Featherstone thought about it, he got annoyed. He hadn't even wanted Ruby to get whacked, and now he had to be concerned along with everybody else. Not only were the Italians going to be looking into this Ruby Stein thing, but now there were going to be 'bulls,' or police, all over the neighborhood.

Mickey was pissed for a while, but then he felt ashamed of himself. Coonan had done a lot for him since he'd gotten out of prison, and there weren't too many people he could say that about. This dismemberment thing was

197

weird, as far as he was concerned, but it was no reason to sell out a friend. Now was the time to reaffirm his commitment to Jimmy, to show his loyalty, to be tough.

Fuck it, he thought. If there was gonna be an investigation, bring it on home.

8

WEST SIDE STORY

Across the street from the Market Diner, on the corner of 43rd Street and 11th Avenue, Officer Richie Egan took a sip of coffee from his Styrofoam cup, scrunched down in the front seat of his unmarked police car, and fixed his eyes on the diner's main entrance. It was around midnight, and Egan's partner, Detective Abe Ocasio, had just gone inside to take a look around. There was nothing heavy going on; it was just a routine surveillance. But with what they'd been hearing about the West Side Irish Mob, you never knew. With his partner all alone inside one of the local boys' favorite hangouts, Egan wasn't about to let his attention wander.

Within minutes, Detective Ocasio returned to the car. 'The place is packed,' he said in his unmistakable Bronx accent.

'Yeah?'

'Yeah. One guy I recognized – Ryan. Richie Ryan, the young kid. In there throwin' money around like it was nothing. Said something about a bar in the Village he knocked over.'

'Hey, good. Gotta remember to check that out when we get back home.'

It was December of 1977, more than six months since the decaying, bullet-riddled torso of Ruby Stein washed ashore at Rockaway Beach in Brooklyn. In that time, the NYPD's Intelligence Division had begun conducting full-time surveillances in Hell's Kitchen – though it didn't look like the Stein case would be solved any time soon. As with most mob-related killings, no witnesses had come forward and few people were willing to admit they even knew Ruby Stein, much less did business with him.

But 'Intell,' as the Intelligence Division was known to most cops, was not so much interested in the Stein homicide, per se; their interest had been piqued even before Ruby's death by a slew of other killings. It was the possibility that those killings – Curley, Dugan, Devaney, Cummiskey, and others – might somehow be connected that had caused Richie Egan, Abe Ocasio, and a half-dozen other Intelligence cops to begin spending their days and evenings cruising the avenues of the West Side.

Egan and his partner sat quietly across from the Market Diner for a few minutes listening to a ballgame on the car radio. Then a spanking new Cadillac Coupe DeVille pulled into the parking lot.

'Hey,' exclaimed Egan. 'There's our man with his brand new Caddy.'

Jimmy Coonan, with his familiar shock of blond hair, stepped out of his new Caddy on the driver's side. Another guy stepped out on the passenger side who was about the same height, but much thinner.

'Who the fuck is that?' asked Egan.

'Shit, I don't know,' replied his partner. 'Who the fuck is it?'

'Wait a minute. Is that . . . is that who I think it is?'

'Who?'

'Featherstone . . . it's fuckin' Featherstone.'

'Naaah.'

'It is. It's fuckin' Mickey Featherstone.'

The Featherstone they'd been tailing the last few months had long, straggly hair and usually dressed like a construction worker on a bad day. But now Mickey had a whole new look, including newly trimmed hair and a nice sports coat.

'Shit,' laughed Egan. 'Coonan's really havin' an effect on this guy.'

Egan thought back to the first time he'd seen Mickey Featherstone, in October '77. It was a surveillance photograph passed around at the very first meeting on the West Side Mob. Egan was a bit surprised when his supervisor, Sergeant Thomas McCabe, told him about Featherstone, Coonan, Spillane, and the others. Irish gangsters, he figured, were something that had gone out in the 1930s and 40s. When he saw the photographs, he'd been even more surprised. At five-foot-nine and roughly 140 pounds, Mickey Featherstone sure didn't look like the feared enforcer he was rumored to be.

But then Egan took a look at Featherstone's criminal record. Three homicides by the age of twenty-one; a half-dozen arrests on assorted other charges; five years in prison. Then there was Coonan, another five-foot-nine guy with numerous arrests for violent crimes who'd done time inside. It reminded Egan of something he learned many years ago, probably on his first day of officer's training school: Give a guy a gun or a knife, and he might as well be ten feet tall.

Egan and his partner watched from across the street as Coonan and Featherstone headed into the Market Diner. The cops couldn't have been more pleased. In the few months since October, when they began their investigation, they'd gotten used to going entire shifts without seeing any of the key players. But tonight it looked like they might be getting a full casting call, including the main man and his sidekick.

From here on out, wherever Coonan and Featherstone went, Egan and Ocasio would follow. If Jimmy and Mickey decided to stay put at the Market Diner, so would they – all night, if they had to. No matter what, they were there for the long haul.

The 'long haul' was something Intelligence cops knew all about. Unlike most other divisions in the police department, Intell, by its very nature, had the luxury of allowing their investigations to evolve slowly, detail by detail. Since the Division was designed to gather information, not make arrests, there were few of the pressures that many other cops were under to come up with immediate results. Most higher-ups in the NYPD understood that accumulating names and locations and establishing criminal relationships could take weeks, months, sometimes years.

Following the outrageously high number of homicides on the West Side, it was inevitable that law enforcement would take an interest. Of course, each recent West Side murder had brought about its own local investigation. But these various isolated investigations had all been stalled by a lack of witnesses, or, in the case of Paddy Dugan, the lack of a corpse.

Along with an inability to crack the West Side code of silence, what was missing was a larger vision, an investigative approach that dealt with the various killings as part of an overall pattern.

The Intelligence Division not only had the right approach, they had the right men. Egan's supervisor, Sergeant Tom McCabe, was from the old school. Born in 1934, he spent his youth in the upper Manhattan neighborhood of Washington Heights in the days when it was a working-class Irish enclave not unlike Hell's Kitchen. Since joining the force in 1955, he'd heard all about the Irish Mob of the '20s, '30s, and '40s, and he was familiar with Mickey Spillane and other Irish gangsters from his own generation.

With his wavy white hair and no-nonsense manner, McCabe looked and sounded like a real-life Jimmy Cagney. Not one to mince words, he'd told the other Intelligence cops that the fact he was of the same ethnic background as the people they were investigating meant little one way or the other. 'A crook is a crook,' McCabe laid it out to Richie Egan and the other officers in their first meeting at Intelligence headquarters.

Egan, the Irish kid from Elmhurst, Queens, had been given a special word of advice. Said McCabe: 'You'll be getting a lot of wiseass comments from people you know – maybe even other cops – about not causing problems for your own people. You just remind 'em you're a cop first and an Irishman second, and let it go at that.'

As McCabe later explained it to Egan, he'd first gotten wind of the changing picture in West Side criminal circles earlier in 1977, during an altogether unrelated investigation of old-time Jewish and Italian gangsters from the Garment District. As part of that investigation – known as OPERATION FASHION – the Intelligence Division's Monitoring Unit had been conducting a surveillance on the Stage Deli, the venerable Manhattan bistro at West 54th Street and 7th Avenue favored by show people and assorted old-time New Yorkers. From their observation post across the street at the Sheraton Hotel, a handful of detectives had photographed the comings and goings of, among others, Rocco Santamarie, an aging loanshark with Fat Tony Salerno's Genovese family.

In the midst of these old codgers at the Stage Deli, McCabe and the other detectives began to see three young Irish kids. At first, nobody had any idea who they were. What would these Irish upstarts be doing hanging out with these decrepit Jewish and Italian gangsters from the Garment District? It didn't make sense. But after checking with the Midtown North precinct, which took in Hell's Kitchen, the detectives were able to ID Coonan and Featherstone. Much later, they learned that the third guy was Robert Michael 'Pete' Wilson, a convicted felon from Boston whom Coonan had done time with in Sing Sing.

It was also around this time that McCabe first heard about three West Side-related killings. The first was the Tom Devaney murder on July 20, 1976. Then came the Eddie Cummiskey murder on August 20th of that same year. And later, on January 27, 1977, Tom 'the Greek'

Kapatos had been gunned down in the middle of the afternoon on West 34th Street.

These murders, which had taken place within six months of each other, seemed to suggest a pattern. All three victims had been born and raised in Hell's Kitchen. All three had been shot gangland style. And all three were known associates of Mickey Spillane.

McCabe checked around and began to hear stories about how Spillane was having problems. The word on the street was that Devaney, Cummiskey, and Kapatos were killed at the behest of Fat Tony Salerno, who was looking to establish control over the soon-to-be-built Jacob Javits Convention Center. At the time, the building was only in the planning stages. But the construction of one of the largest convention halls in the nation promised to be a gold mine for organized crime. Since Mickey Spillane controlled the neighborhood where the Javits Center was going up as well as many of the unions that would be involved in its construction, he figured it was his baby. Never a great friend of the Italians, Spillane had let it be known he wasn't going to let the Genovese people anywhere near the Convention Center other than as a junior partner.

Salerno responded by eliminating Devaney, Cummiskey, and Kapatos, three of Spillane's closest underlings. The scuttlebutt was that Spillane himself would be next.

Sergeant McCabe had heard these reports about Salerno and Spillane and the Convention Center, and as he watched the Stage Deli from their observation post at the Sheraton Hotel, he found himself wondering if there was any connection between them and these young West

Side Irish kids meeting with Rocco Santamarie, one of Salerno's shylocks. It was only a hunch. But in his more than twenty years on the force, McCabe had learned to go with his hunches, even if they sometimes seemed a bit off the beaten path.

The Sergeant wasn't able to do anything about it, though, until OPERATION FASHION was wrapped up and he was transferred to Intell's Syndicated Crime Unit, or SCU. Even then, McCabe's premise that these young Irish kids were somehow connected to the Spillane/Salerno power struggle went untested for months. To get an okay from his supervisors to pursue the matter full-time, he needed something that indicated definitively that the West Side Mob was in a state of flux.

He got his wish on the night of May 13, 1977, around the same time Ruby Stein's mangled torso floated ashore at Rockaway Beach . . .

On 59th Street in Woodside, Queens, a black Cadillac pulled up in front of building number 47-50. The driver got out of the Cadillac, buzzed apartment 5-J and spoke briefly into the intercom. Then he returned to the car.

A few minutes later a handsome forty-three-year-old man wearing dark-blue slacks, a white V-neck T-shirt, and a brown leather jacket appeared from the building and walked over to the car. As he bent down to talk to someone in the car, a shot rang out. Then another and another and another and another. Five shots in all, hitting the man in the face, neck, chest, abdomen, and left arm. The body fell to the street and the car sped away.

A police officer responding to the scene found the victim lying next to a parked car. His body looked like a sieve, with blood flowing freely from the multiple gunshot wounds. His face was half blown away by a bullet that had hit him in the right eye.

The cop carefully reached inside the leather jacket and extracted a wallet. Opening the wallet, he found a driver's license.

The name on the license was Michael J. Spillane.

To the Intelligence Division, the Spillane hit was the most promising development so far, but to many in Hell's Kitchen, it was a cause for grief. On the afternoon of May 16th, mourners had gathered on West 47th Street at the McManus and Ahern Funeral Parlor, owned and run by 'the McMani.' Mickey's widow, Maureen, was there, as was her brother, Jim McManus, leader of the Midtown Democratic Association. Many found it especially ironic that Spillane, a gambler and a superstitious man, had been gunned down on Friday the 13th.

To the older residents, the saddest fact of all was that Spillane's murder was so totally unnecessary. At the time of his death, Mickey was no longer a 'mover' in West Side criminal circles, and hadn't been for months. There was even a story circulating in Hell's Kitchen that following the gangland killings of Devaney, Cummiskey, and Kapatos, Spillane was understandably worried. He took a trip to Florida to see Eddie McGrath, one-time ruler of the West Side docks. When Spillane was a kid, McGrath was friends with all the big-time gangsters, Italian and otherwise. If the Mafia was behind these recent West Side killings, as Spillane suspected they were, he was certain McGrath would know all about it.

In Florida, Spillane had found an old and enfeebled Eddie McGrath, now well into his eighties. Spillane asked Eddie if he knew anything about this recent pattern of killings, in which he was rumored to be next. But McGrath was completely out of touch. His contacts in the New York underworld had dried up long ago. Mickey was on his own.

When he returned to New York, a frightened Spillane moved his family from Hell's Kitchen – where he was born, raised and had risen to a position of prominence – to Woodside, a pleasant, working-class Irish neighborhood in Queens. Now, five months after moving to Queens, Mickey had come home to 10th Avenue – in a box.

At the same time the Spillanes, the McMani, and other long-time Hell's Kitchen residents were mourning the passing of one of their own, Jimmy Coonan, Mickey Featherstone, and a few others were having a sit-down a few blocks away at the Skyline Motor Inn. Roy Demeo, Coonan's contact in the Gambino family, had requested a meeting with Coonan and his people.

'Bet you're wondering what happened with Spillane,' Demeo told Coonan after they'd all settled in at the bar area of the motel.

'I was, kinda,' replied Jimmy.

'Well,' said Roy with a smile. 'You got an early birthday present.'

At five-foot-ten, with slicked-back hair and a sizable paunch, the thirty-seven-year-old Demeo had established a reputation as a feared Mafia enforcer. A former butcher's apprentice, Demeo had yet to be 'made,' or

208

officially initiated into *La Cosa Nostra*. But he was well on his way. His crew was thought to be responsible for dozens of murders, including many in which the victims' bodies had disappeared without a trace.

Naturally, Demeo and Coonan hit it off well. Ever since their initial meeting at Ward's Island, they'd been courting each other. Apparently, the gift of Mickey Spillane's death was Roy's latest overture.

'Yeah,' Demeo added. 'Wanna know what his last words were?'

'Sure,' said Jimmy, his eyes beginning to twinkle.

'He started yellin', "No, no, you was supposed to get Mickey and Jimmy, not me!"'

They all had a good laugh, then Jimmy asked, 'What the fuck did he mean by that, anyway?'

'How the fuck should I know?' answered Demeo.

Jimmy was ecstatic, of course, and he told Roy and his sidekick, Danny Grillo, that from now on, anything they needed from the boys on the West Side was theirs for the asking.

'You don't trust those bastards, I hope,' Mickey said to Coonan after the two Italians had driven off.

'I don't know,' answered Jimmy. 'I ain't sure yet.'

Afterwards, Featherstone began to get worried about the Spillane murder. It wasn't that he cared about Mickey Spillane; he agreed with most of the young guys in the neighborhood that Spillane was over the hill. But he knew how popular Spillane was with some of the legitimate people in Hell's Kitchen. And he knew that he and Coonan would be the prime suspects in Spillane's murder. He didn't want that over his head. So he called

209

Jim McManus, Spillane's brother-in-law, to wash his hands of the whole thing.

'I just want you to know,' he told the district leader over the phone, 'I had nothin' to do with Mickey gettin' killed.'

McManus said he appreciated the call.

Although Egan and the other Intelligence cops didn't have a complete sense of the hierarchy just yet, it was clear that with the death of Spillane on May 13, 1977, the West Side Irish Mob had entered a new phase. Coonan, they knew, was the leader, and Featherstone his number-two man. After that were a whole host of small-time hoodlums, some of them younger guys around Jimmy and Mickey's age, some of them holdovers from the Spillane years. There was Jimmy McElroy, the good-looking ex-boxer; Billy Beattie, the lanky bartender at the 596 Club; Tommy Hess, the muscular kid who also worked at Coonan's bar; Tony Lucich and Tommy Collins, both older gangsters from Spillane's generation; and Richie Ryan, the youngest of the bunch.

As had always been the case on the West Side, the backbone of their operation seemed to be loansharking and the policy games. After that came the unions. Coonan, the Intelligence cops were hearing, had his teeth into the ILA – a traditional neighborhood racket. Where Jimmy seemed to be breaking new ground was with the various entertainment unions, especially theatrical Teamsters Local 817, which delivered props and equipment to film and television studios throughout the city.

Through hours and hours of surveillance, Egan and

the boys from SCU began to amass an updated West Side dossier. Not only were they getting a sense of the key players, but also of their daily routines and where they conducted their business. Although the cops heard plenty of barroom gossip about the recent rash of killings – all of which they passed on to local Homicide detectives – their own focus was much broader. The strategy was to keep methodically collecting details until events kicked the investigation into a higher gear.

Each day, after a long surveillance, Richie Egan would return to Intelligence headquarters on Hudson Street in lower Manhattan and fill out his daily log. Traditionally, an investigation is given a name by one of the detectives involved. Sometimes, there's even a friendly competition to see who can come up with a name that sticks. This time, however, there was little argument. WEST SIDE STORY was the name Egan wrote down on the top of his surveillance report, and the other detectives immediately followed suit.

The first big break came in February 1978. Through Frank Hunt, a police officer at the Midtown North precinct who was well connected in Hell's Kitchen, Intell got a lead on a possible confidential informant, or 'C.I.' Hunt tipped them off that there was a kid in his late twenties who was up to his neck in debt with three or four neighborhood loansharks, including Tommy Collins, Tony Lucich, and a freelance operator named Harry 'the Hat' Wedgemont. The kid was soft, Hunt thought, and might be willing to cut a deal if the right pressures were brought to bear. When the kid got arrested for beating up his girlfriend, Intell made its move. They pulled the kid out of arraignment and gave him an option: He could take his chances back in the neighborhood, where he might wind up dead. Or he could go in with them.

The only way he would cooperate, the kid said, was if they could give him twenty-four-hour protection. 'That,' replied Sergeant McCabe, 'is definitely out of the question.' After further prodding, the kid caved and reluctantly agreed to make a $100 loanshark payment, with cash provided by the cops, while wearing a body recorder.

Over the next few weeks, the C.I. made many more recorded loanshark payments. Lieutenant George Ahrens, McCabe's supervisor, passed the recordings along to Michael Carey, an assistant U.S. attorney for the Southern District of New York. Carey thought they might constitute the beginnings of an indictment. He made a call to the FBI, which also thought the investigation looked promising.

To McCabe, Egan, and the others at SCU, it was an exciting development. The trick with any Intelligence investigation is to acquire enough data to lure one of the big operational agencies into the picture. That's when the arrests get made. If the FBI was going to come on board, as they were now indicating they would, it meant the case would go federal – a feather in everybody's cap.

The decision was made to take the investigation to the next stage. The Intelligence Division, now working with the U.S. Attorney's office, felt their C.I. should open a candy store in the neighborhood, which they could then use as a virtual intelligence headquarters. The regional

FBI contact liked the idea – an important approval since it was the FBI that would be funding the operation. An application was filed at the FBI headquarters in Washington for approximately $3,600 to set up the candy store – a relatively small sum for such potential big returns.

Meanwhile, Egan and the other Intelligence cops on the street were running their C.I. ragged. They would follow him to places like Fran's Card Shop, a candy store at 746 9th Avenue owned by Tony Lucich's wife, where he would make loanshark payments and settle gambling debts. Another frequent drop-off spot was the Westway Candy Store on 10th Avenue, run by Donald Mallay, who was beginning to figure more and more prominently in their surveillances.

Before long, the C.I. started to get nervous. The plan was to have him make his payments regularly at first, then act less and less able to come up with the money. Presumably, this would anger the loansharks and set events in motion. Things had, in fact, proceeded as planned, which is exactly why the C.I. was scared.

'You don't understand,' he said to Egan after one loan-shark warned him that he'd have Mickey Featherstone take care of things if he didn't get his money. 'These guys'll cut my nuts off if they find out what I'm doin'.'

The C.I. operation came to a crashing halt one afternoon when Egan and Ocasio spotted Featherstone with his newborn baby in a neighborhood park near St Clare's Hospital. The detectives had information that Featherstone was selling marijuana out of a baby carriage on the street. While they watched Mickey from an undercover taxi, the detectives told the C.I. they wanted him to attempt a drug deal with Featherstone while wearing the body mike.

The kid became apoplectic. 'There's no fuckin' way you're gonna get me to go near that guy with a wire,' he stated emphatically. 'No fuckin' way!' When the cops insisted, the C.I. ripped the wire from his chest, taking off some flesh in the process. When the cops *still* insisted, threatening to expose him as an informant if he didn't cooperate, the C.I. wet his pants in the backseat of the cab.

Shortly after that the kid fled the neighborhood. Then word came down from FBI headquarters in Washington that the request for $3,600 had been inexplicably denied. As a result, the FBI dropped out of the investigation and the U.S. Attorney's office lost interest.

For the time being, things had stalled. But with such a 'glamorous' investigation, one that included murders, extortion, and old-time racketeers, Richie Egan and the other Intelligence cops knew it wouldn't stay that way for long.

Detective Sergeant Joe Coffey walked into Paparazzi, an elegant restaurant/saloon on Manhattan's Upper East Side, and took his favorite seat at the bar. The commanding officer of an elite, citywide unit known as the Organized Crime Homicide Task Force, Coffey was the living embodiment of the cop as celebrity. In recent years, through his association with many high-profile crime cases, he had become a familiar figure on the local TV news. But even without this, Coffey was the kind of guy you noticed when he walked into a room. With his impeccably tailored suits and six-foot-two-inch frame, he looked like the kind of detective you might see on an NYPD recruitment poster.

On this particular October evening business was the last thing on the Sergeant's mind. Along with his chauffeur, he had stopped into Paparazzi looking to unwind after a long day's work. But while there, he met a boyhood acquaintance he hadn't seen in years. They got to talking about the old neighborhood in Queens, where Coffey's family had moved from an apartment in Manhattan when he was a kid.

'Hey,' said his old neighborhood buddy, 'did you hear about Toby Walker's kid?' Toby Walker was a mutual acquaintance from the old days.

'What about him?'

'He got murdered on the West Side.'

Something in Coffey's mind clicked. He had seen a homicide report a few days earlier in Chief of Detectives James Sullivan's office about somebody named William Walker, whose body had been found at the West 79th Street Boat Basin on October 3, 1978.

'Was that Toby's son?'

The acquaintance nodded. 'And what makes it worse, everybody knows who did it.'

'Yeah?'

'Yeah. He was playin' shuffleboard in a West Side gin mill with this kid McElroy. Jimmy McElroy, West Side Irish. They had an argument. He left the place with this McElroy. That's the last they seen him.'

'No shit?'

'Ask around, Joe, you'll see.'

'I might just do that.'

The next day Coffey pulled the file on the Walker homicide. Just like the guy said, Walker had last been seen at the Sunbrite Bar with James McElroy. There was also a notation that McElroy hadn't been spotted in the neighborhood for a week; he'd apparently gone on the lam. At the time, the focus of Coffey's Homicide Task Force was almost exclusively *La Cosa Nostra*. But he told Chief Sullivan, 'Look, I know it's not mafioso, but let me take a look at this one. I got a personal interest.'

Joe Coffey knew a thing or two about the Irish Mob. Most of it he'd learned from his old man, who drove a beer truck during Prohibition and was a boyhood chum of Eddie McGrath. After Prohibition, McGrath took over the West Side docks, but Joe Coffey, Sr forswore his criminal contacts and drove a delivery truck for Macy's, Saks Fifth Avenue, and some of the other large department stores. In 1946, he co-founded Local 804 of the Teamsters Union.

Coffey had grown up hearing stories from his father about the West Side Irish Mob. In fact, in the late 1940s the murderous John 'Cockeye' Dunn, McGrath's trigger-man, had made efforts to take over Teamsters Local 804 by threatening the life of Joe Coffey, Sr. The only thing that saved Coffey was that he knew McGrath, who intervened on his behalf. Joe Jr always remembered this story. He remembered how the gangsters were always trying to intimidate legitimate working people. It was one of the reasons he had become a cop.

After seven years as an investigator in Manhattan District Attorney Frank Hogan's office, Coffey was

216

selected to head the city's first Organized Crime Homicide Task Force. When Chief Sullivan approached him to form the unit following a rash of gangland slayings in February and March of 1978, he was told he could handpick his own team. Not surprisingly, he turned to cops like himself – high-rolling, streetwise operators who didn't mind if their names or pictures wound up on TV or in the newspapers. They had citywide jurisdiction to go anywhere and do whatever it took to crack the Mob, and they behaved with the sort of brashness you'd expect from superstar cops.

Among other things, Coffey didn't hesitate to use the press in his investigations, a technique that earned him the nickname 'Publicity Joe.' He knew that many cops and prosecutors didn't care for his methods, but he wrote that off as jealousy. 'The fact is,' Coffey used to say to anyone who would listen, 'if properly used, the press can play an important role in the investigative process' – and if they doubted him, they could just look at his record. It had worked in the infamous 'Son of Sam' serial murder case when Coffey made a direct plea to the public for information. In fact, it worked a lot. (In seven and a half years of existence, the Organized Crime Homicide Task Force helped solve over eighty murders.)

Coffey chose Frank McDarby and John McGlynn as his partners in the West Side investigation. He'd first worked with these two detectives twelve months earlier on a case involving a terrorist bombing at Fraunces Tavern, a historic landmark in Manhattan's Wall Street area. Like Coffey, McDarby and McGlynn were Irish Catholic, and they shared Joe's outrage that these West Side toughs were using their ethnic heritage as a framework for their criminal deeds.

McDarby and McGlynn shared another trait with Coffey: they were well over six feet tall. Together, the three of them looked as much like linebackers with the New York Giants as detectives with the NYPD.

The first thing Coffey and his men did was call the Intelligence Division, where McCabe was happy to provide them with all the necessary background material, including files on the murders of Paddy Dugan, Ruby Stein, Mickey Spillane, and a half-dozen others that were still unsolved. The most recent case, McCabe noted, involved a young neighborhood gambler named Rickey Tassiello. He was last seen leaving Tom's Pub on 9th Avenue with Coonan and Featherstone. According to a recent police interview with Tassiello's brother, Rickey Tassiello owed Jimmy Coonan money. There were rumors all over the neighborhood that Tassiello had been murdered, dismembered, and disposed of.

'Jesus Christ,' exclaimed Coffey. 'Are these guys fuckin' monsters or what?'

McCabe just shook his head. 'Joe, you ain't gonna believe some of the things we been hearing.'

With Coffey's unit on the scene, there was mild resentment among some members of the Intelligence team. No doubt the Homicide Task Force would be creating waves and making headlines, an approach that was antithetical to the very nature of intelligence work. And there was the matter of Coffey's reputation – a 'hambone,' one Intelligence cop called him. But McCabe was not one of the begrudgers. Sure, Coffey had led a charmed life as a member of the NYPD. But he was a cop after all, and a good one at that. Besides, said McCabe, 'You can't be an Intelligence cop and worry about that kind of crap.' As long as he had anything to do with it, Coffey's Task Force would get everything they needed to pursue their investigation.

It didn't take Coffey and his people long to make their presence felt on the West Side. Frequently, the Intelligence cops watched from their surveillance posts as the three strapping Irish detectives strutted into some well-known neighborhood hangout like the Market Diner and started asking questions. Within weeks, most of the area's criminal element knew who they were – which was just the way Coffey and his guys liked it. Sometimes they would even walk right into a well-known neighborhood social club and place bets at the gambling tables.

Initially, there were attempts by certain West Siders to bring Coffey and his boys into the fold. When Coffey's partner, Frank McDarby, was brought into the investigation, he was approached by an old friend named 'Mike' who he had worked with years ago in the Metal Lathers union. In a neighborhood diner, Mike asked McDarby why he was messing around with 'his own kind' when there were so many mafiosi at large in the city.

'Because these guys happen to be criminals,' McDarby said.

'Aw c'mon, Frank,' replied Mike. 'They're not bad kids. Maybe a little wild, but they're on our side.'

'Mike, even if I believed you, it wouldn't make any difference. Murder is murder. I gotta do my job.'

When Mike suggested he could possibly set up a meeting

between the cops and Jimmy Coonan to straighten things out, McDarby said, 'Hey, if you wanna set up a meeting, great. But there's nothin' to straighten out, Mike. It's too late for that.'

'I'm sorry to hear that, Frank, I really am. I'd hate to see anybody get hurt.'

McDarby unfurled his six-foot-two-inch frame and glared at his former friend. He knew this routine inside out. First they try to bribe you; then they try to intimidate you. 'Hey, Mike, I got something to say to you and whoever else it is you're talkin' for. We ain't scared of you fuckin' guys, okay? We got a job to do here and it's gonna get done. And if you or anybody else gets in the way you're gonna get taken down just like the rest of 'em. You hear me, you little shit?'

After that, nobody from the West Side made any more attempts to 'influence' the detectives from the Homicide Task Force.

As expected, not long after Joe Coffey and his boys began their own version of *West Side Story*, the investigation entered a new phase. Egan and the other Intelligence cops on the street often found themselves following in Coffey's wake as he stormed around the neighborhood. Occasionally, his antics captured the attention of the local press.

Such was the case one evening in late October of '78. It seemed that Coffey, on a tip from an informant, had learned that the old New York Central railway tracks between 10th and 11th Avenue were being used as a dumping ground for West Side murder victims.

Specifically, he'd been told the heads of Paddy Dugan and Rickey Tassiello were buried near the mouth of the West 50th Street underpass, directly behind the Skyline Motor Inn.

Coffey immediately called in an Emergency Service Unit to begin excavation on the fourteen-block stretch of track. Then somebody tipped off two reporters from the *New York Daily News*, who jumped on the story. That morning, an article in the paper stated that while raking through mounds of debris scooped from beneath the underpass, 'police discovered bone fragments which they hope will substantiate reports that a Manhattan railroad cut has been used as a burial ground by a Hell's Kitchen gang of hit men and racketeers.'

When McCabe, Egan, and the other Intelligence cops first heard about the diggings, they had to chuckle. Nothing like a dramatic operation involving lots of manpower to make sure everybody knew what you were up to. It was vintage Joe Coffey.

But like many of Coffey's more outlandish efforts, it had its residual value. High-profile activities sometimes brought about high-profile reactions. Already the diggings had attracted a wide spectrum of interested observers, including neighborhood people and, according to a telephone call the boys from Intell received from Coffey that morning, some rather ominous-looking black sedans driven by well-dressed Italians from Brooklyn.

Intell had been hearing a lot lately about Jimmy Coonan's Italian connections. The word was out that since Spillane's murder, Coonan had established contact with either the Genovese family, based on Pleasant

221

Avenue in Spanish Harlem, or the Gambino family, located primarily in the Bay Ridge and Bensonhurst sections of Brooklyn. Intell stepped up its surveillance schedule – there were now four two-man teams working around the clock – but they hadn't been able to land any solid intelligence on the alleged Mafia connection. The diggings could be the break they needed.

When they arrived at the site, Egan and his partner for the night, Detective James Tedaldi, could hardly believe their eyes. Not only were a dozen cops from the Emergency Service Unit, a half-dozen plainclothes detectives, and about twenty neighborhood onlookers there, but so was a local television crew. It was late at night, and there were mounted klieg lights all over the place, making the site look like a movie location. Dressed in a dashing trenchcoat, Coffey was holding a press conference, supposedly to downplay some of the more outrageous claims that had been appearing in the papers since the diggings began. (One *Daily News* report quoted a source 'close to the investigation' as saying there were '60, 70, maybe 80' bodies buried near the railroad tracks.)

Egan listened as Coffey explained to the press that 'there might be at least two bodies or parts of bodies' buried in the soil near the railroad tracks. He said that the remains they were looking for belonged to two recent murder victims of a Hell's Kitchen gang known as 'the Westies.'

Egan did a double take when he heard that. The Westies? It was a new one on him.

For days afterwards, the West Side diggings were an ongoing item in the New York press. The notion of a

Hell's Kitchen Irish Mob proved to be an irresistible angle, evoking as it did innumerable gangster movies from the 1930s. One TV report used footage from Prohibition days as the lead-in to their story.

What finally brought the festivities to a halt were the police lab reports, which came in a few days after the bone fragments were unearthed from behind the Skyline Motor Inn. It seemed that the remains were not those of a human being at all. They were dog bones.

Some of the cops connected with *West Side Story* found the whole episode embarrassing. Why call the press in when you've got a lead that might turn out to prove absolutely nothing? But Richie Egan defended Coffey's actions. 'After all,' he said to the other Intelligence cops as they gathered for drinks at Ronell's, their favorite lower Manhattan watering hole, 'Joe had a tip from two different sources that there were human remains buried near the tunnel. Whaddya want him to do? Ignore it?' As for the press, said Egan, chances are they found out about it on their own and Coffey was only doing his best to control the situation.

The only thing that bothered Egan and McCabe was that the diggings hadn't yielded any intelligence on the Italian connection. Recently McCabe had become obsessed with the idea that Coonan had hooked up with the Italians. The forces at play were still somewhat confusing, but he believed, at least initially, that the tie was probably with Fat Tony Salerno's Genovese family. It was Fat Tony, after all, who supposedly eliminated Devaney, Cummiskey, and Kapatos. The cops didn't know yet who killed Spillane, but it seemed possible that was also Fat Tony's handiwork. If so, Coonan would now be in debt to Salerno.

This theory was complicated somewhat by the fact they figured it was Coonan who'd killed Fat Tony's main man, Ruby Stein. In that case, Fat Tony would be mad at Coonan, and Jimmy would be forced to establish ties with the Gambinos out in Brooklyn.

It was a tangled web, no doubt about that. And there were already enough bodies in the morgue to set some kind of record for an SCU investigation. Even so, McCabe was convinced the main event was yet to come.

'Mark my words,' he said to Egan, Tedaldi, and anyone else who would listen. 'This guy Coonan is up to somethin'.'

9

LINGUINI AND CLAM SAUCE

'I need some shoes,' yelled Alberta Sachs, looking down at her dirty white sneakers. 'I can't wear these shoes with this dress.'

It was late February 1978, several months before Joe Coffey's highly publicized railyard diggings. Alberta was standing in the bedroom of Mickey and Sissy Featherstone's apartment. Sissy had just lent her a colorful two-piece outfit. Now she needed the appropriate footwear. She and Sissy wore the same size and had similar tastes, so Alberta figured Sissy could deliver. Something in dark brown, perhaps, or a pair of black pumps.

Alberta, now sixteen, was so excited she could hardly stand still. Just forty-five minutes earlier she and her boyfriend, Raymond Steen, who lived in the apartment right next door to Mickey and Sissy, got a call to come over. When they arrived, Alberta's uncle Jimmy Coonan was there, along with Mickey, Sissy, Richie Ryan, Billy Beattie, Dick Maher, a neighborhood kid, and Jimmy's brother Jackie Coonan. Jimmy, Mickey, and Dick Maher wore suits – definitely not their usual attire – and everyone seemed to be in a serious mood. Alberta didn't have

225

a clue what was up until her Uncle Jimmy explained that he and Featherstone had been called to a sit-down out in Brooklyn at the behest of Paul Castellano. The name didn't mean anything to her at first, but when they showed her a picture and told her who he was, Alberta thought she might just have a heart attack.

Castellano was the head of the Gambino crime family, the largest of New York City's five Mafia families. As the nephew of the legendary Carlo Gambino, he took over the family business in 1976 after the seventy-four-year-old Gambino died of a heart attack. For all intents and purposes, 'Big Paulie' was now king of the underworld, the *capo di tutti capi*, godfather of all godfathers. Getting called to meet with Paul Castellano and his people could be either extremely good or extremely bad, depending entirely on how Paul Castellano looked at it.

This was the moment Jimmy Coonan had been working towards for the last ten years, but under the circumstances he didn't know whether to be excited or wary. He knew that Castellano and the heads of the other four New York families were concerned about the death of Ruby Stein. Jimmy considered it very possible that the Mafia intended to exact retribution.

So Jimmy and Mickey had devised a plan, sort of. They would send a scout team ahead to Tommaso's Restaurant in Bay Ridge, where the meeting was scheduled to take place. In the event that anything looked even the least bit suspicious, the scout team would telephone back to Featherstone's apartment, where the rest of the group would be on call.

It was decided that Alberta and eighteen-year-old Dick

Maher would be the scout team, since they were young and looked the least suspicious. They were told they had to be nicely dressed, since Tommaso's was a respectable joint. All they had to do was go to the restaurant, order a big meal, and keep their eyes and ears open.

In the bedroom, while Alberta experimented with various ensembles, the two women expressed somewhat different emotions about the meeting at Tommaso's. Sissy was worried sick. As her husband spent more and more time with Jimmy Coonan, she began to suspect he was being used. Whenever she brought it up, Mickey told her she was wrong. He said Jimmy was like a brother, that he was the only one who had ever looked out for his welfare.

But Sissy wasn't buying it. She looked at Jimmy and Edna Coonan and saw a couple who had risen above their station. They were in a whole different social and economic class now. They'd just had a new home custom-built in Hazlet, New Jersey – a palatial, ranch-style house with a huge yard, a gymnasium, a game room, and a state-of-the-art security system. They both drove nice cars. And the Coonan children attended the best schools.

Mickey, on the other hand, never seemed to have any money at all. Sissy even had to work as an usherette at Madison Square Garden to help support their new baby. Not that she minded – she enjoyed working. But it seemed to her that Coonan was using Mickey's name and reputation and not giving him a fair share of the profits.

Now, on top of everything else, here was Mickey being dragged out to Brooklyn, where he might get killed! What kind of shit was that?

Alberta had an entirely different take. Ever since she'd seen Eddie Cummiskey and her Uncle Jimmy carrying Paddy Dugan's head down the stairs of her mother's apartment building roughly three years earlier, she'd become perversely enthralled by the world of Jimmy Coonan. To her, it was more exciting than any movie, more exotic and macabre than any story she might read in a book. Sometimes it was almost dreamlike. Like the previous Christmas, when she was over at Jimmy and Edna's house in New Jersey. She went into the bedroom and saw her aunt's and uncle's beautiful new king-size bed. But she couldn't figure out why the mattress was all tilted. Why would such a beautiful bed have such a lumpy mattress? She went over to the bed, lifted up the mattress and looked underneath.

Alberta's young eyes opened wide as could be. There were literally hundreds and hundreds of $10, $20, and $50 bills. Some of them were bound together, but most were loosely tossed about, forming a huge pile on top of the box spring. She would never forget the sight of all that money; for years, it would be her own little secret.

Sometimes, Alberta's excitement at her Uncle Jimmy's antics caused problems with Sissy. They got along okay, on the surface. In fact, it was through Sissy's father that Alberta had gotten a job at Madison Square Garden. They often walked to and from work together. But Alberta knew Sissy's feelings about Coonan; she knew Sissy resented Jimmy and Edna. So Alberta usually tried to keep her enthusiasm to herself.

Today, however, in the heady excitement of going to Brooklyn to see the Godfather, she couldn't contain it.

She preened and giggled in front of the full-length mirror like she was getting ready for her high school prom.

While Alberta and Sissy were in the bedroom, Coonan spoke to the male members of the group gathered in the front room. 'Me and Mickey gonna go to the restaurant,' he said, 'just like we're supposed to. See what these guys gotta say for themselves. But if you don't hear from us in two hours – *two fuckin' hours* – there's a social club next to Tommaso's. Vets and Friends, it's called. You come in there blastin' with everything we got.'

The group looked at each other without saying a word. There was a tension in the air, a tension made all the more palpable by the determination in Jimmy's voice. 'We got no choice,' he was saying. 'We been called. If we don't go, we's gonna get whacked. If we do go, we might still get whacked. But I swear to Christ, if we do, I want this to be the biggest fuckin' slaughter since the St Valentine's Day Massacre.'

Coonan picked up a large laundry bag that nineteen-year-old Ray Steen had brought over from his apartment next door. Inside was a staggering arsenal, the product of five years' worth of steady accumulation. There were .25s, .32s, .38s, and .45s with silencers; there was a 9mm machine gun; there were hand grenades; there were two Japanese machetes; there were ski masks, handcuffs, holsters, bulletproof vests, walkie-talkies.

Jimmy began to spread the contents of the bag out on a coffee table. He handed a .25 and a .38 to Mickey and took two of the same for himself. He explained exactly where Tommaso's and Vets and Friends were located: straight through the Brooklyn-Battery Tunnel to the

229

Gowanus Expressway, exit at 86th Street, and take a left. Just a few blocks down, at 1464 86th Street, was the restaurant. The social club was right next door.

'Remember,' he added sternly. 'Two goddamn hours.'

Outside, walking towards Jimmy's car, Coonan turned to Featherstone. 'Mickey, you know, I'd perfectly understand if you don't wanna make this trip. You been with me up till now and that's somethin' I appreciate. But you don't gotta go. I mean, anybody'd understand that.'

Mickey thought about it for a second. In a way, this whole Italian thing was Jimmy's doing. The guineas were somebody Mickey had never really wanted to deal with. For one thing, they were always sneaky about the way they killed people, so you never really knew who was behind it. Mickey found it hard to respect anybody who didn't have the balls to at least look a guy in the eye when they killed him. As far as he was concerned, that was the difference between them, the Italians, and us, the Irish.

But he would never back down when Jimmy needed him. That was out of the question. 'Nah,' he told Coonan. 'I'm with you, man. I mean, if they're gonna whack you it means they're gonna whack me too, right? So what's the fuckin' difference?'

Jimmy just smiled. He seemed to understand completely.

It was a twenty-five-minute drive through the tunnel and along the expressway to Bay Ridge. As they made the journey, Jimmy and Mickey were mostly silent. For Coonan, it was a time of reflection. Ever since the May 13th death of Mickey Spillane, he had known that the Italians were going to have to do business with him one

230

way or the other. He'd spent years positioning himself for this moment, trying to make it clear that he was not like Spillane, that he could be dealt with. Through his friendship with Roy Demeo he had established all the right contacts. If Castellano was the kind of person everybody said he was – a man of reason and understanding – Jimmy knew this meeting might just be the biggest moment of his life.

Featherstone knew how much the meeting meant to Jimmy, which was why he was going along. But secretly he saw it as the latest in a series of events that stretched his allegiance to Jimmy about as far as it could go.

Just one month earlier, on January 18, 1978, Mickey had been with Coonan when Rickey Tassiello, one of Jimmy's loanshark customers, was lured up to Tony Lucich's apartment on 10th Avenue. Featherstone knew that Coonan was having problems with Tassiello. Rickey was a sick gambler who was chronically late with his payments. He was making Jimmy look bad in the neighborhood. Since the amount Rickey owed at the time wasn't exorbitant, it wouldn't cost Jimmy much to use Tassiello as an example – which is exactly what happened.

Mickey stood up and played his part, though Jimmy had promised him just hours before it went down that he wasn't going to kill Rickey that night. When it happened, Mickey reacted on instinct. He grabbed Rickey Tassiello in the kitchen when the kid reached for a knife. That's when Jimmy shot Rickey three times in the head.

Later, Coonan and Lucich dragged Rickey's body into the bathroom and dumped it in the tub. Then they cut it up. They stuck the body parts in plastic garbage bags,

231

loaded them into cardboard moving boxes and took them out to Ward's Island, or 'Tony's island,' as it was known to Coonan & Company.

They arrived around six o'clock in the morning. 'I got one for you,' Coonan told Tony, the foreman at the sewage treatment plant.

Tony had this thing about having to see the face. Whenever Coonan brought a body out to be discarded, he would open one of the boxes, unfasten the plastic, and peer inside. This time he held the head aloft and said, 'Gee, I know this guy. He's only a kid.'

Mickey had to laugh, it was so morbid. It reminded him of those goddamned vampire movies he used to watch all the time when he first came back from 'Nam.

Sometimes Featherstone thought of all this violence as a kind of baptism, or maybe a test that Jimmy was giving him. God knows, there were enough times when Mickey had initiated violence on his own. Especially in those years when he came back from the war, he seemed unable to get through the day without an altercation. But in more recent times, most of the violence was initiated by Jimmy, and many times Mickey didn't know it was going to go down until the moment it happened.

Each time he and Coonan engaged in a violent act that disturbed him – like the beating of some neighborhood person he'd known all his life – Mickey felt Jimmy was watching and judging him. When he made it through yet another episode without bugging out, it brought them closer together. At times, it seemed like there was a concrete ratio at work: the more violent and dangerous the act, the tighter and more interdependent they became afterwards.

Featherstone sometimes felt wired and angry after these episodes, which usually led to more violence. After the Tassiello murder, he'd come home and punched a hole in the wall of his apartment. But in the end, he never allowed himself to feel doubt or even remorse. He just put his trust in Jimmy.

Trusting Jimmy was a big reason he was driving out to Brooklyn now to meet with a group of people he didn't even like. Or trust.

They arrived at Tommaso's around 7 P.M. and parked on a side street. They went inside, sat at a small bar to the left of the entrance, ordered drinks, and waited.

Tommaso's was a sizable restaurant by Bay Ridge standards, with plenty of greenery, red-checked table-cloths, and a low-key neighborhood ambience. Its most noticeable feature was a huge brass coffee urn that adorned the bar area. Beyond that, it was your typical Italian-American bistro – clean and quiet, with a reputation for an exquisite linguini and clam sauce.

After Coonan and Featherstone had been at the bar for four or five minutes, Roy Demeo approached from the rear of the restaurant dressed in a suit and tie.

'You guys ready?' asked Demeo in his deep, gravelly voice.

Jimmy and Mickey nodded.

'Okay,' said Roy, moving in close and speaking in a near whisper. 'Whatever youse do, don't admit nothin' about Ruby Stein. Okay? They gonna ask you about Ruby. You say, "I don't know nothin'." They gonna ask you about Ruby's black book. You say, "What black book?" Alright?'

Again they nodded.

'Good. Everything's gonna be just fine.'

Demeo led Jimmy and Mickey through the restaurant. Near the back, to the right, there was a hallway leading past the restrooms to a door that was kept closed at all times. As they headed towards the door, Featherstone took a quick look around the restaurant. The last thing he saw before they disappeared down the hallway was Alberta and her companion, Dick Maher, seated at a table near the far wall.

When they walked into the back room, Mickey and Jimmy could hardly believe their eyes. There was a huge horseshoe-shaped table arrangement that took up almost the entire room. A quick scan of the table revealed more than a dozen of the most powerful men in *La Cosa Nostra* circa 1978.

There was seventy-year-old Carmine Lombardozzi, known as the financial wizard of the Gambino family. There was Joe N. Gallo, the family's aging *consigliere*, or advisor, going back to the days of Carlo Gambino. There was Anniello Dellacroce, who, at the age of sixty-eight, was second in power only to Paul Castellano. There was Anthony 'Nino' Gaggi, another aging Gambino under-boss. There was seventy-eight-year-old Funzi Tieri, a representative of Fat Tony Salerno's Genovese family.

And finally, at the head of the table, wearing wire-rimmed glasses, with thinning gray hair and a quiet, grandfatherly manner, was Paul Castellano, arguably the most powerful criminal in the United States of America.

Jimmy Coonan, whose blond hair was a marked

contrast to the dark Sicilian and Neapolitan Italians who filled the room, presented Castellano with a box of Cuban cigars as a gesture of goodwill. Castellano smiled and passed the box around the table for all to see. Then Coonan and Featherstone were formally introduced to each and every person at the table.

Once the two Irish kids were seated, the meal commenced. From a door leading directly into the kitchen a steady stream of salads, pastas, and seafood appeared and disappeared. At first, there was only small talk. Nino Gaggi sat next to Featherstone. He wore black-tinted glasses and wanted to talk to Mickey about Vietnam. He had a nephew who'd been in the Green Berets, and he wanted to know how Mickey had gone about getting 100 per cent disability pay. He was greatly impressed by that. After Mickey told him, he was convinced that Featherstone and his nephew should meet.

Suddenly, without any sign or warning, Funzi Tieri, Fat Tony's delegate, leaned over and whispered something in Paul Castellano's ear. Then Castellano cleared his throat and the room became silent.

'Jimmy,' began the Godfather, who then hesitated and asked, 'You don't mind if I call you Jimmy?'

'Of course not.'

Castellano smiled politely, then began to speak in a polished monotone that belied his Brooklyn roots. After a brief rundown on why the death of Ruby Stein was of such concern to all of them, he asked point-blank, 'Jimmy, did you or any of your people have anything to do with this terrible thing, this murder of our good friend, Ruby Stein?'

'No,' replied Coonan, without missing a beat. 'We didn't have nothin' to do with that.'

'Are you sure?' asked Castellano.

'Yes, sir, without a doubt.'

Castellano then asked if Jimmy knew anything about Ruby Stein's black book.

'I don't even know what youse are talkin' about,' was Jimmy's reply.

'Well,' continued Castellano, 'that book has millions of dollars' worth of loans in it, shylock loans. There are people here who need that book.'

'Wish I could help you, Mr Castellano. But I don't know nothin' about Ruby's death or no black book.'

Then Funzi Tieri spoke up in a heavy Italian accent. 'But did not you and your people get *denaro, molto denaro* off this Ruby Stein?'

'Money?' asked Jimmy. 'Sure. But far as I know those loans were paid back in full, every one of 'em.'

There were a few more questions from the table on the Ruby Stein matter. Jimmy held his ground, adding that he liked Ruby and used to work for him and had no idea who might have done 'this terrible thing.' After everyone had their say, Castellano spoke again.

'Alright Jimmy, this is our position. From now on, you boys are going to be with us. Which means you got to stop acting like cowboys, like wild men. If anybody is to be removed, you have to clear it with my people. *Capisch?* Everything goes through Nino or Roy. You'll have our permission to use the family name in your business dealings on the West Side. But whatever moneys you make, you will cut us in ten percent. Except, of

236

course, for the shylocking. That you'll work out with Roy.'

At this point, Jimmy spoke up. He told Castellano that lately they'd been taking a bath on the numbers business and would need time to build it back up.

'That's okay,' replied Big Paulie in his formal tones. 'We won't have any problems over money, of this I'm sure. But you and your boys have got to end this wild behavior. From now on, every killing must be authorized.'

After that, everyone resumed eating and the mood lightened. '*Mangia, figlio*; eat up, eat up,' said seventy-six-year-old Nino Gaggi when he saw that Featherstone still had food on his plate.

'I already ate a plateful,' said Mickey, laughing. 'What, you want I should wind up with a fat belly like youse guys?'

Mickey felt Jimmy kick him under the table, but the Italians didn't seem to mind the joke; they laughed good-naturedly.

Meanwhile, outside in the main area of the restaurant, Alberta Sachs and Maher were dining among the normal everyday patrons. Ever since she had watched Mickey and Jimmy being led towards the backroom, Alberta's curiosity had been eating away at her. It took constant vigilance on the part of Maher to keep her from trying to sneak a peek.

After they'd been sitting there for more than an hour, she couldn't resist anymore. She told Dick she was going back to the ladies' room, but she had every intention of trying to find out what was going on behind that closed door.

237

Alberta walked down the short hallway past the restroom doors. After looking around to make sure no one was watching, she put her ear against the door. She could hear the muffled sounds of men talking and laughing but couldn't make out what they were saying. Frustrated, she went into the ladies' room to freshen up.

When she stepped out of the bathroom, an elderly Italian gentleman was just coming out of the backroom. Alberta didn't see him at first and as she opened the door she accidentally bumped into the man, knocking his cigar out of his mouth. Flustered, Alberta bent down to pick it up, but the man bent down also.

Thwack! went their heads.

Alberta was embarrassed now. She tried to make it look like she was drunk and didn't know what was going on. When the elderly gentleman just smiled politely and continued on into the men's room, she finally got a good look at him. For a second, she thought she was going to pass out.

The man she'd smacked heads with was none other than Paul Castellano, the Godfather himself.

After everyone at the meeting had finished eating, Jimmy and Mickey were taken to the Vets and Friends social club, a nondescript storefront two doors down from the restaurant with the shades pulled shut and an American flag in the window. Inside, the club was populated with thirty or forty immaculately dressed mafiosi. There were a few card games underway and some people were watching a hockey game on TV, but mostly it was just gangsters drinking, laughing, and talking.

Jimmy and Mickey were introduced as 'the kids from

238

Manhattan' to a number of people in the room, including Nino Gaggi's nephew Dominick Montiglio, the former Green Beret who Mickey had heard about earlier.

After a while, Castellano took Jimmy and Mickey aside and talked to them more about their new alliance.

'If ever you are called to come to Brooklyn,' said Big Paulie, 'you must come – no questions asked. And you don't bring weapons. No weapons allowed inside the club.'

Mickey could feel the sweat begin to run down his back when Castellano said this, since he currently had a .25 stuffed in the crotch of his pants and a .38 in his belt at the small of his back. As far as he knew, Jimmy did too.

'Another thing,' continued Castellano, 'I do everything I can to keep my name out of the newspapers. You boys been attracting too much attention. Publicity is not good for us. I once had to buy a story from a reporter just to keep it from being published. I was happy to spend the money and the reporter was smart enough to accept . . .

'Because when I get a thorn in my side, it's never a problem for me. I just pull it out and get rid of it.'

After they were in the club about thirty minutes enjoying the Cuban cigars, fine whiskeys, and general hospitality of the Brooklyn Italians, Jimmy and Mickey realized it was well past nine o'clock. They had told the boys back in Hell's Kitchen they were supposed to come in shooting if they didn't hear from them in two hours, and the time had already elapsed.

'Holy shit,' Mickey whispered to Jimmy. 'We gotta get outta here and make a phone call.'

'I know,' replied Coonan. 'Least we gotta get outside.

This way, they drive by they see us and know we're okay.'

Trying to stay cool, Jimmy and Mickey said their goodbyes and maneuvered Roy Demeo, Nino Gaggi, and a few of the others they were talking with out to the sidewalk, where they'd be easily spotted by any cruising car.

It was a clear, pleasant evening. They stood in front of Vets and Friends for a while engaging in small talk, but Jimmy and Mickey were hardly paying attention. They were on the lookout for their own people, armed with machine guns and hand grenades, bent on revenge.

Finally, the group split up. Sweating, Jimmy and Mickey rushed to a phone booth and called Featherstone's home number.

Back in Hell's Kitchen, Jackie Coonan, Richie Ryan, Billy Beattie, and Ray Steen had spent the evening sitting around Mickey's apartment, drinking beer and watching TV. When two hours were up, someone suggested they better head out to Brooklyn. 'Nah,' Jackie said, nervously, 'give 'em another few minutes.' Before long, those 'few minutes' had stretched to a half-hour.

'Where the fuck you been?' Mickey asked incredulously when Jackie answered the phone.

'Where the fuck *you* been?' replied Jackie.

'No, where the fuck you been!?'

'Hey, where the fuck you been!?'

'Okay, forget about it. Tell your brother.' Mickey shoved the phone at Jimmy.

Coonan listened for a few seconds, then told Jackie to 'shut the fuck up,' adding, 'I shoulda known better'n to

March 22, 1966 – Little Bobby Lagville after an early morning rendezvous with Jimmy Coonan.

Owney 'The Killer' Madden
(*left*) leaves Sing Sing prison
circa 1931.
Daily News Photos

Vincent 'Mad Dog' Coll,
Madden's nemesis, with
his customary toothy grin.
Daily News Photos

Jimmy Coonan.

Mickey Featherstone.

The 596 Club,
Jimmy Coonan's
saloon at 43rd Street
and 10th Avenue.

Ward's Island in the East River where Jimmy Coonan first met Mafia capo Roy Demeo (*inset*), also site of numerous body disposals.

Mickey Spillane, circa 1974.

Eddie Cummiskey, circa 1968.

Jimmy McElroy, circa 1986.

Billy Beattie, circa 1968.

Jimmy Coonan (*centre*) making the rounds in Hell's Kitchen. To his right is Anton 'Tony' Lucich.

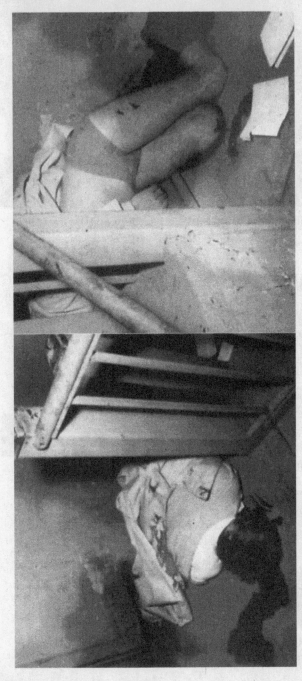

22 November 1978 – Harold 'Whitey' Whitehead left to die in the basement of the Opera Hotel. Note the greeting card addressed to Bobby Huggard lying next to the body.

THE COPS

Detective Frank McDarby (*right*) brings Mickey Featherstone into central booking in Queens following his arrest for the murder of Mickey Spillane. *Daily News Photos*

Detective Richie Egan of the NYPD Intelligence Division.

Detective Sergeant Joe Coffey, head of the Organized Crime Homicide Task Force.

Edna Coonan.

Alberta Sachs.

Ray Steen.

One of two line-ups that Mickey Featherstone (*second from left*) was required to stand in following the murder of Michael Holly.

leave somethin' like this with you lame brains.' He hung up.

Jimmy and Mickey laughed about it in the car on the way back to Manhattan. For Jimmy, the meeting had been successful beyond his wildest dreams and nothing could spoil that. He'd thought they were gonna get whacked. Instead they were now directly tied in with the most powerful organized crime group in the United States. It was a fantasy come true.

He promised Mickey he was going to 'take care of him' for making the trip. There was going to be lots of money now – additional money from the piers, loansharking, extortion of the unions, gambling, hijackings, burglaries, and more. Supposedly, Mickey would be getting a sizable cut.

'You'll see,' said Jimmy. 'This is gonna make us big, bigger'n anybody on the West Side's ever been.'

Mickey had enjoyed the meeting, and he certainly liked the idea of making more money. But all he could think about was what would have happened if Jackie Coonan, Richie Ryan, and the others had shown up like they were supposed to and opened up on the Vets and Friends Social Club. Most of the big-time Mafia leaders in New York City had been there. No doubt it would have been one of the most apocalyptic hits in the history of organized crime.

'Man, can you imagine?' asked Mickey, who smiled gleefully every time he thought about it. 'Now *that* woulda been somethin'.'

* * *

241

Over the course of the next few months, Jimmy and Mickey met often with members of the Gambino hierarchy. There were a few meetings with Paul Castellano and his bodyguard, Thomas Bilotti, in Little Italy. There was a meeting with Nino Gaggi at the Vets and Friends Social Club in Brooklyn. There were many more meetings with Roy Demeo and members of his Canarsie crew, both in Brooklyn and on the West Side of Manhattan.

Mostly, these were meetings to exchange information. When they met with Castellano and Bilotti, Coonan wanted to pass along information he'd heard concerning a planned hit against one of Castellano's underlings. In the Gaggi meeting, it was information about a series of hits that had already taken place. And with Demeo, there were a broad range of topics revolving mainly around money. Following the death of Ruby Stein, Demeo had become Coonan's primary financier. So there was always money to be borrowed or loanshark payments to be made.

For Jimmy, it was a comfortable arrangement. The Italians seemed to expect very little from him, other than a commitment to share 10 percent of his profits – a nebulous demand given the nature of underworld book-keeping. In exchange, Coonan and his people were now able to go around saying they were 'connected,' thereby strengthening their position on the West Side.

But to those who now comprised the inner circle of Jimmy Coonan's crew – Featherstone, Billy Beattie, Jimmy McElroy, Richie Ryan, and a half-dozen others – the Italian connection was met with something less than overwhelming enthusiasm. As far as they were concerned, it was the latest in a series of moves Coonan initiated on his own and then expected gang backing on.

There had been grumbling ever since the Ruby Stein hit. One of the reasons everyone had quietly played along with that killing was Jimmy's claim that once Ruby was gone, it would wipe everyone's slate clean. But after the murder, Coonan went around the neighborhood telling people that from now on they owed *him* the money. Only three or four guys were in deep enough with Stein to be directly affected by it, but even those who weren't felt Coonan was being devious and cheap.

Furthermore, there were rumors spreading around the neighborhood that Jimmy was giving his Italian buddies more than their share of the neighborhood rackets, and that he treated the guineas better than his own people. As Tony Lucich later put it, 'I never seen Coonan show nobody respect like he did Roy Demeo.'

Whenever Mickey heard about Jimmy and the Italians it gave him an uneasy feeling. On the one hand, Jimmy had treated him right. In March of '78, a few weeks after the meeting at Tommaso's, Jimmy met him on the street outside Tony Lucich's 10th Avenue apartment and told him he'd just put $5,000 into the numbers business for him. From that point on, he said, Mickey was to get 25 percent of the numbers money. In addition, Mickey would now be getting $200 a week for driving Jimmy around on his shylock runs. A guaranteed $400 or $500 a week was a lot of money to Featherstone. And for a long time it kept at bay whatever negative feelings he may have been developing towards Jimmy.

But this stuff about Demeo and the Gambinos really

got to him. Ever since the sit-down at Tommaso's, it seemed to Mickey like he was spending half his life meeting with the guineas. He might as well work in a corporation. At first, he didn't mind. But eventually their fancy clothes, formal manner, and general insincerity started to get on his nerves. They were always hugging each other and talking about how important their friendships were – which Mickey knew was bullshit, since nine out of ten mob hits were a case of one 'best friend' killing another.

In recent weeks he'd even come up with a name for these guys. He called them Al Colognes.

'You mean Al Capone,' Coonan said when Mickey first used the term.

'No,' replied Mickey, laughing. 'Al Cologne. You know the type. They got that hundred-dollar cologne on; them rings on their pinky fingers. Hair slicked back and them thousand-dollar silk suits. Always talkin' outta the side of their mouths.

'Counterfeit tough guys. Wish-I-was guys. You know, fuckin' Al Colognes.'

More than anything, Mickey felt most wiseguys suffered from delusions of grandeur. Because they had such a large army of soldiers behind them, they felt they could do anything. In Mickey's eyes, it made them impossible to trust.

In some cases, Jimmy seemed to agree. And his success with the Stein hit made him brave. He knew that the Italians were afraid of the West Side Irish Mob because of their reputation for crazy, impulsive behavior. That was the main reason they hadn't just whacked Coonan and

Featherstone after the death of Ruby Stein. The Mafia was reluctant to go toe-to-toe in a street-level bloodfest with a group of gangsters whose murderous reputation was growing by the month.

But even though Coonan told his underlings time and time again that he didn't really trust the guineas, to Featherstone and some of the others his actions suggested otherwise. Behind Jimmy's back, some of them were saying he had been blinded by the meeting at Tommaso's; that his need to be 'respected' by the Gambino family was making him stupid.

A prime example was an incident involving Danny Grillo, Roy Demeo's right-hand man. Supposedly, Grillo had been Coonan's good friend ever since they clipped Ruby Stein together in the 596 Club. But Grillo was also a gambler and a coke fiend who always seemed to be deeply in debt. The main reason he had been so enthusiastic about helping Coonan stiff Ruby was because he owed Stein well over six figures.

After the murder, Grillo started borrowing freely from Coonan and had fallen way behind on his payments. Mickey kept warning Coonan that Grillo was going to try to bump him off, just like he'd done Ruby when those debts got out of hand.

One day in the summer of '78, a few months after the meeting at Tommaso's, Mickey was at home when he got a call from Jimmy.

'I gotta go see this fuckin' Grillo,' said Coonan.

'Okay,' said Mickey. 'So when youse gonna pick me up?'

'No. I'm gonna go this one alone.'

'Man, I told you about that guy. He's no good. He's probably gonna try an' whack you.'

'Yeah. Well, do me a favor. Just sit by the phone at the Sunbrite, okay? I'll call if I need you.'

That afternoon Jimmy had coffee with Grillo at a diner in the Sheepshead Bay section of Brooklyn. Grillo told Coonan he needed his help killing someone. Jimmy was suspicious, but he went along with it just to see what was up.

From the diner, they drove to a nearby underground parking garage. Grillo had a gun with a silencer on it in a brown paper bag. He gave the gun to Jimmy and told him to hide out in the far corner of the garage and wait for a car with Florida plates. When Jimmy saw the car, he was supposed to open fire.

While he was waiting, Coonan got nervous. He peeked out at the street through a small, ground-level window and saw the car with Florida plates. Inside were a bunch of people Coonan recognized as Grillo's friends.

Wait a minute, thought Jimmy, *something's definitely not right here.* He popped the magazine out of the automatic Grillo had given him. The gun was empty. Not a single fucking bullet.

'Motherfucker,' Jimmy whispered under his breath.

He quickly left the garage, flagged down a cab and headed back to Manhattan.

'You was right, my man,' he told Mickey when he got to the Sunbrite Bar. 'Fuckin' punk tried to set me up.'

After that, Coonan, Featherstone, McElroy, and a few others made at least a half-dozen trips out to Brooklyn to blow Danny Grillo away. They discussed clearing it first with the Gambino family, like Castellano had said, but decided not to. No telling who was on Grillo's side; if they were to consult with the Italians on this, it might tip their hand.

The closest they came to getting the job done was one afternoon in October 1978 at the Gemini Lounge, a saloon in Canarsie that served as a base of operation for Roy Demeo's crew. Coonan, Featherstone, and McElroy staked out the joint in Jimmy C's latest vehicle, a dark-red van. Inside the van the boys sported an impressive collection of commando paraphernalia: army-issue ponchos, black ski masks, bulletproof vests, knives, numerous pistols, and an old-style Browning machine gun, commonly known as a 'grease gun.'

It was pouring down rain as they waited outside the Gemini Lounge for Danny Grillo. When Grillo finally came outside and headed for his car, Featherstone kicked open the back door of the van and got ready to blast away with the grease gun.

'No!' shouted Jimmy. 'Not here. We'll be spotted.'

They tried to follow Grillo as he drove away, but McElroy couldn't get the van started and they lost him.

Even after he'd been double-crossed by Grillo, Coonan still sucked up to the Italians. Danny, he kept telling Featherstone and the others, was just an isolated case. It was important that they maintain ties with Demeo, he said, even as they tried to eliminate his right-hand man.

Just a few days after another unsuccessful attempt to kill Grillo, Jimmy and Mickey met with Roy Demeo at the Skyline Motor Inn on 10th Avenue. Roy didn't know anything about Coonan's problems with Danny, but apparently he'd been having problems of his own. He told Coonan he'd had to get rid of Danny Grillo for being 'a punk and a lowlife.'

Supposedly, Grillo withdrew $100,000 in cash from the Canarsie crew's safe deposit box and gambled it away. 'The kid was suicidal,' said Roy.

After they killed Danny and disposed of his body, they drove his car to the middle of the Brooklyn Bridge and left it there, with the front door open on the driver's side.

'This way,' surmised Demeo, 'they might think the guy got depressed and jumped off.'

'See,' Jimmy said to Mickey. 'I told you we shoulda let Roy know what was goin' on.'

'What're you talkin' about?' asked Demeo.

Jimmy went on to tell Demeo all the problems he'd been having with Danny; how Danny had fallen way behind on his shylock payments and then tried to set him up.

'Damn,' said Roy, the former butcher's apprentice. 'I wish youse woulda told me. I woulda chopped him up in pieces 'stead of just cuttin' him in half.'

A big grin spread across Jimmy's face when Demeo said that, and from then on Coonan acted like the Irish Mob was more indebted to the Italians than ever before.

In late October '78, when Tom McCabe, Richie Egan, and the other cops in the Intelligence Division's Syndicated Crime Unit first started hearing that Coonan had hooked up with Paul Castellano, they were skeptical. They had been expecting an Italian connection, but not with the top man himself. *La Cosa Nostra*, as they knew it, had a strict caste system. At the top was the boss of the family, in this case Castellano. Immediately below were the underbosses and the *consiglieri*, or counsellors. Then came the *caporegimes*, or crew chiefs, like Roy Demeo. Finally, the lowest members of the family were the *soldati*, the soldiers who made up the various neighborhood crews.

In theory, very little got done within this structure that wasn't authorized by at least a *capo* or an underboss. Castellano was known to be one of the most cautious and judicious mob bosses in recent history. Although it was not unprecedented that he would associate himself with a crime group whose ethnic origins were different from his own, why would he hook up with a bunch of crazy Hell's Kitchen Irishmen?

If it was true – and the boys from Intell weren't certain yet that it was – the only thing they could figure was that Castellano thought he might be able to neutralize Coonan's crew by bringing them into the fold. At least this way he'd be able to impose some control over what happened on the West Side. And if anybody got killed there would definitely be some accountability.

Partly, the Intelligence cops' skepticism was based on the fact that for the time being, all they had to go on were unsubstantiated claims from various neighborhood sources. In the thousands of hours worth of surveillance they'd conducted on the West Side so far, they had yet to make visual contact with Castellano, Demeo, or any other member of the Gambino hierarchy. All they could do was keep on gathering intelligence and hope it might eventually lead to a telltale meeting or phone call, something that would establish a definitive link between Coonan's crew and the boys from Brooklyn.

Detective Sergeant Joe Coffey's Homicide Task Force wasn't so patient. When Coffey first heard through Intelligence sources that the Irish Mob was using Castellano's name around the neighborhood, he decided there was only one way to find out if it was legit. He would check with Castellano himself.

Although Coffey had listened to Castellano's voice on wiretaps many times, he'd never met the man face to face. He did have a connection, however, through Funzi Tieri's nephew Francois, who he'd once served with a subpoena. He knew that Tieri felt he'd been dealt with squarely and would probably give Coffey a good recommendation.

Sure enough, once Coffey put out the word that he wanted to meet with Big Paulie, he got a call one morning in his office. 'Joe Coffey the cop?' asked the voice on the line.

'Yeah.'

'Seven o'clock tonight. Tommaso's.'

Sergeant Coffey and his partner, Frank McDarby, arrived at Tommaso's at exactly 7 P.M. They sat in the bar area near the huge brass coffee urn, right where Coonan and Featherstone had waited several months earlier.

Three minutes after seven, in walked Castellano with an entourage of seven or eight wiseguys. An exceedingly polite man, Castellano introduced Coffey and McDarby to each of his bodyguards. Then Castellano and Coffey made their way to the back of the restaurant while McDarby waited in the bar area with the others.

After those who were dining near Castellano's table had been politely relocated to another part of the restaurant, Big Paulie and Coffey were seated.

'I just want you to know,' said Castellano. 'The only reason I'm meeting with you is because Francois says you're okay.'

Coffey thanked Castellano for taking the time, then got right to the point. 'The reason I'm here is that there's a couple Irish kids that are causing a lot of havoc; and they're throwing your name around and it's causing us many, many problems. I think it would kind of behoove you if you would tell them to cease and desist using your name. We have every intention of taking these kids out, and you might just get dragged into it.'

Castellano listened carefully. When Coffey finished, he smiled. 'Yes, I know these two kids. Two nice Irish kids.'

He admitted having a meeting with Coonan and Featherstone, but when Coffey asked what the meeting was about he just smiled again. 'What happens in this place is private, just like this meeting now is private.'

They continued talking, with Coffey trying to lure information out of Castellano and Castellano deflecting all inquiries in a gentlemanly manner. Eventually, the conversation drifted to Castellano's Staten Island home, the food at Tommaso's, the weather. Coffey liked the aging Mafia don; he felt he was respectful and engaging. But he knew two minutes after he sat down that he wasn't going to get anything of any value out of him.

Meanwhile, in the bar area, Frank McDarby found himself surrounded by seven or eight wiseguys. They stood there for five minutes or so in an atmosphere that was less than congenial. Finally, McDarby figured he would try to break the ice. So he asked the Italians if they wanted to hear a joke.

They looked at each other like they couldn't believe this big dumb mick cop, but no one voiced any objections. So McDarby went right ahead with the joke. 'There's just one thing,' he said as a preface. 'You got to let me finish this joke before you make a decision, okay? Don't get upset before you hear the punchline.'

They looked at McDarby suspiciously, then looked at each other and shrugged.

'Okay,' began the detective enthusiastically, 'it goes something like this: Paddy the Irish cop leaves the precinct to go out on his post. He's just starting his tour. On the way out he comes to a street corner and he sees a little black kid sitting in the street playing with dogshit. So he says, "Eye now son, what in the name of Jaysus are you doin' with that? What are ye doin' playin' with that stuff?"

'So the little black kid looked up and said, "I'm making a policeman, sir."

'Paddy says, "Yer makin' a policeman? Well what kinda policeman are ye makin'?"

'The kid says, "I'm making an *Italian* policeman, sir."

'"Aw Jaysus," says Paddy. "Hold on a minute now, son. You stay right here. I'll be right back. I'm goin' up the road t'get Tony the Italian cop . . ."'

By this time McDarby noticed a few of the wiseguys were starting to look troubled. They were glancing at each other – and at McDarby – in utter amazement.

'Hold on now,' he said. 'Relax. I told you, don't pass judgment till I'm done with the joke.'

He straightened his tie and continued.

'So Paddy goes down to the adjoining post, and he says

to Tony, "Hey, Tony, run down with me. I want t'show you somethin' down at me post."

'"Yeah," says Tony, "whaddya got?"

'"Aw Jaysus now, just come down to me post now and I'll show ye."

'So he takes Tony the Italian cop down to his post and he says to the little black kid, "Son, tell this officer here what you were doin'."

'The kid's still playing with the dogshit, and he says to Tony, "I'm making a policeman, sir."

'And Paddy says, "Tell him what kinda policeman it is yer makin'."

'"I'm making an Italian policeman," says the kid.

'So Tony the Italian cop gets all bent outta shape and he says, "Eh, Paddy, whatsa matter with you, what the hell is wrong with you, tellin' a kid to say somethin' like that?"

'He turns to the kid. "Eh, son, why you talk like that? Why you say you makin' an Italian policeman?"

'"Well," says the little black kid, "because I don't have enough shit to make an *Irish* policeman."'

At this, Castellano's henchmen broke out in raucous laughter, catching the attention of just about everyone in the restaurant. They were still laughing when Big Paulie and Sergeant Coffey reappeared from the back of the room.

'Eh,' said one of the wiseguys, 'Paulie, you gotta hear this joke, you *gotta* hear this joke.

'Frankie, go ahead, tell Paulie the joke.'

So McDarby went through the whole joke again. This time the wiseguys were squealing with delight at each line until McDarby arrived at the punchline and they, along with Castellano, cracked up laughing.

On the way out to the car, Coffey and McDarby were still marveling at how easy it was to disarm Castellano's so-called tough guys.

'Yeah,' said McDarby to his partner, 'but did we get anything off Big Paulie?'

Coffey turned suddenly serious. 'No, not really. You couldn't pry that bastard open.'

Coffey's frustration continued, as did that of Egan, McCabe, and the other Intelligence cops. As the investigation proceeded into November 1978, they rummaged for more information, knowing that an alliance the likes of which they were hearing about could mean only one thing.

It was going to be a rough Christmas in Hell's Kitchen.

10

HAVING A DRINK ON WHITEY

One thing about the Italian connection: It certainly clarified the standing of Coonan and his boys in the community. If in the fall of '78 there were still people doing criminal business in Hell's Kitchen who felt an allegiance to the memory of Mickey Spillane, the news of Jimmy's alliance with the Gambino family put an end to it once and for all. Throughout the criminal underworld, Coonan and his people were more than just another gang on the streets; they were now *the* organized crime entity on the West Side of Manhattan.

To most people, they were known simply as the Hell's Kitchen Irish Mob or Coonan's Crew. Some knew them as the Westies, a term first used by the cops in the Midtown North precinct, then picked up by Sergeant Joe Coffey and immortalized in the newspapers around the time of the railyard diggings. Whatever the name, Coonan, Featherstone, and their followers had attained a dubious legitimacy. And their presence in neighborhood saloons and restaurants began to engender new levels of respect and fear.

Of course, some were slower to catch on than others.

In early November, John Bowers, president of the ILA in Manhattan, put out the word that Local 1909 was no longer going to make its weekly extortion payments. Bowers was the son of the late Mickey Bowers, leader of the ILA's notorious West Side 'Pistol Local' in the 1950s. Apparently, the younger Bowers had retained little of his father's underworld acumen. When he issued his edict, an irate Jimmy Coonan immediately called for a meeting. As a courtesy, John Potter, an ILA official, was dispatched to meet with Coonan and Featherstone at the Landmark Tavern, one of the neighborhood's more upscale saloons, at 46th and 11th Avenue.

'Bowers says the payments gotta stop,' Potter told Coonan.

'Jesus,' replied Jimmy, 'don't this prick know nothin'? You go down there and you tell John Bowers if he thinks the checks is gonna stop, I'll blow his fuckin' brains out.'

Potter gagged on his food.

Bowers asked around.

The checks continued.

In the eight months since the sit-down at Tommaso's, Coonan had become more and more brazen. He was still meeting every week with the Italians, sometimes in Brooklyn, sometimes at the Skyline Motor Inn. As folks in the neighborhood who were close to Jimmy realized, this was clearly more than just business. Jimmy actually liked spending time with the wiseguys. He even began to copy their ways: the fancy threads, the elaborate protocol and, most of all, the way they threatened and brutalized anyone who failed to show them the proper 'respect.'

At one point, Coonan had even tried to get Mickey,

Jimmy McElroy, and a few others to *socialize* with Roy Demeo's crew, with predictable results. After a night on the town together, Featherstone had gotten in a heated argument with one of Demeo's underlings, which Roy eventually had to break up.

Coonan backed off a little after that. Perhaps he realized he could only go so far when mixing business with pleasure – at least when it involved the rest of his crew. On a personal level, Jimmy was as solicitous of the Italians as ever, acting as if he himself were a made member of La Famiglia.

The night that really brought it all home for Mickey came in mid-November of '78. He and Jimmy had gone to see Spider Tassiello at Sonny's Cafe on 47th and 9th Avenue. It was nearly ten months since they had killed Spider's son, Rickey Tassiello. Throughout the summer and into the fall Spider's other son, Arthur, had been telling people in the neighborhood he was going to get revenge by wiping out the entire Coonan family. Specifically, he had been saying he was going to drive by Coonan's Tax Service and throw a hand grenade in the window.

Jimmy had a bug up his ass about the Tassiello family long before Rickey's murder. Years earlier, Angelo Tassiello, Spider Tassiello's brother, had had an affair with Coonan's mother. Everyone in the neighborhood knew about it, and it had been a source of great humiliation for Coonan's father. Within a few months of the affair, the elder Coonan died of natural causes. But Jimmy and his brother Jackie felt their old man had died of a broken heart, and they blamed the Tassiellos for it.

When the murder of Rickey Tassiello went down, Mickey had a feeling it was for more than just the $1,250 Rickey owed Coonan. It was Jimmy Coonan settling an old score on behalf of his father.

When Coonan and Featherstone arrived at Sonny's Cafe, Spider Tassiello was behind the counter.

'We got somethin' to talk about,' Jimmy told Tassiello, motioning towards the back of the bar.

As the two of them walked into the backroom, Mickey stayed at the counter and sipped on a bottle of beer. From where he was seated he could only see Coonan's back, but old man Tassiello was facing him. The TV was on, so Mickey had to strain to hear what was being said. He could see Jimmy motioning with his hands, and he got the distinct impression he was telling Spider Tassiello how they'd killed his son Rickey.

Occasionally, Jimmy's voice rose above the sound of the TV. 'If I hear any more bullshit about your kid threatenin' my family, we're gonna come back here and take care of every one a youse. Do y'know what I'm pointin' out?'

Spider Tassiello was in tears, nodding his head in agreement.

Featherstone found the whole scene pathetic. Wasn't it enough to kill the guy's son? Did they now have to berate and humiliate him on top of it?

Mickey turned away to watch the television, hoping it would take his mind off things. To his amazement, there on the tube was *The Godfather*. He sat transfixed for a full minute watching these Hollywood mafiosi on the TV perched high above the bar counter; then his eyes would drift down to Coonan threatening Spider Tassiello.

If there were such a thing as an epiphany, a supreme moment of awakening, for Mickey this was it. It was like a light bulb flicked on in his head . . .

Jimmy Coonan thought he was the fucking God-father!

At 12:30 on the morning of November 22, 1978, Featherstone, Coonan, and Jimmy McElroy arrived at the Plaka Bar, a saloon connected to the lobby of the Opera Hotel at 2166 Broadway, between 76th and 77th streets on the Upper West Side. It was a bar not unlike those in Hell's Kitchen, only slightly cleaner and less populated. As you entered, a long wooden counter ran the full length of the left wall. At the far end of the bar a doorway led into the kitchen. On the right wall another doorway led into the lobby of the Opera Hotel. There were no restrooms in the Plaka Bar. To go to the can, you had to pass through the hotel lobby and go down a flight of stairs.

It had been a long day for Featherstone, Coonan, and McElroy, and they were beat. Most of the day had been spent trying to find a union official they were supposed to whack. In fact, they'd been trying to whack the guy for months without any luck. It was fast becoming a contract hit they wished they'd never taken.

The whole thing began as a favor to Billy Murtha, the guy whose shower Jimmy was hiding in the morning he got busted in his underwear for the Canelstein/Morales hit. It was Murtha who drove the car the night of the shootings in Queens twelve years earlier. Both he and Coonan had done a few years in prison for that one. Since then, Murtha had gone into the construction trade with two good friends from Hell's Kitchen, Buddy Leahy and Mickey Cahill.

With his old buddy Jimmy Coonan now firmly established as the premier gangster on the West Side, Murtha and his sidekicks had approached him with a proposition in July 1978. They were having trouble with a guy named James Maher, who had just been elected business manager for Local 46 of the Metal Lathers Union. Murtha, Leahy, and Cahill were members of the Local, and during an acrimonious campaign for the business manager's position, they had supported Maher's opponent. Now, to add insult to injury, Maher was promoting a collective bargaining agreement they were bitterly opposed to.

What they proposed was this: $10,000 if Coonan and Featherstone killed Maher, and $20,000 more if they made the body disappear. Jimmy and Mickey agreed to do the job and accepted $5,000 as a down payment.

As Jimmy would say later, 'We shoulda known from the start it was a turkey.' The day after they agreed to do the hit, they were sitting in the restaurant area of the Hyatt-Atlantis Hotel, across the street from the union hall at East 76th Street and 3rd Avenue. Coonan, Featherstone, and McElroy were there, as was Billy Murtha. They were waiting for the union official, Maher, to come out of the Local 46 offices so that Murtha could identify him. But they wound up sitting there for a long time drinking, and everybody got a little stewed.

When Maher finally came out of the union offices, Billy Murtha, in a moment of drunken bravado, grabbed

McElroy's gun. 'You guys don't think I got the balls to do it myself? I'll do it right now, goddammit.'

Coonan, Featherstone, and McElroy didn't know whether to laugh or be pissed off. 'Just sit down and stop being a jackass,' Coonan finally said.

Over the next four months there were a number of harebrained attempts to kill this guy Maher. Once, Billy Murtha sketched out a map of Maher's home and the route he took to drive into Manhattan for work. The idea was to ambush him in his car. But that was too elaborate a plan and it never panned out.

Finally, they got tired of playing cat-and-mouse games and decided to wear disguises and just gun the guy down right in front of the union hall. That's where they had been that very day, before they walked into the Plaka Bar. They'd waited across the street from Local 46 in the red van they'd used to stake out Danny Grillo at the Gemini Lounge. It was an invaluable vehicle for transporting weaponry, disguises, and the various dismembered body parts of murder victims. Coonan was especially fond of his red van. As a joke, he'd started calling it 'the Meat Wagon,' a nickname even some of his own people found a tad ghoulish.

'That's the guy,' Coonan blurted out when a man who looked like James Maher, partly obscured by other pedestrians, crossed the street and headed towards the union hall.

'You sure?' asked Mickey.

'Sure I'm sure.'

Coonan and Featherstone got out of the Meat Wagon on East 76th Street, leaving McElroy behind the wheel.

They crossed the street and hurriedly tried to catch up with the guy Coonan had identified as Maher.

Mickey was having a hard time moving very fast. As a disguise, he'd worn a pair of shoes a couple of sizes too big over his regular shoes. He'd also gotten a pair of dirty old pants and worn them over a pair of clean pants. Topping off this grungy ensemble was a long black trenchcoat, also a few sizes too big, that hung all the way down to the ground. The idea was to do the hit in this getup, and then if need be, shed it and escape in his regular clothing.

Jimmy was also dressed down-market, in a pair of dungarees and a blue windbreaker with a hood on it to hide his blond hair.

When they finally caught up with the guy in front of the entrance to Local 46, Jimmy began to ease the .32-caliber automatic with silencer out from under his windbreaker.

'No, no,' said Mickey, tugging on Coonan's jacket from behind. 'That ain't him.'

'What?'

'Forget about it. It ain't the guy.'

They watched as the man they had been following opened the door to the building. Before he disappeared inside, he glanced up the street and they got a good look at him. It was definitely James Maher.

'What the fuck?' asked Coonan, dumbfounded. 'What'd you do that for? That was the guy.'

Mickey shrugged sheepishly. 'I thought it wasn't.'

By the time they arrived at the Plaka Bar, all three of them were in a foul mood. They'd been trying to do this goddamned killing for months. Today, once again, they had whipped themselves into the kind of emotional frenzy that was required to kill someone in broad daylight. Now they had to suppress these emotions and deal with the frustration of having again bungled the job.

Once they were inside the Plaka Bar, the mood lightened somewhat. There were a number of familiar faces there. William Comas, a career burglar and hustler in his fifties who they knew as 'Billy Uptown' was there. Comas kept a room next door at the Opera Hotel and frequently drank at the Plaka Bar. It was Comas who'd first introduced Coonan and Featherstone to the Plaka Bar years earlier.

Featherstone, especially, liked Billy Uptown, who was short, with longish gray hair on the sides of his head and nothing but skin on top. Although Coonan didn't know it yet, Mickey had even hatched a little something with Comas all on his own: a counterfeit operation that was beginning to look like it might pan out.

Also there with Billy Uptown was the solidly built Bobby Huggard, the same Bobby Huggard who helped Jimmy and Jackie Coonan knock over a bar in the Bronx in the spring of '66. At the time, they'd plotted many other crimes together, all in anticipation of a planned showdown with Mickey Spillane. Those plans all went down the drain when Jackie gunned down a bartender in Brooklyn. After that, Jackie went to prison and Huggard went on the lam. Now, thirteen years later, Huggard had reappeared on the West Side.

After everyone said their hellos, Comas introduced Coonan, Featherstone, and McElroy, who was wearing a red painter's cap, to a friend of his named John Crowell.

Crowell was a former heroin addict and small-time criminal whom Comas and Huggard had met at the Clinton Correctional Facility in upstate New York. Short and slight, with stringy black hair, Crowell spoke in a whiny Bronx accent. Although he had traveled with tough guys most of his adult life, he looked like a little weasel, with shifty eyes and a shifty manner to match.

The group proceeded to drink convivially, sharing prison stories and waxing nostalgic about days gone by. Occasionally other patrons came and went, but for the most part they had the bar to themselves.

After thirty minutes or so they were joined by yet another Clinton prison alumnus, Harold 'Whitey' Whitehead. Whitehead had grown up in Astoria, Queens, along with Bobby Huggard. He knew Crowell and Comas from prison and assorted other criminal ventures. Years ago he'd done some drinking at the 596 Club, so he knew Jimmy Coonan and some of the other Hell's Kitchen crowd.

Coonan recognized Whitehead as soon as he walked in the door. Thirty-eight years old, with curly brown hair, Whitehead was remembered at the 596 Club as a loud, arrogant prick. One night he even got in a fight with Richard 'Mugsy' Ritter, one of the bartenders. When Jimmy's brother Jackie intervened, Whitehead ran outside and called the cops from a phone booth at 44th Street and 10th Avenue. Whitey Whitehead had been on Jimmy Coonan's shit list ever since.

After a while, Coonan walked over to Whitehead and began chatting him up. It started out civil enough, but before long it seemed to be getting heated – at least on

Whitehead's part. The only person close enough to hear anything was John Crowell. Crowell heard Whitehead telling Coonan, 'Mugsy's fulla shit. He's a fuckin' fag.'

Then Whitehead said: 'And your brother Jackie, he's a rat bastard. I got no beef with you, Jimmy, it's that brother of yours.'

The conversation continued a while longer, then Jimmy walked back over to Featherstone and McElroy. Coonan had remained calm so far, but his ears were a bright red. Featherstone knew what that meant. Jimmy's ears always got red when he was mad enough to kill.

'What's that guy sayin'?' asked Featherstone.

'He called my brother a rat,' replied Jimmy.

'Yeah?'

'Yeah.'

'Scumbag,' interjected McElroy.

'Yeah,' said Jimmy. 'My brother may be a fleabag, but he ain't no rat.'

Crowell could also see that Coonan was steamed. He'd brought some marijuana along to smoke and figured now might be a good time to torch it up. It might chill people out.

'Hey,' he said to Whitehead, Huggard, and Comas, 'let's go downstairs and smoke a joint.'

While the three Irishmen stayed at the bar, the four Clinton prison alumni headed through the lobby of the Opera Hotel and downstairs to the men's room.

Dank and musty, the men's room in the Opera Hotel was in bad need of repair. The tiling on the floor and walls was dingy and the low ceiling was stained, with peeling paint and corroded plaster. There were two sinks to the left as you entered, and beyond that, separated by a marble partition, two porcelain urinals. To the right was a slop sink, with a mop and a bucket nearby, then three wooden toilet stalls. There were bare waterpipes running from the floor to the ceiling, and the cheap lighting cast a sickly yellow pallor throughout the room.

Crowell and Whitehead stood with their backs to the urinals. Across from them were Comas and Huggard. They fired up a joint and passed it around, laughing and getting stoned.

After a few minutes, Jimmy Coonan walked into the men's room. The group acknowledged his presence, but nothing was said. Coonan walked around them and went to the urinal.

Crowell was standing the closest to the urinals. Once the joint was passed his way, he leaned over and offered it to Coonan. Coonan glanced at him, then reached down to zip up his fly – or so Crowell thought.

Suddenly, from his crotch area, Coonan produced a black .25-caliber Beretta. He took one step forward, put the gun to the base of Whitey Whitehead's skull behind his right ear and *BAM!* The shot reverberated throughout the men's room.

John Crowell was looking directly at Whitehead when the shot was fired. The life didn't drain from Whitehead's face – it evaporated instantly. Then he slumped to the ground.

Coonan, his eyes ablaze, stood over Whitehead's rumpled body. 'There, you bastard,' he snarled. 'Now you can burn in hell.'

With the noise from the shot still echoing in their ears,

Crowell, Comas, and Huggard ran frantically for the door.

Mickey Featherstone and Jimmy McElroy, meanwhile, had been sitting at the counter of the Plaka Bar, sensing that something heavy was about to go down. Coonan had smoldered quietly after the others had gone down to the men's room, then headed off in the same direction. Featherstone and McElroy knew that Coonan, unlike them, wasn't into marijuana. He definitely wasn't going downstairs to get stoned. They sat sipping their drinks for a few seconds, then decided to go see what the deal was.

As they went down the stairs leading to the men's room, they heard a sound they immediately recognized as a gunshot. They looked at each other, pulled their guns, and started running down the stairs. By the time they reached the base of the stairs, Comas, Huggard, and Crowell were practically tripping over each other trying to get out of the men's room.

'Hey, hey, hey,' yelled Mickey. 'Up against the fuckin' wall!'

As Featherstone and McElroy hustled Crowell, Comas, and Huggard against the wall, they heard two more shots from inside the men's room. Mickey opened the door to see Coonan, gun still in hand, standing over Whitehead. Blood was percolating from Whitehead's skull, forming an expanding pool on the dirty tile floor underneath his body.

'C'mon,' Billy Comas said excitedly, 'there's a dumpster out back. We gotta get rid of this goddamn body. Now!'

There was a lot of confusion after that. Coonan told McElroy to watch the stairwell to make sure nobody came downstairs. Featherstone was told to mop up the blood in the men's room. The others, with no choice but to go along, grabbed Whitehead's body and began dragging it towards the back of the basement.

Whitey Whitehead was only 175 pounds, but dead body weight can make a corpse seem twice as heavy. Even with three people, they were having trouble. Crowell had Whitehead's left leg and his belt. Coonan was on the right side, holding the body around the right shoulder. Huggard had it by the right leg. Comas had let go of the body and was leading the way through a basement hallway.

The basement of the Opera Hotel had once been a restaurant, and they passed a dusty old counter with stools, vinyl booths set against the wall, and a decrepit kitchen area. To get to the exit, they had to go up a short flight of stairs and through a set of double doors. Crowell got winded quickly, huffing and puffing before they had even reached the stairs.

At one point, Whitehead's pants began to rip apart at the crotch. Crowell lost his grip entirely and the body fell to the floor.

The others cursed him and regrouped, this time dragging the body instead of carrying it, leaving a trail of smeared blood behind them. When they got within a few feet of the stairs, Comas heard a muffled voice.

'The cops!' he yelled instinctively, touching off a spasmodic reaction. Crowell, Huggard, and Coonan dropped the body, tripping over it. They ran for cover, smacking into each other like they were in some kind of slapstick movie routine.

By this time, Featherstone had appeared, mop and

bucket in hand. 'What the fuck?' he shouted, as the others seemed about ready to run him over.

Comas had put his ear against the back door. 'No,' he turned and announced. 'It's alright; it ain't the cops.'

Through the door, the muffled voice identified itself as being that of a resident at the hotel. As Comas and the others listened, the person explained how he'd attempted to leave the hotel by way of the basement, but there was a metal gate just outside the door, and it was locked. When he exited the basement, the double door had closed behind him. It too was locked – from the inside. Now he was stuck in the area between the double door and the gate.

'Oh shit,' cried Comas, pointing at the door. 'How do we get the body to the dumpster with this fuck out here?!'

Featherstone volunteered to run outside and see if he could get the guy out.

'Yeah, okay,' said Comas, 'you do that.' After Featherstone left the room, Comas turned to the door and spoke loudly. 'Don't worry, pal, we're gonna have you outta there in no time.'

Comas, Crowell, Huggard, and Coonan waited downstairs for a good eight or nine minutes, each glancing nervously at Whitehead's body as a stream of blood now trailed aimlessly away from his head. There was another moment of panic when they thought they heard someone from a freight elevator down the hall.

'Fuck this,' said Coonan, finally. 'We'll leave him here. Pull his pockets out, take his pants down. Make it look like a robbery.'

And that's how they left Whitey Whitehead – his pants

down around his ankles, his pockets turned inside out, a pool of blood beginning to congeal on the floor underneath his head.

Coonan, Comas, Huggard, and Crowell – joined now by McElroy – went back upstairs to the Plaka Bar. They were drained from the excitement and the tension, and exhausted after dragging the body through the basement of the hotel. They avoided looking at each other, and no one spoke as they walked through the lobby of the hotel and back into the bar.

Just two hours had elapsed since Coonan, Featherstone, and McElroy first entered the Plaka Bar. It was now 2:30 A.M. and the bar was empty. Jimmy Coonan took the money they had pilfered from Whitehead's pocket and tossed it on the counter. 'The bastard only had $5,' he said, 'but let's have a drink on Whitey.' They all gathered around for a much-needed shot of whiskey.

Featherstone, meanwhile, had gone out to the back of the hotel, just like he was supposed to. When he got there he pulled the collar of his coat up and spoke in a fake Spanish accent to the guy who was locked behind the gate. But there was nothing he could do, since the gate had a chain lock on it. So he went back into the hotel and told the desk clerk that there was a guy locked behind a gate out back, and he'd better send someone to help him.

Then he went back into the bar. Coonan and McElroy were seated at the counter. The other three sat at a table, still in a mild state of shock and uncertain whether they were allowed to leave now or what.

'Who picked up the shells?' Mickey asked Coonan. The cold-blooded determination Coonan had shown during the shooting was gone now. The adrenaline had left him. He looked shaken, more shaken than Featherstone had ever seen him.

'The casings?' Mickey asked again when Jimmy hardly acknowledged the question. 'The casings from the bullets, did anybody get 'em?'

Jimmy shook his head.

'Get rid of the shells,' Mickey said, turning to McElroy. 'There should be three of 'em.'

After McElroy got up, Coonan walked over to a sink between the counter and the door to the kitchen. He coughed and gagged for a few seconds, then threw up violently. Mickey was surprised. Many times in recent years he himself had vomited at the sight of murder and dismemberment, but this was the first time – and would be the only time – he saw Jimmy Coonan do it. Mickey didn't know whether to laugh, be disturbed, or what. He watched in utter fascination for a few seconds until he was jarred back to reality by McElroy's return.

'You get 'em?' Mickey asked.

'Yeah,' answered Jimmy Mac, the red painter's cap pulled low on his forehead.

'Where are they?'

'Flushed 'em down the toilet.'

'All three?'

'Yeah, yeah. Don't worry.'

They finished their drinks and got ready to leave. As the entire group made for the door, Huggard began to pat himself down. 'Hey, my card! I had a greeting card from my girl. In an envelope. Where the fuck is it?' He looked around for a few minutes but couldn't find it anywhere.

'Bobby, forget it,' Comas finally said. 'You probably left the bastard somewhere and it got thrown out.'

It was late and the streets outside were nearly deserted. For a moment, the entire group stood awkwardly on the sidewalk in front of the Plaka Bar. Then, without anyone saying good-bye, the Clinton prison alumni went their way and the Hell's Kitchen Irishmen went theirs.

In the van on the way back down to the neighborhood, Coonan, Featherstone, and McElroy began to wonder aloud about the trustworthiness of their uptown buddies. The shock of the killing had receded, and another instinct had kicked into gear – survival. Nobody liked the idea of having so many witnesses to the killing. It was going to make it awfully difficult to get a cohesive alibi together.

When they reached Mickey's apartment building on West 56th Street, they went upstairs and entered quietly, so as not to wake his wife and child. As the early morning dawn cast a somber light through the apartment windows, they stood in the kitchen discussing their options.

'I don't think we gotta worry about Comas and Huggard,' Coonan was saying. 'We're dealing with professionals there. Real stand-up.'

'Yeah,' said Mickey, 'but what about Crowell?'

Nobody really knew much about John Crowell. As they parted, sallow and exhausted after another long night, that was the question that dogged them the most. How could they be certain they weren't going to have problems with Crowell?

Later that same day, the body of Harold Whitehead was found in the basement of the Opera Hotel by a janitor.

272

When detectives from the NYPD's 4th Homicide Zone arrived, they found Whitehead pretty much as he had been left the night before. Only now there was a white envelope resting next to the body. On the envelope, in clear handwritten letters, was the name 'Bobby.'

Inside was a greeting card with a picture of a woman looking out at the ocean and a glorious golden sunset. 'I've been thinking of you all day,' it read on the front.

On a piece of paper accompanying the card was a hand-written message that read:

'Hello my love. It's me. There are so many thoughts going on inside of me I had to try and express a few . . .

'Honey, I can't say in words how happy you and the relationship we have has made me feel. Dear God it feels good! Every way. Mentally, physically and spiritually.

'You know, it's funny. I spent a year and 3 mos. with a man because of what I believed the relationship could be. Not what it was – And you and I have it automatically!

'Babe, I'm a fool in a lot of ways – but I'm not going to give up filet mignon for hamburger!!

'Honey, I'm really starting to feel close to you and it feels good and right. I can only hope you feel the same.'

It was signed, 'Hey Babe, I love you, Elena.'

After the area had been secured, detectives from the Crime Scene Unit traced the smeared blood and scuff marks leading from the body back through the basement to the men's room. They found more traces of blood, both on the floor and on the doorjamb. Detective William Nasoff got down on his knees and checked behind the toilet bowls. Behind the one closest to the door he found the brass casing from a .25-caliber bullet. Later, the bullet itself would be found in one of the sinks against an adjacent wall.

Nasoff shook his head in amazement. Some murder scenes revealed nothing, not a single shred of evidence. But on this one, in less than thirty minutes, they had already secured two potentially devastating pieces of evidence. In his more than eighteen years as a member of the Crime Scene Unit, he had learned this usually meant one of two things: It was either an incredibly sloppy murder, or the evidence had been deliberately planted.

Judging from the way the body had been haphazardly left behind, with the bullet and casing carelessly left in the men's room, it certainly had elements of the former. But there was also the greeting card left oh-so-conveniently next to the body. The detective figured that had to be a plant.

Nobody, he thought, could be that stupid.

In Hell's Kitchen, news of Harold Whitehead's murder wafted through the saloons along 9th and 10th Avenue like a malodorous breeze. Unlike the murders of Paddy Dugan, Ruby Stein, and Rickey Tassiello – murders that had been undertaken with a specific purpose in mind – the Whitehead killing was spontaneous and inexplicable. It was a murder unlike anything Coonan had done in recent years – totally impulsive, with a reckless disregard for everyone involved. The killing was especially terrifying to those closest to Coonan. If he was willing to stiff someone for as trivial an offense as Whitey Whitehead's, just imagine what he would do to those who owed him, as most of his underlings did.

Inevitably, many of them blamed it on the Italians. Since the meeting at Tommaso's, Jimmy seemed to believe that he could kill with virtual impunity. Here, finally, was the proof: He had blown a guy away for calling his brother a 'rat' or a 'fag' or some fucking thing.

Billy Beattie, especially, did not take the news of the Whitehead murder well. Formerly a part-time bartender at the 596 Club and Edna's ex, Beattie had been on thin ice with Coonan ever since they first met ten years ago. Nothing he did, including helping Jimmy murder Paddy Dugan and Ruby Stein, seemed to make him any more secure. To make matters worse, he'd also run up huge debts with Coonan. Just a few months earlier he'd gotten Jimmy to front him $5,000 for a dope deal he wanted to make with a supplier in Florida. The deal had gone down but had yielded little or no return. On top of that was the money Beattie had been borrowing from Coonan to finance his shylock operation. All told, he must have owed Coonan at least $100,000.

But the money was only part of it. There was another reason Beattie knew he was in trouble with Jimmy, and the Whitehead murder reminded him of it.

Weeks earlier, Jimmy had ordered Beattie to whack Tommy Collins. Collins, then in his late forties, was not an easy guy to kill. It had been nearly thirteen years since Collins, along with Mickey Spillane and others, had ducked into a doorway on West 46th Street as young Jimmy Coonan sprayed them with machine-gun fire. In the intervening years, Collins continued to live on the fringe of organized crime without ever doing violence to anyone. Most West Side gangsters, including Beattie, thought of Tommy as an uncle; he was universally well liked.

Unfortunately for Tommy, he had a drinking problem that often got him into trouble. He'd developed the habit in the early Seventies, after one of his seven children was killed in a freak fireworks accident on the 4th of July. The tragedy took its toll. Within months, Tommy put on forty or fifty pounds and his hair turned completely white. Every year thereafter, around July 4th, he'd go on a drinking binge, piling up gambling debts and letting his business commitments slide. As the years passed, the drinking binges became more and more frequent.

In early November '78, Coonan told Billy Beattie he was tired of Collins's always being behind on his shylock payments, and he wanted to use him as an example. The order was simple: Kill Tommy Collins and make his body do the Houdini. No payment was mentioned for Beattie. The way Billy understood it, Jimmy just considered it to be the price of their friendship.

It put Billy in a tight spot, to say the least. Not only did he like Tommy Collins, but Tommy owed him something like $25,000. If he killed Collins, how the hell was he going to get his money? And if he didn't get his money, how the hell was he going to settle his debt with Coonan?

Beattie had no choice but to go through the motions. He got a .32 automatic with a silencer from Jimmy's twenty-four-year-old brother, Eddie, a little squirt who was trying to follow in his older brother's footsteps, but who nobody liked very much. Then Beattie drove around

Collins's apartment building a few times, not knowing what the hell he would do if he actually ran into him. But he never saw Tommy Collins. After a week or so he gave the gun back to Little Eddie Coonan and told him to tell his brother he'd been unable to pull it off.

Billy knew he was in deep shit after that. He'd been trying to run two businesses at one time – the drugs and the shylocking – both of which were losing big-time bucks. To make matters worse, in recent months he'd become a regular cocaine cowboy, shooting into his own veins what he was supposed to be pushing on the street. Then he'd backed out on this killing Jimmy had assigned him.

He'd been having Jimmy Coonan nightmares. *Then* came the Whitehead murder. When he first heard about it from Mickey Featherstone, he had to laugh. It was so fucking crazy. He was reminded of something Jimmy had told him around the time of the Rickey Tassiello murder. Beattie asked Jimmy why he had to kill Tassiello over such a small amount of money.

'It's to prove a point,' Jimmy had said. 'Where we're headed, it's good business.'

'I still don't get it.'

'See, the people we're dealin' with now, the more bodies we got the better we look. That's what they're into.'

The more bodies the better. This was becoming Jimmy Coonan's professional credo. And after the Whitehead thing, Billy Beattie had this queasy feeling he might just be next on the hit parade.

Well, he thought, I ain't going to wait for a friggin' invitation. I ain't that dumb.

'What about the money you're owed?' one of Beattie's

shylock customers asked when Billy told him he was going to take a permanent vacation.

'Hey,' said Beattie, 'just tell everybody Billy Beattie's givin' 'em a free ticket.'

Then Beattie headed for the mountains, intending never to return to Hell's Kitchen.

11

THE FEDS AND
LITTLE AL CAPONE

In the wake of the Whitehead homicide, the Intelligence cops began their most concerted initiative yet. Ironically, it had nothing to do with the events surrounding Whitehead's November 22, 1978, demise in the basement of the Opera Hotel. By early December, detectives from the 4th Homicide Zone were still investigating the murder, running evidence through ballistics and trying to track down the 'Bobby' whose love letter had been left next to Whitehead's corpse. As of yet, nobody had connected anything to Coonan or Featherstone.

But even as Homicide continued pursuing the Whitehead matter, the Intelligence Division was following up on a totally unrelated lead of their own – one that would eventually overtake the Whitehead investigation, incorporating it in a barrage of criminal charges designed to get the Hell's Kitchen Irish Mob off the streets once and for all.

Intell's latest line of investigation had actually begun roughly six weeks before Whitehead's death, in September '78, when Greg Derkasch, a Special Agent with the U.S.

Secret Service's New York Field Office, called Sergeant Tom McCabe. 'Hey,' said Derkasch, 'we're holding a guy here named Coonan, James Coonan. Possibly a counterfeit rap, definitely gun possession. We know all about him, but we're trying to track down a possible partner of his. All we got is a first name, Mickey. Know anything about it?'

'Oh, man,' replied McCabe, 'are you kiddin'?'

After McCabe gave Derkasch an extensive rundown on Featherstone, the Secret Service agent let out a loud, sustained whistle. 'Wow. That's some file you got.'

'Yeah,' said McCabe. 'We been hopin' to nail these guys for months. So what's this about Coonan?'

Derkasch told McCabe that a few days earlier, on the morning of September 14th, he'd gotten a call from the manager of Bowery Savings Bank on Lexington Avenue in midtown Manhattan. The manager was holding a woman who had just tried to deposit what looked to be two counterfeit $100 federal reserve notes. Derkasch went to the bank immediately and examined the bills. They were counterfeit alright, and not particularly good ones at that. He recognized them as part of a series that had recently started circulating in the New York metropolitan area.

The woman who'd tried to deposit the notes identified herself as Joanne DePalma. She'd gotten them that night at her place of business, the Spartacus Spa #1, an up-scale massage parlor located at 146 East 55th Street. Ms DePalma, it seemed, was a high-class hooker, and she'd received the bills for services rendered.

Derkasch escorted DePalma back to Spartacus, where he was introduced to the night manager and another working girl named Felicia 'Monique' Ledesma. It was around 6 that morning, Derkasch was told, that two guys, one named Jimmy and the other Mickey, entered the club and had a few drinks. Then they had 'sessions' with Joanne DePalma and Monique. DePalma remembered that the guy she was with had a tattoo on his right arm with the name 'Mickey' written underneath it. Mickey and Jimmy gave the girls a $100 bill apiece and paid the club's fee with a third C-note.

The night manager recalled that the two guys left Spartacus around 9 that morning. A few minutes later they came back to the club cursing under their breath. Apparently their Cadillac was missing from in front of the building. When the guy who called himself Jimmy mentioned where they had parked it, the manager said it had probably been towed away by the city.

Derkasch made a quick phone call and found out that a brown Cadillac Coupe Deville, New Jersey license number 377 JLB, had indeed been towed that morning from East 55th Street. Another quick call and he'd identified the car as being registered to a James M. Coonan.

Derkasch hauled ass over to the city's impound lot, a huge warehouse straddling the Hudson River at West 37th Street. He was barely there long enough to locate Coonan's car when he was informed by a cop on the premises that two people had just arrived looking for the car. It turned out to be Tony Lucich and Tommy Collins, two names which meant nothing to Derkasch at the time. He identified himself as a Secret Service agent and asked which one was the owner of the car.

'What car?' they both replied.

They were brought into the impound lot's main office and searched. At first, Derkasch was surprised to find that neither was in possession of any Cadillac keys. But then he spotted a shiny object on the floor between Tony Lucich's legs.

'Gee,' said Derkasch, picking up the keys, 'what have we here?'

Derkasch was half expecting to find a trunkload full of counterfeit currency, so he was somewhat disappointed when he opened the Cadillac's trunk and found nothing but a cardboard box full of baby's clothing. Then he dug down into the box. At the bottom, wrapped in a diaper, was a fully loaded .32-caliber Colt Special with silencer attached. Also in the box was a police-issue bulletproof vest.

As arrangements were being made to have the car taken to the Secret Service offices downtown, a cop approached from the front desk. 'Excuse me, Agent Derkasch, but we got two more guys out here askin' about that Caddy.'

Derkasch smiled. At age thirty-seven, after ten and a half years with the Secret Service, he'd been up against his share of dead ends. A skeptic by nature, he knew that a smart counterfeiter was almost impossible to catch. There were so many ways to cover your tracks. But these guys had passed bad bills in a cathouse and gotten their car towed with an unregistered gun in the trunk. Now they were walking into the middle of a nest of Secret Service agents? Derkasch loved crooks like this. They tended to make his job a lot easier.

At the front desk, Jimmy Coonan and a friend of his named Bosco Radonjich stood nervously near a water cooler. After flashing his ID, Derkasch confronted the two of them with the fact that a loaded automatic had been found in the trunk of Jimmy's Caddy.

'Ain't mine, sir,' said Coonan politely. 'I didn't even have my car last night. Friend of mine did.'

'What's the friend's name?'

'Lucich,' volunteered Bosco Radonjich. 'Tony Lucich.'

'Uh-huh,' said Derkasch, looking at Coonan. 'So can you account for your whereabouts last night and early this morning – say around six A.M.?'

'Well . . . for that I think you'll need to talk to my lawyer.'

Both Coonan and Radonjich were loaded into a Secret Service car and taken downtown. The agent who drove Radonjich's car after them found yet another pistol – a .25-caliber Astra – resting handily in a utility tray between the front seats.

Gun possession charges were filed against Coonan and Radonjich; both were out on bail within hours.

After talking to Tom McCabe, Derkasch called the U.S. Attorney's office for the Southern District of New York, where he spoke with Assistant U.S. Attorney Ira Block. Derkasch told Block what they had so far regarding the counterfeit bills.

'Sounds promising,' Block said. 'But you need more before we can even think about empaneling a federal grand jury.'

That was exactly what Derkasch had been hoping to hear. It didn't make sense to bust two guys for possession of a few counterfeit notes. Since they'd confiscated other bills in recent months that looked to be from the same batch, chances were good that the source was somewhere in the New York area. If they were to set up an investigation, and were allowed to take the time to do it right, they had a shot at unearthing the entire network – a much more impressive bust than what they had at the moment.

It was ambitious, of course, and maybe not even feasible. If they hoped to trace these bills backward through perhaps dozens of intermediaries to the source, they'd probably have to go undercover. And to go undercover, they'd need a point of entry, always the most difficult part of any operation. At the moment, they knew very little about Coonan, Featherstone, or the circles in which they traveled. What they needed was a knowledgeable source to familiarize them with their subject on short notice.

Enter the NYPD's Intelligence Division.

For McCabe, Egan, and the other cops with Intell's Syndicated Crime Unit, the prospect of working with the Secret Service was a dream come true. Unlike, say, the FBI, who preferred to control their investigations from top to bottom, the Secret Service liked to work in tandem with local law enforcement. Partly, it was because their criminal focus was much more limited than the FBI, making them more dependent on regional intelligence sources. But also, agents with the Secret Service and their sister agency, Alcohol, Tobacco and Firearms, seemed to be under a lot less pressure from higher-ups in the Treasury Department than their fellow agents at Justice.

Like the Intelligence Division, the Secret Service was willing to allow an investigation to evolve slowly. They knew from experience that a counterfeit conspiracy had many tentacles, and if they moved too quickly in one area they might blow their chance to trace the notes to their source.

Unlike the Intelligence Division, however, the Secret Service had a sizable budget. This meant that not only were they willing to assign the necessary manpower, but they also provided the necessary tools – like technologically advanced surveillance equipment, the latest weaponry, and plenty of cash for those costly counterfeit buys. Also, with a federal agency like the Secret Service it was a hell of a lot easier to secure the proper court authorization for phone taps and other eavesdropping strategies.

Once the feds had committed themselves to a full-scale undercover operation, it hadn't taken the boys from Intell long to come up with a point of entry. It was Frank Hunt, the same cop who'd given Intell their first confidential informant back in late 1977, who got the ball rolling. A rotund and gregarious guy known as Fat Frankie on the streets, Hunt had a 'mole' in the neighborhood who was willing to introduce an undercover agent to nineteen-year-old Raymond Steen, Alberta Sachs's boyfriend and Mickey Featherstone's next-door neighbor. The word on the street was that Steen had been pushing counterfeit $100 notes up and down 10th Avenue.

What the cops didn't know yet was that the counterfeit operation was basically something Mickey Featherstone had cooked up all on his own. Along with Billy Comas, the West Side Mob's uptown contact, Mickey had been looking to establish some independent financing. Nothing elaborate, he had told Comas, just something where he might be able to make a quick killing. After all, by 1978 Mickey had expenses; he was a married man now with a recently born son and an increasingly expensive cocaine habit.

Comas, who was of part-Greek extraction, told him about a counterfeit ring he knew of run by a handful of Greek-Americans from New Jersey. It all sounded good to Mickey, who agreed to purchase some notes from Comas.

To peddle the counterfeit bills, Featherstone turned to Steen, a virtually illiterate young hood who had given himself the pathetically inappropriate nickname 'Little Al Capone.' Mickey knew Steen was inexperienced and a potential fuck-up, but he figured, what could go wrong? As with most of the neighborhood gangsters who'd risen to prominence in recent years, Mickey had begun to think he was invulnerable. After all the unsolved homicides in Hell's Kitchen, it was hard to take the NYPD seriously.

What Mickey didn't really stop to consider was that a counterfeit operation, which came under the jurisdiction of the feds, would up the ante considerably.

'How long's he been in there?' asked Richie Egan, seated at the window of an empty classroom at John Jay College, across the street from the Westway Candy Store at 827 10th Avenue. It was a clear winter day just before Christmas, 1978. Egan's binoculars were focused on a black van parked just south of the candy store on the far side of West 55th Street.

'I'd say about an hour,' replied Secret Agent Donald L'Huillier. 'Hasn't stopped talking either.'

the next few weeks Steen and Malfi made four more transactions, the largest being a sale of two hundred $100 notes on January 9th. They eventually agreed to lower the price to 27 points – or $27 for each $100 note – which Steen, lying through his teeth, told Malfi was about half what he was charging other people in the neighborhood.

In the same deal, Steen sold Malfi stolen American Express traveler's checks, and told him if he wanted to buy cocaine he could handle that too.

There always seemed to be long delays between buys. Steen claimed that Coonan and Featherstone, who he described as 'his people,' were worried about dealing with complete strangers. Malfi was constantly trying to get Steen to introduce him to his people so he could 'put them at ease.' But Steen wasn't going for it.

'That can't work,' he said. 'I already found that out. These guys don't want to talk with nobody.'

'What's Featherstone's big problem?' asked Malfi. 'How come he won't meet with us?'

'Look, there's too much trouble with that. A lot of things been happening. It's so hot, if these guys even knew I used their names I'd get my head chopped off.'

As backup on the undercover operation, there were always at least a half-dozen cops and agents down on the street and up in the observation post, linked by walkie-talkie. Everyone was armed and ready to move if Malfi seemed to be in danger.

The closest call came on the afternoon of January 15, 1979, nearly two months after the Whitehead murder. Malfi and another undercover agent, John Libonati, were scheduled to purchase $6,900 worth of counterfeit.

Arrangements had already been made to meet in front of the Westway Candy Store at 4 P.M. When Malfi pulled up, Steen came out and hopped in the back of the van. Agent Libonati was introduced to Steen as Malfi's cousin 'John.'

They drove around the corner and parked the van on West 55th Street between 10th and 11th Avenue. Steen handed Malfi a white envelope secured with two rubber bands containing the $6,900 in counterfeit bills. As previously agreed, Malfi gave Steen $400 in partial payment, with the understanding that the remaining $1,463 would be paid within the next two days.

Steen was on some kind of wild cocaine high that afternoon, talking a blue streak about some good acid he had for sale. He sold a lot of acid in Hell's Kitchen, he said, ten to fifteen tabs to a customer at a price between $3 and $4 per tab. He also sold guns. To illustrate this, he produced a .25-caliber Beretta. He said he liked to purchase as many guns as he could because they were so easy to sell around the neighborhood. 'I mean, four or five or ten ain't nothin',' he said, waving the Beretta around. 'They go in one day.' He added that Donald Mallay, the owner of the Westway Candy Store, was an expert gunsmith. 'He's got a lathe right there in the back of the store where he makes silencers. And you wouldn't believe them fuckin' silencers. I got two or three of 'em in my apartment right now.'

Malfi asked if they could take a look at the silencers. Steen was reluctant at first, but they finally got him to agree. They drove around the block to the entrance of his apartment building at 520 West 56th Street.

The other cops and Secret Service agents were worried. Malfi and Libonati's van was wired, but the undercover agents were not. Once they walked into the apartment building, they would no longer be within the realm of surveillance. Derkasch, who was in an undercover vehicle monitoring the van, radioed to Richie Egan and the Intelligence cops to be on alert.

Steen, Malfi, and Libonati got off the elevator on the fifteenth floor. 'Wait here,' said Steen, pointing towards a stairwell. 'And stay outta sight. My man Featherstone lives right there, 15-B. If he knew I was showin' you these silencers . . . forget about it.'

Steen entered apartment 15-C. Within minutes he returned, a cockeyed grin on his face and a .22-caliber Hi-Standard automatic with a silencer already screwed on. They all went up one flight to the roof, where Steen stood silhouetted against the late afternoon sky and popped off two shots, shoulder level.

'Wow,' said Malfi and Libonati. 'Incredible. Can't hear a fuckin' thing.'

'Yeah, yeah,' said Steen, barely able to contain his glee. 'Twenty-two automatic. Best fuckin' gun for whackin' people, know what I'm sayin'?' A short time later, the two undercovers and Steen came back out of the building smiling, and the cops on the street relaxed.

In the weeks following the meeting on the roof, Steen continued to provide juicy morsels of information on the inner workings of West Side crime, most of it captured on what would come to be known as 'the van tapes.' The cops and agents weren't sure yet how much of it was reliable. But as an insight into the mind of an aspiring young gangster from Hell's Kitchen, it was a fascinating study. Steen's views, which ranged from comical to delusionary to casually brutal, often left them shaking their heads in amazement.

Here, for example, was Steen on why the West Side Mob cut up their murder victims: 'Take for instance, somebody came over and shot your sister, right? That guy, you can't go over and kill him 'cause they gonna have a feeling it's you or somebody in your family. So you do a disappearing act [on him]. Nobody knows where he is or what he's doing, you know? Nobody knows. Nobody.'

Steen on Jimmy Coonan: 'The President, he owns everything, he fucking runs everything. All your theatrical unions? Coonan. The metal lathers and the constructions . . . I mean, this guy walks into the biggest unions in the world and says to the other guy, "I'm taking over now." You know? That's the type of person he is . . . He tells those other fucking people "no" and there ain't nobody in their right mind that's gonna stand up to him.'

Steen on his own exploits: 'Well, I shot him in the chest with a shotgun, sawed-off. No, I couldn't cut him up. This guy was fucking seven foot tall . . . Fucking hit missed him. I'm lucky the shotgun killed him. I shot him right in the chest, man. He died.'

After weeks of listening to Steen over the transmitter, the investigators developed a backhanded affection for the pudgy young gangster. They usually referred to him as Ray or Raymond, never by his last name. There was something almost endearing about Steen's pathetic desire to prove what a tough guy he was.

'Okay,' Ray would constantly lament, 'I'm a young guy.

That's what they look at me as, a kid. Well, fuck that kid shit. I do anything in the notebook.'

Yes, he was a two-bit punk and possibly a killer. The cops knew this. But he was *their* two-bit punk, their most valuable link yet with the West Side crime scene. For the time being, that made him as important as Coonan himself.

One afternoon late in January '79, Mickey Featherstone met with Ray Steen at Amy's Pub on 9th Avenue. Amy's had been a favorite of Mickey's ever since he first met Sissy there years earlier, and lately he'd been conducting a lot of business at a table in the back of the bar.

'That guy you're dealin' with?' he said to Steen, sipping on a Seven & Seven and smoking a Kool.

'Yeah?'

'It's the Man.'

'No way.'

'Yes. It's gotta be.'

Mickey explained to Steen how he had Jimmy McElroy run a check on the van's license plates. McElroy had a friend who was a cop, he said, and his friend had discovered that the plates were registered to a stolen Dodge Dart.

'There ain't nobody with any sense that's gonna drive around armed with stolen plates and counterfeit money in the car. Nobody 'cept the law. Plus, who the fuck would pay twenty-seven points on the shit? I mean, these guys is supposed to be wiseguys, right?'

Steen looked dumbfounded. 'Mickey, no way. I been dealin' with this motherfucker. He's cool.'

'I'm tellin' you Ray, it's the Man.'

293

It wasn't even dinnertime yet and already Featherstone had a good buzz going. Ever since Coonan blew away Whitehead in the basement of the Opera Hotel, Mickey had been getting coked up on a daily basis. It wasn't that the murder bothered him so much. He could handle that, just like he'd handled the Ugly Walter and Rickey Tassiello murders. What bothered him was that before that night he'd been priming himself to confront Coonan, to tell him how everyone felt he was selling out to the Italians. But then the murder went down and everything got tense. Once again, it was time to show loyalty, to keep your mouth shut and go along with the program.

But Mickey was getting tired of it all. He'd started this counterfeit business even though Jimmy and Roy Demeo were against it. It was a federal charge, they warned him. It just wasn't worth the risk.

But Mickey didn't give a fuck about that either. In fact, he was beginning to think prison might not be such a bad idea. There'd been something in Jimmy's eyes the night of the Whitehead murder, something that made Mickey realize there would never be a way out of all this. Except maybe prison.

With the wizard, Larry Hochheiser, as his attorney, Mickey figured he'd get the best deal possible on a counterfeit rap. Two, maybe three years max. He could handle three years. Then he'd be able to take Sissy and Mickey, Jr, and get the fuck out, with no strings attached.

Lately these thoughts had festered inside Mickey's head whenever he got juiced, and it was causing him problems. His resentment towards Jimmy was always followed by intense feelings of guilt. Loyalty, he knew, was what the

294

West Side Mob was supposed to be all about. That's what Jimmy always told him. Loyalty had kept them strong through the generations.

But loyalty was a two-way street, thought Mickey, and Jimmy had violated their loyalty by trying to act like he was an Italian. The emotions this caused in Mickey made him confused. The confusion translated into self-loathing, and sometimes that translated into self-destructiveness.

But just because he was feeling self-destructive didn't mean he was going to be an idiot. With the profits from the counterfeit sales, he would cover his ass. Of the $27 per $100 note they were getting from Malfi, $7 went to Steen, $10 went to Mickey, and $10 went to Mickey's private 'lawyers fund.'

Featherstone knew a guy had to take precautions when dealing with someone like Ray Steen. Steen liked to brag that he'd killed people, but Mickey knew that was bullshit. In fact, Ray was a notorious bullshitter, one of a half-dozen or so teenage toughs in the neighborhood who worshiped Mickey Featherstone. Ever since Mickey returned from prison in '75, they'd treated him like some kind of hero. Sometimes this hero worship made them stupid.

Mickey had realized this years ago. Not long after he got out of prison, he'd fallen into a deep depression. Sometimes back in those days when he was high enough he would pull out his revolver and start playing Russian roulette. Once, he'd done it in front of Steen, who was sixteen at the time. To prove what a tough guy he was, Steen had picked up the revolver, put it to his own head, and pulled the trigger.

That's when Mickey realized what an impressionable little fucker Ray Steen could be.

So now here he was, four years later, in the middle of a business deal with Steen that he knew was about to blow up in their faces. He could feel it.

'Don't worry,' Ray was saying. 'I got this under control.'

'Well,' replied Mickey, stabbing his cigarette into an ashtray. 'If they are agents, they got you already. So you might as well go ahead.'

'Right.'

'But when this fuck starts wavin' a badge in your face?'

'Yeah?'

'Don't come cryin' to me.'

On the evening of February 9th, Richie Egan strapped on his bulletproof vest, secured his .38 Special safely in its holster, and waited for instructions. Once again, he was in the John Jay College observation post across the street from the Westway Candy Store. Along with fellow officers James Tedaldi, Abe Ocasio, Don Gurney, and their supervisor, Sergeant Tom McCabe, Egan was waiting for Mickey Featherstone to arrive at the store. Once he did, the cops were ready to boogie. Search warrants had been secured, the Secret Service agents were in place and an all-out raid was about to get underway.

Simultaneous with their operation, just down the street a half-dozen other federal agents – along with four or five members of the NYPD's Emergency Service Unit – would also be conducting a raid. Both front and back entrances to 520 West 56th Street were being secured as the agents made ready to search apartments 15-B and 15-C – Featherstone's and Steen's.

And there was more. Undercover agents Malfi and Libonati, along with four or five *more* Secret Service agents, would be carrying out the most important part of the night's festivities – the arrest of Ray Steen.

The decision to stage the raids and arrest had come suddenly. In recent weeks, there had been a complication in Steen's supply of counterfeit. The cops got wind of it through a bug on the phone at the Westway Candy Store (by that time, they also had wiretaps on phones in Featherstone's and Steen's apartments). On the afternoon of February 5th, Agent Malfi called Steen at the candy store and asked why their planned transaction of the night before hadn't gone down.

'The guy got busted,' said Steen, referring to his source.

'The guy got busted with our stuff?'

'Yeah.'

'Holy Jesus! So what does that do to the deal?'

'No, no, no, wait, wait. The guy got busted, but not with the stuff.'

'Well, what is this, the guy got busted 'cause of counterfeit or what?'

'No, he didn't get busted for counterfeit. No, a jewelry heist.'

'Oh, so what'd he have, the stuff with him or something?'

'No, he didn't have nothin'. He just had his body with him there.'

'C'mon, Ray, what the fuck is this?'

Steen was reluctant to reveal the name of his and Featherstone's source, but before the conversation was over he'd told Malfi just about everything the cops needed to know. The source, said Steen, had been arrested on a burglary charge and would be arraigned that night at 8 P.M. in lower Manhattan. SCU immediately dispatched an Intelligence unit to set up surveillance at 100 Centre Street, the New York municipal courthouse. Sure enough, at 7:45 P.M., Mickey Featherstone arrived with the bail money for Billy Comas and a sidekick of his named Johnny Halo.

The cops were familiar with Comas. They knew him as a veteran hustler who had been dealing with the West Side Mob for years. What's more, detectives from the 4th Homicide Zone had recently informed the Intelligence Division that Billy Comas was believed to be a witness – if not a participant – in the brutal murder of Harold Whitehead at the Opera Hotel.

Now that they had Steen's and Featherstone's supplier, the investigators were inclined to play their last card. Things had heated up in the neighborhood considerably. It seemed to be common knowledge that the phones were bugged, which meant that Malfi might be in danger. They certainly had the evidence to arrest, indict, and convict Ray Steen, which they hoped would provide enough leverage to enlist his cooperation in the investigation.

What's more, earlier that week Steen had told Malfi he'd seen the counterfeit plates for the $100 notes in Featherstone's apartment. The investigators had used this bit of information as the pretext to file for a search warrant.

At about 7 P.M., as Richie Egan and the other Intelligence cops watched from across the street, Mickey Featherstone arrived with a package at the Westway Candy Store, where Ray Steen was waiting to meet him. In twenty minutes, Steen was scheduled to sell $50,000 in counterfeit to Malfi. The package Featherstone was delivering contained the bogus bills, which Billy Comas had delivered earlier that day.

At 7:07 Mickey called his apartment from the candy store. He told Sissy to tell Billy Uptown to stay put; he'd be right over as soon as he was done. The investigators, listening to the conversation over a transmitter, were pleasantly surprised. They had not known Billy Comas would actually be on the premises when they made their raid. It was icing on the cake.

At 7:30 Malfi drove up in front of the candy store in his black undercover van. Steen slid back the side door and got in. Within minutes the van drove off. The cops waited to make sure it was safely out of the area, then Derkasch gave the order for the raids to commence.

Egan, his heart pounding, hit 10th Avenue running at full speed. Alongside him were McCabe, Tedaldi, Gurney, and Ocasio. Given the Intelligence cops' usual role as backup players, it wasn't often they got to take to the streets like this. Egan had to admit, it felt good. It made him feel like a rookie all over again.

It was freezing outside and there were large ice patches on the street and sidewalk. As he crossed the avenue huffing and puffing, Egan inadvertently stepped on one of the ice patches and almost slipped on his ass. He righted himself without falling just as a half-dozen feds pulled up in two unmarked cars with flashing lights on top.

Mickey Featherstone had just stepped out of the candy store and was standing on the sidewalk in front of the door. In the store behind him were the proprietor, Donald Mallay, Tommy Collins, and three or four other neighborhood people. As soon as he saw the cars hurtling towards the store, Featherstone backpedaled through the door.

'It's a raid!' he shouted, as the small army of law enforcement officers – shotguns and revolvers drawn – descended on the tiny store. Quickly, Mickey took a .25-caliber Beretta he had tucked in his belt and tossed it. It hit the ground near a glass-encased counter just as four of the agents burst in the door.

There was pandemonium, with everyone shouting and bumping into each other. The phone in the candy store started ringing. Featherstone was ordered to get down on the floor, and one of the agents stood over him with a shotgun pointed at his head. Forty-one-year-old Donald Mallay, standing behind the counter, looked like he was about ready to have a heart attack. Along with Tommy Collins and the others, he was told to stand against a back wall near the pinball machines. Instructions were being shouted – 'Hands behind your head!' 'Feet spread!' 'Don't say a fuckin' word!' – as the agents and cops frisked everyone in the store.

'Whose is this?' asked one of the cops loudly, pointing at the gun on the floor.

Nobody said a word.

After an agent from the Drug Enforcement Administration read everyone their rights, a thorough search of the store got underway. Based on what Steen had been telling Malfi, the investigators were hoping to find cocaine and a lathe for making silencers on the premises. But it was soon apparent that neither was there. The cops confiscated the .25 Mickey had tossed on the floor, then lined everyone up and began asking questions – or 'taking their pedigree' as the cops liked to call it. For the time being, they had nothing to hold anyone on. After turning the place upside down and asking their questions, they let everyone go.

'We'll be seeing you again,' one of the agents said to Featherstone as he sneered at the cops on his way out the door.

Meanwhile, down the block at 520 West 56th Street, six federal agents and a four-man Emergency Service Unit had arrived at apartment 15-B. 'This is the police,' announced one of the agents, knocking on the door. 'We have a search warrant for this apartment. Open up.'

The agents heard rustling inside, but no one came to the door.

'Go ahead,' said the agent to one of the Emergency Service cops, who began smashing at the door with a sledgehammer.

Inside the apartment, gray-haired Billy Comas heard the pounding and didn't know what to do. There were no fire escapes on the building and he sure as hell couldn't jump from the fifteenth floor. He ran through the bedroom, past Mickey Jr's crib, and started banging on the bathroom door.

'Sissy! We got a fuckin' problem here!'

Sissy came out of the bathroom and went to the front

301

door. As soon as she opened it, the agents flooded in, shotguns and revolvers pointed in all directions. Sissy and Billy Comas were told to sit on a couch in the front room. Sissy's six-year-old niece, who had been in the kitchen, came into the room, terrified. Sissy grabbed her and brought her over to the couch. They could hear Mickey, Jr, crying loudly.

'Tell your son to get out here!' one of the agents told Sissy.

'He's eighteen months old, he's an infant! Whaddya want him to do!?'

Sissy went into the bedroom, where three or four agents had already begun turning things upside down, and lifted Mickey, Jr, from his crib.

Over the next two hours the Featherstone apartment was vigorously searched. Among the items confiscated were two bayonets, one machete, 30.06 rifle shells, two blank New York State driver's licenses, an honorary Westchester County detective's shield, and a fully loaded .25-caliber Beretta. Underneath a cushion on the couch, right where Billy Comas had been sitting, they found a small black address book. But there were no counterfeit plates.

Nor were there any plates next door in Ray Steen's apartment, which was unoccupied when the cops arrived. They had also hoped to find a large arsenal of weapons which Steen told Malfi was stored in his closet. But earlier that day, Mickey Featherstone, sensing a raid was imminent, had told Ray to move the guns to his aunt's apartment. By the time the agents arrived there was a .25 and a 12-gauge shotgun, a nice cache but hardly an arsenal.

Five blocks uptown, at 61st Street and 11th Avenue, the third and final stage of the night's operation was going down. After Steen got into Malfi's van, they drove around the corner to 55th Street between 10th and 11th avenues. Another undercover agent was in a car that pulled up behind the van. Malfi told Steen he was going to give the counterfeit money to 'his man' in the car behind them.

Steen looked nervous. 'Well, you know, my people ran a check on your plates. They come back registered to a whole different car, man. This is why they're suspicious.'

'These plates?'

'Yeah.'

'Registered to a different car?'

'Yeah.'

'Hey, my man, your people must've made a mistake on the plate check.'

Malfi stepped out of the van and took the two brown-paper bags containing the counterfeit notes to the agent parked behind him. He and the agent talked for a few minutes, then the agent radioed to two more agents in another car, telling them he now had the counterfeit money in his possession.

Malfi got back into the van. 'Okay, Ray, we just gotta drive up here a few blocks to get the bread.'

Steen was even more nervous now. Beads of perspiration were beginning to form on his brow. 'Hey, Ronnie, you said this guy was gonna have it.'

'Hey, relax, Ray. Are we friends or what?'

Steen laughed nervously. 'Alright, but I don't feel too good about this.'

Malfi and Steen drove to 61st and 11th, followed by the agent who had just received the counterfeit. It was dark now and the streetlights on 11th Avenue were a pale yellow. Malfi parked, got out of the black van, and walked across the avenue to a dark sedan, where two armed agents were waiting. Without saying a word, the two agents got out of the sedan and walked over to the van. By then the third agent was out of his car. The three of them surrounded the van and placed Steen under arrest.

Later the agents counted the counterfeit money Steen had given them. There was $48,000 – $2,000 less than there was supposed to be.

They had to laugh. Little Al Capone had tried to stiff them.

That night, high above Manhattan, at the Secret Service's New York Field Office in the World Trade Center, Steen sat in a leather chair surrounded by five or six agents. At first, Steen claimed that Mickey Featherstone had nothing to do with the counterfeit operation. He'd only used Featherstone's name to make himself look big, he said. As for the counterfeit money itself? He'd stolen it from the Town and Country Pub on 49th Street and 9th Avenue.

Nobody believed Steen's story, but he persisted. Eventually, they brought in a tall, bearded man in a nicely tailored suit.

'Raymond,' said Agent Derkasch, 'I have someone I want you to meet. This is Ira Block. He's an assistant U.S. attorney for the Southern District of New York. He's going to explain to you what the charges are and how much

304

time you'll be spending in prison after you're convicted. Have you ever spent time in prison, Raymond?'

Steen shook his head.

'Okay. You just listen to this man.'

After Block told Steen he might be facing fifty or sixty years for counterfeit currency, gun, and narcotics possession charges, Raymond began to waver. Sensing that he was about to turn, Derkasch went for the clincher. He knew it was always risky to confront a prospective stool pigeon with the undercover agent. Sometimes they got agitated and refused to cooperate. Other times they melted before your eyes and signed whatever agreement you put in front of them. With Steen, Derkasch was banking on the latter.

'Hello, Ray,' said Malfi, after he was brought into the room. He was still wearing his street clothes from when he'd met with Steen earlier that night.

The color drained from Steen's face. 'Man, they told me you was bad, but I stuck by you.'

Ray said he wanted to meet with his girlfriend, Alberta Sachs. Within thirty minutes, the agents brought her into the room. For five or ten minutes the two teenagers sat off to one side of the office and talked in private. Occasionally their voices rose; Ray looked distraught, Alberta frightened. Eventually, on the verge of tears, Steen came forward and said they would both be willing to cooperate.

While Ray and Alberta were signing their agreement papers, down the hall Billy Comas was being interviewed by several other Secret Service agents. After the agents had finished searching the Featherstone

305

apartment, they brought Comas downtown, sat him in a chair and gave him a cup of coffee. They told him they knew he was Featherstone's source for the counterfeit $100 notes, but they wanted to hear his side of the story.

'I know what you guys really want,' said Comas. 'I been 'round the goddamn block. You got my record.'

Unlike Ray Steen, fifty-five-year-old Billy Comas was a hardened criminal with a long list of arrests and convictions. Over the years he'd weathered beatings, homosexual assaults, and inmate uprisings in a wide variety of penal institutions, both state and federal. Prison did not scare him. What did scare him was Jimmy Coonan and Mickey Featherstone.

'They're bad guys,' he told the agents, as if that were all that needed to be said.

The agents told Comas that, for the moment, they weren't interested in his dealings with Coonan and Featherstone. They just wanted to know where the counterfeit notes were coming from.

'Yeah,' said Comas. 'Then what?'

One of the agents shrugged. 'Then we build a case.'

Before he had even decided whether to cooperate, Comas told the agents his source for the bills was 'the Greeks.' He said his contact was a guy named Nick Daratsakis, although the notes were printed by a Pete Christie, who lived in New Jersey. Comas added that he had been buying the $100 notes off Daratsakis at 6 points and selling them to Featherstone for 12.

They briefly discussed the quality of the bills, which one of the agents mentioned was not that good. Comas agreed, saying the problem was in the way they had been 'treated.' Usually, to give the bills a used look, they were treated by dipping them in coffee. These bills had been dipped in tea.

The agent said they wanted Comas to arrange a meeting with the Greeks and wear a transmitting device.

'Sure,' replied Comas, 'that's good for you guys, but what about me? I once helped the cops and went to jail anyway. So, you know, what're we talkin' about here?'

The agents told Comas they could make his cooperation known to the U.S. Attorney's office and the U.S. Probation Department. As it stood now, he was going to do hard time for his involvement in the counterfeit operation and maybe a few other charges too, like gun trafficking. They weren't making any promises, but if he became an informant there was a good chance he could get out of this with little more than a long probation sentence. Furthermore, his status as an informant would be closely guarded throughout the investigation. Nobody would have to know anything.

'Yeah,' said Comas, with a knowing smile. 'But what happens if it goes to trial? Then what?'

That, replied the agent, was a definite possibility. The case against Featherstone and Coonan was strong. If he were called as a witness, there was nothing they could do about it. But he could go into the Witness Protection Program where he and his family would be guarded around the clock.

Comas shook his head and laughed. For a few seconds he sat mumbling to himself.

'Alright,' he said finally, looking none too pleased about it. 'I'll take a shot.'

Then he put his index finger up to his temple, as if it were the barrel of a loaded gun, and pulled the trigger.

12

THE WESTIES,
ONCE AND FOR ALL

The weeks following the February 1979 raids and arrest of
Ray Steen were marked by a flurry of activity. Once Ray
and Alberta began to tell their tales, it opened a treasure
trove of possibilities for the government. Ira Block and
the U.S. Attorney's office had the federal counterfeit
case, which looked to be strong even without the printing
plates. On the local level, the Whitehead homicide
investigation was beginning to come together. There
hadn't been any formal charges yet for the murder, but
the Manhattan District Attorney's office was about ready
to empanel a grand jury. And there was an assortment of
smaller violations, including gun possession and a parole
violation against Featherstone.

The authorities were still in the dark about a lot of
Coonan and his crew's activities, but from what they
did know, they figured they had enough to wage war
confident of victory. As ammunition, they had informants
like Steen, Sachs, Comas, and whoever else they might
be able to bring into the fold. As evidence, they had
the counterfeit notes Agent Malfi purchased from Steen

and other items seized in the raid on Featherstone's apartment. And they had mounds of incriminating taped phone conversations involving, among others, Mickey, Sissy, and Donald Mallay of the Westway Candy Store.

The only problem, as far as the government was concerned, was ferreting through the evidence and potential witnesses and deciding which cases should take priority.

In other words, it was a prosecutor's dream.

On a cloudy spring day in April 1979, Larry Hochheiser stood in his law office in the elegant Chrysler Building, overlooking the frenzied midday traffic on East 42nd Street. On a clear day, the view from Hochheiser's forty-ninth-floor window was spectacular; it took in the Empire State Building – just eight blocks south – the Manhattan and Brooklyn bridges, the East River and, in the distance, the enormous twin towers of the World Trade Center. Today, however, the view was gray and ominous, as a hovering mass of nimbus clouds hung over the city like smoke trapped in a bottle.

These were busy times for Hochheiser, now thirty-seven years old. He had just finished a staggering succession of trials, one right after the other, in state and federal court. It had been a good ten months since he'd had anything even remotely resembling a vacation. Now, having just closed the book on his most recent case, he was being asked to dive headlong once again into the wild and wicked world of Francis Featherstone.

Not that he had ever been all that far removed. In the seven years since Hochheiser first represented Mickey at the Linwood Willis murder trial, he'd developed a soft spot for Featherstone. Part of it was Mickey's puppylike devotion, which Hochheiser found endearing. For example, only a few weeks ago, when Hochheiser's wife Sandra was planning to attend a Broadway show and Mickey heard about it, he insisted she park for free in one of the many Hell's Kitchen parking lots. He even offered to meet her there and walk her to the theater. When Hochheiser told him it wasn't necessary, Mickey eagerly insisted. 'Hey, believe me, it's not a safe neighborhood. Your wife shouldn't be walking around at night without a bodyguard.'

Hochheiser laughed and said thanks, but he'd make other arrangements.

Featherstone's devotion was rooted in the Linwood Willis verdict. During that trial, Mickey had never expected to see the light of day again. What's more, he didn't seem to care. When Hochheiser pulled a rabbit out of his hat and got him an acquittal with the insanity defense, it literally gave Featherstone a reason to live.

Hochheiser also had fond memories of the Willis case, inasmuch as it more or less launched his career. Not long after that trial Hochheiser left the firm of Evseroff, Newman, and Sonenshine to begin his own practice. As expected, there were lean years spent building a clientele. But before long Hochheiser had earned a reputation as a tenacious courtroom performer especially adept at the fine art of cross-examination.

In the early months of 1975, the attorney had been doing well enough to take on a young, inexperienced associate by the name of Kenneth Aronson. Aronson, like Hochheiser, was Jewish. But that's where the similarities

311

ended. Hochheiser was six-foot-one with a forceful, slightly cynical nature. Aronson was five-foot-six, pale and soft-spoken. Born in 1949, Aronson was eight years younger than Hochheiser, but seemed even younger than that. Raised in a sedate, middle-class neighborhood of Valley Stream, Long Island, he had none of his senior partner's street smarts. Before hooking up with Hochheiser, in his two years with the Legal Aid Society in Brooklyn, he'd come to be known as something of a nebbish.

But Aronson had a dedication and an attention to detail that Hochheiser – the consummate courtroom performer – lacked. Those who knew Aronson sometimes called him 'Talmudic,' because of his willingness to spend hours and hours poring over documentation. Eventually, this became his forte. While other attorneys, including Hochheiser, derived sustenance from some of the more glamorous aspects of the profession, Aronson's satisfaction came in unearthing obscure statutes that often made the difference between conviction and acquittal.

Once the two men had established a rapport, the firm of Hochheiser and Aronson became the ideal legal partnership. Aronson spent his time preparing the cases, frequently working late into the night, and Hochheiser tried them in court. It was an arrangement that allowed both to focus on what they did best.

Aronson had only been with Hochheiser a short time when he first met Mickey Featherstone. It was May of '75, more than a year before Mickey was to form his criminal alliance with Jimmy Coonan. Mickey was about to be released on parole after serving five years for gun

312

possession in the Linwood Willis shooting, but he still faced charges for the John Riley and 'Mio' shootings.

Aronson was surprised when he first laid eyes on Featherstone in Manhattan criminal court, where he had arrived to represent Mickey before Judge Harold Rothwax. As with most people who knew Featherstone's résumé before they actually met him face to face, he was expecting someone bigger. Prison had taken a toll on Mickey, leaving him gaunt and frightened. His knees quivered, his hands shook, and he spoke in a wispy, uncertain little voice. Not exactly someone you would run for public office, thought Aronson, but certainly nobody's image of a Vietnam vet turned street killer.

Since then, the young attorney and Featherstone had spent a good deal of time together; much more, in fact, than Featherstone spent with Hochheiser. It was Aronson who negotiated the plea bargaining agreement that put Mickey back on the street in '75. And it was 'Kenny' who Mickey called, at home or at work, whenever he got into trouble. Aronson had a bit of the Jewish mother in him, and he was constantly doting over Mickey's health and well-being.

Ever since his release from prison in '75, a grateful Mickey had been steering business to his lawyers. Mostly, it was other folks like Mickey – Irish kids from Hell's Kitchen with little or no money. Generally they were burglary cases or barroom assaults, and the fees were based on what the client could afford – which usually wasn't much.

A typical example was a time in 1977 when Hochheiser and Aronson represented Richie Ryan. It was a few months before Ryan, the kid with the soft Irish face, took part in the Ruby Stein murder, where Jimmy first showed him the fine art of vivisection in the back of the 596 Club. This was a simple assault charge. The fee was only $2,500, but Ryan's payments still came in dribs and drabs – maybe $100 one month, $150 three months later. Finally, the lawyers told him to consider it paid. It would have taken a full-time bookkeeper just to keep track of what he owed.

It was also through their association with Featherstone that Hochheiser and Aronson first met Raymond Steen. In the mid-1970s they represented Steen on a mugging and robbery charge. After that, Steen was added to their regular client list.

Because they handled Steen, Aronson and Hochheiser were now able, in April of '79, to determine just how formidable Mickey's current legal predicament was going to be.

Following the police raids and Steen's arrest on February 9th, Aronson had called Rikers Island in an attempt to locate Raymond, assuming he would be needing legal representation. But word came back that Ray Steen was *refusing* to be represented by Hochheiser and Aronson. The way Aronson saw it, that could mean only one thing: Raymond Steen was cooperating with the authorities. The attorney passed his feelings along to Featherstone, who agreed that Ray must have flipped.

Within weeks, their worst fears were realized. On March 9th, exactly one month after the raids in Hell's Kitchen, Featherstone was surrounded by detectives at 55th Street and 10th Avenue. It was the middle of the day, and he was walking from his apartment to a check-cashing store on the corner.

'Okay, Mickey,' said Sergeant Tom McCabe, who was taking part in the arrest along with detectives from the 4th Homicide Zone. 'Let's make this simple as possible.'

'What's it for?' Featherstone calmly asked.

'Whitehead,' he was told.

'Nope,' said Mickey, 'you'll never make it stick.' Then he put out his hands for the cuffs.

Five weeks later, Jimmy Coonan was arrested in New Jersey for the same killing. While in custody at the Tombs, both he and Mickey were booked on federal counterfeit charges.

Days later, in a totally unexpected development, Featherstone was taken from custody by Sergeant Joe Coffey of the Homicide Task Force, driven to central booking in Queens and charged with the 1977 murder of Mickey Spillane – a murder he swore he didn't commit.

At Featherstone's arraignment on the counterfeit indictment in late April, Assistant U.S. Attorney Ira Block laid it all out for Ken Aronson. Block's indictment alone contained a whopping thirty-one counts. Then there were the two homicides, Whitehead in Manhattan and Spillane in Queens. In addition, there was a parole violation, plus other charges. Assuming conviction, Block told the lawyers Mickey was facing a *minimum* of fifty years, but it would probably be more like two hundred. Under normal circumstances, Aronson might have dismissed the prosecutor's claims as hyperbole. But as he surveyed the damage, he had to admit Block's projections were not unrealistic.

Block told the attorney he thought there was a way out.

'Yes?' asked Aronson.

'Get your client to become a cooperative witness.'

Aronson had been expecting Block to make the offer, though he wasn't looking forward to it. The idea of approaching a client with an offer like this was not something that pleased him. For one thing, if he was the messenger it might look to the client like he was the one pushing the idea. By the same token, if the offer was made and he neglected to convey it to the client, and that client later got convicted, he might be understandably upset at not having been given the option.

'Look,' Aronson told Block, 'here's what we can do. I'll bring my client to your office and tell him not to say anything. You tell him whatever you want to tell him.'

The day after the arraignment, Featherstone was brought to Ira Block's office at 1 St Andrews Plaza in lower Manhattan. Block made his pitch. After he was done, Mickey asked to talk to his attorney privately.

'Kenny,' he said firmly to Aronson after the Assistant U.S. Attorney had left the office. 'I'll do anything you and Larry ever want me to do. But never ask me to be a stool pigeon. No. Never. Fuck them.'

With that out of the way, the various legal parties were free to negotiate a plea. Featherstone's main concern was the charges against his wife. The feds had Sissy's voice on the wiretaps sounding a lot like an accomplice in the counterfeit operation. Also, in their search of the apartment they'd confiscated a large cache of counterfeit copper slugs. Apparently, Sissy and Alberta Sachs had been using the slugs in the washing machines in their apartment building and in place of tokens on the New Jersey Turnpike. In other circumstances it might have seemed laughable; but here it gave prosecutors the chance to add one more violation to the indictment.

The U.S. Attorney's office was willing to drop Sissy from the counterfeit indictment and allow her to plead guilty to a misdemeanor charge for possession of the copper slugs. But *only* if Mickey pleaded guilty to counterfeit possession, which carried a possible ten-year sentence. As for Coonan, they were willing to drop the counterfeit charge – not much of a concession, since they really didn't have anything linking him to the crime. But they did have Coonan on a gun possession charge – the gun that had been found in the trunk of his car following the night at Spartacus, the brothel on East 55th Street. For that, they wanted Jimmy to plead guilty to a five-year max.

With the Whitehead trial still pending and the counterfeit case virtually unwinnable, Featherstone and Coonan reluctantly agreed to accept the government's offer. Mickey copped a plea on the counterfeit charges, and Jimmy took the rap on the gun possession.

Hochheiser and Aronson were relieved to have the voluminous counterfeit indictment out of the way. But they were wary. They knew that for the government to allow those charges to go untried after such a lengthy and expensive undercover investigation, they must have felt they had a sure thing with the Whitehead case. Avoid a long and expensive federal trial, then nail 'em in state court on a murder rap. That, apparently, was the strategy.

317

Once again, normally Aronson and Hochheiser might have dismissed this strategy as bravado on the part of the prosecution. But as they began to focus their attentions on the Whitehead case, they got that sinking feeling they sometimes had when the evidence in a case came at them from all sides.

For one thing, there was the murder weapon. During the raid on Mickey Featherstone's apartment, the feds had found a .25-caliber Beretta sitting on a shelf in the bedroom closet. They photographed its location, dropped it in a cellophane bag, and added it to the long list of items seized. Later, during their debriefings with Raymond Steen, Steen was asked about the Whitey Whitehead murder. Steen said he'd never heard of Whitehead, but he did know something about a killing Mickey and Jimmy had done uptown at the Plaka Bar. The gun in that murder, Steen said, was the gun that was found in Mickey's apartment.

Ballistics ran a check, using the empty shell casing and bullet that were found on the bathroom floor where Whitehead was killed. *Bingo!* The casing and bullet matched the Beretta found in Featherstone's apartment.

The fact that the cops were able to ID the murder weapon had surprised the hell out of Coonan and Featherstone. They thought Jimmy McElroy got rid of the casing and the bullet on the night of the murder. In addition, Featherstone later gave the gun to Donald Mallay, their so-called expert gunsmith, and told him to make the gun untraceable. Mallay had altered the threading inside the barrel of the gun and told Mickey it could never be traced.

So much for criminal professionalism. McElroy fucked up, and Mickey and Jimmy should have gotten rid of the gun anyway, since ballistics experts matched the casing with the shooting mechanism, not the barrel.

As if finding the murder weapon weren't enough, it looked like there were going to be multiple eyewitness accounts of the Whitehead murder. Huggard, Crowell, and Comas had been identified as Whitehead's companions that night and would probably be subpoenaed. There was no telling what they would say once they were questioned.

Featherstone and Coonan, still protesting their innocence, told their attorneys that of the three people who might 'claim' to have witnessed the murder, there was only one they could be sure would 'do the right thing' – Bobby Huggard. Huggard, in fact, had originally been arrested as Harold Whitehead's killer. The greeting card from his girlfriend found next to the body had Huggard's fingerprints on it. But Huggard was a stand-up guy, willing to take the rap himself if he had to. Even while in custody, he kept his mouth shut. When Featherstone and Coonan were finally arrested and charged, Huggard was released – with a grand jury subpoena in his hand.

As for John Crowell, he was crazy and high-strung. There was no telling which way he was going to go. He'd been a friend of Whitehead's at one time and could be looking to exact revenge on Coonan and Featherstone. But Crowell was also a lifer who'd done enough time behind bars to have absorbed the jailhouse ethic. He would know that if you rat on somebody in a courtroom, quite possibly you or someone in your family winds up getting the worst of it.

Then there was fifty-five-year-old Billy Comas. Under normal circumstances, Coonan and Featherstone would have been able to vouch for Comas. He was tight with a lot of the West Side crowd, and especially close to Mickey and Sissy. But already they had been hearing disturbing rumors about Comas's cooperating with the cops on the counterfeit investigation. That didn't necessarily mean he would be taking the stand against them, but it sure as hell wasn't an encouraging sign.

It was still early. But as they got deeper into preparations for the Whitehead trial, Hochheiser and Aronson realized that Comas was potentially the most troublesome witness against them. John Crowell alone was not credible. The prosecution would need corroboration. If Coonan and Featherstone were right and Huggard could be expected to toe the line, then Comas was the man in the hot seat. He was the one who could do the most damage.

On March 22, 1979, two weeks after Featherstone's arrest, Officer Richie Egan and his partner, Detective Abe Ocasio, were driving north on 8th Avenue, heading towards Hell's Kitchen.

'You really think we're gonna find anything?' Egan asked his partner.

'Do you?'

'I don't know. You'd have asked me a month ago I woulda said no way. But now . . .' Egan's voice trailed off, the implication being that these days, with the stories they were hearing from Ray Steen and Alberta Sachs, anything was possible.

It was one of these stories that had launched Egan

and Ocasio on their current undertaking, the search of a basement at 442 West 50th Street. The building was a five-story tenement where Sachs used to live with her mother, Catherine Crotty, Edna Coonan's sister and Jimmy's sister-in-law. During a recent debriefing session, Alberta had told the cops about a night in November of '75 when her uncle Jimmy Coonan and Eddie Cummiskey came by the apartment to borrow some kitchen knives. About two hours later, she said, they returned carrying a plastic garbage bag with Paddy Dugan's head in it, and they told her they were going down to the basement to get rid of it. As far as Alberta knew, it was still down there somewhere.

The story about Paddy Dugan's head was just one of many outrageous yarns the cops had been hearing from Alberta and Ray Steen since they began their cooperation. Some of the stories, the cops figured, had to be horseshit – like Steen's claim that Jimmy Coonan had some kind of a machine he used to grind up human bodies.

'What kinda machine?' they asked Steen.

'You know,' said Ray. 'A machinelike thing. But first he drains the blood.'

Under normal circumstances the cops might have laughed, called Steen a whacko, and let it go at that. But there were so many outlandish stories about Coonan and Featherstone, coming from so many different sources, that eventually they had to take them seriously. After all, Paddy Dugan did disappear without a trace, as did Ugly Walter and Rickey Tassiello. Ruby Stein's severed torso did wash ashore out in Brooklyn. And there were about a dozen other known but unsolved homicides. Every lead, no matter how outrageous, had to be checked.

By the time Egan and Ocasio arrived at 442 West 50th there were two or three other cops from Intell's Syndicated Crime Unit there, including Sergeant Tom McCabe. There were also a few cops from the Crime Scene Unit, Detective John O'Connell from the Chief of Detectives office, and Greg Derkasch of the U.S. Secret Service.

Within minutes, Alberta Sachs arrived, accompanied by two armed U.S. marshals. Then the entire assemblage, led by Alberta, made its way to the basement of the building. It was a comical sight, this nineteen-year-old kid leading no less than a dozen cops and agents on what some might have called a wild-goose chase. But here they were.

Once they were in the basement and flicked on the lights, Alberta froze in her tracks. 'No. It's all different. Everything's different.'

The others watched silently as Alberta walked around the basement pointing out where her Uncle Jimmy used to take target practice, and where her boyfriend Ray used to shoot arrows at a dummy dressed up in his father's clothing.

But it was all changed now. Things had been moved around. Even the boiler was new.

The cops did a quick search of the premises. They found a wooden target with bullet holes in it from a small-caliber weapon. There were some holes in a wall that looked like bullet holes. They also found some hair particles that might be human hair, though it looked more like what it later proved to be: animal hair. The cops were out of the basement within an hour.

322

Egan and Ocasio laughed about it later that afternoon. Maybe they would have found Paddy Dugan's head down there, or human bones. Who the fuck knew? With the West Side investigation, just about anything was possible.

They were still chuckling about it when a call came over the radio at 3:45 P.M. They were told to get to a phone and telephone Alpha Base immediately. Both Egan and Ocasio knew it had to be serious if headquarters wasn't willing to put it out over the radio.

'Listen,' said Sergeant McCabe when Egan got him on the phone, 'get over to the Opera Hotel next to the Plaka Bar. You'll meet Donnelly and Aab there.'

'What's up?'

'It's Billy Comas. Some kind of trouble there, we're not sure what.'

As Egan maneuvered through traffic on the West Side, he thought about Comas and his refusal to testify in front of a grand jury investigating the Whitehead murder. Comas said his cooperation agreement with the feds only covered the counterfeit investigation. In fact, he'd already worn a recording device in his meetings with 'the Greeks,' just like he'd promised. But nobody told him the Manhattan D.A.'s office had big plans for him as their star witness in the Whitehead case. Nobody told him that he'd have to take the stand and rat on Jimmy Coonan and Mickey Featherstone, right there for all the world to see.

They were offering him the Witness Protection Program, but Comas wasn't crazy about it. He'd thrown a few temper tantrums already, claiming that the feds lied to him and set him up. But he wasn't getting a lot of sympathy. Now a date had been set for his appearance before the grand jury. There was no way out. He was destined for prison if he didn't show up and tell the full story. And destined for something worse if he did.

By the time Egan and Ocasio pulled up in front of the Opera Hotel at 2166 Broadway, a slew of cops was already there.

'Emergency Services just went up,' Detective Donnelly told Egan. 'We got reports of a shot fired.'

The police had commandeered the hotel elevators. There were at least fifteen cops now, including patrolmen from the 20th Precinct, detectives from Homicide, Intelligence cops, and Secret Service agents – just about everyone with an interest in the West Side investigation.

Egan arrived at Room 1505 within minutes of the Emergency Service Unit. It was a small room with a kitchen off to the right, a hallway to the left with a bathroom, and at the end of the hallway a tiny bedroom.

Egan entered the bedroom; there were three or four Emergency Service cops already there. On the floor, lying propped up next to the bed, was Billy Comas, short, gray-haired and balding. There was a bullet hole in his right temple, a .32-caliber automatic in his right hand.

Egan found out later that Comas had telephoned Ira Block in the U.S. Attorney's office and told him he'd made a decision to 'check out' rather than testify. The cops were immediately dispatched to Room 1505. They had been banging on the door when they heard the shot. When they burst in, this was how they found Comas.

In the days following the suicide, Egan and the other Intelligence cops wondered if Coonan and Featherstone had gotten word to Billy Comas that he better not take the witness stand. Or maybe Comas felt a sense of loyalty to the West Side guys and didn't want to become a rat. Or maybe it was something personal. Maybe his daughter, with whom he had a close relationship, was against the idea of disappearing into the Witness Protection Program, against having to assume a whole new identity and live a life of constant fear.

One thing was certain: Billy Uptown was now out of the picture. For good. And that didn't bode well for the prosecution in the upcoming Whitey Whitehead murder trial.

Billy Comas's untimely death soon became Topic A among everyone with a vested interest in the trial. To Hochheiser and Aronson, it was a godsend. Now that Comas was dead, he could be anything you wanted him to be – including the guy who shot Whitehead in the bathroom of the Opera Hotel.

As for the other potential witnesses in the case, the shot that killed Billy Comas had a particularly meaningful resonance, one that was certainly not lost on John Crowell.

On May 6, 1979, roughly six weeks after Comas's suicide, John Crowell made a trip to Rikers Island penitentiary, where both Mickey Featherstone and Jimmy Coonan were being held. It was a short trip from Crowell's apartment in Astoria to Rikers, just up the Brooklyn-Queens Expressway, near LaGuardia Airport. Crowell arrived in the middle of the afternoon, signed in under the name 'Murphy' and asked to see Jimmy Coonan.

Crowell had a lot of things on his mind. Before the Whitehead murder, his life had been looking pretty good. He'd just landed a steady job as a superintendent at the Ansonia Hotel, a landmark hotel near the Plaka Bar then under renovation. He was in charge of a crew of some thirty maintenance and construction workers. He'd also just begun a relationship with Victoria Karl, a woman he'd met one afternoon in Central Park. It wasn't exactly Easy Street, but Crowell's life was looking about as 'normal' as any ex-con, ex-heroin addict had a right to expect.

Then, purely by chance, he happened to stop by the Plaka Bar on the night of November 21, 1978, and things took a drastic turn for the worse.

In December '78, a few weeks after the murder, in a bar in the Bronx, Bobby Huggard claimed that Crowell was the one who had planted his girlfriend's love letter on Whitehead's body. Crowell insisted he didn't know what Huggard was talking about. From what he'd heard, it was Billy Comas who'd planted the letter on Whitehead's body.

But Huggard wasn't buying it. In the Bronx that night, he stabbed Crowell in the side with a six-inch blade. Luckily for Crowell, it was a short knife and the bar was crowded. The fight got broken up fast enough to let him escape alive – though with his insides hanging out.

After recuperating from the stab wound, Crowell was subpoenaed to appear before the grand jury. On April 18, 1979, he'd gone there like he was supposed to, but when he walked into the courtroom he froze. He wasn't even able to say his name. A judge threatened to cite him for contempt, but he still couldn't speak. Finally, after postponing his appearance for a week, Crowell was given total immunity from prosecution for anything he might say. On April 25th, he appeared before the grand jury and reluctantly told the complete story of what had happened in the Plaka Bar.

Now Crowell was terrified. Last month his old friend Billy Comas had killed himself rather than testify, which is precisely what the government was now asking him to do – in open court. Crowell knew it wasn't too late to run. His grand jury testimony was inadmissible unless he appeared at the trial. The way Crowell saw it, there were three things he could do. Testify in court and *probably* wind up dead; take the Billy Comas way out and *definitely* wind up dead; or go on the lam.

On May 6th, when Crowell arrived at Rikers Island, Coonan and Featherstone were being held in the same cell block and happened to be together in the recreation area when a guard informed Jimmy that there was a visitor to see him. Coonan wasn't expecting anyone, nor did he know anyone by the name 'Murphy.'

'You know who I bet it is?' Mickey said to Jimmy. 'Crowell.'

Jimmy smiled. 'Yeah.'

'Fuck it. This guy could be wired or any fuckin' thing. Don't go out there.'

'Nah, I'm gonna go. I'm gonna see what's goin' down.'

When Coonan arrived in the visiting area, there was Crowell, looking nervous and shifty as ever. Coonan walked over and sat down across the table from him.

'Hey,' said Crowell, by way of a greeting.

Coonan nodded his head. Since he wasn't sure whether

Crowell was wearing a wire, he planned on keeping his verbal responses to a minimum.

'You know,' said Crowell, 'this is some fuckin' jam you got me in.'

Jimmy shrugged.

'Man, this thing has ruined my whole life, you know. This thing is a big goddamn disaster . . . Don't know what I can do here.'

Jimmy studied Crowell. 'Well,' he said, 'what *are* you gonna do?'

'Yeah, alright, here's the deal. If I should decide not to testify . . . First of all, they know everything.'

'Who?'

'The cops, the government. I was in front of a grand jury.'

'So I heard.'

'There were others too, I heard. I dunno . . .'

'I know, I know. It's a real circus, the whole case.'

'Yeah. But I'm really in a mess here, my life.'

Crowell went on to tell Coonan that he didn't want to testify. But if he was going to run he needed 'financial assistance' and a false ID.

'Yeah,' said Jimmy. 'We could arrange that, maybe. If you're serious.'

Crowell let out a nervous laugh. '*Shit* . . . yes, god-damn.'

'Alright. Gonna give you a phone number. You call this number in a couple days. Give me time to work it out. See what I can do.'

For weeks after the May 6th meeting at Rikers Island, Crowell walked around in a daze. He'd called the number

Jimmy Coonan gave him. It turned out to be the number of a lawyer who put Crowell in contact with Jimmy's brother, Jackie Coonan.

Jackie told Crowell he had what was needed. Arrangements were made for Jackie to drop off a manila envelope for Crowell at the Ansonia Hotel. But Crowell got scared and stopped going into work. One day he called in and learned that the envelope had arrived. The next day he called again and asked a fellow worker to look inside the envelope. The guy looked at it and said there was $500 in cash, a blank New York Department of Motor Vehicles license, and other identification papers.

'Hey, Johnny,' his co-worker said. 'I don't wanna have nothin' to do with this, alright? Don't get me involved.'

Crowell never even picked up the money. All through the summer of '79, alone in his apartment, he thought a lot about his options – about going on the run, about suicide, about testifying. He hardly slept or ate or even went outdoors.

He just didn't know what the fuck he was going to do.

From the beginning, it was clear that the Whitey Whitehead murder trial was not going to be your average courtroom proceeding. Already, there had been the Comas suicide. That was followed by John Crowell's nearly having a cardiac arrest in front of the grand jury. Then came the most startling development of all. Judge Edward J. Greenfield, with a reputation as one of the more inventive judges in New York County, decided that the case would be tried before two entirely separate juries – a short-lived idea that nonetheless landed the trial on the front page of the *New York Times* on November 25, 1979.

The problem, as far as the judge was concerned, was the murder weapon. In one of their first 'motions to suppress,' Hochheiser and Aronson had contended that the gun found in Featherstone's apartment was inadmissible as evidence, since it was seized during an entirely unrelated counterfeit investigation. Judge Greenfield agreed that the gun was inadmissible against Coonan, but not against Featherstone. It had, after all, been found during a legally authorized search, and there was going to be testimony claiming the weapon belonged to Featherstone.

The government had given some thought to having two separate trials. But that would have taken too much time and been far too costly. Plus, the prosecution felt that if Hochheiser had a chance to familiarize himself with the witnesses at the first trial, it would give him a tremendous advantage at the second. The best alternative, proclaimed Judge Greenfield, was to have the defendants tried simultaneously by two juries in a single courtroom. When the gun was offered as evidence, the 'Coonan jury' would be excused from the courtroom.

Hochheiser and Aronson were dead set against the one trial, two-jury idea, as was Gustave Newman, Hochheiser's former associate at Evseroff, Newman, and Sonenshine, who they'd selected to represent Jimmy Coonan. The prosecutor, Assistant D.A. John Mullady, was initially for it. But he changed his mind after the judge's ruling began to receive extensive media attention in the *Times* and elsewhere. Assuming Coonan and Featherstone were convicted, the prosecutor felt the defense might have been able to use the highly unorthodox procedure as the basis for their appeals.

What Mullady agreed to do next surprised even Hochheiser, Aronson, and Newman. Not only was he willing to go with a single jury trial, but in order to do so he was willing to drop the gun as evidence against *either* Featherstone or Coonan. The murder weapon – the single most damaging piece of evidence against Featherstone – would not be entered. Mullady apparently felt they had a strong enough case without it.

On December 5, 1979, more than one year after Whitey Whitehead's killing in the basement of the Opera Hotel, the trial began in State Supreme Court at 100 Centre Street in lower Manhattan. An acrimonious tone was set early, as Hochheiser contended in his opening statement that the government witnesses were going to be 'desperate men of the worst possible character,' men who would say anything to 'satisfy their masters.' Assistant D.A. Mullady objected; Hochheiser objected to Mullady's objection. And so it went.

The bad feelings were genuine and had already reached a fever pitch before any of the witnesses ever took the stand. Much of the hostility was based on personality differences between Mullady, a humorless, somewhat priggish practitioner of the law, and Hochheiser, who viewed his profession as something of a contact sport. The die had been cast during a pre-trial conference when, during a heated argument in the judge's chambers, Mullady jumped out of his chair and challenged Hochheiser to a fistfight. From then on, Hochheiser knew he could push Mullady's button at will. He often did, especially with his outlandishly frequent motions for a mistrial (a total of sixty-five during the three-week trial).

One of Hochheiser's first motions created an incident that eventually wound up in the newspapers. Harold Whitehead's wife, an Irish-born waitress who would later be called to testify, stood in the spectator's gallery with her baby. The baby cried frequently, and Hochheiser called for a mistrial on the grounds that the baby was disruptive. He also claimed that the baby had probably been brought into the courtroom as a ploy by the prosecution, a 'pathetic' attempt to win the jury's sympathies.

When Assistant D.A. Mullady took exception to Hochheiser's claims and the judge turned down the motion, the defense came up with a ploy of their own. The next day Sissy Featherstone showed up with two-year-old Mickey, Jr, who also cried frequently. The *New York Post* later dubbed the incident 'the battle of the babies.'

Along with Hochheiser's antics, Mullady had other problems to worry about. He'd lined up an impressive number of cooperative informants as witnesses, people who would claim to have first-hand knowledge about Coonan, Featherstone, and the circumstances surrounding the murder of Whitey Whitehead. But as the assistant D.A. was about to find out, cooperative informants don't always make the best witnesses – especially when they present conflicting versions of the facts.

As his first big witness, Mullady called Raymond Steen. Freshly scrubbed and dressed in a fine new suit, Steen looked almost respectable. He was obviously nervous, and, at the tender age of twenty, seemed an ideal sympathetic character. Until he opened his mouth.

Not only did he sound like a thug, but as the jury, the audience, and a sizable press contingent listened, Steen revealed the first – though certainly not the last – major contradiction in the government's case.

According to Steen, on November 21, 1978, the day before the Whitehead murder, Mickey Featherstone had called his apartment and told him to bring over a .25-caliber Beretta that Steen was holding for him. When Steen gave the gun to Featherstone, Mickey supposedly said, 'Thanks. I gotta use this tonight on a guy in the Plaka Bar.' Weeks later, Steen said, he overheard Featherstone describing the murder to Donald Mallay at the Westway Candy Store. Featherstone laughed as he told Mallay that he was the one who shot Whitehead, and that Whitehead would not die.

'I shot him once,' Steen quoted Mickey as saying, 'and he wouldn't go down. So I hit him. I hoofed him. He turned purple but he still wouldn't go down.'

By itself, Steen's story might have seemed plausible. Indeed, Mullady had already used it in his opening statement to underscore the government's claim that the Whitehead murder had been carefully plotted ahead of time. Yet Whitehead's own wife, who had taken the stand only moments before Steen, said her husband went to the Plaka Bar that night purely on a whim; it had not been planned or premeditated. So how could Featherstone have known Whitehead was going to be there?

Hochheiser seized on this detail in his cross-examination of Steen. But it was still early in the trial and the discrepancy didn't even make the next day's papers. The reporters, almost all of whom were coming into the story with no real

333

knowledge of the West Side, were there mainly to hear what Steen had to say about an entirely different phenomenon – a phenomenon that they would turn, once and for all, into 'the Westies.'

The name had been bouncing around for some time. Ever since Sergeant Joe Coffey had used it last fall during his televised press conference at the site of the railyard diggings, there had been occasional references in the media to a 'loose confederation of West Side gangsters known as the Westies.' Though Coffey was the first to use the term publicly, he later claimed he'd gotten it from the cops in the Midtown North precinct. Whatever its origins, reporters liked the name. It fit nicely into a headline and evoked memories of previous Hell's Kitchen gangs.

Since Coonan and Featherstone's arrest for the Whitehead murder, the *New York Post* and the *Daily News* had written dozens of articles on the Westies, usually with unnamed cops as their sources. One of the first was an article in the *Post* that claimed, with little substantiation, that 'New York's notorious Irish mob, known as the Westies,' were responsible for, among other things, the gangland slayings of Carmine Galante, Anthony Russo, and Angelo Bruno from the Philadelphia mob. This was followed by a number of other articles connecting the Westies to a staggering array of mob hits.

Another *Post* article linked the late Eddie 'the Butcher' Cummiskey, 'the notorious Irish mobster,' with 'at least 30 murders.' The article was typical of many that appeared around the time of the Whitehead trial. Cummiskey's real casualty total was more like ten or twelve, but apparently that wasn't outrageous enough for the tabloids.

Perhaps the most widely read article of all was by *Daily News* writer Jimmy Breslin. In a column dated April 26, 1979, Breslin, already at the height of his fame, related the 'tortured tale' of Mickey Featherstone. Written in Breslin's inimitable style, it was largely a sympathetic piece presenting Mickey as a victim of war.

'Mickey Featherstone,' it began, 'discharged from the Army after serving as a Green Beret in Vietnam, stared at his sister. His face was the wall of a funeral parlor and his eyes were looking at a log fire that was something else.'

Breslin's article didn't mention the Westies by name; it didn't have to. That had been done elsewhere. What Breslin did by identifying Featherstone, at least symbolically, as *the* representative member of the Hell's Kitchen Irish Mob, was catapult the Westies into the city's consciousness, where the idea of an old-style Irish mob turned ugly by the horrors of Vietnam would take seed and eventually flower during the Whitehead murder trial.

As for Coonan, Featherstone, and the other West Side gangsters, they viewed the name with some amusement – at least initially. Although reactions varied from person to person, some gang members took pride in the notoriety they had achieved. But then the Westies began to get linked with mob hits they didn't have anything to do with, and the gangsters cried foul. Many blamed 'Publicity Joe' Coffey, who they felt was trying to advance his career by pinning a bunch of unsolved murders on the West Side Irish.

By the time of the Whitehead trial in December '79, Coonan and Featherstone's official position was to disassociate themselves from the name. The Westies, their lawyers complained to the press, was a media creation, an attempt by the cops and the newspapers to smear the Godfearing, taxpaying people of Hell's Kitchen. But the more they decried the name, the harder it seemed to stick, until many West Siders began secretly using it among themselves.

Later, after the Whitehead trial, the name would reach its apotheosis when a number of strange bumper stickers began to appear around the New York area. Mostly they were affixed to the rear bumper of cars with license plates from New Jersey, home of Jimmy Coonan. Modeled after the 'I Love New York' bumper stickers that used a red heart in place of the word 'Love,' these stickers read: 'I ♥ Westies.'

To some citizens of New York, the stickers might have held no special meaning. If they'd noticed them at all, they might have thought they were a reference to some country-western bar in Passaic. But to most cops, prosecutors, criminal defense lawyers, gangsters – and to those people in the city of New York who read their newspapers assiduously – there was another explanation.

As the cops and the press trumpeted the existence of the Westies, labeling them, among other things, 'the new Murder Inc.,' they catapulted Coonan's crew beyond the headlines into the mythology of the city.

*　　　*　　　*

Larry Hochheiser stood as close to John Crowell as he could; another two feet and he would have been sitting in the witness's lap.

'Sir,' he commanded. 'It is your claim, isn't it, that Mr Coonan, who you claim shot Mr Whitehead, it is your claim that he put the pistol to his head, isn't it?'

'Yes,' replied Crowell. 'He put the gun to his head.'

'What do you mean by that?'

'Just that it was pointed towards the head, and it was fired.'

'Tell this jury what your sworn testimony is today. Demonstrate on me, if you will, please, what you mean by putting a gun to his head and pulling the trigger. Would you like to step down? Assuming I am Mr Whitehead, show what you meant by that.'

John Crowell was flustered. In fact, he'd been flustered ever since he first took the witness stand the day before, on December 13, 1979. Just like the time he appeared before the grand jury months ago, Crowell was overcome with fear. As the entire courtroom watched silently, Judge Greenfield asked him to give his name and place of birth, but he couldn't. He couldn't speak at all.

A recess was called and Crowell was taken into a back room. After the jury filed out of the courtroom, Crowell's voice could be heard from behind the closed door.

'I don't wanna get killed! I got a family! They're gonna kill them!'

Hochheiser, Aronson, and all the other attorneys and spectators listened. In the back row of the gallery, Crowell's girlfriend, Victoria Karl, wept openly.

Two hours later Crowell was brought back into the

courtroom and put on the stand. Tentatively, in a voice barely audible even with a microphone, he began to give his version of what happened on November 22, 1978, in the basement of the Opera Hotel. He remembered going downstairs to the men's room to smoke a joint with his old prison buddies, Bobby Huggard, Billy Comas, and Whitey Whitehead. They were standing in a circle getting high. Then Jimmy Coonan came in. A few seconds later, Coonan stepped forward and shot Whitehead in the back of the head.

'What happened to Whitehead when you heard the shot?' the prosecutor asked.

'What happened to Whitehead?'

'Yes.'

'Whitehead's face went blank.'

'What did his face look like before he was shot?'

'Well, everybody was more or less in good spirits and laughing.'

'And then after? Describe what you mean by "blank".'

Crowell squirmed. 'Just went lifeless.'

'Can you show?'

'It was, pow, just dead.'

Crowell's description of the Whitehead murder and its aftermath had the ring of truth. Yet it presented the jury with a dilemma. Already they had heard Ray Steen say it was Mickey Featherstone who planned to kill Whitehead and then bragged about it afterwards. Following Steen, the prosecution called another witness, Robert Bruno, to back him up. Bruno claimed that he, Featherstone, and Mugsy Ritter – the guy Whitehead called a fag on the night in question – got together shortly after the killing

338

went down. Again, Featherstone supposedly bragged that he was the one who had shot Whitey.

Now here was Crowell, who had actually seen the murder take place. But if the jury was to believe Crowell, then the testimony of Steen and Bruno was contradictory at best, and at worst, just plain untruthful.

For the better part of a day, Hochheiser, and then Coonan's attorney, Gus Newman, banged away at Crowell. Of particular interest to the defense lawyers was an incident in 1972 when Crowell had slit a guy's throat in the backseat of a taxi when a methadone deal he was making went bad. There were other arrests for assault and drug use. Even Crowell's personal life was portrayed as being outside the bounds of normal behavior. At one point Hochheiser asked him, 'By the way, your girlfriend, Victoria, does she carry a whip?'

'Yeah, she had a whip.'

'What was her business or occupation?'

'From what I know, it's dominatrix.'

'I was just curious.'

As he had with Steen and Bruno, Hochheiser wanted to show the jury that Crowell was a witness 'of the lowest possible character.' Yet he also knew that Crowell's version of the murder may have raised the specter of reasonable doubt, which was alright with him. The jury had been hearing for days that Mickey Featherstone was the killer. Now Crowell was saying in no uncertain terms that it was Coonan. Hochheiser used this turn of events not only to bolster Mickey's position as a 'maligned innocent,' but to characterize the government's case as 'specious' and the prosecutor as totally incompetent.

339

The jury, apparently, was buying it, and during the second week of testimony they took matters into their own hands. They were being asked to choose between the Steen/Bruno version and the Crowell version of the murder, but there was another person they kept hearing about. A person who all of the witnesses claimed had been in the bathroom when Whitey Whitehead got shot.

The day after Crowell's testimony, the jury foreman passed a note to the clerk, who passed it to the judge. It contained three simple words: 'Where is Huggard?'

Currently, Bobby Huggard was being held at Rikers Island. He'd been called before the grand jury to testify on the Whitehead shooting and had given a version of the facts that didn't quite square with the other testimony. Subsequently, the grand jury had indicted him for perjury.

'Is there some way we can accommodate the jury?' Judge Greenfield asked the lawyers.

Mullady had no intention of calling Bobby Huggard. He already had his hands full with Steen, Bruno, and Crowell. Even with immunity, he knew, chances were that Huggard would stick with his original testimony. In fact, Mullady had asked Huggard after his grand jury appearance whether he was going to 'straighten up and fly right' in time for the trial. Huggard had answered, 'I got a cock. I got balls. Know what I mean? I'm a man. You do what you gotta do.'

As for Hochheiser and Newman, it was obviously to their advantage to have Huggard take the stand and give his version of the facts. Except for one thing: They had based their entire defense on denigrating the government's witnesses as 'scumbags' and 'lowlifes.' They couldn't very well call Huggard, who had a criminal record even more unsavory than the others, and say to the jury, 'Now listen to *my* scumbag; he's telling the truth.'

After both the defense and the prosecution made it clear that they would not call Huggard, Judge Greenfield came up with a shocking alternative. *He* would call Huggard. *He* would ask the questions. Then the prosecution and the defense would have a chance to cross-examine.

Greenfield waited until both the prosecution and defense had rested their cases to call Bobby Huggard to the stand. As Featherstone and Coonan had predicted, Huggard 'did the right thing' – and then some. He testified that he had been in the Plaka Bar on the night in question. He'd had a few drinks with Whitey Whitehead at the bar, then left. At no time did he see Mickey Featherstone, Jimmy Coonan, or John Crowell. Furthermore, he claimed to have had a discussion with Billy Comas a few weeks after Whitehead was murdered in which Comas had said that he, Comas, was the one who did the killing.

The jury was stunned. This was the first time anyone – the defense, the prosecution or the judge – had heard of this alleged meeting between Comas and Huggard.

'Exactly what was said?' asked Judge Greenfield. 'Tell us how the conversation began, how the subject was raised.'

'Yes, Your Honor. Mr Comas said that he had information that I was going around getting drunk, talking in bars about the Whitehead incident.'

'What did you say?'

'I denied it.'

'What did he say?'

'He said, "Well, you know, I took care of him and if there is any more conversations the same thing will happen to you."'

By the time Mullady got up to cross-examine Huggard, viciously attacking his credibility, the damage was already done. Huggard had fingered a dead man. And the jury had yet another possible scenario to contend with.

As the jury deliberated, Featherstone, Coonan, and their counsel waited anxiously. Throughout the trial Featherstone and Coonan had sat next to each other, Mickey usually dressed in his blue suit, Coonan in brown. At times they acted like brothers; one would have his arm around the other. They seemed to have grown even closer as the trial wore on.

No one could be certain what the verdict would be. But just in case, Aronson thought he'd better prepare his client.

'You know, Mickey,' he said one afternoon. 'It could happen that the jury might come through with an acquittal for you but a conviction for Jimmy. That's very possible.'

Featherstone had paid close attention to the proceedings. Ever since he and Jimmy had been arrested for the murder, Mickey had felt guilty as hell. Yes, he had been pissed off at Coonan before. He had gone ahead and sold the counterfeit notes even though Jimmy told him it was too risky, even though he knew Ray Steen was dealing with an undercover cop. But he had never expected Steen to flip. That had touched off a series of arrests and a lot of 'innocent' people had been dragged into this mess.

342

Mickey never wanted it to turn out this way. If Coonan were convicted and he wasn't, he'd never be able to show his face in the neighborhood – or in prison – again. In criminal circles, he'd be seen as a classic fuck-up.

'No,' he told Aronson, emphatically. 'That's no good, Kenny. That can't be.'

On the evening of December 21st, after nearly six hours of deliberation, the jury filed back into the courtroom. As Hochheiser waited, he could feel the tension mounting. He wanted an acquittal in this case more than any he had ever tried. He felt he owed it to Gus Newman, his friend and former associate, who had agreed to represent Coonan as a favor to him. Also, throughout the trial Hochheiser's dislike for the prosecutor, Mullady, had grown. As far as he was concerned, the constant gibes had gotten personal. At one point during a recess Mullady had even suggested that Hochheiser was being paid by the Brooklyn Mafia to represent the Westies. Hochheiser had to laugh at that; he would be lucky to get any money out of his client at all.

As the jury members filed past the defendants and took their seats in the jury box, they seemed to be avoiding eye contact. Hochheiser took this as a bad sign. 'Look,' he said to the others at his table, 'whatever happens, let's be gentlemen, alright? This guy Mullady expects us to act like scumbags. Nothing will piss him off more than us just walking out of here like gentlemen.'

Then, to Hochheiser's surprise, Mullady, standing no more than twenty feet across the aisle, began to let him have it.

'Hey, Hochheiser,' he said under his breath. 'You told the jury all about our tricks. You think you know. Well, you been out of the D.A.'s office for a long time, my friend. We got new tricks.'

Hochheiser was astonished. Judging by the way the jury looked, he thought he had lost the case. Now here was this prick rubbing it in.

The jury took their seats and the clerk called for quiet. The jury foreman handed the clerk a sheet of paper. Speaking in a voice that echoed to the far corners of the room, the clerk announced, 'The jury finds the defendant, Francis Featherstone . . . not guilty.'

A loud gasp of relief came from the audience. Many of Mickey's family were there, including Sissy. The rest of the gallery was made up largely of Jimmy and Mickey's Hell's Kitchen friends.

The clerk cleared his throat and spoke again. 'The jury finds the second defendant, James Coonan . . . not guilty.'

Some in the audience cheered. Coonan and Featherstone embraced. The reporters seated in the first two rows of the gallery swarmed towards the attorneys, notepads in hand.

Larry Hochheiser turned to congratulate the assistant D.A., who looked stunned, his face drained of color, his shoulders slumped.

'Well, John,' said Hochheiser, sarcastically, 'you tried a good case. It could have gone either way.'

Mullady attempted to raise his arm to shake hands, but his arm was limp.

The following day, all three daily newspapers carried reports on the verdict. In the *New York Post* one of the jurors was quoted as saying, 'It was a weak case.' The

344

jury *knew* that Coonan and Featherstone were somehow involved in Whitehead's death. They knew it was possible they were pardoning two people who had perhaps killed a man in cold blood. But what could they do?

'The government witnesses,' the juror said, 'that was the problem. We thought most of them were lying through their teeth.'

Within months of the verdict, another of the government's key witnesses 'did the right thing.' John Crowell, who, though terrified, had given the only honest firsthand account of the Whitehead murder, followed in Billy Comas's footsteps after all. On October 29, 1980, Crowell was found in his apartment in the Ansonia Hotel with a self-inflicted bullet hole in his right temple.

After Whitehead and Comas, Crowell was now the third casualty from that lone night of brutality in the basement of the Opera Hotel.

To the cops and the prosecutors, the Whitehead verdict and related suicides were a shocking defeat. The whole West Side investigation had reached a crescendo during the trial, with frequent revelations about the dreaded Westies in the *Post*, the *News*, and the *Times*. The Whitehead verdict was supposed to be the grand finale, with the criminal justice system once and for all smashing the Hell's Kitchen Irish Mob. Instead, the trial had been a disaster, with a key witness killing himself beforehand, the murder weapon getting thrown out, and people flagrantly perjuring themselves on the stand.

It was a fucking travesty, as far as Egan, Coffey, and

345

the other cops close to the investigation were concerned. It was an example of everything that was wrong with 'the system.'

But that was only the beginning. Six months after the Whitehead verdict, in June of 1980, Mickey Featherstone was acquitted of the Mickey Spillane murder. Unlike the Whitehead case, which initially appeared to be solid, the Spillane case was thin from the start. All the government had to offer as witnesses were Ray Steen and Alberta Sachs, both of whom claimed that Mickey told them he was the one who did the shooting. Once again, Hochheiser built his defense around the government's use of 'disreputable witnesses.' It took the jury less than three hours to deliver its verdict.

Then came a trial that, to the cops, was the most maddening of all. Also in the summer of 1980, Hochheiser and Aronson represented Jimmy McElroy, who, after months on the lam in Arizona, had been caught and sent back to stand trial for the murder of William 'Billy' Walker. The trial was of special interest to Joe Coffey's Homicide Task Force, since this was the murder that had gotten Coffey involved in the West Side investigation in the first place.

It looked like an open-and-shut case. In the Sunbrite Bar on 10th Avenue McElroy had gotten into an argument with Billy Walker, who he knew from their work together in the stagehands' union. Then, along with Jack Paulstein, McElroy took Walker for a ride in his van to the West 79th Street boat basin, where he stuck a .32 in Walker's mouth and pulled the trigger.

As their main witness, the government produced

Paulstein, who gave a devastating firsthand account of the shooting. Larry Hochheiser went home that night thinking he had lost the case. Then he came back the next day and did a truly creative number on Paulstein, attacking him for being *too* certain of the facts to be telling the truth. The jury took nine hours to deliberate. When they came back they not only exonerated McElroy, but one of the jurors was quoted as saying he thought Paulstein was the murderer; he wanted to meet McElroy and shake his hand.

With three razzle-dazzle courtroom victories in a row, Hochheiser and Aronson became folk heroes in criminal circles on the West Side of Manhattan – and the scourge of the NYPD.

As crushing as the defeats may have been for the cops and prosecutors involved, there was one major consolation. In early 1980, Coonan and Featherstone had been sentenced on the respective gun possession and counterfeit charges they'd pled guilty to before the Whitehead trial ever began. On January 15, 1980, before Judge Lawrence Pierce in U.S. District Court, Jimmy Coonan was given nearly the maximum sentence on his charge, four years and six months. One month later, on February 14, Featherstone was also brought before Judge Pierce. Pierce listened as Larry Hochheiser pleaded for leniency due to Mickey's 'troubled psychiatric history.' The judge was not swayed.

'Mr Featherstone,' said Pierce, after giving Mickey a six-year sentence. 'The war in Vietnam is over.'

For the first time, Mickey Featherstone and Jimmy Coonan would be serving simultaneous prison terms.

It wasn't as definitive as the various cops, agents and prosecutors had hoped for. They wanted to put Coonan and Featherstone away for life. But with the two most renowned West Side gangsters going off to prison, they felt reasonably certain that the Westies, so recently lionized in the press, were now a thing of the past.

They could not have been more mistaken.

PART THREE

PART THREE

13

BAD BLOOD

By January 1981, Coonan and Featherstone may have been safely tucked away in federal prisons – Coonan in Pennsylvania and Featherstone in Missouri and then Wisconsin – but the publicity surrounding the Whitehead trial helped elevate Jimmy and Mickey's reputations to unprecedented heights. The Hell's Kitchen Mob had always been known within the city's criminal underworld. But now, with blaring headlines about dismemberment murders, suicidal witnesses, and stunning courtroom victories, the Westies were known and feared in virtually every saloon and union hall west of 5th Avenue.

Coonan's and Featherstone's incarceration also marked the departure of full-time police surveillance on the West Side. Even though it had not been as conclusive as the cops had hoped, the investigation, which lasted over two years, was considered a success. Richie Egan, who along with Sergeant Tom McCabe had spearheaded *West Side Story* from its inception, was relocated to Brooklyn, where he immediately went to work on a case involving Colombian drug traffickers. Sergeant Joe Coffey and his Homicide Task Force also moved on, turning their attention back to the Italians. Soon they would become enmeshed in a massive racketeering investigation involving, among others, Paul Castellano and the Gambino family.

The cops may have moved on, but the rackets remained the same. There was still loansharking, gambling, narcotics, tribute from the piers, extortion of the ILA and the Teamsters.

And even from prison, Jimmy Coonan still controlled the purse strings. Given that his four-and-a-half-year sentence was likely to be shortened with parole, it would have been fatally shortsighted for anyone to try and move in on Coonan's territory simply because he was gone from the neighborhood for awhile. Consequently, the proper respect was accorded Jimmy's wife, Edna, who now made the rounds in Hell's Kitchen collecting Jimmy's weekly payments. Just in case, she sometimes took along Richie Ryan or Jimmy McElroy for protection.

In Coonan's absence, one of the Westies' most lucrative rackets continued to stem from their relationship with Vincent 'Vinnie' Leone, business manager of ILA Local 1909 and a long-time shill for the Gambino family. Leone had gone into business with the Irish Mob following Coonan and Featherstone's meeting with Paul Castellano at Tommaso's Restaurant. A loud and gregarious old-time union official, the silver-haired Leone helped lead the Westies into new areas of extortion.

First, there was the outdoor concert season on Pier 82, sponsored every summer by the Miller Brewing Company. Leone saw to it that every stagehand and carpenter who worked the concerts kicked back a portion of his or her wages to the Local, part of which was passed on to Edna Coonan when she made her weekly rounds. She also picked up a portion of the proceeds from the concerts, which were almost always sellouts involving top name acts such as Elton John, Miles Davis, and Diana Ross.

Then there was the USS *Intrepid*, docked directly across from the Local 1909 offices at West 48th Street. A massive aircraft carrier that had seen distinguished service in World War II and in Vietnam, the ship was opened as a museum in early 1982. Through Temco Service Industries, the ILA controlled some thirty jobs on board, including ticket takers, engineers, and general maintenance personnel.

Almost from the day it opened, the *Intrepid* Air-Sea-Space Museum became the Westies' private bounty. Sissy Featherstone and some of the other gang members' wives worked there as ticket takers. In time, Sissy and the girls devised a little money-making scam of their own. They would save previously sold tickets, resell them, and keep the profits for themselves, sometimes taking home an extra two or three hundred a day. After another Westie, Kenny Shannon, became the timekeeper at the *Intrepid*, Sissy stopped coming to work altogether – except, of course, to pick up her weekly paycheck.

The *Intrepid* also became a great way to dole out favors and settle old scores. In August of 1982 Bobby Huggard was put to work on the *Intrepid*. Huggard had been an okay guy with the Westies ever since he perjured himself at the Whitey Whitehead murder trial and almost single-handedly secured an acquittal for Coonan and

Featherstone. After the trial, in a holding pen at Rikers Island, Jimmy Coonan thanked Huggard and told him if ever he needed a job he would have no problem getting one on the West Side of Manhattan.

Once on the *Intrepid* payroll, Huggard was told to do absolutely nothing, for which he was paid a handsome $227 a week. A couple of times he even showed up for work. But he quickly became bored and only showed up on Fridays to get his paycheck – one of a growing list of Westie-related 'no-shows.'

Of all the extortions that flourished in Jimmy's and Mickey's absence, perhaps the most lucrative came from Teamsters Local 817, the theatrical truckers union that delivered props and cameras to and from movie locations. In the early 1980s, with the dramatic increase in movies and commercials being filmed in New York, the Teamsters signed a new contract with the entertainment industry. As a result, drivers for 817 became among the highest paid of any Teamster local in the city. The captain or field boss on an individual job earned somewhere around $2,000 for a five-day week; a driver just under $1,800; a helper just over $1,700.

Local 817 had always been good for something. Back in the mid and late 1970s, when the Local's main offices were located on 9th Avenue between 41st and 42nd streets, Coonan frequently suggested to his people that they sign on with the Teamsters. That way they would have documented employment, which would keep their parole officers happy and give them a better shot at getting bail if they were ever arrested. Not many took him up on it at the time, but through Coonan the West Side

Mob had always kept one foot in the door. When Local 817's wage rates increased in the early '80s, the Westies sought to make the Local their own.

For a legitimate worker, full-time membership in the union took years to secure. First you had to be sponsored by a union member. After that, you could begin shaping-up for work at one of the many prop and trucking outlets on the West Side affiliated with Local 817. Eventually, if you stuck with it long enough, you might be eligible for one of the Local's seven hundred or so union cards or 'books,' which guaranteed you work without having to shape.

In 1982, while Coonan was away in prison, Thomas 'Tommy' O'Donnell, long-time president of Local 817, proclaimed that he was going to purge the union's membership of its traditional gangster element. To do this, O'Donnell turned to what he believed to be a *rival* gangster element, the Italians, and took out a contract on Jimmy Coonan – or at least that's what the Westies were told by the Italians.

In response, Jimmy McElroy and Kevin Kelly, a relative of Jimmy Mac's through marriage and an up-and-coming Westie in his own right, made a trip out to Local 817's new offices in Nassau County, Long Island. They pistol-whipped O'Donnell in his office and slapped around Edward Fanning, the Local's vice-president, out in the parking lot. The two men were told that from now on, whenever Jimmy Coonan or one of his people needed a union book, it was to be given to them immediately. O'Donnell said that there were only so many union books; the best he could offer was that Coonan's people would be given preferential treatment when they shaped-up for a job.

'Oh yeah?' McElroy replied. 'Well then, we're gonna kill one union member a week till there's enough openings for our people.'

The West Side boys had no trouble getting union books after that. McElroy, Kelly, Richie Ryan, Coonan's younger brother Eddie, and others became card-carrying union members with erratic work records. As Jimmy Mac later joked, 'You gotta be a sleeper, a drinker, or a card player to be a member [of Local 817].'

Throughout the early '80s, the Westies' fortunes grew in other areas as well. Narcotics, which Jimmy Coonan had always frowned on, became a profitable racket in his absence. Fifty-year-old Tommy Collins, his wife Florence, and their son Michael became neighborhood coke dealers, selling grams out of their apartment in the Clinton Towers building on 11th Avenue and 54th Street. Mugsy Ritter, forty years old, black-haired, and mustachioed, and a young neighborhood kid, Billy Bokun, whose distinguishing characteristic was a garish red birthmark that covered the right side of his face, also went into the cocaine-selling business.

Sports betting also became a more organized and lucrative racket in the early '80s. James 'Jimmy' Judge, superintendent of a building on West 55th Street just off 9th Avenue, ran a thriving gambling business in his basement office. It was bankrolled by, among others, Vinnie Leone, Jimmy McElroy, Kevin Kelly, and Kenny Shannon – the timekeeper at the *Intrepid*.

As the rackets flourished, the specter of violence

continued to hover over Hell's Kitchen, though the backdrop had changed. In November of '81, Edward I. Koch was reelected to a second term as mayor. In the previous four years, he'd presided over a hectic period of development throughout the city. His reelection assured more of the same. Gentrification, a by-product of the Koch years, became a common word in the city's lexicon as wealthy real estate barons, in the absence of strict zoning laws, ran roughshod over long-standing communities.

As a low-income neighborhood in close proximity to the theater district and midtown Manhattan, Hell's Kitchen was ripe for development. In the late 1970s and early '80s, huge office towers servicing some of the most powerful law and advertising firms in the world went up along 8th Avenue. Condominiums and co-op apartment buildings were being constructed to house the financial analysts, lawyers, and investment bankers who now worked in the area. Inevitably, long-time residents were displaced.

But the violence that had characterized the area for generations continued, as if the neighborhood were going through its last death throes before being reincarnated as 'Clinton,' the name for Hell's Kitchen now favored by real estate interests. Between 1981 and 1983 there were at least seven unsolved homicides believed to be Westie-related.

One involved Henny Diaz, a low-level neighborhood gambler. In January of '81, Diaz was last seen heading to a party at Manhattan Plaza, a recently built forty-six-story apartment complex on 43rd and 10th Avenue. The next time Diaz was spotted, he was flying through the air after having been tossed out the window of Manhattan Plaza in the middle of the afternoon. He landed on a car parked on 10th Avenue.

The autopsy showed that Diaz had been dead for days, possibly even a week, from multiple stab wounds. The rumor around the neighborhood was that Diaz had been murdered during a gambling dispute. His dead body lay in the bathtub of an apartment at Manhattan Plaza at least three days before the killer decided to toss it out the window.

Police questioned nearly every tenant in the building, but nobody knew nothin'. It would go down in the books as one more unsolved homicide in Hell's Kitchen, the neighborhood where dead bodies literally fell out of the sky.

An even more outrageous killing, one that sent shock-waves through the neighborhood more than any murder since Paddy Dugan blew away his best friend Denis Curley in August of '75, was the murder of Tommy Hess in the 596 Club. Hess, who'd been a bartender in the saloon since the early 1970s, supposedly had slapped a girlfriend of twenty-eight-year-old Richie Ryan's one night in another neighborhood bar. Ryan and Hess were once good pals. They'd both been in the 596 Club the day Ruby Stein got whacked. Hess had stood guard outside while Jimmy C showed Richie how to dice up a human body. But in recent years Richie Ryan had become uncontrollable. He was shooting dope into his veins and drinking a fifth of whiskey a day. Once known for his pleasant good looks, he was now bloated, burned out, and more violent than ever.

In retaliation for Tommy Hess's having smacked his woman, Ryan came into the 596 Club on the night of February 26, 1982, and pistol-whipped his former friend. Then, in front of numerous unnamed witnesses, he pulled Hess's pants down around his ankles, stuck a revolver up his rectum and squeezed the trigger.

Everyone fled from the bar. By the time the cops arrived, Hess was dead and there wasn't a witness in sight.

It was an act worthy of the bar's previous owner, Jimmy Coonan, who'd divested himself of the 596 Club in 1979. Not long after the murder of Tommy Hess the bar closed, then reopened under the name T-Bags as a respectable 'fern bar' geared towards the neighborhood's newer residents. Long gone were the memories of Denis Curley, Ruby Stein, Tommy Hess, and dozens of others whose blood had been shed at the same location over the generations.

At the same time that Hell's Kitchen was undergoing its latest transformation, Mickey Featherstone had been shipped out to Springfield, Missouri, and then a federal penitentiary in Oxford, Wisconsin. He was doing his time quietly for a change. It was his first stint ever in the federal system, and he was surprised by the amount of time devoted to actual therapy and rehabilitation. Among other things, he wasn't immediately pumped with psychotropic drugs designed to neutralize his behavior, as he had been in his earlier stays in hospitals and prisons throughout New York State.

His daily routine included regular afternoons of group therapy. It had taken him awhile to get used to the idea of acknowledging his problems even to himself, much less to a group of inmates. But after a few months, he began to look forward to these sessions. He had never really talked freely about his life with people like himself, people from the street. He was amazed to find other inmates who felt the same way about things as he did. In one session, he even wept openly – something he'd never done in front of anyone, other than Sissy, in a long, long time.

Far from the streets of Hell's Kitchen, Featherstone began to feel an optimism and peacefulness that seemed overwhelming at times, as if it were part of some purification process he did not, or could not, fully understand. On one occasion, he tried to explain these emotions when he wrote to his friends and lawyers, Larry Hochheiser and Ken Aronson.

'Hi all,' he began, in a letter dated July 28, 1982. Mickey had just come from a parole hearing, and he wanted to let Hochheiser and Aronson know how well it went. 'I'm really shocked,' he wrote. 'I can't really believe the way things are starting to turn out for me!' After promising his lawyers that he was determined to stay out of trouble from now on, he thanked them for all they'd done to help him. 'I don't know how I could ever pay you back in the way of money, but if there were a way I would. But you didn't save me for money reasons, but for a very rare kind of love for which I'll always love and remember you.'

It was signed, 'I love you all, Mickey.'

On July 26, 1983, after serving just over four years of his six-year sentence, Mickey Featherstone was paroled and released to a halfway house in Newark, New Jersey. He spent a few weeks there before being reunited with his wife and family, which now included their ten-year-old niece, Esther, who had moved in with Sissy following the suicide death of Sissy's sister.

Shaken by her sister's sudden death – the sixth of Sissy's eleven brothers and sisters to die from either an overdose, murder, or suicide – she and the two kids had moved out of the neighborhood and into a small apartment in New Milford, New Jersey. Sissy had a steady income from her job at the *Intrepid* and other assorted financial dribs and drabs: $100 a week from white-haired Tommy Collins, who owed Mickey $5,000 from a shylock loan; $1,000 every now and then from Mugsy Ritter's coke business; and $150 a week from the neighborhood bookmaking operation, which she received from Edna.

The pittance from Edna was a source of bitterness that had festered inside Sissy since the day Mickey was arrested in early 1979. While she was constantly hustling around to make ends meet, Edna was raking in thousands every week just by making Jimmy's old rounds. Initially, she had even accompanied Edna on her shylock runs just to make sure she and Mickey got their cut. In the months during and after the Whitehead trial, she and Edna would come back from Rikers Island after visiting their husbands, and spend the afternoon trying to hunt down the likes of Tommy Collins, Tony Lucich, and dozens of others.

'It's funny,' Edna would say, munching on a hot dog while driving the Coonans' big Caddy. 'When your husband goes away, nobody wants to pay. They always seem to disappear on you. Well, when Jimmy gets back, he'll take care of 'em.'

Eventually, Sissy got fed up with the whole thing. She grew tired of watching Edna stuff her face and brag about all the possessions they had in their New Jersey 'mansion.' Sissy finally cut her ties with Edna and, after moving to New Milford, with just about everybody else in the old neighborhood as well. She knew that Mickey was getting screwed out of money just because he was away in prison. She knew that people were using his name in their various criminal dealings and not paying him for it. But she tried not to let it bother her. She had been trying to get Mickey to cut his ties with Coonan and his people for a long time anyway. So maybe this was all for the better.

When Mickey got back in August of '83, they talked about it. He was upset that his wife had not been taken care of. In Hell's Kitchen, it had always been understood that if one of the neighborhood people wound up in prison, the other gang members were supposed to look out for his family. It was a tradition that had existed since the earliest days of West Side gangsterism. It annoyed Mickey that Coonan and the others had not lived up to their end of the bargain. But, like Sissy, he was not going to let it bother him. Still basking in his new 'positive attitude,' which he had acquired in the prison therapy sessions, he was determined to try and make it on his own, away from Hell's Kitchen, away from the Westies.

Mickey's first big test came in September '83, just a few weeks after he returned from the halfway house in Newark. Late one afternoon he drove into Manhattan to pick up Sissy from work at the *Intrepid* Air-Sea-Space Museum. He was waiting outside, leaning against his car when along came silver-haired Vinnie Leone, whose office was less than two blocks away.

The burly forty-eight-year-old union boss gave Mickey a big hug and said how nice it was to have him back. He asked Mickey to come over to the office to say hi to 'the guys.'

There were three or four men playing cards at a table in the front room when Leone and Featherstone entered the red-bricked ILA offices. Mickey recognized John Potter, who he and Coonan had once shook down at the Landmark Tavern, and Tommy Ryan, whom he also knew from his dealings with the ILA. Mickey shook hands with Potter and Ryan, then Leone led him into a back office.

'I was just up to see Jimmy a week ago,' said Vinnie, as they sat down across the desk from one another.

'Yeah,' answered Mickey. 'How is he?'

'Good, good. You know Jimmy.'

'Yeah.'

'Hey, Mick, everybody's real happy to have you back here. No shit. Things've been goin' good, real good.'

To illustrate his point, Leone pulled a wad of bills out of his pocket and peeled off a few twenties.

'Here,' he said, handing some money to Mickey. 'Here's a hundred. But that's chickenshit. Just some chump change to get you started. They'll be more from now on. Way more.'

'Nah,' said Mickey, 'that's alright.'

'What?'

'No, thanks. I don't want it.'

Leone laughed and tried to stick the bills in Mickey's shirt pocket. 'C'mon, take it, you crazy bastard.'

'Nah. Look, Vinnie, I appreciate what you're doin'. Don't get me wrong. But I got a clean slate right now; I'd rather just go my own way.'

Leone stared at Featherstone. 'Wait. Am I hearin' this? Mickey-fuckin'-Featherstone? This is a fuckin' joke, right? That's what this is.'

'No, Vinnie, I'm serious. I just wanna give it a try.'

Leone stuck the bills back in his pants pocket. 'Okay, Mick, but I gotta tell ya, Jimmy C ain't gonna like this one bit.'

Mickey just shrugged.

For a while, Featherstone did his best to maintain the pact he'd made with himself and his wife. His brother-in-law got him a job as a bartender at the Cameo Lounge, a catering hall in Garfield, New Jersey, where he made a modest living wage. Mickey and Sissy's most immediate problem was their apartment. It was far too small to accommodate a family of four.

Ever since they'd had their first child, the Featherstones dreamed of having a big house far from Hell's Kitchen. Both Mickey and Sissy knew all too well what it was like to grow up amidst the street violence, drugs, and assorted other perils that plagued the West Side. They'd seen how Jimmy Coonan, by moving away from the neighborhood, was able to insulate his family not only from the daily violence of Hell's Kitchen, but from the constant threats and dangers they might have faced because of his life as a gangster.

Jimmy Coonan's children, they were sure, didn't

get ostracized at school because their old man was a well-known criminal in the neighborhood. Jimmy and Edna Coonan, they were sure, didn't have to deal with landlords who wanted to evict them for being undesirable tenants.

For weeks following Mickey's return from prison, he and Sissy spent their weekends driving around New Jersey looking for a house. They didn't really have enough money to buy anything at the moment, but they could dream.

One day in the fall of '83, they saw a house they both loved on Newbridge Road in Teaneck, New Jersey, just thirty minutes from midtown Manhattan. It was a split-level Colonial, with a separate room for the baby, a swimming pool, and a big front yard. The mortgage was a reasonable $92,000, and the realtor said he would give it to them for $5,000 down.

That night they discussed their options. They knew they weren't likely to find anything that suited their needs as well as this house. But the money was a problem. They had so little saved up that if they were to spend it all on the down payment and closing fees they would be totally wiped out.

The way Mickey saw it, there was only one way to go. 'Let me try Jimmy,' he said. 'Just this one time.'

Sissy was against the idea. As bad as she wanted the house, she knew that if they borrowed the money from Coonan, it would come with a price tag that far exceeded the money itself. But Mickey was persistent. He was certain there would be no problem getting a loan from Jimmy on the up-and-up.

'Jimmy owes me,' reasoned Mickey. 'He knows he owes me. Besides, if it does come with any strings attached, I'll just say no.'

Reluctantly, Sissy acquiesced.

A few weeks later, in October, Mickey went to see Edna Coonan at her home in Hazlet. In a way, he was upset he had to beg like this, though he was trying not to think of it as begging. As far as he was concerned, it was money Jimmy had promised him. After the Whitehead verdict three and a half years earlier, just before Mickey was shipped out to Missouri, he and Jimmy had said their farewells at Rikers Island. 'Don't worry,' Jimmy told him. 'I'll take care of your wife and kids. We been through hell together. When you get out? There's gonna be fifty grand – cash – just waitin' for you.'

When Mickey got out, he asked around. No fifty grand.

Now, here he was sitting in Edna's kitchen asking to borrow forty grand. And he was even offering to pay it back once he went to work with Teamsters Local 817, like he was planning.

Edna's response? 'Gee, Mickey, I don't know. I gotta talk to Jimmy about that.'

Two weeks later Mickey got his answer, and it didn't even come from Edna. It came from Bobby Herman, a neighborhood guy. Herman told Mickey that he heard from Edna's brother, Joe Crotty, who heard from Edna, who heard from Jimmy, that the answer on the loan was 'No.'

At first Mickey was shocked. 'After all the shit I been through with Jimmy Coonan?' he asked himself. 'After all the times I put my life on the line for this guy? Ain't

366

nobody knows what I done for this guy except me and one person: Jimmy Coonan. And this ungrateful motherfucker tells me no? Unreal.'

Sissy said she wasn't surprised at all; she had expected it. But Mickey just couldn't believe Jimmy would treat him this way.

In November of '83, just four weeks after Mickey's meeting with Edna, he and Sissy received an invitation to an engagement party for the Coonans' oldest son, Bobby. The party was to be held in a large room at the Hazlet, New Jersey, firehouse, and everyone from the old neighborhood was expected to attend. Edna had even rented a bus to pick up a group of people in front of the Skyline Motor Inn on 10th Avenue and transport them to and from Hazlet.

'I can't believe this bitch,' said Sissy when they got the invitation. 'She treats us like dogs then expects us to come to an engagement party?'

Mickey, on the other hand, was anxious to go. He knew there would be a lot of people there from the old neighborhood, some of whom he hadn't seen in years. And there was the pride factor. 'We can't let her think she controls our lives,' he said. 'We'll go there and hold our heads up just like everybody else.'

There was snow on the ground that night as over one hundred West Siders gathered at the firehouse in Hazlet. Edna had hired a live band, so there was dancing, and tables had been set up around the room for people to sit and talk. It was a festive atmosphere, with everyone drinking and getting reacquainted.

The only thing missing was Jimmy Coonan. Jimmy had recently received parole and was actually out of jail for a few months. But then the Manhattan D.A.'s office nabbed him on an old assault conviction stemming from the Vanderbilt Evans shooting way back in 1975. As a result, Jimmy would be spending at least another twelve months behind bars.

Midway through the evening Edna Coonan came over to Mickey and Sissy's table. She was dressed in a bright-red gown and had her dyed-black hair fastened with a bow. Edna had never really been what anyone would call a knockout, and in recent years she had put on a lot of weight, so much so that behind her back some neighborhood people called her a 'cow.'

'Mickey, do you need a drink?' she asked.

'Sure,' he replied. 'I'll take a spritzer.'

When Edna returned, she handed Mickey his drink and asked, 'Can I talk to you, Mickey?'

He turned his chair slightly so it was facing Edna, who took the vacant seat to his left.

'Jimmy told me to talk to you,' she said, sounding deadly serious.

'What's up?'

'He's got a proposition for you, seein' as you need money and all. He's willin' to turn over the piers to you, the whole thing. But you gotta do somethin' for him.'

'Yeah?'

Edna explained how there were three people Jimmy wanted Mickey to kill. The first was Bull Maher, a neighborhood guy who'd been seated at Mickey's table just a few minutes earlier. According to Edna, Jimmy had found out that Maher, who sometimes picked up ILA envelopes for Jimmy in New York, had been steaming open the envelopes and reading private correspondence between Coonan and his criminal associates.

'Jimmy wants him put outta business,' declared Edna. 'Bull wouldn't even be in the shylock business if it wasn't for Jimmy. Jimmy says, "Youse do whatever you gotta do, but his shylock days is over."'

The second person was Edna's own ex, Billy Beattie. Rumor had it that Beattie, who'd fled from Hell's Kitchen years earlier after failing to kill Tommy Collins, was recently seen in one of the neighborhood bars. As far as Coonan was concerned, Beattie had run out on his debts, which were somewhere in the six figures at the time.

'Jimmy wants him dead,' said Edna, stone-faced, 'and so do I.'

The third person was Vinnie Leone, who, even as Edna spoke, was seated with his wife directly across the table.

'This bastard's been rippin' us off,' she said under her breath. 'I seen it myself. I been over at his house last week. He's got these antiques, statues like, and artwork all over the place. Stuff that's worth thousands, maybe millions. Now where's he gettin' the dough-ray-me, huh? You oughta see this stuff. It's like a damn museum!

'Jimmy wants him dead,' she said. 'The sooner the better.'

Mickey listened to all this impassively without saying a word.

'Edna,' he finally said when she was done, 'I don't want it. Don't want no part of this shit.'

'Mickey, this is serious. This is business.'

'I know what it is. I don't want it.'

Edna stared into her drink. 'Okay, Mickey. But Jimmy's gonna be very disappointed.'

Mickey shrugged.

'I mean,' she added, 'you know this is gonna get done, whether you do it or somebody else. It's gonna get done.'

'That ain't my problem. That's your problem.'

After Edna went back out on the dance floor, Sissy turned to her husband. She'd heard bits and pieces of the conversation and was barely able to contain her anger. 'Are you gettin' involved with these fucking people? Are you gettin' involved again?'

Mickey and Sissy argued at the table for awhile. Mickey was trying to explain that he'd said no to Edna's proposition, but Sissy was so upset she was hardly listening. 'That treacherous bitch!' she kept saying over and over.

Things got even stranger later on, when Mickey and Sissy drove through the snow to the Coonan house, where the party continued with a smaller group of neighborhood people. They were all in the kitchen drinking, waxing nostalgic about the old days, when Edna said she needed to talk to Mickey again. Edna and Mickey went downstairs to the recreation room.

At first, Edna started in again on the people Jimmy wanted to have whacked. Mickey remained adamant, saying he was on his own now. Then Edna started to act weird. She was standing rubbing her back up against the wall, striking what she thought was a seductive pose.

'See those matches?' she said, nodding towards a clear glass bowl filled with matchbooks from dozens of different bars and restaurants. 'Collected all those since

370

Jimmy's been away. I ain't sittin' around doin' nothin' this time. I been havin' a good time.'

Just then Sissy came downstairs. She looked at Edna, who'd walked over to the couch and was now stretched out, and at Mickey standing nearby with his drink.

'What the fuck is goin' on here?' she demanded.

'Nothin's goin' on,' said Mickey, as Edna sat up. 'Just the same old shit.'

By then Sissy could no longer contain herself. She laid into Edna, calling her a 'fat cunt' and a 'treacherous bitch' and every other insult she could think of. Edna just sat there like she was above it all.

'You just remember,' snarled Sissy, grabbing Mickey to leave. 'You keep that fuckin' husband of yours outta our lives or I'll come back here and burn this goddamn house to the ground.'

Things quieted down for the Featherstones after that, at least temporarily. Mickey's brother Henry got him a job at Erie Transfer, a garage affiliated with Teamsters Local 817 that rented trucks and automobiles to the entertainment industry. It was located at 52nd Street and 11th Avenue in Hell's Kitchen. Mickey didn't have his union book yet, but he was getting work almost every day by shaping up.

Soon, however, he was back to using cocaine, which fueled his bitterness towards Edna and Jimmy. 'He's got some balls havin' his wife give me an order like that,' he would say of Jimmy over and over again.

Mickey could feel the anger and hatred eating away at his insides. After all the bloodshed, all the trials and prison time, this is what he got in return?

The cocaine and alcohol were supposed to help ease the pain. But what they really did was draw him back into the same frame of mind he'd been in before he got 're-habilitated.'

Jimmy McElroy was standing on the balcony of his 11th Avenue apartment, looking out at the Hudson River and the banks of New Jersey to the west. In his hand was a .25 with a silencer on it. From the couch in McElroy's front room, Mickey Featherstone and Jimmy Mac's young in-law, Kevin Kelly, watched as he raised the gun and started firing, as if he were trying to shoot holes in the clear blue afternoon sky. It was mid-February 1984, three months since Edna's party in Hazlet.

Kevin Kelly laughed. 'Get in here, you bug. We know the fuckin' thing works.'

There was a half-gram of coke spread out on the coffee table, and they'd all done a few lines. McElroy and Kelly were giggling, and so was Mickey. It had been a long time since Mickey had hung out in the neighborhood and gotten high. It felt good, just like the old days.

In the years since Mickey went away to prison, both McElroy and Kelly had made considerable inroads with Jimmy Coonan. McElroy had always had a reputation as one of the neighborhood's most feared tough guys. But he had no business sense whatsoever. Everybody knew that. A self-styled ladies' man who'd recently given himself the nickname 'Studs,' he was the kind of guy who never thought more than four or five hours ahead. 'A bell-head,' one of McElroy's girlfriends, Fran Mostyn, used to call him – though never to his face.

Jimmy Mac liked to tell stories about when he worked briefly as a doorman at the luxurious Plaza Hotel on 5th Avenue. A couple of Arab sheiks, he claimed, were regular customers at the hotel. When they heard Mac used to be a boxer, they gave him $100 and asked him to come by their room late one night.

'What for?' asked Mac.

'Just come by,' said one of the sheiks, clad in traditional Arab dress.

When he arrived at the room that night, one of the sheiks asked McElroy to slap the other one around.

'Wait a minute,' said Mac, 'what're youse two? Wackos?'

But they offered him another $100, so, as requested, Jimmy slapped one of the sheiks around the room while the other one watched.

Featherstone used to ask McElroy to tell this story time and time again. He always got a good laugh out of it.

Only McElroy could have gotten away with a stunt like leaving the shell casing and bullet in the bathroom of the Opera Hotel the night Coonan stiffed Whitey Whitehead. McElroy had been told by Featherstone to get rid of *all* the casings that night, but he panicked. Mickey asked him about it later. McElroy replied, 'Gee, Mick, I *thought* I got 'em all. Honest.' Anybody else and Mickey would have thought it was a deliberate plant. But you had to make allowances for Jimmy Mac.

Kevin Kelly, on the other hand, was considered to be a cut above the average thug. In recent years, he'd come out of nowhere to assume a position of leadership in West Side criminal circles. Born in 1955, he was eight or nine years younger than McElroy and Featherstone – a member of the generation that had grown up hearing stories about Jimmy Coonan and Mickey Featherstone, dreaming of the day when they would get their shot at the neighborhood's lucrative rackets.

Kelly was born on West 56th Street just off 9th Avenue. His godfather was James McManus, the district leader. With his neatly trimmed black hair and thick black eyebrows, Kevin had been told he looked like Matt Dillon, the handsome young actor. Since his marriage to Kim McElroy, Jimmy Mac's niece, he and the elder gangster had gotten close. Kim was expecting a baby, and Kevin had already told Jimmy he wanted him to be the godfather. Sometimes they also did business together, like, for instance, the day they smacked around O'Donnell and Fanning of the theatrical Teamsters Local 817 at their offices out in Long Island.

At five-foot-seven and 140 pounds, Kelly wasn't much of a physical threat. On top of everything else, he was an epileptic – not exactly the kind of guy you'd want at your side in a neighborhood rumble. But like so many of the smaller guys in Hell's Kitchen, Kelly rarely went anywhere without a gun. And he knew how to use it.

When Mickey first returned from Wisconsin, he'd been hearing that Kevin was now thought of as Jimmy's protégé. Mickey had always been wary of Kevin, and this only reaffirmed his suspicions. The way he saw it, the kid was a bit *too* ambitious.

There was that time on 11th Avenue just after Mickey returned from prison. A group of neighborhood guys were hanging out in front of McElroy's apartment building.

Everybody was telling Mickey how well the rackets had been going since he went away. Eventually, Kevin had taken him aside and asked, 'Hey, Mick, next time we whack somebody, I was hopin' maybe you could show me how you and Jimmy made those guys do the Houdini. Know what I'm sayin'?'

'That's not my thing,' Mickey replied. 'I can't, you know, I can't handle it.'

Kevin started laughing and slapped Mickey on the back. 'Yeah, come to think of it Jimmy told me that once. He said you get sick like a dog every time they cut open the belly.'

Kevin reminded Mickey of Jimmy Coonan when he said that – something about the way he laughed when he talked about dismemberment.

Now, months later, Featherstone found himself seated next to Kelly in McElroy's apartment, and he knew exactly why they had called him here. He'd heard about it a few days earlier. It was a killing. Vinnie Leone had finally been whacked out in Jersey. Edna was right. It got done one way or another. And from the moment he heard about it, Mickey had a sneaking suspicion that the ambitious pretty-boy, Kevin Kelly, had something to do with it.

'You know what this is about?' asked Kelly, bent over the coffee table to do another line.

'Yeah,' said Mickey. 'I got a pretty good idea.'

'Vinnie Leone.'

'That's what I figured. You wanna tell me about it?'

'The fuck deserved it,' said McElroy, jumping into the conversation. 'That guinea bastard's been rippin' us off since day one.'

McElroy explained how Leone, who was their partner in the sports-betting operation being run out of Jimmy Judge's basement, had been 'past-posting.' He would call in after certain games were over and claim he had accepted late bets from various bettors and lost. Then he would take money out of the business, supposedly to pay off the losing bets. But really, McElroy said, it was going back into Vinnie Leone's pocket. Over the last few months alone he'd taken out something like $30,000.

'How'd you find out about it?' asked Mickey.

'This fucking guy,' said Jimmy Mac, 'was running his mouth off out in Jersey, to people in Jersey bars; saying he's making assholes out of us, that he's robbing the Irish kids blind.'

When Kelly and McElroy heard that Mickey had turned Edna down, they visited Jimmy at the Clinton Correctional Facility in upstate New York and offered their services.

'We wanted this guy dead, Mick,' said Kelly. 'Somebody had to do it.'

'Yeah,' answered Mickey, not wanting to commit himself one way or the other. 'So how'd it go down?'

With great enthusiasm, McElroy and Kelly explained how a week earlier, on the afternoon of February 11th, they met Leone at the Local 1909 offices on 12th Avenue. Leone lived out in Jersey near one of McElroy's girlfriends, and they had asked if he'd be willing to drop them off on his way home. 'Sure,' Leone said.

In the car, McElroy told Vinnie they had some good coke they wanted to try out. Vinnie was game, so he pulled off the expressway in Guttenberg, New Jersey, and stopped on Bellevue Avenue, an idyllic tree-lined suburban street. Kelly was in the backseat, McElroy in the passenger's seat, and Leone behind the wheel.

From the back, Kevin handed Vinnie the packet of coke. Vinnie carefully opened the pyramid paper, talking nonstop, as he was sometimes known to do. He dipped the corner of one of his car keys into the coke, put it to his nose, and inhaled. He leaned his head back to savor the effect. The coke worked its way through his sinuses to his brain, stimulating his nerve endings and causing a sudden rush of stark clarity and euphoria.

Just then, from behind, Kevin Kelly put a small-caliber automatic to the base of Vinnie's skull and began firing. He emptied the chamber, firing six shots when one would have easily done the job. Leone's head and brains sprayed like watermelon over the inside of the windshield. Particles of flesh splattered on Jimmy McElroy, who had his fingers pressed to his ears, trying to block out the deafening sound of gunfire. Kelly hadn't even used a silencer.

McElroy had almost panicked, but he laughed about it now as he related the story to Featherstone. The windows in the car had all been rolled up, he said, and the shots were so loud that they rang in his ears for hours afterwards.

After the shooting, they fled to McElroy's girlfriend's place, where they quickly changed clothes. Then they met Billy Bokun, the young kid with the birthmark on his face, who was waiting for them at an agreed-upon spot nearby. Bokun drove them back into Manhattan, where they destroyed the clothes and got rid of the gun they'd used on Leone.

'Yeah,' McElroy told Featherstone. 'Then we went to visit our man. You know, Blondie, Jimmy C. We told him we took care of that fuck and now we wanted the piers, just like he said.'

'And?'

'He said, "You got it, you know. Long as Mickey's in it with youse."'

Okay, thought Mickey, so they finally got to the point. He had suspected this was why they called him here in the first place. Ever since he turned Edna down, he'd known it was coming. There was no way Jimmy Coonan was going to let him walk away from the Westies. No way. McElroy and Kelly were trying to make it sound nice, like the piers were being handed to him on a silver platter. But what this really was, he knew, was his last chance.

Without saying so, they were letting him know that if he didn't go in with them now, he would be following in Vinnie Leone's footsteps.

Featherstone was ready for this – so ready he even had a little speech prepared.

'Alright, youse two listen to me for a minute. You fuckin' guys wouldn't be nowhere if it wasn't for me and the sweat off my balls that made Jimmy Coonan what he is today. All the time I put myself out for this guy? Everybody used my name, and youse know it. Everybody. People get rich using my name, they don't even tell me. Nothin'.'

'Hey,' said Jimmy Mac, 'that's why it's gotta be different this time.'

'Definitely.'

'Mickey, that was Coonan, not us.'

378

Featherstone could feel the cocaine loosening his tongue; his words poured out in a nonstop torrent. 'Let me tell youse. Nobody took care of my wife and kids when I was inside, that's another thing youse know is true. Nobody. You want me back in the crew? Okay. But things is gonna be different, see? 'Cause I ain't in it for friendship this time. I ain't in it for loyalty no more. I'm in it for money. Youse people used me enough, man.'

Kelly and McElroy both assured him that things would be different this time, that the piers were now theirs to do with as they pleased. From now on, anytime Mickey's name was used by any member of the crew for any transaction, Mickey would get his cut.

'We'll make sure of that,' promised Kelly.

As for Mickey's family and kids, never again would they be hung out to dry. That was Jimmy Coonan, they said over and over. Everybody knew he'd done wrong.

Hours later, on the drive back to New Jersey, Mickey thought about what he'd done. The 'positive outlook' he'd had in those months when he first returned from prison had been slowly eroded by the alcohol, the cocaine, and the rage he was feeling inside. By the time the moment finally arrived – the moment where he was faced with the crucial decision of what he would do with his life – there was never any question. He wasn't about to just sit there and let them take advantage of him. He wasn't about to 'take it up the ass.'

Mickey thought about loyalty. Loyalty was the thing Jimmy Coonan had always talked about. It was the thing that supposedly made the West Side gang invulnerable. And it wasn't just Coonan. The entire neighborhood had demanded loyalty, and Mickey felt he had come through for them. At one time, he would gladly have taken a bullet for Jimmy if he'd been asked to, and he'd have taken a bullet for the rest of the Westies.

But all that was bullshit, and now Mickey knew it. He'd been used, that was all. And he felt like a douche bag for having taken so long to figure it out.

It made him feel depressed, too, in a way. This was not what he had wanted. For the last few years he had harbored dreams of a halfway normal life. But that was all down the toilet now.

Within days Mickey's sadness disappeared and was replaced by anger. Anger at those who, he felt, had forced him into this position.

The first order of business was ILA Local 1909. McElroy and Kelly had long suspected Tommy Ryan, who Mickey shook hands with when Leone brought him around the shop, of skimming their waterfront profits with Vinnie. John Potter, who seemed to have forgotten his encounter with Coonan and Featherstone at the Landmark Tavern six years earlier, might also have been in on it, though they weren't sure about him.

In late February 1984, two weeks after the Vinnie Leone murder, Featherstone, McElroy, and Kelly set up a meeting with Potter and Ryan at the Madison Diner, one of the neighborhood's oldest diner/bars, at 57th Street and 11th Avenue. The meeting was set for one in the afternoon. Potter and Ryan were already there when Featherstone arrived.

Both in their fifties, the two veteran union officials

were well aware of the brutal interplay that often went on between the mob and organized labor. But still, to have their business manager disappear overnight had been an unsettling development. Now, at the Madison Diner, the sight of Mickey Featherstone taking a seat across the table reduced them both to helpless, quivering old men.

'Hey, Mick,' said John Potter, his hand trembling as he tried to maneuver a cup of coffee from its saucer to his mouth.

Tommy Ryan chose not to speak. He put a cigarette in his mouth and attempted to light it. But his hand was shaking so bad he accidentally knocked the cigarette from his mouth into his lap.

'Take it easy, man,' said Featherstone. 'Nobody's gonna hurt youse.'

There was terror in Tommy Ryan's eyes. He stared at his broken cigarette, unable to look Mickey in the face.

Featherstone spoke sternly. 'Just don't lie, Tommy. They know you was part of, you know, stealin' with Vinnie. If you're straight with Kevin and Jimmy, nothin' bad'll happen.'

When Kelly and McElroy arrived, they sat down at the table with Potter, Ryan, and Featherstone. There was a sizable lunchtime trade in the diner, including many dock-workers and neighborhood folks who recognized one or all of the guys seated at Mickey's table. Occasionally, someone passing by would say hello.

'You're lucky,' said Kevin Kelly, pointing a finger at Tommy Ryan. 'You're lucky you didn't go too. We know what you and Vinnie were doing.'

Kelly went on to explain that from now on Jimmy

Coonan didn't want Ryan handling the money at all. John Potter would now be responsible for the proceeds from illegal activities along the waterfront. Kelly told Ryan, 'You just . . . you don't touch nothin' no more and you'll still get yours, you know, your end of the money. But this is it. One more fuck-up and you might wind up just like that other bastard. Okay?'

The very next day, they each got their first envelope, which contained $1,100 in cash. Thereafter, Featherstone, Kelly, McElroy, Coonan, Potter, and Ryan received the same amount each week. Eventually, this group would be expanded to include Kenny Shannon. Thirty years old, slender, with a thick head of sandy-blond hair that was turning prematurely gray, Shannon was originally from Manhattan's Upper East Side. It was Kevin Kelly who'd first introduced him to the Hell's Kitchen crowd and gotten him his job as a timekeeper on the *Intrepid*. Since then he was known to almost everyone as Kelly's 'gofer.'

With the ILA taken care of, the next problem was Jay Gee Motor Homes. Jay Gee was a West Side business that rented large campers to film and television companies. Kevin Kelly had heard that at a recent meeting with organized crime figures, some hotshot from Jay Gee was saying he had the Westies under his control; there would be no union problems or anything like that, he said, because the Westies were his own private crew. According to Kelly, this person from Jay Gee had the balls to specifically mention Mickey Featherstone as being 'his guy.'

Mickey was pissed. This was exactly the kind of thing he was determined would never happen again.

Featherstone, McElroy, and Kelly hopped in a car and drove to Jay Gee's garage, located on 59th Street between 11th and 12th avenues. McElroy came out of the front offices with a guy named Joe, who was supposedly the president of Jay Gee, and another guy named Vic.

Mickey told Jimmy Mac and Kevin to take Vic 'for a walk.' Then he turned to Joe. 'Listen, man. I understand you was usin' my name with some of your business people, and I don't even know you.'

'Holy fuck. Who told you?'

'Don't worry 'bout who told me. I wanna know why you're usin' my name. You don't know me.'

The color drained from Joe's face. 'Uh, look, I just thought we, you, 'cause of the West Side and all . . .'

'Hey, I don't wanna hear about that. You don't know me, and if you're gonna use my name in your business, then you *sure as fuck* are gonna pay me for it. And if you don't pay me for it and I understand you've been usin' my name, I'm gonna put you out of business.'

By this point, Joe had started trembling. There were tears in his eyes.

'Don't start cryin' now,' said Mickey. 'Don't start puttin' on an act. That don't mean nothin' to me.'

'Smack the fuck in the face!' shouted McElroy, who was standing near the garage entrance with Kelly.

'You remember my words,' said Mickey to Joe.

The third and final order of business Mickey had to take care of was with Bull Maher. Maher was the older brother of Dick Maher, the kid who accompanied Alberta Sachs to the sit-down at Tommaso's Restaurant in '78 (but no relation to James Maher, the union official Coonan and Featherstone plotted to kill later that same year). In recent years, Bull had been helping Edna Coonan pick up loan-shark proceeds in Jimmy's absence. But he'd run afoul of Coonan when Edna determined he was opening the envelopes and reading Jimmy's private correspondence.

Apparently, Maher had heard that Coonan put a contract out on him for 'moving in on his shylock territory.' Maher immediately started calling in his loans, with the intention of recouping as much of his outlay as possible before splitting town. When McElroy – never a business whiz – and Kelly heard what Maher was up to, they decided to kill him for Jimmy Coonan.

'Look,' Mickey told them. 'You kill the guy, you don't get nothin'. What if I make him give us $30,000? We leave him alone, we get $30,000 plus we get his business.'

Kelly and McElroy agreed.

The next day Maher agreed to meet them near the baseball fields on 11th Avenue at 52nd Street. They found him sitting in the shade, sipping on a beer and watching a softball game.

Featherstone had known Bull Maher all his life, as had Kelly and McElroy. Mickey always liked Bull. They had been in a bar softball league together and played often at this very park. When Mickey saw Bull sitting there watch-ing a bunch of kids playing ball, it reminded him of how he and Bull had practically grown up together.

'Let me talk to him alone,' Mickey said to the others.

Maher was over thirty years old, but he looked like a helpless child as Mickey walked over and sat down next to him. Featherstone rested his hands on his knees and spoke firmly. 'You know what this is all about, I'm sure, Bull?'

'Yeah, Mickey.'

'We all know about you pullin' in your loans to recoup your money, and I'm tellin' ya, if you don't own up thirty grand, plus your shylock book, you're gonna get killed, man.'

'You want thirty grand plus my book?'

'That's it.'

'Man, Mickey, you know that's gonna wipe me out. I'm in a bit of a situation here.'

'Hey, Bull, I may be the only friend you got. Since I get back from prison, everybody in the neighborhood's been tellin' me they want you dead. Coonan. His fuckin' wife. Kevin and Jimmy Mac. Believe me when I say it – this is the best deal you're gonna get.'

Bull's eyes began to well up with tears.

'Hey,' said Mickey, 'it ain't so bad. We'll get you a job with the Teamsters.'

The next day Maher forked over thirty grand, along with his list of shylock customers and what they owed. There was around forty grand or so in outstanding loans, which, once collected, was to be split between Mickey, Jimmy Mac, Kevin Kelly, and Kenny Shannon.

Everybody was pleased with the score, except Mickey. Sure, the money was great. The problem was seeing Bull Maher sitting there crying like a baby. It reminded him of all those times, years ago, when he'd gone with Coonan on his shylock runs and seen the neighborhood people reduced to tears. At one time he got off on it. But times had changed.

Mickey was making about $4,000 a week now, more money than he'd ever made in his life. But he'd become something he did not want to be, something he had promised himself and his wife he would never become.

He had become just like Jimmy Coonan.

And yet, unlike Coonan, Mickey was not able to reconcile his life as a gangster with his new suburban home life. With the money he'd been making through his illegal activities, he was able to buy his and Sissy's dream house in Teaneck. Each night, after running the various neighborhood extortions, he would drive home to his family. Sissy had given birth to another baby boy, Danny, in early '84, and they'd just learned she was pregnant again. It was all supposed to make Mickey proud – the wife, the kids, the nice house.

But the old dreams had started up again. Dreams of horror and violence.

Around this time, in November of '84, Mickey spoke to Charlie Boyle, his father, on the phone. Boyle, now a U.S. Customs agent, had been hearing stories about how his son was back on the West Side. Mickey and his dad had never really been close. Since his parents moved to the Bronx way back in the early '70s, Mickey had hardly ever spoken to them.

Charlie Boyle sensed Mickey's agitation and despair. He had a feeling that now that Mickey was living the gangster's life again, he was sure to wind up in prison – or dead.

'The cemetery's fulla tough guys,' he told his son. 'What about your family? What are they gonna do when you disappear one day?'

'Whaddya want from me?' Mickey snapped back. 'There ain't no way outta this, you know that.'

Boyle suggested that Mickey offer to make a deal with the government.

'You mean be a rat?'

'Let me at least look into it, Mickey. Let me check it out. You don't gotta do a thing.'

Much to Charlie Boyle's surprise, Mickey did not get upset at the suggestion. 'Look,' Mickey replied, 'I ain't callin' no government people, okay? You do what you gotta do.'

Boyle took this to mean that maybe, just maybe, Mickey was willing to come in from the cold.

The very next day he called the New York office of the FBI. Without mentioning Mickey Featherstone by name, he said he was Charlie Boyle and he had a son who was looking to give information on New York organized crime figures. The person on the phone took his name and number and said an agent would get back to him.

The FBI, perhaps unaware that Charlie Boyle was the father of Mickey Featherstone, never returned the call.

Meanwhile, Mickey continued to get himself in deeper and deeper. In less than a month, Jimmy Coonan would be returning home from prison. When he did, Mickey knew that a lot of old wounds would be reopened. He knew that he'd now be seen as a threat to his old friend and might just wind up dead.

Unless he acted first.

387

14

BETRAYAL

On a grim, drizzly Thursday morning in April 1985, Michael Holly spent the last few minutes of his life strolling along West 35th Street, heading towards Clarke's Bar on 10th Avenue. A laborer currently working on the nearly completed Jacob Javits Convention Center, Holly, aged forty, had received his weekly paycheck earlier that morning. It was now 11:45 A.M., lunch-break time; he hoped to cash his check at Clarke's and maybe get a cold beer. He was dressed in his usual construction attire – blue jeans, a T-shirt, a lightweight jacket, and a white plastic hard hat.

A one-time bar owner from the West Side of Manhattan, Holly used to be a well-known face in the saloons and diners along 9th and 10th avenues. Then, one night in 1977, there was a shooting in his bar. John Bokun, a neighborhood gangster, was gunned down by an off-duty transit cop. But a lot of John Bokun's friends held Michael Holly responsible; they felt Holly had set John Bokun up. After numerous threats on his life, Holly was forced to close his bar and leave the neighborhood. He was lucky enough to land a union job as an ironworker, and even luckier still to be placed at the Convention Center, a long-term construction project if ever there was one.

Holly stopped to buy a hot dog from a street vendor across from the Convention Center, then continued east on 35th Street, past the old brick warehouses that lined the block. He paid little attention as a beige station wagon with New Jersey plates approached, headed in the opposite direction. The station wagon passed him, then came to an abrupt halt, forcing a van that was behind it to slam on the brakes.

Seconds later, in a flickering moment of intense clarity, Holly heard what sounded like a muffled gunshot and felt an excruciating pain in his upper back, near his right shoulder. Then, in rapid succession, he heard another shot, another, another, and another. The pain exploded throughout his body before his mind had a chance to register what was happening. All but one of the bullets hit home, piercing his flesh and puncturing his right lung and his aorta. One of the bullets passed all the way through his body. Another grazed his temple, sending his hard hat flying.

Riddled with bullets, his body contorted but still upright, Holly was able to turn and face his attacker. He caught a glimpse of a man standing roughly ten feet away, holding a gun with a silencer attached still pointed straight at him. As the life rushed from Holly's body, there was a glimmer of recognition.

'Aaaargh . . .' he gasped, his knees beginning to buckle. 'You dirty motherfucker!'

In the middle of West 35th Street, Michael Holly collapsed to the damp pavement.

The assailant quickly ducked back into the beige station wagon on the passenger side. Before the door was even closed, the car speeded west on 35th Street towards 11th Avenue.

By the time an ambulance arrived, siren wailing, a pool of blood had already formed underneath Holly's body. A small gathering of onlookers stood in the drizzle and watched as one of the paramedics checked Holly's vital signs. There was no blood pressure, no pulse, no sign of breathing.

Before they had even loaded him into the ambulance, Michael Holly, the former bar owner from Hell's Kitchen, was a dead man.

Early on the morning of the Michael Holly shooting, Mickey Featherstone was home in bed when he got a call from his friend and neighbor, Pat Hogan. Like Mickey, Hogan was a West Sider who now lived in Jersey and worked at Erie Transfer. That morning, Hogan was calling to see if Mickey was going in to shape up for work. If so, Hogan wanted to hitch a ride.

'Nah,' Mickey mumbled into the phone. 'I feel like shit.'

It had been a few days since Mickey had been to work. In fact, it had been a few days since Mickey had done much of anything except get high. Since Monday of that week, he'd been on a serious cocaine bender. Finally, after two or three sleepless days and nights, he'd vomited a few times and crashed. Now, here he was in bed with his pregnant wife, Sissy, barely able to see straight, with some guy asking *him* for a ride to work.

390

A few minutes later, with Mickey still in a semi-conscious state, the phone rang again. This time it was either Kevin Kelly or his gofer, Kenny Shannon – Mickey wasn't sure which. Whoever it was, the person told Mickey about a meeting they were supposed to have that day at the Skyline Motor Inn. Mickey mumbled something incoherent into the phone and hung up.

A few minutes later, the phone rang again.

'Goddammit,' Mickey growled, fumbling for the receiver.

This time it was his brother, Henry, who was telling him if he got his ass into Erie by early afternoon there was work to be had. Mickey sure as hell didn't want to go in to work, but he knew he might be pushing his luck if he didn't. Besides, Henry was the shop steward at Erie. Mickey figured he owed it to his brother to try to show up at least one day out of the week.

After he showered, shaved, and dressed, Mickey called Sam Beverly of Lifestyle's Transportation. Lifestyle's was another West Side rental agency that provided vehicles to the entertainment industry. One of the largest in Manhattan, it had a sizable fleet of Ford compacts, both station wagons and sedans. Mickey had borrowed a beige Ford Tempo wagon a few days earlier, and was calling to let Lifestyle's know he was bringing it in.

After first running Sissy to the grocery store and back, Mickey drove into Manhattan. As he made his way along Route 9 and onto the George Washington Bridge he had no way of knowing that just moments earlier, on West 35th Street, Michael Holly had been riddled with lead.

Mickey arrived at Erie Transfer on West 52nd Street

around 12:30. Before he returned the car to Lifestyle's, he wanted to clean up some soda he'd spilled on the front seat the day before. One of the workers at Erie put the car in the 'barn,' or garage, where Mickey planned to scrub it down. But before he could get to it, a friend of his named Bobby drove up in a van.

'Bobby,' asked Mickey, 'can you do me a favor and drive me down to Lifestyle's? I wanna tell 'em I got their car. Just gotta clean it up first.'

'No sweat,' said Bobby, 'but first I gotta run by my Uncle Vinnie's place.' Bobby's uncle, Vinnie Russo, was a caterer who provided food to movie and television sets.

On the way to Vinnie's place on West 50th Street, Bobby and Mickey lit up a joint. Mickey had been feeling a little grim that morning, his nerves still on edge from three solid days of cocaine abuse. The smoke was just what he needed to relax.

When they arrived at Vinnie's place, Mickey ran into his brother Henry. Henry said he was on his way down to Lifestyle's himself, so he could give Mickey a ride.

As they were driving south on 9th Avenue, Mickey suddenly remembered the phone call he'd gotten that morning from either Kevin Kelly or Kenny Shannon. He was completely out of it when he got the call, but he remembered something about a meeting at 12:00 or 12:30 at the Skyline Motor Inn. 'Hey,' he told Henry, 'drop me off at the Skyline, will ya? I'm supposed to meet Kevin and Kenny there, I just remembered. I can walk to Sam's place from there.'

At the Skyline, Mickey asked Vic, who managed the bar, if Kelly and Shannon had been around that day.

Vic said they'd been there earlier and left. So Mickey continued on foot down to Sam Beverly's garage on West 38th Street.

He was still feeling the effects of the joint he'd smoked when he walked into Lifestyle's around 2 P.M. Sam was in his office, and when he spotted Mickey, he furrowed his brow. 'Come outside for a minute. I gotta tell you something.'

'Yeah,' said Mickey when they got outside to the sidewalk. 'What's up?'

'Detectives was just here. They was lookin' for one of our cars. I ain't even sure which one.'

'They say why?'

'They said a stickup, but I got a feeling . . .' Sam held his hand in the shape of a gun and pointed it at his head.

Mickey grabbed his brother Henry. They hopped in his Bronco and drove directly to Erie Transfer.

Mickey was still wondering what the hell was going on when he got to Erie. When he saw twenty-six-year-old Billy Bokun walk out of the men's room, it all came back to him. He remembered how, yesterday, he'd talked to Bokun, Kevin Kelly, and Kenny Shannon about Michael Holly. Even though it had been eight years since the death of Billy Bokun's older brother, John, they still wanted revenge. Never mind that eyewitness accounts revealed that John Bokun brought about his own death that night in 1977 by first shooting Holly in the shoulder, then firing at an off-duty cop; the Westies were convinced it had all been part of some elaborate arrangement between Holly and the cops to eliminate Bokun.

Just a few days before Mickey talked with Billy Bokun,

Kelly, and Shannon, Kelly had spotted Holly down by the Jacob Javits construction site and told Billy about it. For years, Bokun had been bragging that he was going to avenge his brother's death, but he'd never been able to track Holly down. When he heard where he was now working, Bokun enlisted Kelly and Shannon in a plan to gun him down.

Mickey had been told all about this the day before. In fact, he'd had a drink with Bokun near Erie Transfer.

'The fuck set my brother up,' Billy told Mickey. 'I'm finally gonna get my revenge.'

'Hey, Billy,' replied Mickey, who had himself once plotted to kill Michael Holly. 'You been sayin' this for years, man. Why don't you just fuckin' do it and stop talkin' about it?'

Later that same day Mickey met with Kelly and Shannon. They wanted to use his car – the Ford Tempo station wagon borrowed from Lifestyle's – to scout out the location where Holly was working. They even made plans to meet the following day at the Skyline.

All of this came rushing back to Mickey as he spotted Billy Bokun, his hair and face dripping wet, hurriedly coming out of the bathroom at Erie Transfer. He was carrying a car mat and a few other items Mickey couldn't really make out. Bokun looked stunned when he saw Mickey, and he froze in his tracks for a few seconds.

'Hey,' Mickey said to Bokun, realizing he must have just murdered Michael Holly. 'Congratulations.'

Bokun smiled nervously and shook Mickey's hand.

'What you got the car mat for?' asked Mickey.

'Uh, yeah, I spilled some makeup on it.'

Mickey nodded. He knew that Bokun usually wore makeup and a disguise to hide his facial disfiguration whenever he was doing criminal business. Although Bokun was a little guy – about five-foot-seven and 150 pounds – his birthmark gave him a slightly demented look. Some people in the neighborhood referred to Bokun by the nickname 'Indian.'

Before Mickey had a chance to ask Bokun anything more, Billy said, 'I gotta run.' Then he dashed off to his car and drove away.

Mickey was curious about how the murder went down, but he figured he would probably learn the details in due time. He ran a few more errands in the neighborhood without giving it any more thought. He and Henry got back to Erie Transfer an hour later, around three.

The place was crawling with detectives.

'Aren't you Mickey Featherstone?' asked one of them excitedly as Mickey strolled into the parking lot.

'Yeah. So what?'

'Where were you at eleven forty-five this morning?' asked another detective who had just walked over.

'Is this your car?' asked another, pointing towards the beige Ford Tempo parked in the barn.

'Mickey,' said his brother Henry. 'Don't be stupid. You don't gotta tell these guys nothin'. Call your lawyer.'

After he'd made a call to the offices of Hochheiser and Aronson, Mickey told one of the detectives, 'Look, I got nothin' to say to youse people. I been advised against it.'

The cops let Mickey go, telling him they'd be in touch shortly.

That night, Mickey tried to act as if everything were

normal. He decided to wait before he called around to find out what had happened. He and Sissy took a meat-loaf over to a neighbor's house and spent much of the evening there. But as the evening wore on, Mickey became more and more distracted. Something was not right, he felt. There was something about Billy Bokun, the way he had looked so surprised when he saw Mickey. And the detectives.

The events of the previous twenty-four hours stoked his paranoia. There was no reason for him to be worried, Mickey knew that. But he couldn't help it. He knew all those cops swarming around Erie Transfer must have had something to do with the Michael Holly murder. But why had they started asking him all those questions? Even if there had been witnesses, Mickey knew he didn't look anything like Billy Bokun. So why had they reacted as if *he* were a prime suspect?

There were too many unanswered questions. And these days unanswered questions made Mickey think, and thinking made him nervous. For good reason. In recent months, Mickey had hatched a plan so audacious that the very thought it might somehow become known had touched off his current cocaine binge, and kept him on edge for the last two months.

To Mickey, it was the most ballsy criminal act he had ever conceived . . .

A plot, planned and put in motion by him, to murder Jimmy Coonan.

Four months before the Michael Holly shooting, in late December of 1984, Jimmy Coonan had returned home from prison after serving his time for gun possession and for the old Vanderbilt Evans assault. Initially, Mickey and everyone else tried to act as if nothing had changed. There'd been a few meetings on the West Side with Mickey, Jimmy McElroy, Kelly, and Shannon in which Coonan sought to lay out his new agenda for the Eighties. Jimmy had been gone just over four years, and there were a lot of loose ends to be addressed, including an eight-year-old contract on the life of Michael Holly. The fact that Holly had not been taken care of was a source of embarrassment to Coonan – one he wanted dealt with as soon as possible.

One of the personal duties Coonan resumed when he came back from prison was collecting the tribute from the ILA. As soon as he did, everyone else's share dropped drastically. There was a lot of grumbling about that, from Mickey as well as McElroy, Kelly, and Shannon (who'd now risen in status from gofer to partner with the ambitious Kevin Kelly). But what bothered Mickey and the group most of all was that since Coonan's return, he'd rekindled his romance with the Italians.

One of the first times Mickey saw Coonan after he got out was in the lobby of an office building on Madison Avenue in January. Jimmy had summoned Mickey there to meet with a high-powered defense attorney named James LaRossa. LaRossa was the attorney for none other than Paul Castellano, boss of the Gambino family. Recently, Castellano had been ensnared in a massive federal racketeering indictment, and LaRossa was planning his defense.

In the lobby of LaRossa's ornate office building,

Mickey met up with Coonan, Mugsy Ritter, and an up-and-coming *capo* in the Gambino organization named Danny Marino. While Coonan was away in prison, his good buddy Roy Demeo had been murdered by his own people, and Marino had taken over as Coonan's 'Italian connection.'

Marino and Coonan were concerned about Castellano's upcoming trial. Specifically, they were worried about Dominick Montiglio, the former Green Beret and nephew of Nino Gaggi whom Mickey had been introduced to after the sit-down at Tommaso's Restaurant. Since then, Montiglio had flipped and was set to testify against Castellano.

What they wanted Mickey to do was come up with damaging personal information about Montiglio to help discredit him on the stand.

'Mickey, you talked to the guy,' said Coonan. 'Whaddya know?'

'I don't really know nothin'. We talked about 'Nam a little bit . . .'

'Okay, what'd he say?'

'Just about things he seen there and nightmares he been having.'

'What else?' asked Danny Marino.

'Nothin' else.'

'Look, Mickey,' said Coonan. 'It don't have to be true, know what I'm sayin'?'

They all went up to the lawyer's office and sat in the waiting room. Mickey was getting steamed. He knew what they wanted him to do. They wanted him to put himself on the line, to sign a bunch of papers saying

Dominick Montiglio was a scumbag and a killer. They wanted him to perjure himself and risk doing prison time for Big Paulie.

Mickey was called into LaRossa's office along with Coonan and Danny Marino. The lawyer asked Mickey what he knew about Montiglio, and Mickey repeated what he'd said in the lobby.

'What else do you know?' asked LaRossa.

'That's about it.'

'C'mon, Mickey,' said Marino. 'Tell us more.'

'Look, I only talked to the guy a few times and I told youse all I know. Now, if what you wanna do is make it up, whaddya need me for?'

Mickey could tell Coonan and Marino were annoyed with him when he left LaRossa's office. But the way he saw it, *he* was the one who had a right to be annoyed. Why should he be asked to put his freedom on the line for the guineas?

Mickey was still incredulous about it the next day. 'Those people,' he told black-mustachioed Mugsy Ritter, in reference to the Italians. 'Sometimes they think they can do whatever they want just because they're ginzos.'

It was the same deal a few weeks later, when Mickey found a message waiting for him at Erie Transfer after he'd put in a long twelve-hour day on a movie set. The message said to meet Jimmy Coonan at Visage, a nightclub/disco on the West Side partly owned by Danny Marino.

Mickey was still dressed in his work clothes – blue jeans, a heavy leather jacket, and a navy-blue knit cap. When he arrived at Visage, a burly doorman told him there was no way he could let him in dressed the way he was.

'Look,' said Mickey. 'I'm a West Sider, a friend of Jimmy Coonan's and Danny Marino's. They're expecting me. Why don't you go inside and check?'

The doorman disappeared for a few minutes, then returned. 'Sorry,' he said, pulling back the rope so Mickey could enter.

There were disco lights glittering amid flashy dresses and expensive suits as Mickey made his way through the club carrying his cap and leather jacket. Finally, he spotted Coonan and Marino seated at a booth and walked over.

'Jesus,' said Marino when he saw Mickey. 'No wonder they wouldn't let this guy in. Look at the way he's dressed.'

'Yeah,' replied Coonan, sheepishly. 'Well, you know, he was out doin' a piece of work.'

Mickey couldn't believe the way Jimmy was kissing Danny Marino's ass. Here was this fucking Al Cologne from Brooklyn making comments about the way he was dressed *in his own fucking neighborhood*, and Coonan was practically apologizing for it.

Mickey's dissatisfaction with Jimmy had been festering ever since Edna refused him that loan he'd asked for. Then, a year later, Jimmy comes back to the neighborhood and starts cozying up to the Italians again. Add to that Mickey's refusal to carry out the murders he'd been assigned through Edna, and he and Jimmy's 'friendship' could not have been more tenuous – on both sides.

The way Mickey saw it, there was only one way to go. In the early weeks of 1985, Mickey sought out Billy

Beattie, who, after many months on the lam in the Catskill Mountains had been trying to work his way back into the neighborhood. As soon as Coonan heard about it, he'd put out a contract on Beattie's life, forcing him back into hiding.

Mickey knew he could get a message to Billy through his brother Tommy. He made arrangements to meet Billy one afternoon near Central Park, away from Hell's Kitchen.

It was a brisk day as Mickey greeted Billy, who he hadn't seen in nearly five years, since before the Whitehead trial. They strolled south on Central Park West, in the shadow of some of the city's most stately apartment buildings.

'I just wanna tell you one thing,' said Billy, wasting no time getting to the subject that was on both their minds. 'If Coonan's gonna kill me, I want you to know why. The real story.'

Mickey smiled. 'Hey, don't tell me. I'll tell you, man.'

Beattie looked startled.

'I'll bet,' said Mickey, 'Edna tried to hit on you.'

'How the fuck did you know?'

'I don't know, man, I just figured.'

Beattie explained how Edna, who he'd dated years ago before she married Coonan, had found out where he was staying. With Jimmy away in prison, she'd started calling up and making sexual advances. Beattie would hang up on her, but she'd call again the next night.

'That's the whole reason she wants me dead. And that bitch probably told Jimmy I'm the one that was comin' on to *her*!'

Mickey laughed. 'Billy, I don't wanna kill you, okay?

401

I don't intend to kill you. Neither do any of the other guys, 'cept Jimmy. I believe he wants to kill me too. So, you know, what else can we do? It's like, kill or be killed, know what I'm sayin'?'

'Yeah.'

'Besides, Jimmy don't wanna be an Irishman no more. He's forgot where he come from, you know. He just wants to be an Italian now.'

'Yeah, that's his thing.'

'Has been for a long, long time, I believe. We just didn't wanna admit it.'

Mickey and Billy Beattie stood silently for a few minutes looking out at the heavy traffic on Columbus Circle. A chilly breeze whisked through the treetops along Central Park West, and mothers, bundled in their winter clothes, pushed babies in strollers to and from the park.

'I can't say I like this,' said Billy, shaking his head. 'But I guess we got no choice.'

One week later, on the movie set where Mickey was working, he met again with Billy Beattie. The movie was 9½ Weeks, starring Mickey Rourke and Kim Basinger, and the crew was filming a scene right on 10th Avenue, in the heart of Hell's Kitchen. During a break they met in a camper and Mickey gave Billy a .32-caliber pistol wrapped in a towel.

The gun was supposed to be used on Jimmy Coonan.

But Billy Beattie didn't have the nerve to do it alone. So other members of the Westies were brought into the conspiracy. McElroy, Kelly, and Shannon had all recently told Mickey they were fed up with Jimmy Coonan. To them, the idea of eliminating Jimmy certainly had its advantages: profit and survival. They'd all get more control over the neighborhood's criminal bounty this way. And they knew how upset Featherstone was with Coonan. If he carried through on his plot to kill Jimmy, anyone too closely associated with Coonan might be next in line. Even if they didn't agree with Mickey, it would be smart to at least act like they were on his side.

Mickey, Beattie, McElroy, Kelly, and Shannon all met one evening in March '85 and talked about how to get rid of Coonan. Someone raised the possibility of having a black guy they knew dress up as a Rastafarian, go out to Hazlet, and gun Jimmy down in his neighborhood. With a black dude as the shooter, the cops would never think to trace it to the Westies. Everybody liked that idea until they realized there probably wasn't a single black person in all of Hazlet. Any Rastafarian seen in that neighborhood would probably be arrested just on general principle.

The whole thing reached a low point, of sorts, one afternoon later in March when they all put on bulletproof vests, piled into a car, and drove out to Hazlet, hoping to catch Coonan at home. 'The house that Ruby built,' they called Coonan's home at 15 Vanmater Terrace, because Jimmy had purchased it with the money he saved by murdering Ruby Stein. They drove around the neighborhood for an hour or so bitching about Jimmy and Edna, passing a joint around and getting high. They never saw Jimmy that day.

Although everyone was trying to act tough, the thought of killing Jimmy Coonan was not a pleasant one. It wasn't that he didn't deserve it. It was the uncertainty that lay ahead. After Coonan was gone, who would control the rackets? Who would give the orders?

No one dared ask those questions aloud, but they were heavy on the minds of all five men that day as they drove around the immaculate suburban streets of Hazlet, half-heartedly looking to kill their lifelong friend and leader, Jimmy Coonan.

Although it hadn't happened by April of '85, there were those who felt it was imminent. Maybe it would take place right on 10th Avenue when Jimmy drove by in his brand-new Mercedes. Maybe it would happen in a restaurant when he was eating pasta with one of his Italian friends. Or maybe it would be quiet. Maybe Jimmy Coonan would just disappear one day, his body made to 'do the Houdini,' just as he had made so many other bodies disappear over the years.

The fact that Coonan knew nothing of this plot was an indication of just how far removed he had become. Since his return, he'd been spending less and less time with his West Side crew, which contributed to their resentment towards him. Jimmy didn't seem to want to associate with his old pals anymore. The way they saw it, he was on the verge of just turning the neighborhood's rackets over to the guineas in return for a spot in their organization.

The very idea of Coonan's demise had created a high level of paranoia among those Westies who were in on the plot. Who knew what bloodshed might result from even thinking about such an outrageous act?

These thoughts were definitely on Mickey Featherstone's mind on April 26, 1985, the day after the Michael Holly shooting. That morning, Sissy, who was six months

404

pregnant, and their niece Esther rode with him in the family Oldsmobile to Erie Transfer, where he was going to pick up his paycheck. For the first time in a long time, he hadn't gotten high the night before. He stayed straight so he could mull over all the sinister possibilities of the previous day's events with a clear head.

The Holly murder was just too goddamned suspicious, he kept thinking as he crossed the massive span of the George Washington Bridge and headed south on the West Side Highway towards the old neighborhood. Why did they use a car from Erie Transfer? Why didn't they let him know exactly when and where it was going to go down so he could establish a clear-cut alibi?

When Mickey pulled up in front of Erie Transfer he hardly noticed the car that was double-parked in front of him. And he wasn't really paying much attention to the sedan behind him either, though he could see it plainly in his rearview mirror. It wasn't until he spotted a car with four men in it driving the wrong way on West 52nd Street that he realized what was happening.

Then all hell broke loose. More cops than he'd ever seen in one place in his life, both detectives and uniformed officers, descended on his car.

'Oh my God!' gasped Sissy.

'Stay in the car!' Mickey shouted at his wife and niece, as he opened the door and stepped out into the street.

The cops, guns drawn, swarmed around the car. They pulled Sissy and Esther out on the passenger side and led them away.

'You're under arrest, Mickey,' one of the detectives

barked, pushing Featherstone up against a chain-link fence and slapping on a set of cuffs.

'Mind tellin' me what the fuck for?' asked Featherstone.

'Wouldn't you like to know?'

An unmarked police car pulled up. As he was being led away, Mickey peered past the sea of cops towards Erie Transfer, where many of his fellow workers had gathered.

'Call my lawyers!' he yelled as he was pushed into the detective's car. 'They ain't tellin' me what I'm under arrest for!'

On May 13, 1985, two and a half weeks after Featherstone's arrest, Ken Aronson got a call from a detective in the 10th Precinct.

'Is this Mickey Featherstone's attorney?' asked the detective.

'Yes.'

'We located the witnesses. Today's the lineup. You're here, you're here. You're not, you're not.'

Then he hung up.

Aronson was suitably annoyed. Since Mickey's arrest, there had already been one such lineup. It had taken place within hours of the bust, and Hochheiser and Aronson had not been notified. Apparently, that lineup involved two people who had been driving a delivery van on West 35th Street the day Michael Holly was shot. Their van was forced to stop when a beige station wagon in front of them came to an abrupt halt. They watched in amazement as a man got out of the station wagon on the passenger

406

side, screwed a silencer onto a chrome-colored pistol, and fired five shots at a pedestrian dressed in construction clothes. Then the shooter hopped back in the car and it drove off.

One of the witnesses swore he saw the shooter plain as day. The other was slightly less certain of the assailant's appearance, though he'd definitely seen the guy. They both described the shooter as roughly five-feet-seven-inches tall and about 150 pounds. He had sandy-blond hair about collar length, a mustache, and was wearing a white painter's cap and sunglasses.

The two witnesses had identified Featherstone from the lineup as the person they'd seen shoot Michael Holly.

Now, two more witnesses – construction workers who'd been walking on West 35th Street and observed the entire incident from start to finish – had finally been located by the police. They, too, would now get a chance to pick Featherstone out of a lineup.

Aronson got over to the 10th Precinct as fast as he could. From what he'd been hearing from Mickey, the cops had been mistreating him since the day of his arrest. Featherstone was something of a legend in law enforcement circles, and the attorney didn't doubt for a minute that the NYPD was making the most of having him in custody. Aronson also felt it was entirely possible that the cops, pissed that Featherstone had beaten so many cases in the past, might try to railroad him by establishing bogus witnesses to the shooting.

At the station house, the attorney was led into a small, narrow area – more like a hallway than a room – with no windows. There were two file cabinets along one side, and along the other a large plywood panel with hinges on the top. The detectives lifted up the panel to reveal a two-way mirror which looked out onto the lineup room.

Aronson stood against the back wall, near the file cabinets. The only light was from the lineup room, where a couple of detectives waited patiently for the order to bring in Featherstone and the assorted crooks and cops – 'fillers' – who would stand next to Mickey in the lineup. But first, a gruff-sounding detective called for the witnesses to be brought in.

Given the reputation of Mickey Featherstone and the Westies, the cops were taking no chances. The Whitehead murder trial had resulted in two suicidal witnesses, and they were determined that would not be the case this time around. Even Aronson wasn't told the names of the witnesses.

As they were led into the room, the attorney, who had been present at many police lineups in his career, observed something he had never seen before. Both witnesses had paper bags over their heads. Small holes had been cut in the bags so they could see.

With a cop on each side, the witnesses stood directly in front of the two-way mirror.

'Bring 'em in,' a detective shouted to the cops in the other room.

Mickey Featherstone and five other people were led into the room and stood against the wall. The fillers were all about Mickey's size, with mustaches like his and hair of a similar sandy-blond color. They were all wearing painter's caps of the type the witnesses remembered the shooter wearing on the day in question. The lights in the lineup room were doused, except for a fluorescent light on the ceiling, which shined down on Featherstone and the others.

The witnesses, their paper bags still securely in place, peered through the glass partition.

'Turn to the left,' one of the cops commanded to the six men in the lineup. 'Turn to the right,' he commanded a few seconds later.

Within minutes, one of the witnesses said he was unable to make an identification. But the other, his eyes still fixed on the lineup, had no doubts at all.

'The guy on the left,' he said. 'Second from the end. Number five. That's the guy.'

'You're sure?' asked the detective.

'Yeah. No question about it.'

The person he identified was Mickey Featherstone.

Ken Aronson didn't know quite what to make of it. This was the third time Mickey had been picked out of a lineup, and two of the three witnesses had been absolutely certain of their choice. Normally, Aronson might have thought it meant that maybe, just maybe, his client was guilty. But in the few times he'd talked to Mickey since his arrest, Featherstone had sworn adamantly that he had not done this killing.

'You gotta believe me on this one,' he'd told Aronson, practically in tears. 'I didn't do it.'

The guilt or innocence of his clients was not something Aronson usually spent a lot of time thinking about. Unless you were told otherwise, you acted on the assumption they were innocent, often as the evidence piled up against you. In Mickey's case, Aronson had no illusions. Initially, he

409

suspected Mickey may have indeed done the shooting. He thought so because he'd been hearing through the Westies grapevine that, in the last year or so, Mickey had reverted to his old ways. At first the attorney had been saddened. Then he grew angry, and finally disgusted.

In the years he'd known Mickey, Aronson, the 'nebbish' from Long Island, had grown emotionally attached to this Hell's Kitchen tough guy who was so drastically unlike himself. He'd been charmed by Featherstone and was willing to put in ungodly amounts of time to help him out. Not just legal time, either, but hours on the phone trying to convince Mickey he could make it in the 'legitimate' world. Often, his senior partner, Larry Hochheiser, joked that Aronson could claim Mickey Featherstone as a tax exemption.

At times, Aronson, who was single and without any family in the area, lived vicariously through Featherstone. He fondly remembered afternoons when Mickey would bring his son, Mickey, Jr, over to his office and play with him in the foyer. Aronson would watch them laughing together and say to himself, 'I should be this good with a child if I had one.'

The fact that Mickey had fallen back into a lifestyle of gangsterism affected Aronson on a personal level. Over the years, he'd done everything he could to help straighten Mickey out. Now Mickey, he felt, had let him down. Even if Featherstone *was* innocent of the Michael Holly shooting, as he so vehemently claimed, Aronson had reluctantly come to the conclusion it was only a matter of time before Mickey Featherstone would be back in court on some other charge.

Aronson's disillusionment persisted, even though two weeks after the lineup he heard a version of the Holly shooting that exonerated Mickey – at least as the person who had pulled the trigger. He was given this version at Billy Bokun's wedding in Sacred Heart Church, the same church where Mickey Spillane had tied the knot with Maureen McManus some twenty-five years before. The Irish community in Hell's Kitchen was nearly nonexistent by now, but Sacred Heart still held a special place in the hearts of those old enough to remember the glory days.

Aronson was invited to Bokun's wedding not only because he was a friend of the community's, but also because there were rumors that Billy might be arrested as an accomplice in the Holly murder. Bokun's future mother-in-law, Flo Collins, wife of white-haired coke dealer Tommy Collins, told the attorney she didn't want any 'wiseguy detectives' interrupting the ceremony.

Aronson arrived at the church around 4:30 on the afternoon of May 26, 1985. The ceremony was not scheduled to begin for an hour or so, and few people were there. Inside the cathedral, Aronson spotted Bokun and approached to offer his congratulations.

'Kenny,' said Billy, looking anxious, 'I gotta talk to you.'

Bokun was dressed in a white tuxedo which accentuated his red birthmark. He led Aronson to a quiet corner near the front of the church, just to the right of the altar. A soft late-afternoon light cascaded down from the high stained-glass windows, bathing the entire church in a golden hue.

In these somber and dramatic surroundings, Billy

Bokun confessed to the Holly shooting. Nearly in tears, he told Aronson that Mickey hadn't killed the guy, though, Bokun claimed, Mickey knew the murder was to take place that day.

'So what am I gonna do, huh?' Billy asked Aronson. 'I'll turn myself in if I have to.'

'Billy, as your lawyer, this is what I'm going to suggest . . . First of all, who knows about this?'

'A lot of people, you know. This is what I don't understand. Mickey knew all about this. He knew. He didn't fuckin' cover for hisself.'

'Okay. Look, Billy, I can't *tell* you what to do, okay? There's a conflict. But I can tell you if you try to turn yourself in, they'll just charge you as being the driver or something. It doesn't mean they'll let Mickey go. They have witnesses that identified him.'

Billy began to cry. 'I can't just let this happen . . . Fuck, motherfuck . . . why didn't he cover hisself?'

Kenny took a hard line. 'Billy, look, this is your wedding day. Try to cheer up.'

Throughout the wedding ceremony and over the next few days, Aronson was in a mild state of shock. Both Bokun and Featherstone were clients of his. How could he exonerate one without convicting the other?

In the weeks following the confession at Sacred Heart Church, Aronson and Larry Hochheiser discussed their options.

'As the guy's counsel,' cautioned Hochheiser, 'we sure as hell can't tell him to take the stand. It's not exactly in his best interest.'

'You know,' replied Aronson, 'we don't even know if

412

this confession is for real. I mean, what if he was put up to this? I don't think we could count on this confession even if we did put him on the stand.'

Hochheiser sat at his desk and glanced out the window of his forty-ninth-floor office. It was a reasonably clear day, and in the distance he could see a small private plane soaring over the concrete peaks and caverns of Manhattan. Hochheiser, himself a licensed pilot who loved to fly in his off hours, was jealous. He would have liked to be out there right now.

He was not a kid anymore. At forty-four, Hochheiser's once wild mane of brown hair was now speckled with gray. After fifteen years as Featherstone's attorney, he was finally beginning to think maybe Mickey was more trouble than he was worth.

'Well,' said Hochheiser, asking the question he knew was on both their minds. 'So who do we tell about this?'

Aronson didn't look pleased. He knew they were trolling in murky legal waters. Already he'd checked the Canon of Ethics. There were no provisions that directly addressed their dilemma.

'The way I see it,' said Kenny, 'we don't tell anyone. If Bokun wants to turn himself in, that's his business. But the confession itself is privileged.'

With that, the matter was closed. They agreed they would proceed with the case regardless of what Bokun intended to do, based on the evidence that was at their disposal. In the meantime, they would tell Mickey about the confession, but no one else – not the judge, not the prosecution, and certainly not the press.

But news of Billy Bokun's confession to Aronson spread

through Hell's Kitchen like wildfire. Sissy Featherstone, for one, couldn't believe that the attorneys weren't going to make Bokun turn himself in. In June, a few weeks after Bokun's wedding, she confronted Ken Aronson in a Chinese restaurant near the courthouse in lower Manhattan. They'd spent the morning in court during one of Mickey's pre-trial hearings, and Sissy was uptight.

'I told you Mickey was innocent,' she said to Aronson.

'No,' replied the attorney, 'Bokun didn't say *innocent*. He just said Mickey didn't pull the trigger. He knew, Sissy. It was his fault he went to Erie. He shouldn't have been so nosey. He should have stayed away.'

'Wait a minute. Mickey wasn't being nosey. He was told by Kevin and Kenny to meet them at the Skyline.'

'He should have had an alibi, Sissy. He shouldn't have been anywhere near Erie.'

As the conversation continued, Aronson found himself getting more and more upset. He could see how he had boxed himself into a corner. All those years he spent getting close to the West Side community were backfiring on him. All the weddings, engagement parties, and funerals he'd attended had led people to think of him almost as a member of the gang. It had all seemed so exotic to him at the time. But now Mickey and Sissy were expecting him to 'do the right thing,' to do whatever he had to in order to make sure Mickey didn't take the fall.

'So Billy confessed,' said Sissy. 'What're you gonna do about it? He wants to turn himself in.'

Aronson pursed his lips. 'Sissy, that's entirely up to him. I don't know what he intends to do. Frankly, I wouldn't hold my breath. This is real life, you know, this isn't Perry Mason.'

In the many months leading up to his trial, Mickey Featherstone sat in Block C-95 at Rikers Island, his mind working overtime trying to untangle all the sinister forces that had landed him where he was. The stress was wearing him down. In July of '85 Sissy gave birth to a baby girl, Gillian, her and Mickey's third child. But with all that was going on, Featherstone hardly noticed. Through the summer, fall, and into the winter, he was constantly on the phone with his lawyers and fellow gangsters from the neighborhood, especially Kevin Kelly and Billy Bokun.

At first, Mickey couldn't understand how or why these eyewitnesses had fingered him. He knew that Bokun, who had dark-brown hair and a chunky physique, had been the shooter. How could anyone think Bokun looked like him? Then Mickey talked with Billy Bokun on the phone, and Billy told him he'd worn a disguise that day. Along with the makeup he normally wore over the large red birthmark on his face, he'd worn a sandy-blond wig, a painter's cap, sunglasses, and he'd darkened his normally wispy mustache with brown eyeliner. All of which made it conceivable that an eyewitness might later identify Mickey Featherstone as the assailant.

'Why?' Mickey had demanded. 'Why'd you wear this fucking disguise?'

'It was Kevin,' said Bokun. 'Kevin planned the whole fuckin' thing. He had Kenny drive the car. He had me wear the goddamn wig, the mustache, everything.'

415

But when Mickey talked to Kevin Kelly about it, he denied that Bokun had worn any kind of disguise at all.

'You want my opinion?' Kelly said. 'That's just somethin' the cops is makin' up to turn everybody against each other.'

Mickey was shocked at first. Sure, he'd sometimes felt Kevin was a conniving bastard who couldn't be trusted with his own mother. But he didn't want to believe he'd deliberately set him up. Still, nothing else fit the facts.

In all his ruminations, Mickey tried not to think about his own screw-ups. Yes, he'd heard that the Michael Holly shooting was likely to take place that day. But he didn't really give it much thought. Billy Bokun had spent so much time over the years bragging about how he was going to kill Holly that Mickey didn't really believe it was going to happen. He was stoned the day before the shooting when Kelly and Shannon told him to meet them at the Skyline Motor Inn. And he was burned out from four straight days of debauchery on the morning of the shooting.

Maybe I was wrong for not having an alibi, thought Mickey, but does that mean I should get pinned with a murder I didn't do?

For months, Mickey's paranoia seethed. In time, an elaborate conspiracy theory began to take shape in his mind. From his conversations with Bokun, he didn't think Billy had been in on the setup. Billy was a bit like Raymond Steen – a not-too-bright kid who'd do almost anything to endear himself with the neighborhood's gangster element. Chances were, figured Mickey, Kelly and Shannon had used Bokun.

As for the larger conspiracy, the moving force behind the whole thing – that was easy. There was no doubt in Mickey's mind. It had to be Jimmy Coonan.

Maybe Coonan had found out about the plot against his life, and he'd told Kelly, Shannon, McElroy, and God-knows-who-else that if they got rid of Featherstone he'd forget about their disloyalty. Or maybe Coonan was just getting his revenge for Mickey's having refused to murder Vinnie Leone and the others. Or maybe it was the goddamned Italians. Maybe they'd told Coonan if he really wanted to be one of them he'd have to get rid of Featherstone, his crazy Irish partner.

By the early months of 1986 Mickey's conspiracy theory had expanded to incorporate yet another person – his one-time friend and lawyer, Kenny Aronson.

Again, it was a phone call with Billy Bokun that got him thinking. Tearfully, Bokun had told Mickey there was no way he was going to let him go down. He'd turn himself in if he had to. Mickey had suggested that if he were going to do that, he'd better not go to the cops. They couldn't be trusted. Mickey wanted him to turn himself in to Jimmy Breslin or Michael Daly, two journalists who'd written about him in the past.

But Bokun said he had a better idea. He'd wait till the trial was underway, then he'd walk right in the door, right in the fucking door with the same disguise on that he'd worn when he shot Michael Holly.

Mickey liked that idea; it had a certain style. But when he asked Bokun about it a few days later, Bokun said Ken Aronson had told him not to do it.

Now Mickey was certain Aronson was in on it. First

Bokun confesses and Aronson says they can't tell anybody about it. Then Billy says he wants to turn himself in and Kenny says no. Sometimes Mickey thought it was all a bad dream. Here was his own attorney knowing who really whacked Holly, and he was still going to let this fucking thing go to trial!?

There could be only one explanation, figured Mickey. Jimmy Coonan must have gotten to Aronson, too.

By the time the trial got underway, Mickey was so strung out he could hardly focus on what was happening. He'd been getting high almost every day, using coke and marijuana Sissy had smuggled in to him at Rikers Island. She would wrap the illegal substance in a tiny rubber balloon, then when she kissed Mickey in the prison visiting room, pass the balloon from her mouth to his. Mickey would swallow it, retrieve it later when he defecated, and snort or smoke whatever Sissy had been able to get her hands on.

For three straight weeks in March of 1986, Mickey watched in a semistupor as his life went up in flames. In the criminal courts building in lower Manhattan – familiar terrain for Mickey Featherstone – three eyewitnesses took the stand and identified him as the person they'd seen shoot Michael Holly. The last one, a black construction worker who just happened to be on West 35th Street on the day of the shooting, was terrified when he took the stand. Larry Hochheiser asked him, 'So, as you sit here now you are one hundred percent positive that you were correct in your identification [on the day of the lineup], right?'

'Yes,' the construction worker answered, hesitantly.

'Heaven and earth wouldn't change that view now, is that correct?'

'Yes.'

'Are you absolutely certain?'

'Yes.'

It was an old Hochheiser ploy, one he'd used successfully in 1980 when he savaged Jack Paulstein – the main witness at the William Walker murder trial – by making him seem *too* certain to be telling the truth. But it wasn't working here. The more he pressed the construction worker, the more confident he became, until it started to sound like Hochheiser was part of the prosecution.

Not only was the government able to deliver eyewitness testimony, but as the trial unfolded the alleged motive for the shooting was established by none other than Raymond Steen, who'd long since disappeared into the Witness Protection Program. On the stand, Steen told of a time seven years earlier when Mickey Featherstone had given him a bottle of poison – or what he'd been told was poison – to drop in Michael Holly's beer. Featherstone, Steen related to the jury, believed that Holly was responsible for the death of his friend, John Bokun.

'Mickey explained to me,' said Steen, 'that he owed the family of John Bokun this killing of Michael Holly.'

At first, Mickey watched with some amusement as Ray Steen jabbered away on the stand. He knew that for once in his life, Steen was telling the truth. He had, in fact, given Steen a bottle of knockout drops, telling him they were poison. But Steen, Mickey was certain, was a totally unreliable witness. Without corroboration, who in their right mind would believe fast-talking Ray Steen? The prosecution rested.

Days later, to Mickey's utter astonishment, his own attorneys put Kevin Kelly on the stand. Hochheiser and Aronson explained that since all the eyewitnesses had described the shooter as holding the gun in his right hand, they wanted to use Kevin, who would identify himself as a lifelong friend of Featherstone's, to establish that Mickey was left-handed.

'But you can't put a guy like this on the stand,' argued Mickey. 'He's from the street. He's got rough edges, man. I'm tellin' ya, this fucker sounds like a hood.'

Hochheiser believed it was better to have a witness who was weak on elocution than one who was liable to wilt under cross-examination. 'Look, Mickey,' he explained, 'it's a lot easier to smooth rough edges than it is to grow a pair of balls on a guy.'

'What the fuck does that mean?'

'Mickey,' Larry sighed, 'just let us try the case, alright?'

As it turned out, Featherstone was right. When Assistant D.A. Jeffrey Schlanger cross-examined Kelly, he sat on the stand sounding like the tough guy that he was, claiming disingenuously that he'd never even *seen* a gun in his life. Furthermore, the assistant D.A. was able to use Kelly to more or less corroborate Steen's claim that everyone in the neighborhood, including Mickey Featherstone, blamed Michael Holly for the death of John Bokun back in 1977.

Mickey watched from the defense table as the guy *he knew* had planned the murder of Michael Holly gave damaging testimony against him. Not only that, but the motherfucker had been put on the stand by his own attorneys.

Mickey was stunned as he watched their case slip away. He'd seen Hochheiser work his magic in the courtroom so many times, he'd come to think he was invincible. But this time Hochheiser's tactics kept backfiring, and his cross-examination seemed shoddy and lackluster.

In his heart, Mickey couldn't believe that Hochheiser had anything to do with the conspiracy against him. He'd worshiped him his whole adult life; there was no way that Larry would sell him out. But Mickey did believe that somewhere along the line Hochheiser had come to realize that he, Mickey, was being set up. Rather than take sides with Mickey, he'd apparently gone with Coonan, Aronson, and whoever else was behind the conspiracy.

As the trial wound down, Mickey began to rely more and more on Bokun's promise to walk in the door and give himself up.

'Where's Bokun?' he kept asking the attorneys. 'What's he gonna do?' Hochheiser and Aronson just shook their heads, as if they didn't have a clue.

What Mickey didn't know yet was that Bokun *had* shown up in the courthouse one afternoon. He'd delivered word to Aronson that he wanted to see him in the hallway outside. When Aronson arrived, Billy was distraught and his breath smelled of alcohol. Once again, he asked the attorney what he should do, and Aronson told him basically the same thing he had on the day of the wedding. Bokun left the courthouse that day, and it was the last anyone would see of him until after the verdict.

Later, when Mickey heard of Bokun's visit, he saw it as further proof that his attorneys had conspired against him. Mickey was angry. Angry and scared.

Along with the stress of watching his life go down the toilet, Featherstone had physical dues to pay during the trial. After each day of testimony, he was tossed into a jam-packed holding pen in the criminal courts building. He'd stand up for three, four, sometimes five hours before he got on a Bureau of Prisons bus back to Rikers. There he was held in another pen. At Rikers, you didn't dare close your eyes for a second or you risked being groped by another inmate. By the time Mickey got back to his cell it was usually some ungodly hour of the morning. Then they got him up at 6 A.M. to start the process all over again.

When Mickey arrived in court his attorneys could see he was a complete wreck. He was running on three, maybe four hours' sleep. Sometimes, as he tried to focus on the testimony – testimony he knew might put him behind bars for the rest of his life – he couldn't help drifting in and out of consciousness.

It was in this state that Mickey stood for the verdict on March 29, 1986. When it came, he couldn't say he was surprised, though the sheer finality of it was numbing.

The jury found him guilty as charged.

Sissy Featherstone cried as Mickey was led out of the courtroom and back to Rikers Island, where he stared at the bars of his cell. Even he had to appreciate the irony: In the past, he was found innocent of killings he'd definitely been involved in. Now, he had been found guilty of a murder he did not commit.

The setup was complete. Mickey had watched it slowly evolve over the months, and now whatever final doubts he might have had were gone. The final tipoff was when the black construction worker who had identified him in the lineup testified against him. Mickey knew that if he were still a valued member of the Westies, that construction worker would have fallen off a scaffolding somewhere either before or after he took the stand. But that never happened. The construction worker lived. For all Mickey knew, right this minute he was sitting in some far-off country sipping on a Piña Colada, spending the money he had no doubt been paid to finger Mickey Featherstone.

It wasn't even necessary for Mickey to go over his options. He had done it so many times already it made him nauseous to think about it. He knew all along that when the guilty verdict came in, he would have only one alternative left. It was not an alternative he relished, but it was one he was willing to consider.

As the entire West Side was about to find out, Mickey Featherstone figured he had nothing left to lose.

15

IN THE INTEREST OF JUSTICE

In late April 1986, three weeks after the verdict in the
Michael Holly murder trial, Mickey got an early morning
visit at Rikers Island from two plainclothes detectives.

'You know what this is all about, I take it,' said one of
the detectives after Mickey had been brought from his cell
to the receiving room.

'Yeah, I know. And I don't wanna go.'

'Look,' said the detective, 'everyone went to a lot of
trouble to set this meeting up. We had to get a court
order, for Chrissake. So just come and listen to what they
have to say, alright? What do you have to lose?'

'Whaddo I got to lose? My fuckin' manhood, that's
what.'

'C'mon, Mickey. If nothin' else, you can stretch your
legs.'

Featherstone sighed. 'Alright. Shit. Let's go and get it
over with.'

Still clad in his prison overalls, Mickey was handcuffed
and led by the two detectives to a black four-door sedan
outside the main gate. From there, they drove through the
streets of Queens to a half-empty parking lot, where he

and the detectives were met by another car. Featherstone was transferred quickly from one car to the other. In the front seat of this car, on the passenger side, was Jim Nauwens. In his early fifties, with thinning blond hair, Nauwens was an ex-cop currently working as a special investigator with the U.S. Attorney for the Southern District of New York.

'How you doing, Mickey?' asked Nauwens.

'Not so good.'

'Don't worry. We'll be there in thirty minutes. No sweat.'

Featherstone shrugged. He wasn't exactly sure *where* they were headed, but he knew all too well why they were headed there.

Ever since the Holly verdict, Mickey had been thinking about how shocked his friends would be if they knew he had 'reached out' to the government – not once but twice. Throughout the 1970s, no Westie was considered more of a stand-up guy than Mickey Featherstone. He'd stuck by Jimmy, even defended him, when other folks felt Coonan hadn't done right by the neighborhood. Even in recent years, as Mickey's dissatisfaction with Coonan became well known, no one would have ever believed that Mickey Featherstone would turn canary.

In truth, Featherstone's attempts to get out went back months *before* the Michael Holly murder. After trying to make it on his own, he'd come to realize that the gangster's life was not one you were allowed to walk away from. It was late 1984, a few weeks before Jimmy Coonan was scheduled to arrive home from prison. Mickey knew that when Jimmy came back everything would start up again, only now there would be deadly rivalries within their own gang. Folks would get whacked. Bodies would accumulate.

It was then that Charlie Boyle, Mickey's father, phoned the FBI. The FBI never returned his call, and Boyle didn't pursue the matter any further.

The second time Mickey made efforts to reach out, he was in a far more desperate state of mind. It was November of 1985, one year after his father's phone call, when he first contacted Ira Block, a former assistant U.S. attorney who had prosecuted him on his counterfeit currency conviction in 1979. He'd always felt that Block dealt fairly with him and was a man who could be trusted. Block, no longer with the U.S. Attorney's office, put Mickey in touch with Nauwens.

In a meeting at Rikers Island three months before the Holly murder trial got underway, Featherstone told Nauwens that he believed there was a conspiracy afoot. Nauwens was dubious. The term most often used to describe Mickey Featherstone throughout his criminal career was 'paranoid schizophrenic,' and the government investigator, at least for the moment, had no reason to believe Featherstone's claims.

'In any event,' said Nauwens, 'I can tell you right now the government isn't likely to give up something for nothing. You'll have to plead guilty to charges.'

A few days later, Featherstone met a government-assigned attorney named John Kaley at Rikers Island. Kaley, a former assistant U.S. attorney sometimes used by the government to facilitate their cooperation deals, told Mickey basically the same thing Nauwens had.

'But I didn't do it,' Mickey replied angrily. 'Why should I have to take a plea? I'm tellin' you, there's a frame goin' down. Don't that mean nothin' to youse people?'

Kaley was adamant. 'Look, Mickey, if you want to co-operate with the government now, that's fine. But with your record, you're going to have to take a plea. That's just the way it is.'

Featherstone refused. He insisted he was innocent, and he'd rather take his chances in court.

Five months later, Featherstone was convicted.

Mickey knew the government would come calling again, only this time they held all the cards. He also knew that unless he wanted to rot away in prison the rest of his life, he had no recourse but to at least listen to what they had to say.

As the car crossed the Whitestone Bridge, Mickey stared blankly at the soft blue expanse of the East River. He sat quietly as they continued north along the Hutchinson River Parkway through the Bronx, past the city limits, and into Westchester County. After exiting the expressway and driving through the streets of some suburban area Mickey was not familiar with, they arrived at a nondescript hotel at a remote outpost.

Still in handcuffs, he was taken from the car into a hotel room. One of the detectives patted him down, then removed the cuffs. Coffee and buttered rolls were brought in while Nauwens and the detectives disappeared into an adjoining room.

After sitting alone for ten minutes, Mickey was joined by John Kaley, his newly assigned government attorney.

'Hello, Mickey,' said Kaley, dressed in a crisp new

suit and tie. 'Your wife'll be in in a minute. She's being searched by an FBI agent. Female, of course.'

'Hey,' shot back Mickey. 'Why didn't you tell these people me and my wife didn't wanna come? I told you at Rikers I wanted to talk to her first.'

'It was too late when they called. Everything was set up.'

'That's bullshit.'

'Look. We're here, okay? Let's just see what they have to say.'

At that moment, Sissy walked into the room looking sallow and shaken.

'What's the matter?' asked Mickey.

'I was just stripped naked in there and searched by some woman in the bathroom.'

Kaley, the attorney, interjected, 'That's security, Sissy. They have to do that.'

'Yeah, but she could've just searched me. Not take my clothes off and look inside me.'

'Well . . .'

'Forget it. I don't wanna talk about it no more.'

Mickey and Sissy sat together on the couch, across the coffee table from Kaley.

'Okay,' said the attorney. 'Look. Here's what I'm going to do. Mickey, you claim you're innocent, right? That you didn't do this killing. I'm going to ask them to look into that.'

Sissy could hardly contain herself. She knew that Mickey had already been told if they were to look into his innocence, he would have to plead guilty to a federal racketeering charge, which carried a possible twenty-year

428

sentence. 'Hey,' she declared, 'Mickey ain't gonna take no twenty-year charge just so's he can get help to prove his innocence. No way.'

'I understand that. Let's just tell them you want help and see what they say.'

Kaley called the government people into the room. It was a large group led by Walter Mack, a rangy, blond-haired federal prosecutor. With him were Mary Lee Warren, another federal prosecutor, Jeffrey Schlanger, the assistant D.A. who prosecuted Featherstone for the Holly homicide, and Nauwens. Behind them were a half-dozen other men and women, a mix of FBI agents and NYPD detectives; all people with investigations – and careers – that would benefit greatly from the cooperation of Mickey Featherstone.

'Alright,' said Kaley, after they'd all taken their seats. 'We know why Mickey and his wife are here, so let's get to it. He says he's innocent and he's looking for help to prove it.'

'Okay,' replied Mack, who was acting as chief negotiator. 'We can do that. But first he'll have to plead to a racketeering charge, a RICO charge, and agree to cooperate. Then we can proceed from there.'

'No way,' Mickey said fiercely. 'This is the same old shit. Why should I have to plead to anything? I was set up by my lawyer, man, and everybody else too. I can prove it.'

Sissy, who'd been on the verge of tears ever since she walked in the room, began to cry.

'Look,' Kaley said to Mack. 'Will you be willing to tap their phones, have Sissy and Mickey wear a wire so they can get the real killers on tape? Would you do that?'

'Certainly. We'll do all that.'

'And the Witness Protection Program? Sissy and her kids will be relocated and cared for when this is all over?'

'Certainly. They'll have the full benefits of the Witness Program. But listen, I reiterate, none of this is going to happen unless Mickey agrees to take a plea.'

For the next twenty minutes the negotiations went back and forth with little headway. Mickey and Sissy couldn't believe the government wasn't the least bit interested in Mickey's claims of innocence unless he was first willing to plead guilty to a federal racketeering charge.

'It's the only way,' Mack insisted. 'If we were to help you establish your innocence, and you were able to do so, what guarantee would we have that you'd cooperate? Your plea is the only backup we've got.'

Eventually, Kaley asked the government people to go into the other room.

'Look,' he said, when he and Mickey and Sissy were alone again. 'Let's be realistic, Mickey. You're thirty-seven years old – right? – facing twenty-five years to life for a murder you say you didn't commit. Now, there's no way you're going to win on appeal, if that's what you're thinking. Let's face it – you are who you are. There's no judge alive that's going to reverse that conviction. You're going to get twenty-five to life for this murder.

'Now, the government is offering a twenty-year RICO, okay? If you cooperate with them, it's not likely you'll get twenty years. Not likely at all. So if we can prove your

430

innocence on the murder charge, get rid of that twenty-five to life . . . and your wife and kids'll be taken care of in the Witness Program . . . I don't know, that's not such a bad deal.'

'No,' cried Sissy. 'Maybe I can find a way to prove his innocence on my own.'

'And who's going to believe you, Sissy? C'mon, let's not be naive here. The only way you're going to *prove* anything is if the government oversees it.'

When the government team returned, the argument resumed with little or no progress until the issue of bail was brought up.

'You can get me bail?' Mickey asked Mack, a glimmer of hope in his voice.

'If your murder conviction is overturned,' said Mack, 'and all you're facing is the racketeering charge, I wouldn't object to bail.'

After the issues of bail and furloughs and conjugal visits had been tossed around for a while, Mickey and Sissy were left alone to make their decision. As Sissy tried to compose herself, Mickey glanced around at the empty room. For a brief second, he thought of just walking right out the door and starting to run. But there were cops and FBI agents all over the place. He'd just be caught and laughed at.

'Sis,' said Mickey, as depressed as he could ever remember feeling. 'What the fuck else can we do?'

The most important thing, as far as both were concerned, was somehow proving Mickey's innocence in the Holly murder. It was hard for them to think beyond that, to the hours of debriefings and grand jury hearings and trials that were sure to follow. They'd been told what might lie ahead, but it all seemed so remote. If they were somehow able to clear Mickey of the murder charge, and if at the same time he'd get bail and furloughs so he could be with his family, what else was there?

Everyone was called back into the room. Kaley conferred briefly with Mickey, then turned to Mack and the rest of the government team. 'Now let's get this straight. If Mickey cooperates, you'll investigate his innocence on the murder charge. You'll recommend bail, and once he's sentenced on the racketeering charge he'll get furloughs a few times a year. Also, his family will be placed in the Witness Protection Program. They'll be cared for during and after the period of cooperation. Is that it?'

'That's it.'

'Mickey?'

Featherstone looked up from the couch at the group, most of them middle-aged men dressed in conservative suits and ties. 'I don't know . . . you people got me in a situation here. I guess I got no choice.'

The government people all stepped forward to shake Mickey's hand. A few of them told him reassuringly that he'd 'done the right thing.'

'Alright,' said Mack. 'No sense wasting time with this. If we're all agreed, I'd like to start the debriefings right now.'

'Now?' asked Mickey.

'Sure. Why don't you just start by telling us everything you know?'

Mickey took a deep breath and tried to get his head together. He didn't have the faintest idea where to begin.

From the moment they made their pact with the government, Mickey and Sissy were obsessed with establishing Mickey's innocence. The key players, they knew, were Kevin Kelly, Kenny Shannon, and Billy Bokun. All three had been in contact with Sissy on a semiregular basis since Mickey's conviction. With her husband going away for a murder they committed, they'd gone out of their way to assuage Sissy. As was the Hell's Kitchen custom, a benefit had been held to raise money for her and the kids, and there'd been numerous phone calls and commiserations – none of which altered Sissy and Mickey's conviction that the same people now showing so much 'concern' were the very people who'd set Mickey up.

On the afternoon of May 6, 1986, two weeks after Mickey and Sissy cut their deal with the feds, Kelly and Shannon came to visit Sissy at her home in Teaneck. The Featherstone children played noisily in the next room while the three of them sat in Sissy's kitchen. Kelly, the handsome young gangster who looked like Matt Dillon, was rarely seen these days without Shannon, his fair-haired partner. Since Mickey's arrest, they'd become the most active Westies in Hell's Kitchen, with their fingers in everything from loansharking to cocaine sales.

Anxious to put Sissy at ease, Kelly and Shannon spoke freely, not knowing that just inches away, resting on the arm of a nearby chair in Sissy's pocketbook, was a small six-by-six-inch FBI-issue recorder.

'Alright, Sissy,' said Kelly, tossing an envelope onto the table. 'There's two here, you know, from us. And an extra six. We got another payment from the guy – three hundred from the pier.'

'Uh huh.'

'And that three hundred from last week, from the pier. So that's twenty-six there.'

The $2,600 was Mickey's monthly share of the loan-sharking money on the West Side piers. Kelly, Shannon, and Billy 'the Indian' Bokun had also agreed to put up $11,000 for an appeals lawyer, but that money, Kelly said, had not yet been collected.

Then Kelly launched into a tirade against Bokun, who was slow coming up with his share.

'When we talked to Billy,' said Kevin, 'Billy says, "Look, I wanna do the right thing." I said, "Well, Billy, mine and Kenny's nut comes to seven thousand now. Five thousand for the lawyer, two for Sissy." I said, "So, you wanna do the right thing? Get it on with us. Give me five hundred for Sissy, right? And two thousand for the lawyer." So he makes his first payment, right? And he tells me, he goes, "I'm gonna sell my car at the end of the month so I'll have next month's payment." I said, "Hey, Bill, whatever you wanna do . . ."'

'Yeah.'

'Because, I mean, if he don't come up with the money, you know, the kid has a fuckin' accident or somethin'. I mean, what the fuck.'

Sissy was only half-listening to Kelly; she kept worrying about the recorder. Was it picking up the conversation? Was there enough tape? Was it even on? On top of all that, there was the constant fear that somehow Kelly and Shannon might become suspicious. She'd been instructed by FBI agents on how to use the recorder, but *when* she used it was totally up to her. There were no agents backing her up in the event she was found out. It was just her and the children alone in the house with Kelly and Shannon.

'You know what always bothered me?' she asked Kelly and Shannon. 'Mickey said that when you spoke with him, you said youse didn't tell Billy to wear a mustache that day.'

'It's bullshit,' said Shannon.

'That's nothing,' agreed Kelly.

'Yeah.'

'That's fuckin' bullshit.'

'Why did he make it up then?'

'Look, Sis,' said Kelly. 'I mean, even if there was a mustache, what's the difference? He don't look nothin' like your husband.'

'He can't grow a fuckin' mustache,' added Shannon.

Sissy was miffed. 'Well, I wonder why he even wore one then. Oh, I could choke this guy.'

In their eagerness to convince Sissy, Kelly and Shannon began verbally tripping over one another: 'He didn't have one . . .' 'He didn't have a mustache . . .' 'He didn't have one that day.'

'Yeah,' said Sissy. 'But they identified him as having a mustache. That's why they picked Mickey out. The witness was sayin', "That's him!" because of the mustache and the color of his hair.'

'That's the cops tellin' them,' insisted Kelly. 'That's all that is.'

'Yeah.'

'That's gotta be, Sissy, like, coaching 'em.'

'They couldn't see Billy do it,' offered Shannon. 'Because Holly was behind 'em. You understand what I'm sayin'? And when Billy got out of the car, the car was right there, okay? He got out. He ran right in behind the truck, you know? Bing bing bing! He came out and went right behind the truck and got in the car. And we swung left. There's no possible way they could see, even from the van . . .'

'Yeah.'

'So they didn't even see it happen. They might've heard it. But the van, you know, it's about the size of this room. So if they were in the van – right? – they can't see behind the van.'

Sissy was ecstatic, though she tried hard not to show it. Shannon had admitted his role as the getaway driver, described the event itself, and even cast doubt on the validity of the government's eyewitnesses.

In the weeks that followed, there were other conversations with Kelly and Shannon in which they gave even more details on the Holly shooting. Sissy taped these as well as phone conversations with other gang members using a simple device she purchased from a local Radio Shack. Since the government was interested in more than just the Holly murder, Sissy had been instructed by Marilyn Lucht, the FBI agent assigned to her case, to establish contact with as many other Westies as possible.

It wasn't hard. On May 15th, just nine days after the kitchen meeting with Kelly and Shannon, Jimmy McElroy called Sissy to reassure her that she was going to be taken care of while her husband was away.

'Whatever we do,' McElroy told Sissy, 'you're gettin'.'

'Yeah.'

'I'm gonna make sure of that. I told the other guy – Blondie . . .'

'Who's that?'

'Jimmy.'

'Oh. Mr Coonan.'

'I was with him last week.'

'Yeah.'

'We were drinkin', right? And I told him. I said, "Let me tell you somethin'. Whatever we do, Mickey's gettin' the same." He said, "Oh, yeah, yeah, yeah, yeah." I said, "Or else I ain't doin' anything anymore."'

Sissy still got steamed whenever Coonan's name came up. 'He didn't even give nothin' to his benefit – the benefit they had for Mickey,' she said.

'I know. I know all about that. But he's gonna make it up. He . . .'

'When? In the year 2000?'

'No. I'm gonna . . . I'll take care of that. Because, listen, Sissy . . .'

'Yeah?'

'I tell ya, he knows he did wrong. Because I talked to him, and he says, "Nah, I didn't really take care of none of you guys." He was drinkin', you know? He came out with it. And it ain't even him. It's his fuckin', stinking wife!'

'Edna. Right.'

'She's a bitch, you know that.'

'Yeah, she is. She's treacherous.'

'She fucking hates us.'

437

'Uh huh. Well, she wants more money, more money, more money.'

'That's it. Greed.'

Sometimes, after taping conversations like that, Sissy would get depressed. It was bad enough that she was eliciting damaging information from people she knew; there was also the fact that everyone seemed to have turned against one another. Kelly and Shannon were constantly bitching about Billy Bokun. Bokun, in return, felt that Kelly and Shannon were out to get him. Jimmy McElroy bitched about Edna Coonan and her scheming ways. And God only knew what Jimmy Coonan was up to.

On top of all this was the weight of Sissy and Mickey's feelings of betrayal, and their participation in a plan that might bring the whole neighborhood operation to a crashing halt.

As the implications of what she was doing dawned on her, Sissy began to feel lonely and isolated. At the end of the day, after reporting to Lucht on the conversations she'd recorded that afternoon or evening, after tucking her children into bed and telling them for the umpteenth time that, no, their father was not coming home the next day, she would fall into bed, exhausted. The only way she could keep the fear and anxiety at bay was to think about her husband languishing away in his five-by-seven-foot prison cell. Only then could she muster the anger and indignation that would get her through the night, and on to the next secret recording session.

Mickey's pact with the government did nothing to change his status in general population at the Rikers Island

House of Detention. The FBI, which was monitoring his taped conversations as well, insisted that his life follow the same daily routine as any convicted prisoner awaiting sentencing. Certainly no inmates, and as few members of the prison administration as possible, were to know anything about Featherstone's status as a confidential informant.

The danger, of course, was overwhelming. If there was even the slightest inkling that Mickey Featherstone was cooperating with the government while he was still within the walls of Rikers, he would become an immediate casualty. No one knew this better than Mickey himself, who by now had spent more than ten years of his life absorbing the prison ethos.

On top of the anxiety and paranoia that went along with trying to live as an informant within the prison confines, Featherstone was under pressure from the U.S. Attorney's office to come up with indictable information. Since Sissy was not central to the Westies, the burden was on Mickey to elicit details from his friends on criminal matters other than just the Michael Holly murder. Mickey knew that with people like Kelly, Shannon, and McElroy, to appear too inquisitive would tip his hand. The idea was to ask as few questions as possible, but to ask the *right* questions.

One opportunity came on May 16th, three and a half weeks after Mickey agreed to become an informant. The occasion was a meeting with Kevin Kelly and Larry Palermo, a friend of Kelly's who'd been helping Kevin with his loanshark collections on the West Side. Before they arrived, FBI agents told Mickey they'd planted a transmitting device behind a picture on the wall in the visiting room. When Kelly and Palermo got there, they were seated under the picture.

The visiting room at Rikers Island was an open space, approximately forty feet long and twenty-five feet wide. There were large tables and chairs along the wall and even larger conference tables in the middle of the room. Two prison guards stood by the door, and at the far end of the room was a glass control booth where surveillance cameras kept a steady watch.

Mickey was brought into the room and took a seat across a wallside table from Kelly and Palermo. There were maybe fifty or sixty other people in the room, inmates and their visitors passing time.

Kevin Kelly still had no idea that Mickey believed he'd been deliberately set up to take the rap for the Holly shooting. As far as Kevin knew, Mickey was 'doing the right thing' – sitting out the time as long as he was certain his wife would be taken care of.

'Just so's I can clear my head,' said Mickey, after he'd arrived and taken a seat across the table from Kelly and Palermo. 'What money are you givin' Sissy?'

'We're gonna give Sissy two thousand,' replied Kevin, 'beginning of every month. It never stops.'

'Alright. 'Cause that's all I'm worried about.'

'Oh yeah. I told you that. Your wife's never gonna sell the house . . . just as long as we're alive, you know. Long as I'm on the street, me and Kenny.'

It had been weeks since Kelly last talked with Mickey, so he spent five or ten minutes filling him in on the neighborhood gossip. Billy Bokun was pissing everybody off, said Kevin, because he was stoned all the time and not making his payments to Sissy. And ever since Mickey went away, Kevin said, McElroy had been getting tighter and tighter with Jimmy Coonan.

'Mac's his bodyguard now,' sneered Kevin. 'Can you believe that shit? He's with him all the way, know what I mean? He drives him around. I seen him yesterday with a suit.'

'McElroy!?' asked Mickey skeptically.

'Yeah,' answered Kevin, laughing. 'He was wearing polyester.'

Since they were on the topic of McElroy, Mickey said he wanted to ask Kevin about an item he'd seen in the paper a few days earlier. It involved the shooting of a Carpenter's Union official named John O'Connor. In several phone conversations during the days leading up to the shooting, McElroy had alluded to something that 'might be good,' which Mickey interpreted to mean some sort of criminal business.

The O'Connor shooting had all the makings of a Westies hit, and Mickey had immediately suspected there might be some connection between it and his conversations with McElroy.

Before Mickey could even finish asking about the shooting, Kelly spoke up. 'Fucking guy just asked for it.'

'I swear to my mother,' said Mickey, laughing. 'I knew you guys did it. For some reason, I just sensed it, you know? Papers said a Spanish guy, right?'

'Yeah.'

'But, you know what? The description of the shooter fits your description. It's your height and weight and everything.'

441

'Well, that's what they said on the news; that this guy was a hundred and forty pounds, dark glasses. It said he wore a Band-Aid over his right eye. I've got a scar over my right eye.'

'So who was it for? For Jimmy?'

'Oh yeah. For the greaseballs. Somethin' they needed quick.'

Kevin explained how Coonan and McElroy had attended the funeral of Frankie DeCicco, a Gambino family *capo* who'd recently been blown to smithereens while sitting in his car on a Brooklyn street. Coonan's 'Italian connection,' Danny Marino, was at the funeral, and mentioned that he'd been given an assignment to shoot O'Connor, a business agent for Carpenters Local 608. Supposedly, O'Connor had run afoul of the Mafia when he trashed a Gambino-run restaurant for using nonunion labor. Marino added that he was having trouble getting the job done.

'So they volunteered!' exclaimed Kelly. 'They volunteered their fuckin' services. Him and Mac. So about ten days ago they come up to me and Kenny, fuckin' cryin'. And McElroy said, "What am I gonna do? What am I gonna do?" So I told them, I says, "Don't be doin' that, 'cause I ain't doin' it no more. This is the last time." Then, uh, me and Kenny set it up.'

Kelly, whose jet-black hair and dark complexion could easily be mistaken as being of Spanish heritage, explained how he waited outside the offices of Local 608 near 51st Street and Broadway early on the morning of May 7th. Once O'Connor arrived for work, Kelly followed him into the lobby of the building and proceeded to shoot him four times below the waist. O'Connor fell into the elevator, bleeding profusely.

Kevin chuckled. 'He's a donkey, this guy O'Connor.'

'He's hot-headed like?'

'Yeah, he's got an Irish brogue. You know, one of them guys?'

'Right.'

'He's got a hot ass now,' interjected Palermo.

They all broke up laughing.

'Yeah,' Kevin snorted. 'He's got . . . he's got an extra asshole.'

'Oh, shit,' said Mickey, who was practically bent over laughing.

''Cause, you know what happened was, he was supposed to get kneecapped, not murdered, and the bullets ended up high. One went in his ass, you know, the bullets. So Coonan told Danny Marino, he said to Danny, "One of the kids got pissed off and shot him in the ass for being an asshole." So Marino answers, "Wow!"'

'Yeah?'

Even as Kevin spoke, Mickey was astounded by the implications of what he was being told. He knew that just five months earlier, while he was in prison awaiting trial for the Holly murder, Paul Castellano, the *capo di tutti capi*, and his bodyguard, Thomas Bilotti, had been dramatically gunned down outside Sparks, a midtown Manhattan steak house, during the Christmas holidays. Castellano's murder had set off a series of reprisal killings – including the car bombing of Frankie DeCicco. Once the dust had settled, the new leader of the powerful Gambino family was believed to be John Gotti, a previously unheralded *capo* from Howard Beach, Queens.

Mickey knew that Coonan's buddy, Danny Marino, was tight with Gotti, which could mean only one thing. Now that Castellano was out of the picture, Coonan was already sucking up to the new Godfather. He'd volunteered to do this shooting for Marino knowing it would put him in good standing with Gotti.

'Let me get this straight,' said Mickey, trying to make sure Kevin stated it as clearly as possible on tape. 'What I don't understand, right? Is Danny Marino with Gotti or . . .'

'Danny Marino's with Gotti.'

'He is with him?'

'Danny Marino's with Gotti.'

'See, I wasn't sure.'

'Right. Yeah, he's with him now. He even mentioned that to me.'

Later that night Mickey sat in his cell in C Block and ran it over and over in his mind. He'd had no contact with any FBI agents since his conversation with Kevin Kelly that afternoon. But he could imagine them sitting in a room somewhere, listening over headphones as Kevin bragged about the shooting he'd done for Marino and Gotti. He knew that ever since the Castellano killing the feds had had a hard-on for Gotti, whose sartorial splendor and flamboyant style hearkened back to an earlier era of gangsterism.

Just a few days earlier, one of the FBI agents handling Featherstone's case had given him a stern lecture about not having gathered any useful information.

Well, thought Mickey, if this don't satisfy the pointy-headed bastards, nothing will.

At least once every day, and sometimes three, four, or five times in a twenty-four-hour period, Mickey and Sissy spoke on the phone. Working with the platoon of lawyers and agents assigned to Mickey's case, they had a pretty good idea what was needed to get his conviction overturned. Each week, Sissy pored over transcripts with their attorney, John Kaley, and with Assistant D.A. Jeffrey Schlanger, who would be instrumental if the Holly verdict were to be reversed.

So far, what they had gathered from Kevin Kelly and Kenny Shannon was strong. What they needed to tie it all together was a confession from the person who'd actually pulled the trigger that day.

In the few times Sissy had spoken with Billy Bokun since Mickey's conviction, he'd been stoned out of his mind. Bokun had become convinced that Kelly and Shannon were going to kill him, and his conversations with Sissy were filled with anger and paranoia. One time, on 9th Avenue, he told Sissy flat out, 'They set your husband up and now they're tryin' to set me up too!'

On the afternoon of May 18th, Sissy made arrangements to meet with Billy Bokun at the 9th Avenue International Food Festival, one of the city's largest street fairs, running down the middle of 9th Avenue from West 34th Street all the way up to West 57th.

By the time Sissy spotted Bokun on the corner of 51st Street and 9th Avenue, it was already late afternoon. The sun had dipped low in the sky, and the shadows from the old Hell's Kitchen tenement buildings stretched across the avenue. But there were still thousands of people milling about, shoulder to shoulder, and the smoky aroma of burning grills and fresh-cooked foods was as pungent as it had been all day.

'Billy! Billy!' shouted Sissy as Bokun, a beer in one hand, approached through the crowd. She made sure her purse, which contained the recorder, was hanging in front of her body.

'What's up?' said Billy, leaning on a mailbox on the corner of 51st Street in front of a Spanish bodega.

'Alright,' answered Sissy. 'I just feel funny. Like, I asked the guys, "Have you seen Billy around?" They said, "Every once in a while, like, I'll bump into him." It's like, we look at each other, you know, you could at least say hello.'

'Yeah, I . . . you know, hey, Sis. Well . . .'

'It's ridiculous. I mean, I feel stupid.'

'No . . . I feel, uh, I feel the same way.'

Sissy and Billy Bokun had known each other since they were young kids. Both were born on 9th Avenue, just blocks from where they now stood. Billy had been best friends with Sissy's brother Danny before Danny got busted for assault and sent away to prison. It pained Sissy to see Billy in such a desperate state. It pained her even more to have to lure him into a conversation she hoped would vindicate her husband, and maybe, at the same time, put Bokun away for the rest of his life.

'I'm gonna be honest with you,' said Billy. 'I had one beer. This is my first beer. I'm not drunk, and I'm not high or nothin'.'

446

'Uh huh.'

'I'm straight. I just got outta bed a little while ago. I mean, let me be honest with you, I'm goin' for broke with this, you know, this appeals lawyer for your husband. I'm ready to sell my car. 'Cause I have no money. I'm not working. Everybody's fuckin' makin' money but me. Okay? And I'm not sayin' a fuckin' word. I ain't gonna say nothin'. Listen, I'm not doin' nothin' no more. I mean, I'm not gettin' into horses, killing nobody else. I'm straight.'

'Well, Mickey still feels like, "Why did Billy turn around and say Kenny told him to wear a mustache?"'

'He did. He said, "Wear your wig. Pencil in your mustache and shave it off afterwards."'

'See, now, they never brought up the mustache. Kevin says you didn't wear a mustache.'

'I had a mustache. But it was so light and so thin I had to pencil it in. It was an eyeliner mustache.'

'That's what's messin' Mickey up. Mickey's goin', "Why the fuck?" 'Cause I said to Mickey, "I don't doubt Billy." I said, "Billy says to this day they told him to wear a mustache. I don't doubt that . . ."'

'Oh, Sissy, I did a job on myself. I did a job that you wouldn't believe. They couldn't identify me. They still can't identify me!'

'Yeah.'

'I mean, if eyewitnesses couldn't, you know, I did one hell of a job. If I say so myself.'

'Were you high, though, that day?'

'No, I was straight.'

'I mean, at ten to twelve in the afternoon, go shoot somebody?'

'No, I was straight.'

'Yeah? Did Michael Holly ever see you comin' towards him?'

'Uh, I was in the car. He didn't see nothin'. I jumped out. Boom! I just shot him. One-two-three-four-five. Back in the car. Ten seconds, no more.'

'There was one black guy that day. A construction guy.'

'Well, I aimed the gun at him. Yeah, I was gonna shoot everybody dead. Okay? But, the only reason I didn't was I had no bullets . . . Like, I didn't, well, I'm not ashamed of what I did. I think what I did is absolutely right.'

'Why you did it is, you feel . . .'

'I feel 'cause he whacked my brother. He was responsible for John. Otherwise I wouldn't have done it. Okay? I'm not a go-shooter. I'm not a cowboy. I'm just what I am, right? I'm a workin' guy.'

Sissy knew she had enough to hang Billy already, but she let him go on. Billy seemed to need to talk, to reassure Sissy that he had nothing to do with Mickey taking the fall.

'Far as I'm concerned,' continued Billy, 'I do believe the cops framed your husband. Somebody told them from jump street who did it. They say, "Well, no way we can get Bokun. We can probably frame Featherstone." The way I'm looking at it now . . .'

'Right.'

'They framed your husband. Okay? Your husband added to the frame by going to Erie, which was a mental mistake. Okay? Going to check.'

'But remember when you said, "Kevin fuckin' set me

448

up. And he didn't only set me up, he set Mickey up along with me." Remember?'

'Right. I said that after the fact. After I spoke to your husband, after me and Mickey decided that it was true . . . The only thing I can say is, what I was told is everything was taken care of. Everybody had their place and their alibis. He could've hid hisself, you know? He could've put hisself at the dentist or anything.'

'But he said that they called him that morning to use the car. Kenny, or somebody, called to use his Tempo that he was leasing.'

'But that was the fucking plan! See, the plan was . . . alls I was supposed to do was go over to that corner, you know, and go and shoot the guy. And I didn't know nothin' else about the plan.'

'Yeah.'

'That's what I was supposed to do. And I did what I was supposed to do. And now I get all the repercussions! See, the reason I'm by myself is, I don't know, I'm not the type of guy who can walk around and shoot everybody. I can shoot anyone for my brother, but I can't just go out and whack everybody. It's my personality. I mean, that's my big fault. I guess it's my loyalty to everybody, you know. I'm so loyal, 'cause I can't help it.'

The sun had begun to set, and the booths along 9th Avenue were finally being taken apart. As the crowds thinned out, a soft breeze sent debris and dust flying about. Sissy told Billy she had to get going and pick up her children from her mother's apartment on 56th Street.

'I hope your husband gets out,' said Billy, his voice straining with emotion. "Cause, you know, I sit here . . .'

449

'He'll be alright.'

'I sit here and, more than anybody, it bothers me.'

'Alright, Billy. Take care.'

Sissy watched Billy head south on 9th Avenue. When he was a safe distance away, she peeked inside her purse to make sure the recorder was on. It was.

She didn't know whether to be elated or depressed. In all likelihood, this would be the last time she would see Billy Bokun for a long, long while. And the next time would probably be in court.

On the afternoon of September 5th, Francis Thomas Featherstone was brought before the same judge, Alvin Schlessinger, in the same courtroom where just five months earlier he'd been convicted for the murder of Michael Holly.

John Kaley had just put forth a motion to have his client's conviction vacated. Joining Kaley in that motion was Assistant D.A. Jeffrey Schlanger, the same prosecutor who secured Mickey's conviction.

Schlanger had been promoted to the Rackets Bureau following his widely heralded prosecution of Featherstone. He admitted being 'skeptical' upon first hearing Mickey's assertion that he was not the shooter in the Holly killing. But after listening to the taped conversations with Kelly, Shannon, and Bokun, he'd changed his mind.

'On too many occasions to cite,' he said, reading from a prepared text, 'the New York County D.A.'s office has gone to extreme and extraordinary lengths to investigate claims of innocence by people either charged or convicted of crimes which they claimed they did not do. Usually those claims do not hold water. However, on those rare occasions when they do, our obligation to see that justice is carried out is clear: that conviction must be set aside . . .

'When all the evidence in this particular case is taken together, the People are now convinced beyond a reasonable doubt that it was William Bokun and not Francis Featherstone who shot and killed Michael Holly on April 25, 1985.'

Judge Schlessinger listened dutifully to Schlanger's statement, but for all intents and purposes his decision had already been made. Since the beginning of Mickey's and Sissy's cooperation, the judge had been kept abreast of the investigation. He'd been informed of the Featherstones' ongoing debriefings with the FBI, the U.S. Attorney's office, and the Manhattan D.A. He'd pored over the transcripts from Mickey and Sissy's undercover conversations with Kelly, Shannon, and Bokun. And he'd gone over the legal precedents for the highly unusual ruling he was now being asked to make.

As the judge prepared to deliver his verdict, Mickey stood to face the court. Ever since he could remember, he'd been called 'paranoid' by doctors, lawyers, and even friends. Nobody believed him when he claimed he was not the person who killed Michael Holly, and nobody believed him when he said he'd been deliberately set up. He'd been forced to pursue a path he never wanted to, a path that had isolated him from everyone in his life except for his wife and family.

What he hoped for now was more than just vindication. What he hoped for was deliverance.

'In the interest of justice,' declared Judge Schlessinger with the bang of his gavel, 'I am compelled to overturn this conviction.'

Mickey was asked if he had anything to say. He responded with a simple, 'Thank you.'

Later, he decided what he should have said – loud enough for every cop, prosecutor and judge in New York County to hear – was, 'I told you so.'

16

MICKEY'S NEW FRIENDS

Long before Richie Egan arrived at the offices of the U.S. Attorney, he had a pretty good idea why he'd been summoned. A prosecutor, Mary Lee Warren, had informed him it involved a federal racketeering case they were building against Jimmy Coonan and other West Side crime figures. Egan knew there was no way the Southern District would attempt a case of this magnitude unless they had a big-time witness on their side. Now that Mickey Featherstone's conviction had been vacated, there was only one possible explanation.

Featherstone must have flipped.

Egan's sixteen years as a cop had taught him never to be too surprised by anything, especially the whims and machinations of a professional racketeer. Yet he found it hard to imagine Mickey Featherstone cooperating with the government. In police circles, Featherstone always had a reputation as the ultimate tough guy, the kind of person who would just as soon spit in a cop's face as shake his hand.

In some ways, Egan found it comforting that people

453

like Featherstone existed. It made it that much easier to distinguish the good guys from the bad guys.

But if Featherstone was serving as a government informant, presumably he had decided to forswear his past. Egan wasn't buying that just yet, but one lesson seemed clear: No matter how tough the criminal, there was always the possibility that one day he might join hands with the government, whatever his personal motivations.

At the U.S. Attorney's office, adjacent to the federal courthouse at 1 St Andrews Plaza in lower Manhattan, Egan got a complete rundown on the case from Warren and the other investigators involved. Not only were Featherstone and his wife cooperating with the investigation, but extensive debriefings by the FBI and the Manhattan D.A.'s office had already begun.

In order to put the Westies away for good, the government would have to charge them with the Racketeer Influenced and Corrupt Practices (RICO) Act. And in order to do that, they would need to go above and beyond the individual crimes and establish a 'pattern of racketeering,' which is where Egan came in.

'What we're proposing,' Warren told Egan, 'is that you move in with us full-time. Nobody knows this particular group of criminals as well as you. We could use your expertise on this. You'd have a desk right here with us, and you'd be working in conjunction with all the other branches of the investigation – the FBI, Narcotics, Homicide, and the Manhattan Task Force South.'

Egan had plenty of reasons to say no to the government's offer. For one thing, he'd been promoted to detective in '79 and was currently working on an investigation of

Colombian drug traffickers in Brooklyn. Along with the Drug Enforcement Administration, he'd been gathering intelligence on that case for nearly three years now, and it would soon be entering its crucial final stages. Like most cops, Egan didn't like the idea of leaving an investigation just when it was beginning to heat up.

And there were inherent pitfalls in working with the U.S. Attorney's office. Throughout his career with the NYPD, Egan had heard many horror stories from cops who'd gone to work with federal prosecutors and regretted every minute of it. Federal prosecutors were a different breed – ivory-tower lawyers with no understanding of the streets, much less hard-core criminal behavior. Many had political ambitions of their own and tended to view a member of the city's police department, however distinguished, as little more than a necessary evil.

Egan was aware of this, yet knew immediately what his answer would be. In all his years as a cop, no case had gotten his adrenaline going quite like the West Side investigation. Plus, it was rare for an Intelligence cop to get an opportunity to see a case through to the end. Usually Intell laid the groundwork, then some other division came along and got all the credit when the arrests and convictions got handed down. Here was a chance to make sure the boys from Intell would be given due representation. Egan felt he owed it to himself – and the Division – to say yes.

Within days of his meeting with Warren, Egan moved in with the other investigators assigned to the case on the 9th floor of 1 St Andrews Plaza, just down the hall from Warren and her thirty-one-year-old co-prosecutor, David

Brodsky. The accommodations, of course, were a mere formality. With all the debriefings and surveillance operations yet to come, Egan knew he'd be spending very little time behind a desk.

The first order of business was to join the ongoing debriefings with Featherstone. Art Ruffles, an FBI investigator, along with Detective Steve Mshar from the NYPD's Task Force South, had been questioning Mickey on crimes involving Coonan, Kelly, McElroy, Shannon, and others. Already, they had gathered information on a staggering number of crimes spanning some twenty years.

Where Egan's expertise was needed most was in the area of historical background. Using the Intelligence Division's voluminous files, he might be able to give the investigation the kind of overview necessary for the government to bring all the names and events together in one neat RICO package.

Within days after Featherstone's conviction was overturned, Egan had his initial meeting with Mickey. As had been the case at least once a day for the last few months, Mickey was brought from the Manhattan Correctional Center (MCC), where he was now being held, to a conference room in the U.S. Attorney's office. It was the first time the two men had been face-to-face since March of 1979, when Egan, with about a half-dozen other detectives, had arrested Mickey for the Whitehead murder in front of a check-cashing store on 10th Avenue.

'Mickey,' said Egan, extending his hand, 'for what it's worth, no hard feelings.'

'No,' replied Featherstone. 'I got no hard feelings for

you. You was always straight with me.' Then he laughed and added, 'Wish I could say the same for your fellow officers.'

Egan had not really known what to expect from Featherstone. He'd heard how Mickey felt he'd been framed for the Michael Holly murder by his fellow gang members. There was no telling whether he would be embittered by this, and see his cooperation as an opportunity to settle old scores, or whether he would be contrite, hoping only to clean his own slate and start anew. As an Intelligence cop Egan had interviewed dozens of criminals in similar situations, and there were no set patterns. Some were surly and argumentative. Some felt shame and humiliation. Others were polite, even downright friendly.

Over the following weeks, Egan found that Mickey was a little bit of everything. Often, after he was brought from his cell for his daily debriefing session, Featherstone would start out angry and uncommunicative. Usually his anger had something to do with the U.S. Attorney's office, which he felt was not doing enough to get him a bail hearing. Sometimes it had to do with the treatment he was receiving at the MCC, where, he claimed, inmates in the Witness Protection wing were constantly derided as stoolies and 'cheese eaters' – or rats – by the guards who worked there.

After a while, though, Mickey always calmed down. 'It's not you, Richie,' he would say to Detective Egan. 'I ain't angry with you. It's those other bastards.' Then the two men would begin to burrow back through Mickey's past, dredging up memories of violence and criminal behavior that Featherstone had, over the years, buried deep in his memory.

Egan was particularly interested in reviewing the years when Mickey first hooked up with Jimmy Coonan. That was when Sergeant Tom McCabe, Egan's supervisor, had first begun to push for a full-scale investigation of the Hell's Kitchen Irish Mob. Specifically, it was the murders of Tom Devaney, Eddie Cummiskey, and Tom Kapatos in '76 and early '77 that had first piqued McCabe's interest. Despite the hours and hours of investigation by McCabe, Egan, and others, those murders had never been solved.

'You gotta remember,' Mickey told Egan. 'Coonan kept me in the dark 'bout a lot of things. To tell ya the truth, I was never interested. But I can tell ya who was behind those murders – Fat Tony Salerno. Definitely.'

Just as McCabe and Egan had always suspected, the killings were part of Salerno's struggle with Mickey Spillane for control of the soon-to-be-constructed Jacob Javits Convention Center. Joseph 'Mad Dog' Sullivan, the freelance hit man famed for his Attica escape and long rumored to have been involved in Jimmy Hoffa's demise, did the hits for Salerno, boss of the Genovese crime family, in expectation that he'd get a piece of the Convention Center rackets. But after the killings, Fat Tony reneged on his part of the bargain, and in 1978 a very pissed off Mad Dog Sullivan came to Coonan and Featherstone looking to join their crew.

Egan listened to Featherstone's stories with utter fascination. Over the years, the West Side investigation had always suffered from a certain lack of cohesion.

There had been so many seemingly related homicides that the Syndicated Crime Unit had barely been able to keep track of them all. Now, Mickey was connecting files and files of Intelligence data from more than a decade's worth of surveillances and investigations.

To Egan, some of Mickey's most intriguing revelations involved jobs that went unfinished. Like the plot to murder Fat Tony himself. Apparently, around the time Coonan and Featherstone heard that Salerno was positioning himself to take control of the Convention Center, they decided to take matters into their own hands. On three separate occasions, said Featherstone, he and Coonan, along with Jimmy McElroy and Richie Ryan, armed themselves with an arsenal of weaponry and drove to Salerno's favorite social club at 116th Street and Pleasant Avenue in East Harlem. The idea was to blow him away in broad daylight. Luckily for Salerno, they never spotted him.

Another scheme that never materialized was Jimmy Coonan's grand plan to link up the Hell's Kitchen Mob with an Irish gang in Boston run by Jimmy's friend from Sing Sing, Pete Wilson (one of the original Irishmen spotted at the Stage Deli by Sergeant Tom McCabe in '77). Once, after numerous meetings with Wilson in New York, Featherstone, Coonan, and his brother Jackie flew to Boston to carry out a heist with Wilson and his boys. Together they robbed a pharmaceutical warehouse one night, then returned to Manhattan with the intention of pursuing their Boston connection at a later date. But events in the neighborhood kept getting in the way, and the alliance – which would have been the first known partnership between Irish gangsters in the two cities – never went any further.

Throughout the latter months of 1986, Featherstone was pumped relentlessly for information. Along with Egan, there were federal prosecutors, city D.A.s, FBI agents, and, at one time or another, cops from just about every department in the NYPD. Most had little interest in Featherstone other than as a source of information. In recent years, the Westies had become one of the city's more notorious organized crime cases. Featherstone's co-operation ensured that from here on out, anyone connected with the case could expect lots of free publicity. To those investigators with their sights on career advancement, the Westies case, or, more pointedly, Mickey Featherstone, was their ticket to the promised land.

And what a ticket he proved to be. Before Featherstone was done, he had given the government information on, among other things, thirty unsolved homicides in Manhattan going back some sixteen years. Of the thirty murders, six had been committed by Eddie 'the Butcher' Cummiskey, four by Jimmy Coonan, five by Richie Ryan, three by Kevin Kelly, and three by Jimmy McElroy. On top of all that, Mickey detailed his own involvement in hundreds of beatings, stabbings, and shootings both before and during his time as Jimmy Coonan's right-hand man.

To Featherstone, the debriefing process was long and rough. It wasn't his show. At times, he resented having his brain picked four, five, sometimes six hours a day. He would demand food and refreshments at odd intervals – anything to break the monotony and make him feel like he was in control. But eventually Mickey settled in and began to see the value in what he was doing. Not so much for the government, but for himself. It was his chance to set the record straight.

A few of the investigators, like Egan, Marilyn Lucht, and Art Ruffles of the FBI, were aware of the toll it was taking on Featherstone. Mickey had stayed high or drunk for most of the violence over the years. Now, they were asking him to rehash, over and over again, gruesomely detailed descriptions of brutal killings and dismemberments totally sober. Egan, for one, realized if they pushed Featherstone too hard he might crack before they ever had a chance to get him into court.

Sometimes, usually at the end of a marathon interview session, Egan would attempt to humanize these encounters, to take Featherstone beyond the names, dates, and facts. Once, he asked Mickey how it had gotten so violent; how, as human beings, they had been able to watch arms, legs, and heads being severed without realizing they had gone too far.

'It was no big deal,' Mickey said with a forced bravado. 'It's like a coroner, right? After you've seen it a few times you can deal with it.'

'Yeah,' said Egan. 'But these were people you knew. Some of them people you'd known your whole life. Neighborhood people.'

Mickey thought about this; his voice got quiet and uncertain. He admitted that after a while it got vicious, even evil. 'But youse gotta realize,' he pleaded. 'That wasn't me. I never could stomach that – the cutting up. It was Coonan. Always Coonan.'

461

At one point, Mickey's shame had caused him to almost violate his agreement with the government. He had been warned – in writing – that if he ever withheld information about a crime he was involved in and it later came to light, the agreement would be terminated. Even so, in his description of the Rickey Tassiello murder, Mickey never mentioned stabbing Tassiello. Even though Coonan had told him to do it, Mickey always felt disgraced by that act. Throughout his life, he'd derived a scrap of twisted pride from the fact that he never inflicted violence on anyone who didn't have a chance to defend himself. But sticking a knife in a dead man, that was something different.

Eventually, Mickey was called before a grand jury to tell what he knew about the Tassiello murder. He sat in a holding pen before being led into the jury room and thought about what he was going to do. He reminded himself that he'd made a commitment to give the *entire* truth. After a life of crime, it was not a philosophy he embraced easily. But he knew that Tony Lucich was testifying. Lucich knew Mickey had stuck a knife into Tassiello's chest. Mickey would have to come clean.

Before the grand jury, nervous and soaked with perspiration, Featherstone admitted what he had done. He admitted taking a knife and plunging it into the heart of a dead man.

With Mickey and Sissy Featherstone providing more and more pieces of the puzzle, the government got ready to throw out the net. Now that Mickey was on the side of the law, the Westies were like a wounded animal. And this time, the investigators were determined not to let the gang slip through their grasp. They resolved to eradicate what was left of the West Side Irish Mob, once and for all.

Along with Steve Mshar and other detectives from the Task Force South, Richie Egan took to the streets. Driving around Hell's Kitchen again after all these years was a strange experience for Egan. It made him feel old. The neighborhood was hardly recognizable now. Long gone were the White House Bar, Sonny's Cafe, the Sunbrite, the 596 Club, and the other saloons that Coonan, Featherstone, and their predecessors had frequented. Many of the old tenement buildings had been leveled and replaced by condos and co-op apartment buildings. The grizzled old Irish and Italian faces of a bygone era were few and far between. It was not uncommon to see people in suits and with briefcases hustling to and from Hell's Kitchen, a neighborhood now known almost exclusively as Clinton.

It didn't take a genius to figure it out, thought Egan. After the thousands of hours' worth of surveillance they'd done, and all the trials and investigations, gentrification had probably done more to force the Westies out of Hell's Kitchen than anything law enforcement was able to do.

Once they began their surveillance, the cops were surprised to discover that Jimmy Coonan had all but disappeared. Before it was known Mickey had flipped, they'd heard he was sometimes seen driving around the neighborhood in a black Mercedes 4-door with a cellular phone. Edna, the one-time orphan from 9th Avenue, also had a new Mercedes; hers was blue. She too was often seen cruising along the avenues of the West Side like some upwardly mobile expatriate who just couldn't resist flaunting her wealth back in the old neighborhood.

When Mickey flipped (WESTIES CON SINGS IRISH LULLABY, trumpeted the *Post*), the Coonans were seen less and less frequently. Jimmy had done what all successful gangsters were supposed to do. He'd gone into a 'legitimate' business. Along with his old pals Billy Murtha and Buddy Leahy – the guys who'd hired him and Mickey to whack James Maher of the Metal Lathers union in July of '78 – Jimmy had begun investing heavily in Marine Construction, a sizable contracting firm based just north of the city in Tarrytown. It was a profitable business, but its real purpose was to give Coonan a patina of respectability when the shit finally hit the fan. It also served as an ideal way for him to launder his criminal proceeds.

In Coonan's absence, the remains of the West Side's ground-level rackets were up for grabs. For years, Kevin Kelly – Jimmy Coonan's protégé – had been positioning himself for just such a moment. Now, even though Featherstone's cooperation was headline news, even though there were ongoing state and federal grand juries and subpoenas were being delivered up and down the West Side of Manhattan, Kelly stepped forward to seize what he felt was rightfully his.

Egan had heard about Kelly and Shannon during his interviews with Featherstone. Emboldened by Coonan's inattentiveness, they'd even taken their criminal ambitions beyond the neighborhood by pushing cocaine in some of the swankier bars on Manhattan's Upper East Side, near where sidekick Kenny Shannon had been born and raised.

One time, said Mickey, Kelly told him they'd heard someone was dealing coke out of one of 'their' bars, the Comic Strip Bar and Grill on East 81st and 2nd Avenue. Kelly and Shannon drove to the bar, found the guy, and took him outside at knife point. They handcuffed the dealer, who was a mere novice, put him in the backseat of the car, and issued the usual warnings and threatening suggestions. Then Kelly and Shannon unzipped their pants and masturbated all over the guy.

Even Featherstone, who'd taken part in hundreds of stabbings, shootings, and dismemberments over the years, had to admit this was a new and twisted variation on the accepted rules of intimidation.

Throughout the summer and into the fall of '86, Egan, Mshar, and others gathered hours of incriminating evidence against Kelly, Shannon, and Larry Palermo from a recording device placed in the dashboard of a blue '85 Oldsmobile Cutlass driven by Shannon. One time they even overheard Kelly slapping around one of his loanshark customers on 9th Avenue.

'I don't fuckin' buy this, man,' proclaimed Kelly, who had stepped outside of the car to confront his victim. 'I'm the one you're supposed to pay. I'm the man on the street. You hear me? He ain't the man. I'm the man.'

At the end of a long day, while Egan filled out his surveillance log, just as he had years ago when *West Side Story* first began, he would think about Kelly, Shannon, and others who seemed to be following in Coonan's footsteps. It reminded him of an adage he'd heard many years ago, probably from his Irish-born father:

Old habits die hard.

By the winter of '86, a new kind of paranoia became the rule of the day in West Side criminal circles. With all the subpoenas that had been handed out, the remaining gang members had gotten a pretty good idea of exactly who and what was being investigated. The implications were truly frightening. There were ongoing grand jury hearings on the Paddy Dugan, Ruby Stein, Rickey Tassiello, and Vinnie Leone murders, just to name a few. Search warrants were being executed all over the neighborhood and the feds were accumulating evidence on gambling, narcotics, and gun possession charges. Federal agents had been to the offices of theatrical Teamsters Local 817 and ILA Local 1909 and seized files.

On top of all this, there were rumors floating around about who would be testifying along with Mickey and Sissy Featherstone. Tony Lucich, the old-time loanshark who initiated Jimmy Coonan into the business back in the early seventies and was best man at his wedding, had also flipped. From his hideout in New Jersey, Coonan immediately put out a contract on Lucich, but Tony hadn't been seen around the neighborhood in weeks.

The cooperation of the Featherstones and then Lucich had created a justifiable concern that others would follow suit, and that as the domino effect fell into place, friend would turn against friend, brother against brother.

One person who was a likely candidate for the role of informant was Billy Beattie. Ever since he'd returned to the neighborhood to help Mickey plot the murder of Jimmy Coonan, he had lived in constant fear. Not only was Coonan still after him for debts incurred before he ran away to the mountains, but since his return he'd become more and more dependent on Mickey – half hoping that once they got rid of Coonan, Mickey would take over and he'd be sitting pretty.

But then Beattie had been in his kitchen watching TV one night, and a report came on the news about Featherstone's cooperation. Billy felt like his whole world had just been pulled out from under him. Not only did Mickey know about his involvement in the Paddy Dugan and Ruby Stein homicides, but recently Beattie had been involved in another murder with a guy he knew out in Queens – a cop killing! Although he was reasonably certain Mickey didn't know anything about this one, Beattie had a bad feeling that one thing might lead to another.

With a wife and six kids, it wasn't like Billy could just run off to the mountains again. All through the summer of '86, after he first heard about Mickey's cooperation, Beattie lived in abject terror, fully expecting the cops to come knocking at his door, not knowing what he would do when they did.

In October of '86, Beattie's worst fear finally came to pass. There was a knock on his door one day. He answered. It was Detective Steve Mshar of the Manhattan Task Force South – with an arrest warrant.

One month later, on the afternoon of November 14th, Beattie was seated in Smoke Stacks Lightning, a chic bar and restaurant at West Broadway and Canal Street in lower Manhattan. He was there with a guy named 'Ron,' who supposedly was looking to make a drug deal with Beattie's lifelong neighborhood friend, Jimmy McElroy.

When McElroy walked in the door, he was carrying with him a package of barbiturates, wrapped in a brown paper bag. Beattie, McElroy, and Ron had been trying to consummate the deal for a week, but McElroy, as was often the case in recent months, kept getting stoned and missing the appointed meetings.

This time there was going to be another problem, which Jimmy Mac knew about before he even sat down. Beattie's buyer had ordered a bag of 5,000 pink-colored 'uppers.' But in his haste to make their meeting, McElroy had accidentally grabbed the wrong pills from his apartment in Jersey.

'How's it going?' McElroy asked nonchalantly after walking over to the table where Beattie and Ron were sitting.

'Hey,' said Beattie. 'I was just sayin' I know this traffic's got his fuckin' ass.'

McElroy sat down and got right to the point. 'Uh, you know what happened? The fuckin' kid, the asshole, he sent the green ones over instead.'

'Oh, shit,' mumbled Beattie.

'I can go get 'em, though,' said Jimmy. 'I got the green ones with me, you know. They're better, I think. But I can get the pink ones. It'll take me about an hour.'

It was 4:30 P.M., rush hour, and outside the restaurant the traffic was bumper to bumper on Canal Street.

'Jimmy,' asked Beattie, 'do you know what time it is? You're never gonna get through the tunnel in an hour. It'll take you over an hour just to get to Jersey!'

McElroy complained, 'Last night I told him, "Bring the pink ones." He gave me the green ones, the fucking jerk.'

'This is the second time, Jimmy. I had Ron here with me eight hours last time and you never showed.'

'I know. I'm sorry.'

'You showed me the pink. I gave him the pink ones last time.'

'I know, man.'

McElroy insisted he could have his girlfriend, who was staying at a place on 72nd Street in Manhattan, rush over to the apartment in Jersey and be back with the pink pills in an hour. Ron was dubious, but he said he would come back to the restaurant in an hour. If McElroy had the pills they could make the deal.

After Ron left and McElroy made the call to his girl-friend, Billy Beattie settled down. There was nothing to do now but wait.

'Hey, Jim,' he said, looking around the restaurant. 'Maybe we should sit at the bar 'cause there's people eatin' here. You know?'

As they moved up to the bar and ordered a couple of beers, Beattie noticed that McElroy was not looking too healthy. He'd heard that Mac recently did a stint in the hospital, where he was diagnosed as suffering from severe weight loss and nervous exhaustion.

'So how you feeling, man?' Beattie asked.

'I feel great, man.'

'Yeah? You look like your face is drawn, your eyes . . .'

'This is nothin'. This is gaining weight, man. You shoulda seen me. It's like fucking cancer. I fell into the hospital . . . Had a whole bunch of them green ones, you know? Yellow and then green. Two of each. I was up for like three, four days, man, wide-eyed.'

469

'Yeah. It's a fuck. That can only make you nuts, man.'

'I liked it. I'll do it again.'

'You are fuckin' nuts.'

'No, I'm not. If you can handle it . . .'

'Jim, but that shit you can't handle. It catches up to you. You know that.'

'You can't do it every day. Just, like, once a month.'

'Party time, huh?'

'Yeah, once a month.'

'Your girlfriend get high?'

'Not really. We give her a half gram of coke, it lasts her all week. I do that in one shot!'

Beattie had to laugh. In recent weeks the tension in the neighborhood had reached a fever pitch. Among other things, Kelly and Shannon had gone on the lam. But here was McElroy, with the world caving in all around them, still getting high and cracking jokes. Devil-may-care, that was Jimmy Mac. Beattie had known him just about all his life and he'd always thought of him as a fuck-up. But you had to like him.

Soon the conversation turned to the impending federal investigation. They instinctively spoke in whispers.

'Them other guys got a lot of heat,' cautioned Beattie. 'They ever come for them motherfuckers, forget about it.'

'Who? Kevin and them?'

'Kevin and them. It's fucking all I hear. Every time you speak to somebody, they say, "Oh, the fuckin' heat's on them motherfuckers." I mean, the way it sounds, I don't think they're ever gonna come back.'

'That's what I heard, too.'

470

'They better stay the fuck away, man.'

McElroy mentioned how he'd recently been contacted by Jimmy Coonan, who'd offered him big-time money if he murdered Tony Lucich. Mac, who was definitely in need of capital, had taken Coonan up on the offer and waited patiently one night to kill Lucich.

'Where?' asked Beattie.

'In that building, 747 10th Avenue.'

'Is he still there?'

'Oh, he comes around on Sundays. He's still collecting. The two marshals were with him. They go in the garage and stay there. He goes up by himself in the elevator. I was sittin' in the fuckin' sink. You know that door? It's where the garbage goes. For three hours! Oh, fuck it, man. Fucking Jackie Coonan never shows up with the silencer.'

'Crazy fuck.'

'That's the only one that can hurt Jimmy. Mickey can't. Jimmy told me, "Mickey ain't shit. You need somebody to give you, uh, collaboration. You need more than one." So Tony, he's the guy.'

Billy took a swig of beer. 'Speakin' of Jimmy, I been lookin' to get in touch with his brother, Eddie. The little guy, the fuckin' dwarf.'

'Whaddya wanna get in touch with that prick for?'

'Well, I figured with Jimmy gone, he's taking care of business.'

'Are you kiddin' me? Him?'

'Well, he gave me all this shit: "Yeah, Jimmy says if you go see the lawyer, everything's cool."' Coonan had been trying to get Beattie to sign a legal document

471

swearing there was no such thing as the Westies. 'So I did. I went and saw the lawyer. I said, "Alright, I got no more problems now, right?"'

'No, no. You never had fuckin' problems.'

'Well, you remember. Fuckin' Jimmy was lookin' to shoot me.'

'Well, I told Jimmy that day, "Jimmy, we ain't doin' shit." He wanted me to do the killing. I said, "Are you fuckin' crazy!?"'

Beattie shook his head. 'Man, I did nothin' but earn money for that motherfucker. You know what it was? I know what it was. It was his fuckin' wife.'

'That's what I think. That's why none of us wanted it. We all disagreed with Jimmy. You know why? It ain't him.'

'Yeah, it was his wife.'

'It was her, that cunt. 'Cause he don't know the situation. We do. Me and Mickey. I told him, "Look, forget it. She was in love with Billy. She hates Billy now because he refuses her."'

Beattie smiled. 'I thought you was fuckin' her, you know, at one time.'

'Me? Nah.'

'Yeah. I said this prick ever fucks her, she's gonna try to get him killed, man.'

'Oh, I wouldn't go near her. She don't attract me . . . Fuckin' douche bag, that's what she is. A fuckin' drunk.'

'Yeah.'

'Now she lives high and mighty. That's what I always think.'

McElroy paused. It had been a long time since he'd sat

at a bar and shot the breeze with an old friend from the gang. It felt good. There had been so much tension lately, so much treachery and paranoia. If you blocked everything else out, this was just like old times – sitting and having a beer with someone you'd known your whole life. Someone you could trust.

It wasn't long, though, before the conversation turned to the topic that was uppermost in everyone's mind – Mickey Featherstone.

'The cocksucker,' said McElroy, shaking his head in disbelief every time Mickey's name was mentioned. 'If I was gonna do . . . if they asked me, if they said they'd let me out if I'd rat, I'd spit at 'em. If I was gonna do twenty-five years in the hole. Fuck it.'

'I hear ya.'

'Sure, alright. He's crazy and shit. I betcha he comes around.'

'I'm sure. You know he's a fuckin' nut. He'll be back.'

'I told Kevin, "You know he's still fuckin' bad. So don't think 'cause he's a rat that he's not bad."'

Beattie quickly changed the subject. 'Listen, Jimmy. You need any help collectin' any money or anything? 'Cause I'm fuckin' strapped.'

'I ain't collectin', Billy. Fuck it! I'm not collectin' for nobody. I'm gonna get my own money out there.'

'Yeah? The fuck. You ain't got nothin', you prick.'

'I'll get it.'

Beattie started laughing. 'You're in the same boat I'm in.'

'No, but I'm gonna get it. I wanna go partners, me and you. I need a partner anyway.'

Beattie was still laughing when his friend Ron returned. 'Hey, Ronnie,' he said.

'I can't hang out anymore,' replied Ron, looking annoyed.

'I was gonna give you them pink pills,' offered McElroy, trying not to sound too desperate.

'Maybe a day or two. I got somethin' I gotta do.'

Beattie seemed flustered. 'Jimmy . . . Ron. Well, listen, we'll definitely handle it by next week.'

'How 'bout over the weekend?' asked McElroy. 'Tomorrow?'

'Maybe,' said Ron. 'I'll give you a call. I gotta take care of this.'

'Alright,' yelled Beattie as Ron headed for the front door. 'Get in touch with me, okay?'

McElroy slumped down on his barstool. 'I'm sorry. It's my fault. I'm sorry.'

'He's that kind of guy, man. I tell ya, he can't stand still. 'Cause he's got a pocket full of fuckin' money.'

'Yeah. He don't need us.'

Beattie and McElroy stood in stunned silence for a few seconds.

'So,' said Jimmy Mac, trying to sound conciliatory. 'What a bummer, huh? We coulda had this money. Both of us. We coulda gone out.'

'Jimmy, I was . . . look what I'm goin' home with!' Billy tossed a five and four singles up on the bar. 'That's what I got! That's my bankroll! I gotta, I've fuckin' six kids in my house. I'm lookin' to feed 'em, man.'

'I know.'

'That's fuckin' depressing.'

474

'We'll do it with him tomorrow.'

'I had that money spent, Jimmy.'

'Me too.'

'My fucking refrigerator is empty, man.'

Outside the restaurant's large plate-glass windows, the street lights had come on and the rush-hour traffic had begun to thin out. It was early evening, and the setting sun cast a pinkish glow in the sky to the west. Beattie glanced nervously around the bar and then at McElroy. 'Alright, look. I know some people not too far from here. I might catch 'em in their store. If I do, I'll get some bread. This way I can get a couple hundred. I'll give you a hundred, I'll take a hundred.'

'Yeah. I just wanna get somethin' to eat tonight.'

'I hear you,' said Beattie, picking up his nine dollars from the bar.

McElroy drained the last of his beer. 'Hey, this guy Ron, he want anybody whacked?'

'If he does, I'll ask him.'

'Yeah! Ask him, you know? I'll do that.'

'Give me a figure.'

'I don't know. Whaddya think?'

'I never talked to him on that line.'

'So tell him I'm available.'

'Alright. I'll tell him you said, like, to keep good faith, you'll give him a good package on somethin', if he wants it done.'

With that, Billy Beattie walked out the door of Smoke Stacks Lightning onto Canal Street. By now it was dark outside and there was a sharp winter chill in the air. Beattie glanced inside the restaurant one last time to see

475

his old friend Jimmy Mac sitting alone, ordering another bottle of beer with the last few dollars in his pocket.

Jesus, thought Beattie, walking south on West Broadway. How did it ever come to this? How did it get so fucking pathetic?

He walked around the corner to Lispenard Street, where a black van with black tinted windows was parked. He looked around furtively to make sure no one was watching, then knocked on the side of the van.

The door slid open and Beattie got inside. There, surrounded by surveillance equipment, were three or four New York City detectives, including Ron Stripp, the supposed drug buyer.

'Jesus,' said Ron, reaching over to help Beattie remove the five-by-four-inch Nagra recorder strapped to his abdomen. 'You should get an Academy Award. That was some act.'

'Yeah,' answered Beattie, dejectedly, holding up his shirt.

'Don't worry, Billy,' said another cop. 'There'll be a special place in Heaven for you.'

Beattie raised an eyebrow. 'Yeah? Don't be too sure about that.'

17

WHAT GOES AROUND, COMES AROUND

The arrests went down in late November and December of 1986. Jimmy Coonan was found in his hideaway in Jersey and peaceably taken in. Edna Coonan was arrested in front of the family Christmas tree in their home in Hazlet. Others, including Billy Bokun, Mugsy Ritter, Johnny Halo, and Florence Collins, were arrested in and around Hell's Kitchen. Florence Collins's husband, Tommy Collins, was already incarcerated on a narcotics rap at the time. He too was handcuffed, taken to central booking, and charged with being a member of the Westies.

Jimmy McElroy, after learning that his good friend Billy Beattie had been cooperating with the government, went on the run. But McElroy was a creature of habit. And the NYPD knew of a place in Mesa, Arizona, where he'd gone on the lam before. He was arrested there by federal authorities.

Kevin Kelly and Kenny Shannon could not be found, despite a combined local and federal multistate manhunt. In the few remaining working-class bars in Hell's

Kitchen, rumors circulated that they were either dead or hiding out in Ireland.

Over the next few months a succession of state murder indictments were returned against various members of the gang, with a litany of victims' names sounding like a casting call for a 1930s gangster movie: Paddy Dugan, Ruby Stein, Rickey Tassiello, Whitey Whitehead, Vinnie Leone, Michael Holly.

The murder charges, all of which were brought by the office of Manhattan D.A. Robert Morgenthau, made it possible for a steady stream of cops and assistant D.A.s to claim credit for having brought the dreaded Westies to justice. After all the career-enhancing press conferences had been held and the state indictments announced, the federal government moved in.

On March 26th, Rudolph Giuliani, the highly ambitious U.S. Attorney for the Southern District of New York, announced an indictment that was to supersede all others. Ten people – including those already hit with the state indictments – were being charged on fourteen counts with having taken part in a 'racketeering conspiracy.' The charges dated back some twenty years and included sixteen murders, attempted murders, and conspiracies to commit murder. These charges, assured Giuliani, would finally bring about an end to what he termed – with his usual penchant for dramatics – 'the most savage organization in the long history of New York City gangs.'

Giuliani's strong rhetoric underscored what had, for the Southern District, become something of a religious calling in recent years. Since his appointment in 1983 to head the most prestigious District in the United States, Giuliani had made the pursuit of organized crime groups his number one priority. Not since the days of Estes Kefauver and New York Governor Thomas Dewey's Waterfront Commission had the Mob suffered such a relentless legal assault. Earlier in 1987, Giuliani's office had imprisoned, among others, cigar-chomping Fat Tony Salerno, onetime nemesis of the Hell's Kitchen Irish Mob, who was sentenced to 100 years for his role as leader of the Mafia's ruling commission. Then came the 'Pizza Connection' case, the longest-running trial ever to be held in federal court, in which fifteen defendants were found guilty of an elaborate international narcotics and racketeering conspiracy.

More recently, however, the Southern District's successes had been tarnished somewhat by yet another high-profile mob case. In the Eastern District of New York, which encompassed Queens, Brooklyn, and Long Island, Gambino boss John Gotti was tried in a racketeering case that dominated newspaper headlines for months. Much to the chagrin of the Justice Department, in March of 1987 the trial ended with Gotti's acquittal.

Now prosecutors focused on the Westies case, the biggest mob trial in New York since the Gotti fiasco. A conviction would accomplish two things: It would get the government's pursuit of organized crime squarely back on track, and it would reestablish Giuliani's Southern District as the area's preeminent prosecutorial branch, the first to take the Westies off the streets for good.

As it had in virtually every major mob case in recent years, the Southern District would once again be utilizing the RICO law, which seemed especially well suited to the Westies case. Under RICO's somewhat controversial statutes – which have been attacked in many legal circles for being too far-reaching – the government was able to admit as evidence crimes that the defendants had already been charged, tried, and possibly even done time for. By using these crimes to establish 'a pattern of racketeering,' the government was able to assert the existence of an 'enterprise,' thereby implicating multiple defendants on a vast array of charges.

It also meant that if the prosecution was able to show that a 'relationship' existed between the various defendants, they could use one person's previous convictions to establish the racketeering charge against another. As a result, in the case against the Westies, some of Jimmy Coonan's kidnapping and assault convictions from the late Sixties and early Seventies would be used, as would Tommy Collins's recent narcotics conviction.

Along with these charges, the fourteen counts in the indictment encompassed numerous others for murder, conspiracy to commit murder, gambling, extortion, loansharking, counterfeiting, and, as regards Jimmy and Edna Coonan, income tax evasion. As evidence to support their claims, the prosecution had assembled an assortment of guns, knives, narcotics paraphernalia, bags of amphetamines, gambling and loansharking records, police surveillance photographs and logs, ballistics and autopsy reports, phone records, tax records, and numerous taped conversations from telephone wiretaps, body wires, and recording devices placed in automobiles, restaurants, and prison visiting rooms.

Even more important to the prosecution were the witnesses. There were more than seventy scheduled to testify about crimes that, in some cases, were two decades old. Charles Canelstein, who'd been gunned down near Calvary Cemetery in Queens by nineteen-year-old Jimmy Coonan in April 1966, would be called to testify, as would Paddy Dugan's sister, Rickey Tassiello's brother, and Ruby Stein's mistress. There were loanshark victims like sixty-four-year-old Julius 'Dutch' Grote, one-time bartender and friend of Bobby Lagville and Mickey Spillane, who in the late Seventies once hid inside his Hell's Kitchen apartment for fifteen months for fear of being killed by Coonan.

But the most devastating testimony of all was expected to come from the confidential informants. Just as the West Side criminals had feared, Mickey and Sissy Featherstone's cooperation had opened the floodgates. Tony Lucich and Billy Beattie had followed, with Beattie circulating in the neighborhood for weeks before it was known he'd flipped. In addition, the old standbys, Alberta Sachs and Raymond Steen, were being called to testify again. And finally, there was the most unlikely stool pigeon of all – Bobby Huggard. The 'stand-up guy' who had single-handedly secured an acquittal for Coonan and Featherstone at the Whitehead murder trial by perjuring himself on the witness stand was in prison on an armed robbery conviction when he heard Mickey Featherstone turned stoolie. Knowing that Featherstone had enough on him to have him put away for life, Huggard began singing to the FBI.

It was a staggering collection of evidence on the

government's part, enough to make even the most hardened West Side gangster flinch.

For the prosecutors – assistant U.S. attorneys Mary Lee Warren and David Brodsky – it was an unbelievably strong foundation. And as the proceedings got underway in late September of 1987, they had every reason to feel confident.

In the still, pristine air of Room 506, in the federal courthouse at 60 Centre Street in lower Manhattan, Larry Hochheiser grabbed a seat in the back row of the spectator's gallery. It was November 12th, a gray, ominous day, and the large, wood-paneled courtroom was packed. Since the Westies trial first began two weeks earlier, Hochheiser had talked many times with the defense attorneys involved in the case. He'd followed the newspaper reports, which had already devoted considerable space to the testimony of Billy Beattie, Alberta Sachs, and Tony Lucich. But Hochheiser had avoided making an appearance in the courtroom for many reasons, the most compelling being that the very existence of this trial had caused him more personal grief than any event in his career as an attorney.

To say that Featherstone's cooperation had stunned Hochheiser and his partner, Ken Aronson, wouldn't begin to tell the story. Since 1972, when Hochheiser got Mickey acquitted on an insanity plea in the Linwood Willis murder trial, he'd represented Featherstone time and time again, usually for little or no fee. He did so because he liked Featherstone, but also because, in his mind, Mickey was linked so inexorably with his career as a successful attorney. The Willis case had been his first great triumph, the first time he'd really known that being a criminal defense attorney was the only job for him.

Since then, Hochheiser and Aronson had represented Mickey and his West Side friends on some thirty different occasions. There had been literally hundreds of arraignments, motion filings, bail hearings, parole board appearances, trials, and appeals. In fact, Hochheiser and his partner had come to be known in police and legal circles as 'the Westies' lawyers.' And they had carried that moniker with a certain amount of pride, knowing that it had been acquired against great odds. Every cop, assistant D.A., and county judge was after them from the start.

Then came the Michael Holly trial, a disaster from beginning to end. Hochheiser knew that Featherstone had come to believe he'd been convicted by design, that some unholy alliance had been forged between the attorneys and his perceived enemies. To Hochheiser, this was patently ridiculous. Yes, the trial, in retrospect, had not been handled very well. For one thing, they made a tactical error by putting Kevin Kelly on the stand. But to believe that Kelly's surly performance was part of a deliberate plot to throw the case, to believe that the three eyewitnesses who identified Mickey had somehow all been put up to it by Coonan or Kelly or the attorneys – this, to Hochheiser, was the product of a disturbed mind.

Hochheiser knew very well that Mickey Featherstone was a diagnosed 'paranoid schizophrenic.' On many occasions, beginning with the Willis trial, he'd used this fact to wriggle Featherstone through the clutches of

483

the criminal justice system. If it hadn't helped him beat charges altogether, it often got Mickey preferred treatment in sentencing and in the prisons. But even though he had been responsible, in a way, for Featherstone's being officially designated as 'crazy,' Hochheiser chose not to think of him that way. He and his partner had come to believe the legend of Mickey Featherstone as it was presented at the Willis trial: a troubled Vietnam vet from a tough neighborhood, a little guy whose crimes were all about self-preservation, not profit motive.

Now here was Mickey Featherstone seated on the witness stand – a stool pigeon, a rat. In the world of the high-priced criminal defense attorneys, a fraternity of which Hochheiser and Aronson were now prominent members, there was nothing worse than a stoolie. They were a threat to the livelihood of so-called mob lawyers everywhere. The assumption, of course, was that everything a stoolie said was a lie; that they were desperate people liable to say anything to save their own skin. No criminal defense attorney worth his salt would ever represent a stoolie – on principle. Simply put, a stool pigeon was the lowest form of human life.

'Daddy,' Hochheiser's thirteen-year-old daughter had asked after hearing that Featherstone would be testifying against his own people, 'you mean all this time Mickey Featherstone was a fake?' Many times Hochheiser's family had heard him talk about Mickey as if he were a character from a Dickens novel.

'Yes,' he reluctantly told his daughter. 'Mickey Featherstone is not everything he was cracked up to be.'

Later, after all the indictments were announced and it

seemed possible that Hochheiser might someday be cross-examining Mickey on behalf of one of his clients, he used stronger language. 'Mickey Featherstone is a pimp and a liar,' he told a reporter for the *Daily News*, knowing full well that being called a pimp, in Mickey's mind, would be the lowest possible insult.

As for Ken Aronson, Featherstone's cooperation with the government was, if anything, even more of a blow. It was Aronson, after all, who Mickey was claiming had deliberately brought about his conviction in the Holly case. After Mickey and Sissy began working with the government, Sissy had even gone so far as to secretly tape phone conversations with Aronson, hoping that he might inadvertently reveal his role in the so-called frame-up. To Aronson, this was an unconscionable act of betrayal, one which he still found hard to believe months after it was revealed.

Yes, Aronson would admit, he had begun to give up on Featherstone even before the Michael Holly trial began. And he realized now that those feelings of disillusionment, which he'd communicated to Mickey throughout the Holly trial, had probably contributed to Featherstone's belief that the attorney had somehow joined forces against him. But even with all that, Aronson had never expected Mickey to flip. He had always thought he was a *mensch*, a stand-up guy.

To Aronson, it was now apparent that he'd gotten too close to his client, that he'd put himself in an impossible position by trying to be more than a lawyer to Mickey and Sissy and some of the others. Eventually, it had put him in a place he did not want to be – an unindicted co-conspirator in what the government was now calling a criminal enterprise.

From his seat in the back of Room 506, Larry Hochheiser watched as Featherstone took the witness stand. He recognized Mickey's courtroom look – the slicked-down sandy-blond hair, neatly trimmed mustache, conservative suit and tie. It was strange to see Featherstone on the stand instead of at the defense table. He seemed comfortable, though, cocky even, as he leaned forward to take the questions from Gerald Shargel, the lead defense attorney.

'Mr Featherstone,' said Shargel, standing near the large, rectangular jury box. 'I think you told us that in the year 1984 carrying into 1985, before your cooperation, there was a plan to kill Jimmy Coonan, correct?'

'Yes, sir.'

'And there is no question in your mind, is there, sir, that you, Mickey Featherstone, were a part of that plan, correct?'

'No, I was part of it.'

'There was one time, I think you testified, you went into New York because you heard Jimmy Coonan was in the neighborhood, right?'

'Yes, sir.'

'And you were looking, with others, in the neighborhood bars to see if you could find Jimmy for the purpose of killing him, right?'

'Yes, sir.'

Gerald Shargel was a veteran criminal defense lawyer in the Hochheiser mold – forty-three years old, smooth and wily, with a sharp, sometimes sarcastic wit. He usually dressed in elegant, dark-blue pin-striped suits with a red tie. He was bald on top, with black hair around his ears and a neatly trimmed black beard. He tended to strut like a peacock but was usually exceedingly polite. Occasionally, in the great tradition of high-priced legal talent, he got dramatic.

In the pre-trial stages of the case, when Judge Whitman Knapp declared it would be a conflict for Hochheiser and Aronson to represent *any* of the Westies because of their previous lawyer/client relationship with Featherstone, they'd recommended Shargel to Coonan. The choice seemed especially apt, since Shargel had once been the attorney for the late Roy Demeo, Jimmy Coonan's one-time *paisan* in the Gambino family.

For four days running, Shargel had listened to Mary Lee Warren lead Featherstone through a mind-boggling litany of crimes during his direct testimony. He'd been impressed with Featherstone's demeanor, with his willingness to admit that he had been, at one time or another, a drunk, a drug addict, a killer, and a nut case. Yet Shargel had no intention of allowing this witness – *especially* this witness – to imply that he had in any way been an unwilling participant in his crimes.

His voice rising in indignation, Shargel asked, 'Didn't you tell us, Mr Featherstone, that there was a time when you got better?'

'Yes, kind of – I didn't have the hatred after I came back from prison in 1982. I just lost the hatred I had in the past.'

'You lost the hatred after 1982?'

'Yes.'

'You, sir, had no hatred when you had a gun and a silencer and you went to kill my client on the streets of New York? You had no hatred?'

'Yes. I had it then – definitely.'

'That was in 1984, wasn't it, Mr Mickey Featherstone?'

'Yes.'

'And what about the hundreds of people, according to your testimony, that you assaulted and you stabbed and you beat and you robbed? What about them? Did you *like* them?'

'They were my barroom brawls.'

'Didn't you have hatred when you were in those barroom brawls, Mr Featherstone?'

'Yes, I did.'

Along with Featherstone's propensity for violence, the crux of Shargel's cross-examination – in fact, the crux of his and the other seven defense attorneys' main argument with the government – was that the Westies were a fabrication. In their opening statements, all of the attorneys voiced what had always been the unofficial position of the gang itself – that the Westies were a creation of the police and the media. 'Hell's Kitchen sink,' Shargel called the government's case, a reference to all the crimes that had been thrown together in an attempt to establish a racketeering conspiracy.

Now, to bolster this claim, Shargel used Featherstone's own words. Through Hochheiser and Aronson, he'd gotten his hands on a series of taped interviews Featherstone had done with a would-be biographer in early 1980, following his acquittal for the Whitehead murder. At the time, even though he was incarcerated and awaiting sentencing on his counterfeit conviction, Featherstone was still very much one of the boys. As a result, most of what he told William Urshal, the interviewer, was either half-truths or outright lies designed to protect himself and others from possible prosecution.

Nonetheless, as the entire courtroom listened, here was Mickey's voice, loud and clear, claiming undeniably that the Westies were a fiction. 'Do you really think,' he was heard saying on tape, 'if there was a gang making all this money, like they say, I'd be living in a small apartment [on 56th Street]?'

Over the next several hours, Shargel referred to 'the Urshal tapes' time and time again. The jury read from written transcripts and listened to Mickey Featherstone, sounding exactly as he had under direct examination, telling lie after lie. At one point, Featherstone was heard absolving Coonan of the Whitehead murder, a murder he'd described in great detail just days earlier.

'Is it your testimony now, sir,' Shargel asked incredulously, 'that in 1980 you sat down with this author and you made up a story out of whole cloth?'

'Parts of it were lies, yes.'

'Parts of it were truth and parts of it were lies?'

'Yes.'

'In other words, Mr Featherstone, you took facts you knew to be true, right?'

'Yes.'

'And then you took facts you knew to be lies?'

'Yes.'

'And you jumbled together the truth and the lies to

confuse or deceive the person who was listening to you, is that right?'

'I was a criminal, yes. So I gave the guy a bunch of lies.'

'Is there any way we have of telling when you are lying and when you are not?'

'Right now I'm telling the truth. That's all I can say.'

'How do we know you're telling the truth right now, even as you speak?'

As the afternoon wore on, Shargel's cross-examination gained in intensity, requiring acute concentration from the witness, the jury and anyone else who hoped to follow. Unlike Mary Lee Warren, who had presented Featherstone's direct testimony in neat chronological order, Shargel was all over the place. One moment it was 1967, the next, 1987. One moment he was in Vietnam, the next, Hell's Kitchen. Sometimes subjects changed in midsentence. Crimes began to blur. There were murders, assaults, strategies, vendettas, betrayals . . .

What emerged was a life unlike anything anyone on the jury could possibly comprehend. The violence and depravity was numbing. This man, Shargel was telling the jury, is not a human being at all. This man is a killer.

A psychopath.

A monster.

'Mr Featherstone,' he asked near the end of the afternoon. 'You said at the end of your direct testimony, the very last part, that there was a time in your life when you were, I believe your words were, "vicious and an animal," something like that?'

'Yes, I was.'

490

'No question about it?'

'I was a liar, an animal, a criminal. I woke up every day and committed a crime every day.'

'And when you said vicious and an animal, you used the past tense because you are no longer that way?'

'I'm still angry at a lot of things, but I don't believe I'm as violent as I was in the past.'

'Do you still have that hatred that caused you to kill people in the 1970s?'

'No.'

'But isn't it a fact, sir, that you who are no longer vicious, you who are no longer an animal, called over the phone this past weekend and threatened to kill someone in this audience? Yes or no, Mr Featherstone?'

'That's a lie.'

Shargel's voice was rising now, echoing to the far corners of the room. 'Did you say you would be out in four years, *in four years* you'd be back on the streets and you would kill a certain member of this audience?'

'No.'

'*Did you say it!?*'

'No.'

Mickey knew Shargel's accusation was bullshit, and he was certain Shargel did too. All phone calls at the MCC were monitored, so even if he'd wanted to he would never have made a threat like that over the phone.

Shargel let the accusation sink in, then waved his hand in the air. 'I have nothing further, Your Honor.'

As the jury and the audience sat in stunned silence – the damning implications of the last question left dangling in the air – Mickey felt helpless, totally unable to

491

defend himself. It reminded him of all those times when Hochheiser had destroyed witnesses on his behalf, asking dramatic, incriminating questions, smearing them with innuendo.

Mickey saw the smirks on the faces of Coonan and the others as they slapped Shargel on the back and shook his hand.

For the first time in his life, Mickey knew how it felt to be on the receiving end.

Featherstone's cross-examination continued over the next four days. Each of the eight defense attorneys got their chance to bang away. After Mickey left the stand, a staggering cast of players followed, with their testimony stretching throughout November and December of 1987 and on into the early months of '88. Even to those with a knowledge of the West Side, the flow of names, dates, and events was overwhelming. As the evidence piled up the proceedings took on an air of inevitability, and the long afternoons in Room 506 revealed countless ghoulish and indelible moments.

Sixty-eight-year-old Tony Lucich testified on the Rickey Tassiello murder, explaining how, as Jimmy Coonan was cutting up the body, he severed Rickey's penis, held it in his hand, and said to Lucich in all seriousness, 'See, this is somethin' you gotta get rid of, because this could be identified by his girlfriend.'

Bobby Huggard explained why, even after he had been offered immunity by the government to testify at the Whitehead murder trial, he elected to perjure himself. 'Yeah, immunity,' said Huggard. 'That's nice. Immunity

492

protects me from the state. It don't protect me from other people.'

And thirty-one-year-old Sissy Featherstone, anxious and combative, answered questions about Mickey's plan to murder Coonan.

'You knew,' asked Shargel, 'that your husband Mickey Featherstone hated this man Jimmy Coonan, right?'

'No,' replied Sissy. 'Actually, he loved Jimmy.'

'He loved him?'

'Yes.'

'He just thought he needed killing?'

Sissy looked directly at Coonan. 'No. Mickey loved him in the beginning, and Jimmy knows it.'

Among the numerous law enforcement people who testified was Richie Egan, whose daily surveillance reports became the glue that held many of the government's charges together. On two separate occasions, Egan was called to the stand to lead the jury through a normal day's surveillance, which usually involved following Featherstone and Coonan on their afternoon shylock runs.

As the weeks of testimony wore on, the press couldn't get enough. The trial catapulted the Westies into some strange, exalted place in the city's folklore. For so many years the Westies had been a crime story that wouldn't go away. And now, not only was the full historical sweep of their reign being revealed for the first time, but the whole damn ball of wax was going up in flames.

Of course, not lost on the press was the sordidness of the gang's activities – the dismemberment murders, the number of victims, and the bitter, jealous way in which they had reached their day of reckoning.

One writer, Anthony M. DeStefano of *Newsday*, compared the proceedings to the Grand Guignol theater of 19th-century Paris, where audiences gathered daily to hear sensational tales of murder and mayhem.

On Wednesday morning, February 24, 1988, after eight days of deliberation, the jury passed a note to the judge informing him they had reached a verdict. Over the next hour, relatives and friends of the defendants gathered in Room 506, as they had throughout the four-month-long trial. By 11 A.M. the courtroom was packed, with federal marshals lining the walls and a sizable press contingent, notepads in hand, crowded into the front two rows of the spectators' gallery.

Days earlier, the jury had heard the government summarize its case. David Brodsky – whose short, curly brown hair, conservative suit and tie and well-scrubbed good looks gave him the appearance of a recent prep-school graduate – had delivered a long, comprehensive overview of the charges and evidence against the Westies. As Gerry Shargel would later point out to the jury, Brodsky was ten years old when the March '66 murder of Bobby Lagville – the earliest act in the indictment – took place. Unlike Mary Lee Warren, who approached her task with a severe, unemotional air of inscrutability, Brodsky was not above appealing to the jury with a boyish smile or an offhand comment.

As was traditional during government summations, the young prosecutor thanked the ten women and two men for their patience, acknowledging how difficult it must have been to listen to tales of violence and death in such polite, civilized surroundings. 'But out on the streets of Hell's Kitchen,' Brodsky reminded the jury, 'Jimmy Coonan and his gang were vicious; they were not civilized. And the people of Hell's Kitchen did not hear about the violence from the witness stand, they had to live through it day after day, year after year . . .

'Well, I say to you, ladies and gentlemen, the time has come to end this reign of terror on the West Side.'

At the end of his six-hour summation, the fatigued prosecutor, his voice rich with emotion, cautioned that, 'Jimmy Coonan, on his tax returns, claims to be a carpet installer and a construction consultant, and when Mr Shargel gets up here he might even claim that Jimmy Coonan is one of those things.' Then Brodsky's voice began to crack. His jaw tightened and his eyes moistened. He pointed directly at Coonan, who glared implacably from the defense table, and hollered, 'Ladies and gentlemen, the evidence in this case shows that Jimmy Coonan is no legitimate businessman. *Jimmy Coonan is a damn butcher!* He has killed people over and over again, and he has cut up their bodies—'

Shargel immediately interrupted, moving for a mistrial and calling Brodsky's outburst 'an emotional trick' and 'an act.' After Brodsky shouted back, 'That's a lie,' Judge Knapp quieted the courtroom and overruled Shargel's objection.

In his summation, Shargel did the only thing he could – he attacked 'the content and character' of the government's case, calling special attention to the high number of convicted felons who were used as witnesses. Featherstone in particular, he claimed, was a 'lowlife' who was using the Westies as his ticket to freedom. 'If you examine Mickey Featherstone's past,' Shargel told the jury, 'you will find that when the government entered into an agreement with this man, they were shaking hands with the devil.'

Now, eight days later, with the various summations still ringing in their ears, the jury filed into the courtroom with their verdict. The relatives of the defendants had gathered on the right side of the gallery. Billy Bokun's wife, Carol, who was Tommy and Flo Collins's daughter, was there. So was Billy Bokun's old man. Jimmy McElroy's niece, who was also Kevin Kelly's wife, was there. Also Mugsy Ritter's wife. And in the very back, seated all alone, was Jimmy Coonan's mother. Over the past few months, she'd heard her son being accused of despicable acts of violence. Whether or not she'd heard these accusations before – and what she thought of them – she never shared with anyone, not even neighbors and relatives.

It took the court clerk fifteen minutes to read the voluminous thirteen-page verdict. But within the first few minutes, it was apparent where things were headed. Except for Johnny Halo, who was acquitted of all charges, the rest of the defendants were nailed to the wall – guilty on all fourteen counts of the indictment.

'He never had a chance,' cried Billy Bokun's father when the reading of the verdict had been completed. The elder Bokun had now lost two sons to the Westies. As Billy and the other defendants were led from the court-room, his emotions boiled over.

'Them people shamed themselves!' Bokun called to his son, gesturing towards the jury box.

496

'Don't worry, Pop,' Billy shouted back. 'I'll be alright. Fuck them!'

'Yeah,' the anguished father replied. 'Tell it to the Marines.'

Within thirty minutes of the verdict, Mickey Featherstone got a visit in his cell from one of the marshals who'd been in the courtroom. 'It's all over, Mick,' said the marshal. 'Except for Halo – he was acquitted – they all went down. Pretty much across the board.'

After the marshal left, Mickey stood up from his bed, stretched, and began pacing back and forth. For over a year he'd been waiting for this moment, not knowing exactly how he would react when it finally came. He'd prepared for it, reminding himself over and over that some of these people had framed him for a murder he didn't commit. The others, those who knew nothing about the frame, had used his name and reputation for their own gain as far back as he could remember.

But even with all that, he couldn't say he felt any great satisfaction. To take the stand and testify like he had violated a standard near and dear to criminals the world over. Mickey was reminded of this during the trial, when Shargel played a portion of the Urshal tapes in which Mickey was asked how he felt about informants. 'Even if my life was on the line,' he told the interviewer, 'I still wouldn't rat . . . A stool pigeon would kill his own mother, man. He's worse than a junkie.'

Featherstone burned with shame at the realization that he'd become exactly what he never wanted to be. A stoolie; a rat; a cheese eater.

Mickey had paced back and forth often in his cell during the trial, just like he was now. His thoughts would drift back over the events of his life, and he'd begin to think of all the violence he'd seen. Sometimes, he would close his eyes and he wasn't in prison anymore at all. He was back on the streets of Hell's Kitchen, among the people. Among the victims . . .

Like Ugly Walter. There was one that, along with the Rickey Tassiello murder, he'd spent his entire life trying to forget. It had been early in 1976, and he'd only been out of prison on the Linwood Willis gun possession rap and his parole violation for about six weeks. At the time he was twenty-seven years old and hadn't hooked up with Jimmy Coonan yet. He was still looking for a way to stay out of trouble and make a few extra bucks for himself and his new girlfriend, Sissy.

Together with Jackie Coonan and another neighborhood kid, Mickey had put what little money he had into starting up an after-hours club on 44th Street, between 9th and 10th avenues. It was a grungy old storefront looking in on what used to be an ice cream parlor, the kind of place that might have been a popular Hell's Kitchen gathering place in the 1950s.

The club was barely up and running more than a week, and already Mickey had installed a jukebox and a pool table. The neighborhood's younger tough guys – those loyal to Jimmy Coonan – had quickly become steady patrons. Enthused by the club's financial prospects, Mickey decided to go one step further and install a small stage so they could occasionally host live music.

To build the stage, Mickey had turned to Walter Curtis,

a maintenance man and carpenter who worked in the neighborhood's hotels. Known to most people as Ugly Walter because of his crooked teeth, unfortunate complexion, and notoriously bad hygienic habits, Ugly Walter was nonetheless liked by those who knew him. He was a decent guy who might buy you a drink every now and then, and as far as most people knew, he had little or no involvement with the neighborhood's gangster element.

One afternoon, Mickey and Ugly Walter were in the club deciding where they should put the stage. Ugly Walter had just finished taking measurements, and he'd placed his tool belt on a barstool. The shades covering the club's front windows were pulled, and it was dim and dusty as Mickey poured them both a drink at the bar.

Suddenly, Eddie Cummiskey came in the door. Mickey looked up to see Eddie the Butcher glare at Ugly Walter. When Mickey glanced at Walter, he saw an expression of stark terror come into his eyes.

Cummiskey pulled a pistol out of his jacket and aimed it. *Bam! Bam!* The gunshots echoed loudly throughout the nearly empty room. Ugly Walter never even had a chance to put his drink down. The bullets hit him squarely in the chest.

Ugly Walter toppled off the barstool. There was blood pouring from his chest, but he wasn't dead yet. He started to drag himself towards the back of the club, as if there were still some way he might be able to evade Eddie Cummiskey.

Mickey froze in his tracks, his drink still held to his lips. Cummiskey came over and took a hammer out of Walter's tool belt. With Walter gasping for air and blood seeping from his wounds, Cummiskey looked at Mickey and stammered, 'This motherfucker . . . this cocksucker . . .'

Without finishing his sentence, he walked over to Ugly Walter and began beating him with the hammer over and over. As Ugly Walter raised his bloodied hands in a helpless attempt to protect himself, Cummiskey just kept smashing away.

Mickey knew there was nothing he could do. Cummiskey had a gun in one hand, a hammer in the other, and an expression on his face that suggested if anyone were to get in his way, he'd do to them exactly what he was doing to Ugly Walter.

Cummiskey must have struck his victim thirty or forty times, crushing his skull and bludgeoning the last remnants of life from his body.

'Get me a garbage bag,' he finally called to Mickey, breathing heavily from the exertion.

He pulled it over Ugly Walter's upper body. Then Mickey was instructed to help drag the body up a flight of stairs to the bathroom of a flophouse apartment.

There, Ugly Walter's body was dumped in the bathtub. As they stripped him naked, Cummiskey explained how he'd been waiting five years to kill Walter Curtis, who he said had witnessed a murder that he'd committed years earlier. Cummiskey had been forced to plead guilty to the killing and always believed that Walter talked to the cops.

'Nobody,' said Eddie, 'and I mean nobody, rats on Eddie Cummiskey.'

After Ugly Walter was stripped naked, Cummiskey took Mickey to the Market Diner on 11th Avenue, where they met Jimmy and Jackie Coonan. Eddie explained what happened and told Jimmy Coonan to get his 'tools' and meet them back at the flophouse.

Within minutes they were all back in the bathroom, standing over what was left of Ugly Walter. Cummiskey and the Coonan brothers took a number of large kitchen knives out of a paper bag and rolled up their shirt-sleeves.

'Watch this, kid,' Eddie said to Mickey. 'You're about to get an education.'

Mickey knew what was coming. Weeks earlier, Paddy Dugan had disappeared under similar circumstances, and Mickey had heard all about it. But this was the first time he would witness it for himself.

As Cummiskey stuck a knife in Ugly Walter's stomach, cutting a five-inch diagonal incision, Mickey began to heave into the toilet. The others, deeply engrossed in their task, hardly paid attention as Mickey retched in the background, over and over again.

Eventually, Jimmy Coonan came over and threw an arm around Featherstone. 'Don't worry, Mick,' he said. 'You'll get used to it.'

Now, all these years later, from his small, lifeless prison cell, Mickey thought about Ugly Walter. He thought about all the Ugly Walters.

When he saw the blood and heard the screams, as he had so often in recent months, he didn't feel so bad about what he'd done.

At least now, he thought to himself, there would be no more victims. There would be no more Ugly Walters.

EPILOGUE

Four days before Christmas, on December 21, 1988 (Jimmy Coonan's forty-second birthday), Francis Featherstone was once again led into U.S. District Court. This time he stood before Judge Robert W. Sweet, whose duty it was to sentence Mickey on his RICO conviction.

As promised in their agreement with Featherstone, Mary Lee Warren and other federal prosecutors had already urged the judge to 'consider the scope and value of Mr Featherstone's cooperation' when sentencing. A favorable probation report and a psychiatric evaluation declaring that Featherstone was 'mentally competent' were offered as evidence.

After the U.S. Attorney's office stated their case, the judge spoke. 'Mr Featherstone,' he said. 'You stand before me having admitted to fourteen specific acts of racketeering, including four murders, five conspiracies to murder, loansharking, extortion, numbers, counterfeiting and distribution of drugs . . . During the forty years of your life, you have experienced violence as a child, as a student in our city schools, as a soldier in Vietnam, as a criminal on the streets, and as a killer and an enforcer of one of the most feared gangs in our city.'

Despite this troubled history, the judge told Mickey, 'The Westies have been broken as an organization, largely as a result of your cooperation.' Therefore, Sweet pointed out, the sentence he was about to impose was an attempt to balance 'a violent past, a redemptive present, and an uncertain future.'

Noting that Mickey had already served three and a half years in prison since being wrongfully charged with the Michael Holly murder, the judge sentenced Featherstone to five years probation.

'We want to believe that violence, aggression . . . can be overcome by acts of contrition and redemption,' said Sweet, who concluded, 'Mr Featherstone, you are no longer a prisoner of your past.'

The next day Francis Featherstone disappeared into the Witness Protection Program.

It had been a long, bumpy ride. Since the end of the Westies trial some ten months earlier, Featherstone had been engaged in a vituperative battle with the U.S. Attorney's office. Mostly, it centered around his agreement with the government. Featherstone felt that when he first made the decision to flip – in the hotel room in Westchester County in April of '86 – he had been promised bail. When bail was not forthcoming, Featherstone began to see a new conspiracy. This time it involved various prosecutors, members of the U.S. Marshals' Witness Protection Program, and his government-appointed attorneys.

At one point, Mickey had gone so far as to file a motion

with Judge Sweet to have his guilty plea withdrawn. Later, he changed his mind and the motion itself was withdrawn.

Of course, Mickey's disagreements with the government were put to rest when Judge Sweet handed down his sentence – a sentence that many in the city's law enforcement community felt was outrageously lenient. Egan, Coffey, and many of the cops who had pursued Featherstone for years felt betrayed by the judge. The way they saw it, Mickey had simply found a way to beat the system once again.

The other Westies were not nearly as lucky as Mickey. Eight months before Featherstone's sentencing, the seven convicted gang members had been brought before seventy-two-year-old Whitman Knapp. Each had their attorney deliver a statement asking for leniency. The last to do so was Gerald Shargel, Jimmy Coonan's lawyer. Shargel said that Jimmy Coonan himself had a statement he wanted to read, adding that Coonan was not an educated man and was unaccustomed to speaking before large groups.

Perhaps more than any of the others, Jimmy Coonan's personal life had been a carefully constructed illusion. At the same time he was terrorizing people in Hell's Kitchen, he'd sought to build a home and family life that were entirely separate. With his comfortable abode in suburban New Jersey and his children attending the finest parochial schools, he'd risen from the streets of Hell's Kitchen to achieve a certain 'respectability.'

That respectability was forever shattered during the Westies trial, in which the full extent of Coonan's brutality became known – perhaps for the first time ever – outside the city's criminal underworld.

Now, at his sentencing, Coonan sought to hold on to his final illusion. He began his statement by claiming something the evidence at the trial had already revealed to be untrue – that Edna was guilty of nothing other than having been his wife. Reading from a piece of paper, he claimed that Edna was an innocent bystander and therefore deserved special treatment. Soon his voice began to break. 'There's a lot more here, Your Honor. I can't get through it right now. I would just ask you to take any frustration out and any hatred out on me – not my wife.'

Judge Knapp said that he had no hatred towards Coonan and found his sentiments admirable. Then he sentenced him to prison for seventy-five years without parole, or, as the judge put it, 'the rest of your natural life.' In addition, Knapp fined Coonan $1 million.

Most of the others were given similarly stiff sentences. Jimmy McElroy received sixty years; Billy Bokun, fifty years; Mugsy Ritter, forty years; and Tommy Collins, forty years – all with a recommendation of no parole. Tommy Collins's wife, Flo, whose involvement was limited to the sale of narcotics, was given six months.

The last to be sentenced was Edna, who stood before the judge holding her husband's hand. Along with Jimmy's tearful plea for leniency, Knapp had received a handwritten note from the Coonans' eleven-year-old son asking that the judge not send his mother away. Knapp acknowledged that Mrs Coonan presented him with his most troubling duty, since 'you wouldn't be here if you hadn't married Mr Coonan.' All the same, he sentenced her to fifteen years behind bars and fined her $200,000. Knapp did, however, hint that her sentence might be reduced if she were to turn over the millions of dollars in criminal assets prosecutors claimed the Coonans had buried.

For months after the sentencing, the Westies continued to be an occasional newspaper item. In August of '88, hit men Kevin Kelly and Kenny Shannon, looking tanned and well rested, inexplicably turned themselves in to the FBI after nearly two years on the lam. At the time they surrendered, they were scheduled to be profiled on a national TV program, 'America's Most Wanted.' After they walked into the U.S. Attorney's office the program claimed credit for having pressured the two Westies into giving themselves up.

The real reason was far more mystifying, given that the evidence against Kelly and Shannon was overwhelming. The only answer the public was to get came from Frank Lopez, Kevin Kelly's attorney. 'It's tough being on the run,' he said at their arraignment. 'They wanted to see their families.'

In announcing formally that Kelly and Shannon had surrendered, Rudolph Giuliani identified the two men as 'the last of the ruling structure of the Westies,' and added that his office had, once and for all, crushed this 'violent organized crime group that terrorized and exploited the Hell's Kitchen section of Manhattan for the last twenty years.'

It would be one of Giuliani's last press conferences

before quitting his job as U.S. Attorney to run for mayor of New York City.

Along with these developments, the latter months of 1988 and on into '89 saw the emergence of Mickey Featherstone in his new role as a 'professional witness.' Within the space of ten months, Featherstone was called to testify at three separate trials, two in state court and one in federal.

The federal trial involved what was left of the Roy Demeo crew of the Gambino crime family. In a massive RICO indictment, Joseph Testa, Anthony Senter, and nine others were charged with some sixteen murders, including the killings of Danny Grillo and Demeo himself. Featherstone spent six days on the stand detailing how his West Side compatriots had met often with Demeo, Testa, and Senter to discuss, among other things, how to dispose of murder victims. Testa and Senter were later sentenced before Judge Vincent L. Broderick, who gave them both life plus twenty years.

After he had testified already at the Westies trial, the name of Mickey Featherstone was no doubt high on hit lists everywhere. By testifying against the powerful Gambinos he'd upped the ante even more, becoming perhaps the most wanted man in the underworld.

In April of '89, Mickey was called to testify at yet another important trial. Kelly and Shannon were being prosecuted in state court for their roles in the murder of Michael Holly. Billy Bokun, having heard the evidence against him on this charge at the Westies trial, had already pleaded guilty to shooting Holly.

It had been exactly four years since Holly was gunned

down on West 35th Street, touching off a series of events that would eventually bring the Hell's Kitchen Irish Mob to an end. Mickey, of course, still believed that he'd been set up to take the fall for the Holly murder as part of a power play involving Kelly, Shannon, Ken Aronson, and Jimmy Coonan. In the many days of testimony at the Westies trial, it had never been definitively shown that there was such a frame-up, though the evidence presented by the U.S. Attorney's office suggested that there was one.

By the end of the Holly trial in April of '89, all the old questions were still unresolved. Why had the assailants used a vehicle from Featherstone's place of business as the getaway car? Did Kelly and Shannon in fact tell Billy Bokun to wear a disguise that would make him look like Mickey, and if so, why? And why had the dreaded Westies, known for their ability to persuade witnesses to 'do the right thing,' allowed three different people to finger Mickey Featherstone free of retribution?

Sissy Featherstone was also called to testify at the trial. Her recorded conversations with Billy Bokun at the 9th Avenue Food Festival and with Kelly and Shannon at her home in Teaneck were played for the jury, as were portions of Mickey's chat with Kelly and Larry Palermo in the visiting room at Rikers Island.

After two days of deliberations a jury convicted sandy-haired Kenny Shannon for his role as the getaway driver. As for ambitious pretty-boy Kevin Kelly, although the evidence seemed to indicate that he had, at the very least, known about the Holly shooting, his actual role remained nebulous. He was acquitted.

509

Kelly was not home free, however. Not by a long shot. Six months after the Holly murder trial, in late October and November of '89, he was tried before Judge Whitman Knapp on a multiple-count federal RICO charge. Kenny Shannon, following his murder conviction in state court, had already pleaded guilty, so Kelly was on his own. The five-week trial before Judge Knapp was a virtual replay of the first Westies RICO trial, with many of the same witnesses and much of the same evidence. On November 16, 1989, Kelly was found guilty of racketeering.

Meanwhile, back in Hell's Kitchen, the ravages of gentrification continued to reshape the neighborhood. In the summer of '89, one block east of the building where Jimmy Coonan was born and raised on West 49th Street, Mary Dunn, a forty-year resident of Hell's Kitchen and president of a local tenants' association, placed four ceramic gargoyle masks on the front of her apartment building. The idea, she told a newspaper reporter, was to ward off developers.

The focus of her attentions was a massive structure directly across the street – Worldwide Plaza, a sparkling forty-nine-story office tower and condominium complex then under construction. The building, which takes up the entire block between 8th and 9th avenues, is the most notable of a dozen or so real estate projects that have altered the demographics in Hell's Kitchen, once a bastion of working-class and low-income families.

For those who've remained, there are a few old-time gathering places where the memory of Mickey Featherstone, Jimmy Coonan, and others still lingers.

Before the Westies trial, many West Siders assumed that whatever Featherstone might say on the stand was bullshit, the self-aggrandizing ravings of a government informant. Featherstone, after all, had not only violated the sacred West Side Code, he'd obliterated it, making it possible for others to follow in his wake.

At the trial, however, most of Featherstone's claims had been corroborated by Billy Beattie, Tony Lucich, Bobby Huggard, and the rest. In the end, the level of violence revealed shocked most West Siders, even those who'd heard the rumors about Paddy Dugan, Ruby Stein, Ugly Walter, Rickey Tassiello, and all the others whose bodies had mysteriously disappeared over the years.

There were the diehards, of course, those who still believed – and would always believe – that Featherstone was a bold-faced liar. To these hardened few, the only plausible explanation for what transpired in U.S. District Court was that it was all a power play on Featherstone's part. In fact, as the various Westie-related trials continued throughout 1989, a rumor began to make the rounds – a rumor that was endlessly dissected over cups of coffee and pitchers of beer at the Market Diner, the Madison Cocktail Lounge, and the bar of the Skyline Motor Inn.

The rumor went like this: Featherstone's cooperation had all been a ploy to remove Coonan and the others from the neighborhood. In fact, it was said by some that Mickey had been spotted on 10th Avenue, that he was back in Hell's Kitchen looking to pick up the pieces of the neighborhood's shattered legacy.

It was nonsense, of course. Featherstone's Witness Protection agreement with the U.S. Marshals Service precluded his ever returning to 'the danger zone,' which in Mickey's case included the entire northeast part of the United States. But to some old-timers, it was almost a comforting thought – Featherstone, a criminal through and through, returning to keep the traditions alive, traditions that had withstood the ravages of time since the earliest days of gangsterism.

As terrifying as the Westies had been, for those who'd lived their entire lives in the neighborhood, the alternative was far more unsettling – that the Hell's Kitchen Irish Mob, born of another age, was the last vestige of a culture and a community that would never be seen again.

With Mickey and Sissy Featherstone tucked away in the Witness Protection Program, the other key players in the drama were resigned to their fates. As of 2008, their whereabouts were as follows:

The Gangsters

Jimmy Coonan: In May 1989 Coonan's appeal of his RICO conviction was denied. He is serving his seventy-five-year sentence in the federal prison system.

Edna Coonan: Edna's appeal was also denied in May '89. She served her time and was paroled in the mid-1990s. She and Jimmy Coonan are no longer married.

Jackie Coonan: Contracted AIDS and died at the age of forty-four on April 24, 1988, just two weeks before his brother Jimmy and the other Westies were sentenced. Jackie, known to occasionally inject cocaine, is believed to have gotten the fatal disease from the use of contaminated needles.

Richie Ryan: On September 20, 1983, while Coonan and Featherstone were both away in prison, Ryan was found dead at the bottom of a flight of stairs in a tenement building at 443 West 48th Street, directly across from where Paddy Dugan killed Denis Curley eight years earlier. Ryan was known to have been consuming huge amounts of alcohol; the cause of death was listed as acute and chronic ethanolism. He was twenty-nine years old.

Ray Steen and Alberta Sachs: In 1981, while still in the Witness Protection Program, Steen – once known as Little Al Capone – and Jimmy Coonan's niece were married. By the start of the Westies trial in October '87 they were divorced with a daughter. Sachs has remarried, and while neither she nor Steen is in the Witness Program any longer, they both live far from New York under new names and with new identities.

Billy Beattie: In June '88, one month after the Westies sentencing, Beattie was brought before Judge Morris E. Lasker in U.S. District Court. Beattie's lawyer, Ken Caruso, argued that not only had his client cooperated fully with the investigation – wearing a wire at great risk to his life – but that Billy, though he'd played a role in the Paddy Dugan and Ruby Stein homicides, had never actually taken a life himself. It was a fine distinction, to say the least, but apparently the judge bought it. Beattie was given eighteen months, twelve of which he had already served. In December '88 he was released from prison and disappeared into the Witness Protection Program with his wife and children.

Tony Lucich: In July '88, before Judge Robert Sweet – the same judge who would later sentence Featherstone

– the sixty-eight-year-old Lucich was given 'time served' on his RICO conviction. Along with Featherstone, he was later called to appear at the marathon seventeen-month trial of Gambino family members Anthony Senter and Joey Testa, where he gave testimony on the relationship between the Westies and the Roy Demeo crew. Lucich has since disappeared into the Witness Protection Program.

Jimmy McElroy: In early 1990, McElroy testified in New York State court against Gambino Family boss John Gotti. On the stand, McElroy claimed that he was present in 1986 when Gotti and Jimmy Coonan agreed that the Westies would assault Carpenters' Union official John O'Connor. McElroy also admitted having committed two murders, two attempted murders, and having slit the throat of one man. His testimony was littered with inconsistencies, and Jimmy Mac himself came off as surly, unreliable and downright frightening. In the end, Gotti was acquitted of all charges, and McElroy's sentence was not reduced, as he hoped it would be. He is serving his time in federal prison.

Kevin Kelly: Following his November '89 conviction on federal RICO charges, Kelly was given a sentence of fifty years. Later, citing his 'consistently good to outstanding record' in prison, Judge Knapp reduced Kelly's sentence from fifty to forty years and withdrew his recommendation of no parole. The earliest Kelly is eligible for parole is 2011.

Kenny Shannon: After being given eighteen years to life for his role in the Michael Holly shooting, Shannon pleaded guilty to the federal RICO charge against him. In August '89 he was sentenced before Judge Knapp on the

RICO charge and given twenty years, to run concurrent with his state conviction. He served his time in Sing Sing prison and was paroled in 2006.

Billy Bokun: In May '89 Bokun was sentenced to fifteen years to life in State Court for his guilty plea in the Holly murder, the sentence to run concurrent with his RICO conviction. Two years later, Bokun's sentence was reduced by Judge Knapp, who stated that his opinion of Bokun's culpability had been altered by the Kevin Kelly trial. In particular, he noted, 'Bokun's involvement in the Westies activity seemed considerably less than that of Kevin Kelly, who received the same sentence.' In addition to reducing Bokun's sentence, Knapp waived his recommendation of no parole. In 2003, after serving fifteen years in prison, Bokun was paroled. He currently resides in New Jersey.

Tommy Collins: At the time of the Westies trial, Collins was already serving ten to life in state court on a narcotics conviction. In December 1994, after serving eight years at the Greenhaven correctional facility in upstate New York, Collins was paroled.

Flo Collins: Tommy Collins's wife served the least amount of time of all the Westies defendants – six months. She was paroled in early 1991.

Mugsy Ritter: In May of 89 Ritter's appeal of his RICO conviction was denied. He is serving his forty-year sentence at a federal pen in Terre Haute, Indiana.

The Neighborhood
James McManus: On October 27, 1988, McManus celebrated his twenty-five-year anniversary as leader of the Midtown Democratic Association. Among the 500

celebrants at Gallagher's Restaurant in Hell's Kitchen was then Mayor of New York Edward I. Koch. Five years later, McManus retired from the post of district leader, ending the century-long reign of 'the McMani.'

The Cops
Richie Egan: Retired from the police department at the age of forty-one in October '87. Upon his retirement Egan went to work for the U.S. Customs Department's Regional Intelligence Division in Manhattan, where he remained for fifteen years. 'I'll never forget [the Westies] case,' he says. 'The level of violence, the personalities, the overall scope – it has to be one of the most memorable cases in history.'

Tom McCabe: After thirty-five years with the NYPD, Richie Egan's supervisor retired in 1990. He passed away from natural causes on July 1, 2004, at the age of seventy-three, leaving behind five children, including NYPD Sergeant Phil McCabe, who has been with the department for more than twenty-five years.

Joe Coffey: Retired from the police department in March of '85 and went to work for the statewide Organized Crime Task Force. Known to the Westies as 'Publicity Joe,' in 1992 Coffey published a book chronicling his years in law enforcement entitled *The Coffey Files.*

Frank McDarby: Joe Coffey's partner retired from the police department in 1983 and opened his own carpet cleaning and extermination service based in Queens, with the advertising slogan 'rugs and bugs.' In 1986 McDarby again changed careers and began his own private investigation firm, also based in Queens.

Greg Derkasch: Retired from the counterfeit division of the U.S. Secret Service in 1990 after twenty-two years of service, eleven of those in the New York field office. Derkasch remembers the Westies case as 'one of the most important, not only in my career but in all of New York law enforcement.'

The Lawyers
Larry Hochheiser and Ken Aronson: Throughout 1989 and into the 1990s, the firm of Hochheiser and Aronson continued to represent clients with alleged mob connections, until the two attorneys dissolved their partnership in 1995. Hochheiser went on to represent Bosco Radonjich – Jimmy Coonan's one-time criminal associate – whom the U.S. Attorney's office claimed had 'taken over' the Westies and served as the gang's leader following Coonan's conviction and had continued in that capacity well into the 1990s. It was a dubious charge, at best, given that there were no Westies left for Bosco to lead and he had no known affiliation with anyone in Hell's Kitchen. The government's star witness against Radonjich was to be Sammy 'the Bull' Gravano, right-hand man to John Gotti, who had famously turned against his former *mafiosi* in a series of explosive criminal trials in the late 1990s. Gravano was set to testify that Gotti met on numerous occasions with Radonjich, who presented himself as the new 'boss' of the Westies. When Gravano – by now living under a new name and identity in Arizona – was himself arrested on narcotics trafficking charges in March 2000, the government's case against Bosco Radonjich

fell apart. In 2001, the charges against Bosco were dropped altogether.

Mary Lee Warren: Following her successful prosecution of the Westies, Assistant U.S. Attorney Warren was named to head the prestigious Narcotics Bureau of the U.S. Attorney's office for the Southern District of New York, where she remains today.

Rudolph Giuliani: On November 7, 1989, the former U.S. Attorney for the Southern District was defeated in his run for Mayor of New York by his Democratic opponent, David Dinkins. Four years later, Giuliani defeated Dinkins and went on to serve two eventful terms as Mayor.

AFTERWORD

'I'm glad it worked out the way it did,' says Mickey Featherstone, talking by phone from somewhere in the world.

Since this book was first published in 1990 Featherstone and I had spoken occasionally, though I had no idea where he'd been relocated. Our conversations were set up by a third-party government official who had facilitated Mickey's relocation and stayed in touch with him over the years.

What pleased Featherstone most about the resolution to the Westies story was that he and his wife, Sissy, had found a way to escape 'the life' and were able to create a new existence for themselves and their four children. Says the kid from West 43rd Street in Hell's Kitchen: 'I've seen the other side of the world now, and I love it.'

The degree to which Featherstone has been able to adjust to life after the Westies would probably amaze those who knew him in his former life. Particularly in his early adulthood, Mickey was the toughest of the tough – an alcohol and drug abuser with a hair-trigger temper. The violence that he both encountered and inflicted on others was so prevalent that much of it is now a blur. 'I don't think about it much,' says Featherstone of the past. 'But when I do, a lot of it disgusts me.'

To Mickey, a key turning point in his life came in 1986 when, in an attempt to overturn his onerous conviction for the murder of Michael Holly, his wife, Sissy, undertook the highly dangerous act of wearing a wire and circulating among the Westies, all in hopes of gathering evidence to establish Mickey's innocence. To this day, says Featherstone, he is humbled by his wife's bravery and devotion. It has become the basis of an emotional bond that has made it possible for the Featherstones to achieve the unthinkable: a law-abiding, productive, cohesive family life far from the once-mean streets of Hell's Kitchen.

In the early years of their relocation, Mickey was 'Mr Mom' staying home with the kids while Sissy created a business career for herself. Regular counseling was an important aspect of his and Sissy's adjustment, but Featherstone contends that the main factor was merely being physically and emotionally removed from the old neighborhood; they were now free to ponder a life the likes of which they never could have conceived of before. A big part of their new life involved creating opportunities for their children that had never existed for them. Their oldest son graduated from college, joined the Army, and was stationed in Kuwait in the years before September 11, 2001; he's now married to a schoolteacher. Their oldest daughter is married and owns her own business. Another son recently enlisted in the Army and is currently stationed in Iraq, where he was given a commendation for bravery. Their youngest daughter is currently in college on an athletic scholarship.

For the old Mickey Featherstone, loyalty was a high value – loyalty to the gang, the neighborhood, and to Jimmy Coonan. The betrayal he felt at the hands of Coonan and other Westies may have obliterated whatever loyalty he felt towards the gang and turned him into a 'rat,' but he seems to have found a way to maintain loyalty as a value through devotion to his family. 'We're a tight group,' says Featherstone of his family. He believes the family unit is what has kept him on the straight-and-narrow. 'Any time I've had an instance where my temper rises, where the old Mickey Featherstone starts to surface, I think about my wife and kids. It's the only thing that matters.'

As for his previous criminal impulses, Featherstone claims that is all part of the distant past. Since relocation there have been no crimes, no brushes with the law, nor, says Mickey, a desire on his part to drift back into the old ways. It seems incredible given his criminal history, but Featherstone's claims check out: the facts of his relocation – clean criminal record, the details of his family and home life – were verified to me by current and former law enforcement officials familiar with his life since being relocated.

So how has Featherstone done it? How has he been able to achieve and maintain a new life for himself when Sammy 'the Bull' Gravano, Henry Hill of *Goodfellas* fame and so many other high-profile criminals have reverted to their lives of crime? Much of it has to do with Featherstone's original motivations as a criminal. Although Featherstone was clearly 'a danger to society,' he was never a 'gangster' in the way that Jimmy Coonan, Sammy the Bull or Henry Hill were gangsters. Featherstone's more violent criminal impulses were usually acts of emotion driven by a perverted sense of loyalty, not by a profit motive. It is true that, later, after Featherstone returned to the neighborhood in the 1980s following a stint in federal prison, he became obsessed with making sure he got his fair share of the Westies criminal proceeds. But, he contends, that was due mostly to the resentment he felt that his wife and family had not been taken care of when he went away to prison, and also because people in the gang were using his name and reputation for their own personal gain.

To this day, claims Mickey, he was never 'money hungry or power hungry.' Consequently, he doesn't find himself battling impulses to go on a robbery, make a big score, or use violence as a way to make money because 'I never had those impulses in the first place.'

As for Jimmy Coonan and other leading members of the Westies who were put behind bars by his testimony, Featherstone feels 'they got what they deserved,' though he long ago let go of the hatred and rancor. Despite the remorse he feels at many of his violent acts, Featherstone is no longer a tortured soul haunted by nightmares. He is, he says, 'free from the past.'

Of course, the past is never gone for good. With criminal behavior, in particular, it has long been a contention of psychiatrists, sociologists and criminologists that ingrained antisocial behavior is like alcoholism or any other drug addiction: it may go into remission, but it never truly disappears.

Even so, for nearly twenty years now, by all available accounts, Mickey Featherstone has lived an exemplary life. Against all odds, and contrary to the steadfast beliefs of his enemies and even some of his supporters, he appears to have attained something few ever thought he would: peace-of-mind.

T. J. English

TOUGH GUY
by Louis Ferrante

From an early age, fear and brutality defined Louis Ferrante's world. He made his reputation as a gang leader on the streets of New York and later, hooking up with the infamous Gambino crime family, he pulled off some of the most lucrative robberies in American history. Life was sweet, and most of the time Louis had fun wisecracking his way around town and staying one step ahead of the law.

But when the feds finally caught up with him, Louis faced a long sentence. For nine years, as prisoner 42365053, he lived amongst many of the most violent, not to mention insane, criminals incarcerated in the US prison system. Relying on his wits, his reputation and his wiseguy connections, he battled each day just to stay alive.

But things changed dramatically when Louis had an unexpected exchange with a prison guard – an exchange which forced him to confront and question the dishonest, brutal reality of his past.

As Louis embarked upon an incredible journey of the mind that would provide a form of santuary from the violent chaos of his everyday life, he also began a long and difficult fight to turn his life around.

Gritty, hard-hitting, and yet often hilarious, *Tough Guy* is an extraordinary, powerful true story of hope and transformation that is shocking, inspiring and unforgettable.

9780593060186

NOW AVAILABLE FROM BANTAM PRESS

—— BANTAM PRESS ——

THE LOST BOY
by Duncan Staff

The series of child murders that took place in and around Manchester in the 1960s shocked and scandalised the country. In a sensational case Myra Hindley and Ian Brady were tried and sentenced to life in prison. The horrific nature of their crimes made them two of the most reviled characters in Britain. Four children were murdered by Hindley and Brady and buried on Saddleworth Moor; the body of one of their victims, Keith Bennett, is yet to be found.

With unprecedented access to Myra Hindley's papers combined with the cooperation of the families of the victims, the police and expert witnesses, Duncan Staff has written a definitive account of these terrible events. He casts new light on the motivation for the murders, the nature of Hindley's relationship with Brady and her life in prison. In bringing together this evidence, Staff calls for a renewed effort to find the body of Keith Bennett.

The Lost Boy is a classic work of investigative journalism and the gripping story of the most notorious crimes in Britain of the last one hundred years.

9780553818079

BANTAM BOOKS

THE RESTLESS SLEEP
Inside New York City's Cold Case Squad
by Stacy Horn

**In New York City, since 1985, nearly 9,000 murders
remain unsolved . . .**

These cases are never closed but they can – due to passage of
time, lack of evidence, loss of investigative momentum – go
'cold'. And when this happens and the world seems to have
moved on, it falls to one small, élite NYPD unit to offer hope
of resolution. Its purpose is to rescue these near-forgotten
victims from oblivion, to answer the questions: who were
they? What happened? And who did this to them? – and in
finding justice, lay their troubled ghosts to rest. It is
The Cold Case and Apprehension Squad.

The Restless Sleep is Stacy Horn's riveting, at times
harrowing, account of the two years she spent working
with New York's Cold Case Squad. Revealing the real-
life subculture of crime solving that inspires and informs
television series such as *CSI* and *Waking the Dead*,
it is a new classic of true crime.

'Riveting, moving and haunting . . . you come away with
the deepest respect for these true-life heroes'
Tess Gerritsen

'These cases haunted Horn, and because of her masterful
storytelling, they are likely to haunt her readers too'
San Francisco Chronicle

'The *CSI*s make gripping telly but *Restless Sleep* would be
compulsive viewing too, based on this book . . . fascinating'
Sunday Sport

9780553816075

BANTAM BOOKS

THUNDERSTRUCK
by Erik Larson

The true story of Dr Crippen and the miraculous invention that helped catch a killer and transform the world . . .

The Edwardian age: a time when shipping companies competed to build the biggest, fastest vessels, the rich vied with one another with their displays of wealth, and science dazzled the public with visions of a world made wondrous.

The Murderer: Wanted for what would become one of the twentieth-century's most infamous murders, Dr Hawley Crippen fled England on a ship bound for America accompanied by his unsuspecting mistress disguised as a boy.

The Detective: A veteran of the Ripper case, Inspector Walter Dew found himself strangely sympathetic to the murderer and his young lover.

The Inventor: Guglielmo Marconi drove himself to the brink in his obsessive struggle to perfect his visionary creation, but his 'wireless' would play a pivotal role in catching the killer.

Written with riveting attention to detail, narrative drive and an uncanny ability to bring a bygone era to life, this true story culminates in one of the most spectacular criminal chases of all time, as one luxury liner pursued another across the Atlantic, and recalls an extraordinary and largely forgotten chapter from history.

'Meticulously researched . . . a fascinating read'
Daily Express

'Larson has an exceptional mastery of historical detail and a real flair for suspense'
Observer

'Shines a vivid electric light on the birth of the modern age . . . Larson is a great master of narrative'
Mail on Sunday

'Larson has done it again . . . as in his last book, *The Devil in the White City*, he has taken an unlikely historical subject and spun it into gold'
New York Times

9780553817089

BANTAM BOOKS